Advances in Object-Oriented
Data Modeling

Cooperative Information Systems
Michael Papazoglou, Joachim W. Schmidt, and John Mylopoulos, editors

Advances in Object-Oriented Data Modeling, Michael P. Papazoglou, Stefano Spaccapietra, and Zahir Tari, editors, 2000

edited by
Michael P. Papazoglou
Stefano Spaccapietra
Zahir Tari

Advances in Object-Oriented Data Modeling

The MIT Press
Cambridge, Massachusetts
London, England

This book was set in Times Roman by Windfall Software using ZzTEX and was printed and bound in the United States of America.

Library of Congress Cataloging-in-Publication Data

Advances in object-oriented data modeling / edited by Michael P. Papazoglou, Stefano Spaccapietra, Zahir Tari.
    p.   cm. — (Cooperative information systems)
  Includes bibliographical references and index.
  ISBN 0-262-16189-3 (hc : alk. paper)
  1. Object-oriented methods (Computer science) 2. Computer software—Development.
I. Papazoglou, M., 1953– II. Spaccapietra, S.   III. Tari, Zahir. IV. Series.
QA76.9.O35 A38 2000
005.1'17—dc21   99-045287

Contents

Series Foreword

The traditional view of information systems as tailor-made, cost-intensive database applications is changing rapidly. The change is fueled partly by a maturing software industry, which is making greater use of off-the-shelf generic components and standard software solutions, and partly by the onslaught of the information revolution. In turn, this change has resulted in a new set of demands for information services that are homogeneous in their presentation and interaction patterns, open in their software architecture, and global in their scope. The demands have come mostly from application domains such as e-commerce and banking, manufacturing (including the software industry itself), training, education, and environmental management, to mention just a few.

Future information systems will have to support smooth interaction with a large variety of independent multi-vendor data sources and legacy applications, running on heterogeneous platforms and distributed information networks. Metadata will play a crucial role in describing the contents of such data sources and in facilitating their integration.

As well, a greater variety of community-oriented interaction patterns will have to be supported by next-generation information systems. Such interactions may involve navigation, querying and retrieval, and will have to be combined with personalized notification, annotation, and profiling mechanisms. Such interactions will also have to be intelligently interfaced with application software, and will need to be dynamically integrated into customized and highly connected cooperative environments. Morever, the massive investments in information resources, by governments and businesses alike, calls for specific measures that ensure security, privacy and accuracy of their contents.

All these are challenges for the next generation of information systems. We call such systems *Cooperative Information Systems,* and they are the focus of this series.

In layman terms, cooperative information systems are servicing a diverse mix of demands characterized by *content—community—commerce*. These demands are originating in current trends for off-the-shelf software solutions, such as enterprise resource planning and e-commerce systems.

A major challenge in building cooperative information systems is to develop technologies that permit continuous enhancement and evolution of current massive investments in information resources and systems. Such technologies must offer an appropriate infrastructure that supports not only development, but also evolution of software.

Early research results on cooperative information systems are becoming the core technology for community-oriented information portals or gateways. An information gateway provides a "one-stop-shopping" place for a wide range of information resources and services, thereby creating a loyal user community.

The research advances that will lead to cooperative information system will not come from any single research area within the field of Information Technology. Database and knowledge-based systems, distributed systems, groupware, and graphical user interfaces have all matured as technologies. While further enhancements for individual technologies are desirable, the greatest leverage for technological advancement is expected to come from their evolution into a seamless technology for building and managing cooperative information systems.

The MIT Press Cooperative Information Systems series will cover this area through textbooks, and research editions intended for the researcher and the professional who wishes to remain up-to-date on current developments and future trends.

The series will include three types of books:

- Textbooks or resource books intended for upper level undergraduate or graduate level courses;

- Research monographs, which collect and summarize research results and development experiences over a number of years;

- Edited volumes, including collections of papers on a particular topic.

Authors are invited to submit to the series editors book proposals that include a table of contents and sample book chapters. All submissions will be reviewed formally and authors will receive feedback on their proposals.

John Mylopoulos
jm@cs.toronto.edu
Dept. of Computer Science
University of Toronto
Toronto, Ontario
Canada

Michael Papazoglou
M.P.Papazoglou@kub.nl
INFOLAB
P.O. Box 90153
LE Tilburg
The Netherlands

Joachim W. Schmidt
j.w.schmidt@tu-harburg.de
Software Systems Institute
Technische Universität TUHH
Hamburg, Germany

Foreword

Gio Wiederhold
Stanford University
USA

Object-oriented Modeling has become the prime methodology for modern software design. Not since the conception of Structured Programming appeared has a new software technology had a similar impact. Today many textbooks, professional guides, and CASE tools support object-oriented software design. However, object-oriented data modeling has not kept pace, and the papers in this volume illustrate a range of issues that are still being dealt with.

Object-orientation in software creation is simpler than object-oriented data modeling, because a specific program represents one approach to a solution, and hence one point-of-view. Data are commonly shared, and participants can hence approach the modeling from multiple points-of-view. For instance, early relational systems supported implicitly multiple points-of-view, since they only provided the simple semantics of isolated tables (3). The relational model complements the simple storage structure with algebraic manipulation of these structures. Moving to a calculus allowed automation in processing of "what" queries rather than following programmatic "how" instructions. Having an algebra also enabled the optimizations that were required. Alternate expressions over the tables define alternate views, which are mutually independent. Even now, relational processing capabilities remain weak. The relational SQL language has mainly one verb: "SELECT". UPDATES are severely restricted to the full database, since views, essential to understand subsets of complex data-structures, cannot be updated in general.

To assure consistency among views there has to be more, namely a shared model. Entity-Relationship models provided quantitative structural semantics (2), but, until recently, this information remained in the design phase, and at most provided documentation for subsequent program creation. A formalization of the Entity-Relationship model, allowing matching of the relational transfers, the Structural Model (5) did not have a significant impact, since data modeling remained informal until objects started to emerge as first class data structures (1).

Subsequent additions to relational systems provide the specification of integrity constraints, and these will limit the structural choices. For instance, combining uniqueness and a reference constraint will assure conformance to a 1:n relationship among two tables. Providing constraints is important for consistency and sharability. Still, the methods used to manage conformance remain outside of this model, so that software reuse is not encouraged. Programmers have the freedom of defining semantics through the code they provide, but its sharability is hard to validate, and a certain amount of trust is needed in practice.

In object-oriented programming there is a richness of methods that greatly exceeds the relational paradigm. The corresponding data models must allow much more semantics to be inserted and managed than in relational and E-R modeling, where models remained restricted to static structures. Those models, specifically, do not support the transformation process—the essence of data-processing. When the methods of transformation themselves are shared, interaction among participants moves to a higher level.

The emergence of common business objects, supported by OMG and vendor initiatives heralds an acceptance of sharable object models and their methods. To the extent that this technology becomes accepted the conceptual distance between programs and models will be reduced. Business models must express now functions and relationships that go beyond the static structures easily visualized in tables.

Since until recently relational systems and E-R support has well nigh ignored temporal computation, this area has been especially fruitful for data modeling. Here objects go through transformations over time, without losing their identity. Information in older versions is often of value, even though these objects no longer exist in reality and cannot be validated with respect to the real world. Most data describing these objects does not arrive in storage systems in real time, so that demands for strict consistency conflict with up-to-dateness. We have recently suggested that simulation access may be needed in cases where currency is more crucial to decision makers than consistency (7).

Temporal operations are informally well understood, although their correct formalization requires great care. For instance, consider the handling of open intervals (common in human interaction) and closed intervals (needed for reliable computation if temporal granularities are mixed) (6).

These business objects constrain tasks beyond the realm of traditional programs, since they must share data structures and content. Here interoperation among vendor offerings will remain an issue for some time. Focused software vendors, as SAP, have reaped great benefits by providing domain-specific software with somewhat implicit, but fairly rigid models. Many customers are willing to adjust their processes to those models, in order to gain the benefit of shared software and especially the expectation of shared software maintenance.

Today, at the closing of the 20th century, the world of programming is in a state of unusual ferment. The Y2K problems have brought issues of programming into every home. The economics of dealing with this issue are distorting the expected growth curves in computing. Major resources are being devoted to fixing legacy software, which should have been allowed to die a gradual death. Other software is being replaced, but without much new functionality. Innovation in data-processing, requiring advanced modeling techniques, is at a low state. However, as resources now devoted to the Y2K problem, and to fixing the problems created by those fixes, are freed up, we can expect that the growth curve will resume.

As our systems become larger, more complex, and more interlinked we will also find that we will have to maintain our models beyond the design stage. It will become rare that software systems will be replaced as a whole; the cost and risks of doing so will be too great. But components will be updated and exchanged, requiring a clear understanding of the software that is not available for today's legacy systems and that cannot be accommodated by documenting the code alone. An open question that remains is how to document the decision process—for instance, the assessments that led to a design alternative not to be adopted. We hope that this book, reflecting the state of the art in modeling complex software today, will provide guidance for the creation and maintenance of the computing infrastructure we will be relying on in the future.

Gio Wiederhold
ww-db.stanford.edu/people/gio.html

June 1999

1. Thierry Barsalou, Niki Siambela, Arthur M. Keller, and Gio Wiederhold: "Updating Relational Databases Through Object-based Views"; *ACM-SIGMOD 91*, Boulder CO, May 1991, pages 248-257.

2. Peter P.S. Chen: "The Entity-Relationship Model—Toward a Unified View of Data"; ACM Transactions on Database Systems, Vol.1 No.1, Mar.1976, pp.9–36.

3. E.F. Codd: "A Relational Model of Data for Large Shared Data Banks"; /sl CACM, Vol.13 No.6, June 1970.

4. O-J. Dahl, E.W. Dijkstra, and C.A.R. Hoare: "Structured Programming"; Academic Press, 1972,

5. Ramez El-Masri Ramez and Gio Wiederhold: "Data Model Integration Using the Structural Model"; *Proceedings 1979 ACM SIGMOD Conference*, pp. 191-202.

6. Gio Wiederhold, Sushil Jajodia, and Witold Litwin: "Integrating Temporal Data in a Heterogenous Environment"; in Tansel, Clifford, Gadia, Jajodia, Segiv, Snodgrass: *Temporal Databases, Theory, Design and Implementation*; Benjamin Cummins Publishing, 1993, pages 563-579.

7. Gio Wiederhold, Rushan Jiang, and Hector Garcia-Molina: "An Interface Language for Projecting Alternatives in Decision-Making"; *Proc. 1998 AFCEA Database Colloquium*, AFCEA and SAIC, San Diego, Sep. 1998.

Preface
The Blossoming of Object-Oriented Data Modeling

Data modeling is by virtue of its nature the preeminent factor for the successful development of data intensive applications. An accurate and understandable representation of an application domain is the key to successfully developing complex applications, as developers can ascertain that their requirements have been met. It is also the key to long-lasting solutions, as future developers can comprehend existing implementations and incrementally evolve them to respond to new developments in the business world.

The importance of data modeling can be understood easily when one considers the long-lasting debates about which model best supports database design process. This has been one of the hottest issues that has confronted database researchers and practitioners for nearly three decades. In the early seventies, several conferences were organized for the sole purpose of assessing the merits of the emerging relational data model. Later debates were fueled between proponents of the relational model and proponents of semantic models, whose champion has been the Entity-Relationship (ER) model. The controversy arose between those who favored an implementation-oriented design (directly on the basis of the relational model), and those who favored an enterprise description approach, one that kept as close to reality as possible. The latter consider that transforming specifications into implementation is a subsequent stage in the design process. This approach become known as the *conceptual modeling approach*, to denote that the emphasis is placed on clean concepts rather than on implementation techniques.

Conceptual modeling is about understanding the reality of what is usually called the Universe of Discourse (UoD). To model a particular UoD, data models are used to represent and abstract various types of information, including data and processes, that are related to it. The quality of the resulting representations depends not only on the skills of the database designers, but also on the qualities of the selected data model and the methodology applied.

The ever-growing pace of technological advances has clearly indicated that technology specific solutions that ignore the other components of the business context within which they apply; e.g., operations and strategies do not last for too long. Such considerations are becoming even more important now that businesses are increasingly under pressure to respond quickly to strategic changes and market challenges in order to remain competitive in a global market. Too often organizations find their ability to compete hampered by archaic business process and systems—designed years ago to meet the challenges of a market that no longer exists. Enterprises now begin at a more fundamental level, directing their efforts into re-engineering of their business models and systems. This is the objective of business integration, the preeminent challenge of our times. Enterprises are now discovering the superiority of the conceptual modeling approach. Database and information system design methodologies are now receiving much closer attention than ever before. In particular, a lot of attention is placed on the style of development known as "object-oriented modeling."

The object-oriented modeling approach provides a new way of thinking about problems: it employs modeling techniques that are organized around real-world concepts. Information systems until now have generally been designed around different functions of a business operation, such as accounts payable, inventory control, customer service, delivery, and so on. These functions are, however, very volatile and require periodic adjustments. They also have ripple effects throughout an entire system. Object-oriented modeling, by contrast, structures systems around data—the objects—that make up the various business functions. In this way the system becomes a software model of the business itself. And because knowledge and implementation about a particular function are limited to one place—to the object—the system is shielded from the effects of change. Moreover, object-oriented modeling promotes a better understanding of the requirements, clear designs, and more maintainable systems.

Object-oriented data modeling is based on what is called the "object-oriented paradigm," which is not just a way of programming but most importantly, is a way of thinking abstractly about a problem using real-world concepts, rather than implementation-oriented concepts. There are at least two converging threads which led to the development of object-oriented data modeling. One thread was the need to promote the various phases of application management, which include such important factors as design, development, maintenance, portability, and extensibility. The other is the emergence of new classes of complex applications which require better representational facilities and more elaborate modes of data sharing. Object-oriented data models achieve these requirements by providing appropriate mechanisms to represent the *structure* of application domains with a high degree of accuracy while also placing emphasis on operational, i.e., *behavioral*, abstractions. Object-oriented data models take an abstract data-typing approach to modeling by embedding operations, i.e., methods, within types to support reusability and extensibility. In this way object-oriented technology provides a practical, productive way to develop software/databases for most applications, regardless of the final implementation language.

To provide adequate support for the modeling of complex applications, the *function-oriented* (*process*) design, which is typically the focus of software engineering, and the conventional *data-centered* approach (typically used by database modelers) should be unified, giving rise to object-oriented data modeling techniques. In object-oriented data modeling these two stages can be unified into one as classes encapsulate both data and processes. High-level design can be accomplished in terms of objects which contain both *data and services*. Objects provide services using a client/server model of interaction by employing messages. This leads to the notion of a *contract* between interacting objects and to a *responsibility-driven* approach, which represents a major deviation from the classical structured techniques. This results in models that are able to represent both structure and behavior while addressing software reusability and extensibility issues.

Current object-oriented data models, including the ODMG proposal for a de facto standard, still do not fulfill all of the requirements of conceptual modeling from an enterprise point of view. There are important modeling requirements in the context of complex data-intensive applications, which require highly intricate (collaborative, behavior-oriented or temporal) functionality, or rely on the use of distributed information, conceptual workflow systems, and legacy systems, which need to be addressed by means of enhanced modeling techniques. The power of object-oriented models lies primarily in the ability to support enhancement and extensions that are inherent to the model. Currently, there are many research threads being devoted to such kinds of improvements or extensions of the object-modeling technology. This book is dedicated to advances in object-oriented data modeling, which we expect to have a long lasting impact on the way that modeling is conducted. As a result the book introduces several important problem areas, suggestions, and solutions that target advanced modeling issues.

About This Book

The primary focus of this book is on recent developments in object-oriented data modeling techniques dealing with representational and processing aspects of complex data-intensive applications. The chapters chosen for this book are representative of research work from a growing literature on object-oriented data modeling. They cover "hot" research topics such as behavioral and consistency aspects of data-intensive applications, reverse engineering, interoperability and collaboration between objects, and workflow modeling. The chapters are not intended to represent all aspects of the research work underway, but rather to illustrate useful approaches, novel techniques, and methodologies. Each chapter starts with a thorough review of its subject area and proceeds by covering useful object-oriented data-modeling techniques and methodologies that can be applied to real-life applications.

The chapters in this book were solicited from leading experts in the area of object-oriented data modeling and were formed after face-to-face meetings and several "online" discussions. All chapters are largely original pieces of work that have evolved over the past year and are undergoing thorough reviewing to guarantee high quality, consistency and cohesion, and uniformity of presentation, as well as as in-depth treatment of the topic covered. Each chapter includes a comprehensive overview of the topic/issue covered, proposed solutions to practical problems, and the most recent findings in the topic covered, as well as directions for future research and development.

This book is unique in that it takes a unified view of different techniques and developments in the area of object-oriented data modeling and reports on recent work that can only be found scattered throughout the literature. This book is useful for both researchers, software professionals, and advanced students who are working, or intending to work, on the area of object-oriented modeling. Some familiarity with object-oriented programming languages and database systems is required. The reader will learn a variety of ways of applying the object-oriented paradigm in the context of data modeling. This book has a dual purpose. It can be used in advanced courses on object-oriented data modeling or object-oriented software development focused around database systems. Furthermore, it represents a valuable source of information for software engineers, developers, and project managers who wish to familiarize themselves with object-oriented data modeling techniques and methodologies and apply some of the material covered in this book into practice.

Contents of the Book

The chapters presented in this book cover a wide spectrum of both theoretical and practical issues, and all make use of a common realistic case study that demonstrates how the proposed modeling methodologies can be applied to real-life situations. The case study is based on a standard case study widely used by the European Union (EU) and known as the EU-Rent Car Rentals study. This case study provides an easily understood context for examples that cover several business issues and user requirements that could be easily mapped to other applications and systems. It is described in the next section.

The book is divided into six parts representing broad categories of topical research and development targeted by this book. Each category contains chapters which present novel techniques, methodologies, and tools.

Overview: Advances in Object-Oriented Data Modeling   This chapter provides a thorough overview of the requirements and features of data models with respect to design and implementation of application systems and their underlying data management systems. Following this, the features of object-oriented data models are discussed and related to other earlier modeling paradigms. Finally, research challenges and open research issues in the area of object-oriented data modeling are raised and related to the material of the book.

Behavioral Modeling   This part of the book is dedicated to the topic of behavioral modeling. A main characteristic of an object is its behavior, that is, the set of operations that can be applied to instances of a specific object type. The object type refers to an object's interface, the set of all signatures defined by all the object's operations. In this way we may define (and make visible) a set of services that an object can provide and perform. Objects interact with each other by sending messages and requesting the execution of a particular operation (service). A message typically consists of the name of the operation and identification of the target object. This mode of interaction follows the client/server paradigm in that an object (client) requests another object (server) to perform a specific operation (service) on its behalf. A major requirement is that clients should remain unaware of the specific types of the server objects they use as long as these adhere to the interface that clients expect. This type of modeling is of extreme importance to object-oriented data modeling as object behavior identifies legal sequences of states for objects and guarantees correct execution patterns.

Behavioral modeling is concerned with the patterns of communication between client/server objects. Behavioral modeling is important for large systems where objects need to interact and cooperate to perform a task that no single object can carry on its own. Behavioral modeling is thus concerned with *composability*, i.e., the ability to acquire references to server objects and combine their services dynamically. Behavioral composability provides the ability to obtain new functionality by composing discrete object behavior. Object composition requires that objects being composed have well-defined interfaces and that objects respect each other's interfaces.

Behavioral modeling poses a series of challenges for object modeling. Important issues are how to model consistent composition of object behavior to address complex application functionality; how to compose conditions constraining the triggering of object services; and how to extend server interfaces to cope with slightly differing requirements on behavior.

- The first chapter in this category is by Delcambre and Eklund and provides a behaviorally oriented methodology for identifying aspects of data modeling that need to be included in the analysis phase and those that need to be handled during design. This approach makes use of a use-case-driven methodology during the analysis phase and represents the analysis model using objects and responsibilities, a behavioral approach. It also describes how to represent key aspects of a database in the analysis model. The guiding principle is that user-visible behavior should be present in the use cases and should be modeled during analysis.

- The chapter by Teisseire, Poncelet, and Cicchetti proposes an approach that uses events for capturing behavior and behavioral constraints. Events are characterized by their type. These types can express not only their semantics but also synchronization conditions. Event chaining is captured through functions. To express particularly precise conditions (temporal or constraining event triggering) an algebraic language is proposed.

- The chapter by Schrefl and Stumptner looks at various notions of conformance in connection with inheritance in object-oriented data models. The chapter treats the inheritance of object life cycles by means of behavior diagrams that identify legal sequences of states and operations. It identifies sufficient rules for checking different types of conformance between behavior diagrams of super-types and subtypes.

Modeling of Reverse Engineering Applications   Although the interest in object-oriented databases is growing, a major limitation on their acceptance in the corporate world is the amount of time and money invested in existing databases using the older data models ("legacy systems"). Obviously, the huge undertaking needed to convert from one database paradigm to another is a major expense that few corporations are willing to readily accept. What is needed are tools that allow corporations to generate the conceptual schemata and reveal the hidden semantics of current database applications efficiently and with limited user involvement. This process is known as database "reverse engineering" (or reengineering).

Reverse engineering can be defined as a process of discovering how a database system works. Whether using reverse engineering to migrate between different database paradigms (from hierarchical to relational, relational to object-oriented), elucidating undocumented systems, or using it to forward engineer existing systems, reverse engineering involves a wide collection of tasks. The pivotal feature of all these tasks is the need to identify all the components of existing database systems and the relationships between them.

This part of the book describes advanced modeling techniques for reengineering legacy database applications. The contribution of these techniques relies not only on proposed (reengineering) methodologies but also on the their use in real environments. Two main approaches for reverse engineering are described.

- The first approach, by Missaoui, Goding, and Gagnon, presents a complete methodology for mapping conceptual schemata into structurally object-oriented schemata. The main advantages of such a methodology is the use of an adapted clustering technique allowing recursive grouping of objects (e.g., entities and relationships) from an extended entity-relationship schema.

- The second approach is by Papazoglou and van den Heuevel. The authors describe an access in place solution for building object-oriented applications that access legacy relational data and functionality. This approach is based on the use of abstraction mechanisms and a semantically oriented protocol that provide intermediate abstract constructs that support the coexistence of diverse data models such as the relational and object-oriented.

Temporal and Dynamic Modeling   Most conventional database systems represent a snapshot of the real world at the current instant. Although the contents of a database continue to change as new information is added, theses changes are viewed as updates to the current state of the database, with the old, out-of-date data being deleted from the context of the database. Such conventional databases may serve several applications well, but fall short of applications that require the modeling and management of historical data. This requires the ability to model objects and their relationships over a period of time. The ability to model temporal dimensions of the real world is critical for many applications, including banking, inventory control, stock brokerage, accounting, medical records, and airline reservations. Temporal object-oriented databases add the notion of time to model time-varying types of information. Another modeling dimension of object-oriented databases that is related to time is the ability to model changes in state and behavior. The objects of interest in an application domain usually do not remain static; they must possess the ability to evolve as either groups or individual objects. Of particular importance is the ability to model dynamic behavior, whereby an object may change its behavior periodically while retaining the same identity. Thus the ability to model significant shifts in object behavior and correlate them with existing properties of objects is important for a large number of applications. The modeling of temporal and dynamic aspects improves the versatility and modeling power of object-oriented databases and allows us to model complex applications that challenge the currently available database technology. The chapters in this category provide a good understanding of the use of specialized techniques to deal with more complex requirements that analysts and developers need to master in order to develop complex applications and systems.

- The first chapter, by Jensen and Snodgrass, proposes guidelines for the design of temporal object-oriented databases. The authors describe techniques for capturing the properties of time-varying attributes in temporal databases. These techniques allow the modeling of real-world objects by means of attributes, life-spans of attributes, and derivation functions that compute new attribute values from stored ones. The connection between these temporal object properties and the design of the conceptual database schema are also highlighted.

- The chapter by Papazoglou and Krämer discusses modeling techniques and language extensions for representing object dynamics for objects that may attain many types while retaining a single object identity. This technique allows the modeling of objects whose behavior (roles) changes over time or varies depending on how these objects are viewed by applications. Up-growths of behavior are known as roles that objects play which can be assumed and relinquished dynamically to reflect changing modeling requirements.

Modeling Interoperable Objects   New data processing applications are rarely built from scratch or in isolation. They have to reuse existing data, which are already stored in computer files or databases, most likely spread over several autonomous sources interconnected via an intranet or the internet. To facilitate application development, the data to be reused should be integrated into a single "virtual database," providing for the logical unification of the underlying data sets. This unification process is called "database integration," and its result is termed the "federated database." The process deals with semantic issues, leaving to one side traditional system issues of distributed systems (e.g., distributed concurrency control, query processing, and transaction management).

While there is a majority consensus on the architecture of future federated systems which will provide such an integration, many diverse integration methodologies have been proposed in order to unite existing schemas into a global federated schema. Basic assumptions diverge, as well as technical solutions and overall goals of the database integration process. The overall picture is quite confusing for the inexperienced practitioner or even researcher trying to find out a way to solve the problem.

- The first contribution in this section, by Parent and Spaccapietra, starts with an overview of different approaches to interoperability, from simple gateways to the most sophisticated federated systems. The paper continues with a synthetic, consistent analysis of the various trends and alternatives in database integration. It makes clear the approaches, the differences, and the possible goals. A general perspective over the whole problem area is provided, so that the readers can identify the interactions among the various facets of the problems and the solutions. Emphasis is on basic ideas, rather than on technical details.

- The second contribution, by Gogolla, focuses on the very basic problem of determining an identification mechanism that could support object migration between heterogeneous systems. In an environment of cooperating systems, object identities provided by local object-oriented systems are of no help, as they are by definition only relevant within the system that generated them and only for the duration of a single transaction. Federated systems need to move objects around, from the provider to the requester, and such moves may have to last beyond the limits of a traditional transaction. One way to solve the problem is to introduce long transactions. This approach is not yet operational and raises uneasy issues of data sharing. Gogolla's paper reviews semantic-based solutions to the problem and formulates an alternative proposal using the query facilities.

Modeling Object Collaborations   Owing to the growth of networking technology, software applications are no longer restricted to support only individual work. Now it becomes more and more common to support collaborative activities whereby people and process in different parts of an organization work together. WWW application or Intranet applets are concrete examples where collaborative processing is useful to allow different objects of geographically distributed environment to synchronously collaborate with each other over a network.

Object-oriented technology provides better support collaborative processing than other technologies. Even though there are quite a few proposed methodologies and environments which deal with the problems of designing appropriate infrastructures (e.g., models, languages, etc.) for better collaboration between objects, we believe there are still a lot of limitations with regard to understanding "internals" of object collaboration. For instance, most of these design methods model local individual object behavior, and thus they fall short on modeling coordinated behavior and collaboration between several interacting objects. This part of the book comprises two interesting contributions which address problems related to the design of collaborative objects.

- The first contribution is by F. Casati, S. Ceri, P. Pernici, and G. Pozzi. The authors address challenging modeling issues regarding the use of workflow technology to design a better coordination environment for the execution of tasks. Their workflow-based approach provides techniques for modeling "internal behavior" (i.e., interaction and cooperation between tasks) as well as the relationships to the environment. In addition, they propose a framework to translate workflows into active rules, thereby providing an operational and implementation scheme for many components of a workflow management system.

- The second contribution is by Engels, Groenewegen, and Kappel. It addresses the improvement of existing design methods for collaborative objects. The authors propose a multi-model approach specification of collaboration between object, which deals with (i) the degree of visibility of executed tasks by by collaborative objects, (ii) the design of collaboration constraints, and (iii) the design of cooperation contract. For each of these issues, an appropriate model is provided for enforcing usage collaboration and collaboration constraints. Finally, in this paper, the authors compare the expressiveness of the proposed multi-model approach with existing approaches with respect to four criteria: the number of threads of control, the degree of asynchronism, the number of collaborators influenced, and the degree of freedom within the cooperation.

Beyond Modeling—Unified Language and Model Support   The sixth category of chapters deals with bridging the gap between *modeling* and *language implementation*. This is an important topic as it discusses mechanisms to avoid the disparity between modeling and implementation, which frequently leads to loss of transformations between conceptual and implementation models and cluttered implementations. This category comprises only one chapter contributed by Liddle, Embley, and Woodfield and looks at an approach for unifying modeling and programming through the use of an object-oriented programming language. The authors use a model-equivalent language (a language with a one-to-one correspondence to underlying executable model) to reduce the complexity of advanced-application specification and implementation.

Case Study: The EU-Rent Car Rentals

The case study that follows is based on a case study conducted by Model Systems and Brian Wilson Associates and concerns the rental of cars in European countries. EU-Rent is a car rental company, owned by EU-Corporation, with 1000 branches in towns all over Europe. It is one of three businesses—the other two being hotels and an airline—each of which has its own business and information systems, but with a shared customer base. Many of the car rental customers also fly with EU-Fly and stay at EU-Stay hotels.

EU-Rent has approximately 200,000 cars and makes about 20 million rentals per year, spread across 1000 branches of three types: branches in major airports (100 branches, average 700 cars), branches in major cities (200 branches, average 375 cars), and branches in local agencies such as hotels or garages (700 branches, average 80 cars). Cars are classified in five groups. All cars in a group are of equivalent specification and have the same rental price.

EU-Rent estimates that about 5 million customers per year are served, of whom (approximately): 10% rent frequently from the same branch; 3% rent frequently, but from several branches; 35% rent from EU-Rent between 2 and 5 times per year; and 52% are effectively "one-off renters"—they use EU-Rent once per year or less.

The EU-Rent basic activities include, for example, the delivery of a range of services (rental of cars of different quality and price) at many locations (rental branches) and the capacity planning and resource replenishment (disposal and purchase of cars, moving of cars between branches). EU-Rent aims (i) to maintain customer satisfaction by promoting a high-quality image, (ii) to increase coordination between branches, and (iii) to increase utilization by better management of numbers of cars at branches and better coordination between branches.

The different branches' operations of the EU-Rent are car rentals, purchase of cars, and sale of cars. The activities of the Branch Car Rentals involve: advance reservations (for rentals that are reserved in advance); walk-in rentals (where a customer may walk in and request an immediate rental); provision of cars for rental (were each day, the branch manager must ensure that there are sufficient cars in each group to meet his reservation commitments for the following day.); the return of car (and the car is inspected for fuel level, kilometers traveled and damage); the returns (of cars) to other branches; and the management of late returns. The purchase of cars involves the ordering of new cars, acceptance of new cars, and payment for cars. Finally, the sale of cars involves the decision on which cars to sell, the release of car to dealer, and the receipt of payment for car.

The IT system of EU-Rent is currently being modernized and has as a major aim to support the following main processes.

- Manage Car Pool: The Car Bookings file contains details of the cars currently owned by the branch. A car entry is added to the Car Bookings file when a car is acquired by a branch and deleted when the car is disposed of.

- Control Car Movements: When a car is picked up for maintenance, the time is noted in the Car Bookings file and the driver is given an authorization. When a car is returned from maintenance, the time is noted in the Car Bookings file and the driver is given a receipt.

- Process Car Rental: Advance reservations are recorded in the Reservations file showing a reference, customer details, car group requested, start of required rental and number of days of rental. Each day, booking clerks look through the rentals due to start on the following day, look in the Car Bookings file or the group and book a specific car for each reservation.

- Record Return of Cars: When a car is returned from rental, the time, payment amount, and any comments about the customer or rental are recorded in the Car Bookings file and a receipt is printed. If the car was rented from a different branch, ownership of the car is transferred to the receiving branch; the branch from which the car was rented is notified by telephone.

- Arrange Car Maintenance: A Branch Manager may book a car in for service at the service depot, as long as the car is free and the service depot has capacity for that day. A Branch Manager or a Depot Manager may cancel a Maintenance Booking at any time until the car is picked up. This process requires coordination between the relevant Branch Manager and the Depot Manager, to ensure the Service Diary and the Car Bookings file are in step. When a service has been completed, a description of the work done and the parts and labor cost are added to the car service history, and the parts and labor cost to the service diary.

Mike P. Papazoglou, Stefano Spaccapietra, Zahir Tari

Tilburg, Lausanne, Melbourne, June 1999

1   *Advances in Object-Oriented Data Modeling*

Moira Norrie
Institute for Information Systems
ETH Zurich, CH-8092 Switzerland
norrie inf.ethz.ch

Ideally, both the development and use of an information system should be based on a single abstract model of the application domain. This means that the same information model should support all of the development stages from conceptual modeling through to implementation. It follows that the underlying data model should be semantically expressive and amenable to a refinement process from design to implementation. Further, the model must provide a good framework on which to base a data management system.

Traditionally, it has tended to be the case that different models have been used for application modeling and for system operation. For example, it is commonly the case that an entity-relationship model is used for application analysis and design and a relational model for implementation. This results in a semantic gap between the conceptual and operational models of the application. One of the major aims of research and development in object-oriented database technologies is to eliminate this semantic gap by developing object-oriented data models which support both the development of application systems and the implementation of data management systems.

Here, we review both the requirements and features of data models with respect to the design and implementation of both application systems and the underlying data management systems. We then go on to discuss the features of object-oriented data models and how they relate to other data model paradigms. Finally, we outline some of the major research issues concerning the integration of database and programming technologies in order to attain truly integrated development environments for advanced information systems.

1.1   Schema and Model Duality

The schema of a database plays a dual role in that it is both a description of that part of the real world referred to as the application domain and also a description of that part of the computer world referred to as the database. Thus, it describes not only application concepts, but also their representation within a data management system. It is important to recognise this duality as it is the cause for certain tensions between the two realms of data models—application development and data management system development.

We illustrate this schema duality in Figure 1.1. The upper part of the figure denotes the realm of application development and the role of the schema as an abstract model of the application domain. Primarily, this model must identify the various application entities of interest and their various roles and associations. The database schema

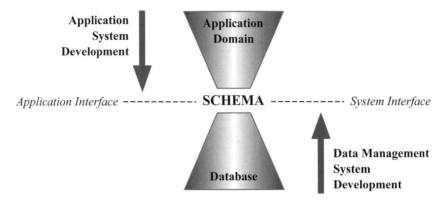

Figure 1.1   Schema Duality

defines the application interface to the database system which will be used by an application programmer or an end-user browsing and querying the database directly.

The lower part of Figure 1.1 denotes the realm of data management system development and the role of a schema as a specification of a database instance. The system interface defines the functionality of the data management system in terms of a set of generic structures and operations. A schema for a particular application specifies a database in terms of these generic structures and the resulting database is accessed using the generic operations defined in the interface.

The set of generic structures and operations that form the system interface are referred to as a *data model*. As described above, we see that, just as a schema has dual roles, a data model has corresponding dual roles. On the one hand, the constructs it provides must be capable of modeling application semantics and here expressibility is a major factor. On the other hand, the constructs must be amenable to efficient implementation and here simplicity and generality are major factors.

The above picture is rather idealistic—in line with our opening remark that both the development and use of an information system should be based on a single abstract model of the application domain. However, the differing requirements of a data model in terms of its dual roles has led to the situation where, frequently, instead of seeking a single data model which satisfies all of our needs, different data models have been developed for specific roles.

In the following subsections, we examine in detail the requirements of data models for application development and also data management. We then discuss the abstraction levels present in application system development and operation in terms of the various data models used.

1.1.1   Data Models for Application Development

The process of constructing an abstract model of the application domain is often referred to as conceptual modeling and has been supported by a number of semantic data models with the entity-relationship models being the most widely used. The

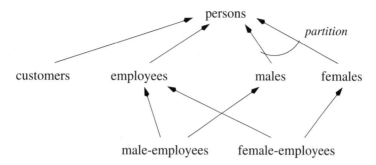

Figure 1.2   Classification Graph

resulting schema is often referred to as a conceptual schema since it describes the main concepts of the application in terms of application entities, their roles and associations. Depending on the model and methodology in use, it may also detail the properties of these entities and also their behavior.

A conceptual schema must be *adequate* in that it captures the relevant features of the application domain. Furthermore, it should be *natural* in that it should correspond to the sorts of mental models that users form to visualise and work within application domains. The general area of study concerned with the construction of models which correspond directly and naturally to our own conceptualisations of reality is known as cognitive modeling. While the precise nature of mental models is still open to much debate and research, there have been some general principles proposed on the basis of psychological and linguistic research (34).

The process of abstraction is fundamental to human information processing and there is strong evidence to support the fact that we make 'order out of chaos' by extensive use of *classification*. We classify individual entities by means of general concepts and then further place these concepts into general classification graphs which relate certain concepts are being *specialisations* or *generalisations* of other concepts. Unlike, biological taxonomies, these classification graphs may not be purely hierarchical and an entity may be simultaneously classified in many different ways.

For example, in the realm of a company, we could classify *persons* into *customers* and *employees*, and also into *males* and *females*. We could further introduce the concepts of *female-employees* and *male-employees* since it may be that employment laws require special facilities depending on employee gender and so these concepts are significant in our application domain. The resulting classification graph is shown in Figure 1.2: The nodes are classifications and a directed edge from node n_1 to node n_2 represents that n_1 is a specialisation of n_2. A classification graph is generally a directed acyclic graph. It can be considered as modeling the different roles of an entity—and note that an entity may have many roles simultaneously and that these roles may change over time. Thus, a person may be both a customer and an employee and, at some future time, continue to be a customer even though they cease to be an employee.

Some roles however may be exclusive and this we can denote by placing constraints over the arcs of a classification graph. For example, in Figure 1.2, we indicate that concept classifications *males* and *females* partition *persons* meaning that every person must belong to exactly one of those classifications. The ability to model entity roles and role-dependent properties and behavior is very important in application modeling and, as we shall discuss later, is something that lacks support in the data models of many existing database management systems.

The basis for the classification of an entity may or may not be well-defined. In accordance with a number of contemporary philosophers (26), linguists (18) and psychologists (33), we consider that it may not be possible to define a set of necessary and sufficient conditions for a concept classification. For example, we may not be able to define precisely the concept of a 'trusted customer'—but we could still choose to classify some of our customers as such. In practical terms, even if a set of defining properties can be established, they may not be of interest in a given information system: We do not need to know anything about the genetic makeup of a person to classify them in *males* or *females*. Rather, we may leave the classification to the entities themselves when filling in forms or simply leave it to the end-user who adds an entity representation to a particular classification group during data entry or update.

In addition to classification of entities into concepts, we form associations between concepts which allow us to navigate through our information space. Classification structures over associations are also possible. For example, a general association may exist between company employees and customers, and this may be specialised into associations representing various forms of contacts, services and agreements.

Conceptual modeling forms the basis for not only the design and documentation of an information system, but also communication between the client and the developer in terms of requirements analysis and contractual agreement. It is the meeting point between the application expert and the method expert and therefore must be easily understood by both, without requiring detailed knowledge of any underlying technology.

A schema is defined in terms of a *data modeling language* associated with the underlying data model. In the case of conceptual schemas, where the focus is on analysis and design, most data models have an associated graphical language which aids understanding through the visualisation of the schema structure. Some data models used for conceptual modeling have only a graphical language, a few have only a textual language—and many have both. Popular data models such as the family of entity relationship models have had many associated graphical and textual languages proposed and these may differ to a greater or lesser extent.

An important distinction between data models proposed solely for conceptual modeling and those for data management is that the former generally have no associated operational model since they are used only for system development and not system operation. This difference stems also from the fact that, traditionally, the development of a database has been considered separately from the development of the application programs. Another major goal of object-oriented database technologies and methodologies is to consider *both* aspects of information system development within a common, integrated framework. More recently, there has been a growing trend, as seen in object-oriented analysis and design methodologies (5, 29, 6), to include the modeling of behavior and transactions at the conceptual level. However, we note that, even with such models, a full operational model is usually not supported, since the models are not executable.

Where one does see full operational models at the conceptual level, is in the case of prototyping systems which support conceptual modeling (15, 20, 23). Rapid prototyping is generally advocated as a means of eliciting and validating requirements (37, 30). In the software engineering community, rapid prototyping usually revolves around the user interface as a means of determining system functionality and interface design. In contrast, rapid prototyping in the case of information systems development usually revolves around the conceptual schema. Ideally, a rapid prototyping system must support full database functionality in terms of a persistent store, querying, behavior specification and execution, database evolution and constraint management. Fundamental to such a system is a data model which incorporates a full operational model.

1.1.2   Data Models for Data Management

We now turn to consider the requirements of a data model from the point of view of the design and development of a data management system. A data management system is a generalised software system that should provide efficient data management for a range of application systems. It must provide methods of representing, storing and processing data such that operational performance will reach a reasonable standard of efficiency regardless of specific data and application characteristics. This can be done through the provision of a small number of general constructs along with various implementations suited to different data and application profiles. Further, operations on a database should be specified at a logical level which is independent of physical representation and implementation: The system can then determine the methods of evaluation through consideration of data characteristics and the current form of representation. Hence, as the database evolves, the underlying representations and implementations can evolve without recourse to the application programmers or end users.

The requirements for efficient data management are in fact not orthogonal to those for conceptual modeling. Both require a data model which provides a small number of general constructs in terms of which one can model the application domain with relative ease. Also, they both require a high-level operational model which is independent of physical representation. We therefore believe that it is possible to realise our goal of a single data model which is both expressive in terms of role and association modeling and provides a good framework for data management (22).

In practice, however, many of the designers and developers of database management systems have tended to focus on the level of the storage model or programming language type model as their view of data management. As a result, the system

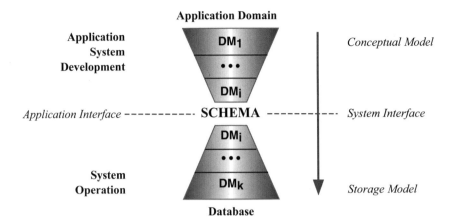

Figure 1.3   Schema Levels

interface is at too low a level of abstraction and, often, too closely bound to the implementation platform. The schema of a database is thus very much a description of a representation of an application, rather than of the application itself. For example, the relational model which consists of a single generic structure—the relation—may be amenable to an efficient implementation, but is very limited in terms of application modeling as it forces us to model everything in terms of flat tables of values.

In the case of most object-oriented database management systems, the constructs and operations of the system interface are basically those of the associated programming language with possibly a few additional generic constructs such as bulk type constructors for sets, lists etc. The problem here is that a programming language type model is designed to model our man-made computer world of values and computations in which everything is well-defined. It is not suited to the sorts of dynamic and flexible role and association modeling required for describing concepts of the application domain. Further, programming languages are often not designed to cater for a persistent environment in which both objects and types can evolve over time (12).

1.1.3   Abstraction Levels

The development and operation of a database system may therefore involve not one, but many, data models as indicated in Figure 1.3. Each data model represents an abstraction level. A schema of one data model will be mapped into a schema of the data model at the level below. Similarly, operations of one data model are implemented in terms of operations at the lower levels.

With respect to application system development, an initial conceptual schema may be mapped in one or more stages into a schema defined in terms of the model corresponding to the system interface of the data management system that is the final implementation platform. For example, an entity-relationship schema may be first mapped into a general relational schema which is then mapped into a schema of specific relational database management system such as the Oracle8 server (4). This schema defines the application interface.

A data management system itself usually also involves several abstraction layers—with each layer offering data management services in terms of a set of constructs and operations. Thus, a data management system may have a number of internal data models—including a basic storage model. At the top level is the model which defines the system interface and this is the same model used at the end of the application development process to specify the application interface.

It is important to distinguish between data models which are 'internal' to system operation and those which are 'external' to application development. Those which are internal are of importance only to the developer of the data management system and are not visible to the application programmer or end-user of a database system. To emphasise this, consider the following two cases. First, there is the case of an application developer who uses an object-oriented data model for conceptual design and then maps the resulting schema to a relational schema for implementation. Second, there is the case of the developer of an object-oriented database management system who uses a relational engine for storage management and therefore internally maps the object-oriented data model defining his system interface to a relational model. Is there a significant difference between these two cases since in both a relational system is used to store the data?

The important difference between these two cases is that the level of the application and system interfaces is radically different. In the first case, application programmers and direct end-users interact with the database system at the level of the relational schema and must be aware of its structure and operations. In the second case, they interact at the level of the object-oriented schema and the relational schema is purely internal to the system.

We consider that our major research goal in the development of object-oriented database systems is not necessarily to remove the different levels of data models, but rather to move the level of the application interface to the conceptual level by providing suitable data models at the system interface which can support both conceptual modeling and effective data management.

1.2   Evolution of Object-Oriented Models

From the foregoing discussion, it should be clear that the notion of a data model is central to both information system development and to the provision of general data management services. During the last three decades, a large variety of data models have been proposed. These vary not only in their form, but also in their intended purpose. Many have been proposed specifically as a conceptual modeling tool with the intention that the resulting application model be later translated into the data model of the chosen database management system. Others have been proposed as the basis for a data management service. However, this distinction is not always a clear one as sometimes a data model intended for use as a conceptual modeling tool is later realised in terms of a data management system and an operational part of the model specified.

Here we present the main features of a number of data models with the intention of showing how object-oriented data models evolved and how they relate to other kinds of data models. It is beyond the scope of this chapter to provide a comprehensive review of all proposed models—or, indeed, of the model families. We rather simply highlight the main influences and directions of development.

Early database management systems were based on the network data model or a restricted version of it known as the hierarchical data model. These models reflect the physical structure of data and are based on the idea of files of records with links between them. Operations are specified at the level of records and a navigational style of programming is supported. Both the structural and operational aspects of these models were criticised for being at too low a level requiring the application programmer to be aware of the physical representation structures and to keep track of navigation through these structures.

Although implementations of the relational model were already in existence, the formal introduction of the model is attributed to Codd in his paper (9). The structural part of the relational model represents an application entity as a tuple of values and entity classifications as relations. Associations between entities are implied by cross-references among the values stored in relations. It is interesting to note that in his original exposition of the model, Codd does not state that values *must* be atomic, but rather introduces it as a secondary restriction that might be appropriate in certain cases. However, the atomicity of values was adopted and considered a basic restriction referred to as the *first normal form*.

The relational model was one of the first data models to have operations at the level of collections and these are given in terms of a relational algebra. The join operator can be used to navigate through the database by means of the associations represented implicitly.

The main criticism levelled at the relational model concerns its lack of semantic modeling capability. We can identify two main areas of development of the model aimed at addressing this issue. The first was the need to express conceptual dependencies between relations and the second the need to extend the limited forms of values supported.

The notion of keys was introduced to provide some form of entity reference. Cross-referencing of keys is the means of representing associations and linking relations together into a database structure. Concepts of referential integrity were introduced to define the semantics of insertion and deletion operations on a database.

The relational model was extended to support further forms of conceptual dependencies so that not only associations between entities, but also associations between classifications such as specialisation relationships could be represented. RM/T (10) extended the relational data model with various metadata relations that described such dependencies. This model also distinguishes between relations which represent entities from those that represent associations.

Proposals for nested relational models remove the first normal form restriction and allow relations as values of attributes. This can be thought of as removing the restriction that the tuple and set constructors can be applied only once and in a specific order—"build tuples and then from these build relations". By allowing tuple and set constructors to be used repeatedly, we arrive at nested relations. If we further relax the restriction that set and tuple constructors have to strictly alternate, then we end up with what is usually called complex objects (2) or extended relations (25). A number of proposals exist for extending the operational part of the relational model to deal with these complex values: these include (16, 1, 39, 25, 31, 32).

Parallel to these developments of the relational model, was the emergence of a number of data models designed specifically to support the conceptual modeling process. We shall refer to these generally as *semantic data models* since their primary goal was to model application semantics. This family of data models can be considered as having two main influences: The entity-relationship model introduced by Chen (8) and semantic nets introduced in the realm of artificial intelligence for knowledge representation (27, 28).

The entity-relationship model was proposed as a database structure design tool and therefore the original proposal had no associated operational model. The model brought to the fore the idea of there being two basic notions of equal importance—entities and associations.

The semantic data models which developed from semantic nets took on board the abstractions which were the basis for relationships between concepts—the *isa* relationship for specialisations and the *part-of* relationship for aggregation. Smith and Smith (38) proposed to introduce these abstractions into the relational model. From these origins, a number of semantic data models evolved including SDM (14) and TAXIS (19). In these models, entities are represented by complex values and associations as reference attributes. Thus, an association is decomposed into two directional, functional components—usually a dependency between them may be declared in order that consistency is ensured.

Later, enhanced entity-relationship models were introduced which combined the basic constructs of the entity-relationship model with the classification structures and complex values supported in other semantic data models. The success of the entity-relationship family of models can be measured by the fact that its use spread into the software engineering community and it strongly influenced current object models used in object-oriented analysis and design methodologies.

From this brief description, we see that there was a demand for data models which were more suited to the task of conceptual modeling in terms of modeling application entities, their roles and associations. While the detail and approach of the models varied—in particular, with respect to whether they placed the emphasis on entities, associations or both—the trend was obvious. Data models were required which provided higher levels of abstraction than those provided by existing data management services.

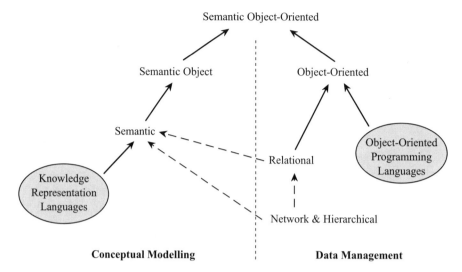

Figure 1.4   Evolution of Data Models

One of the key features of these models is that they are entity-based rather than value-based enabling application entities to be modeled directly. Further, the importance of concept specialisation and property inheritance through some form of *isa* or *subtyping* relationship was recognised. These are often considered as the essential features of object data models and, if we do so, most semantic data models would nowadays be classified as object data models.

The progression of semantic data models to object data models is therefore hard to define in terms of distinguishing constructs. Rather it was a gradual and natural trend which paralleled the new object-based paradigms influencing other areas of computer science. Two papers provide surveys of the first generation of semantic data models. Peckham and Maryanski (24) give a comparative review of a number of semantic data models, while Hull and King (13) examine semantic data modeling concepts through the introduction of a generic semantic data model based on the formal object data model IFO (3). Many object data models for conceptual modeling have been introduced in the last decade. In (21), Mylopoulos discusses the features of many of these and also associated conceptual modeling tools.

In Figure 1.4, we show the main evolutionary paths of object data models. On the left, we show data models used primarily for conceptual modeling and on the right those used primarily for data management.

The solid lines indicate what we might call 'positive influences' on data model development and the dashed lines 'negative influences'. By this, we mean that a solid line indicates a dependency in which the later model adopted notions from the former model. A dashed line indicates that features were introduced into the later model as a result of inadequacies recognised in the earlier model. Thus, the recognition that the early network and hierarchical models were too bound to physical representation and based on single record-at-a-time processing led to the development of the relational

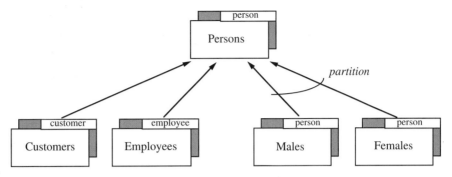

Figure 1.5   Role Modeling in Object-Oriented Databases

model. In turn, the lack of semantic expressiveness of the relational model caused people to develop other semantic models that were suitable for conceptual modeling.

The right side of Figure 1.4 shows the influences in data model development from the point of view of data management systems. A major influence in recent years is that of object-oriented programming languages and technologies. Motivated by the requirements of advanced applications in the scientific, engineering and commercial domains, the functionality of database systems has been extended to support also the behavioral aspects of information systems in terms of storing programs, rules and integrity constraints alongside data. This has resulted in a new generation of object-oriented database management systems which in turn have influenced relational vendors to add limited object-oriented concepts to their relational systems, see for example Oracle8 (4).

Further, these influences are on the increase as more and more developers are choosing object-oriented languages, in particular Java, as their application language. While relational vendors rush to try and integrate object-oriented features into their systems and to support Java language bindings, there still remains a fundamental mismatch in the underlying data models of the relational and object-oriented worlds. This means that an application programmer must continually map between a relational model and the data structures and operations used in his program.

Object-oriented database management systems aim for a seamless integration of the database and programming worlds by offering a data model that is compatible with the programming language type model. This means that the constructs and operations that define the data management services interface are compliant with those of the programming language. The type model of the programming language is usually adopted as the model for defining entity representations in terms of object instances. Bulk type constructors—either of the native programming language or introduced through special data management class libraries—are used to represent entity roles by collections of objects. Thus, a part of the classification graph of Figure 1.2 could be represented as shown in Figure 1.5.

Here, we denote a collection of objects corresponding to a classification as a rectangle. The shaded part of the collection specifies the types of the objects belonging to

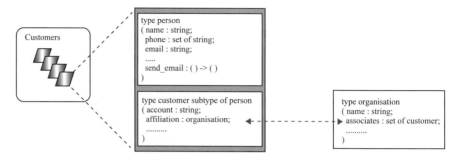

Figure 1.6   Types and Collections

that collection. For example, collection *Customers* is a collection of objects of type *customer*. The classification *Customers* is a specialisation of *Persons*. Thus, each object in *Customers* is also in *Persons*. A person may have several roles as represented by memberships of several collections. For example, a male employee who is also a customer would be a member of collections *Persons*, *Customers*, *Employees* and *Males*.

In Figure 1.6, we indicate how such customer objects might be represented in an object-oriented database. The collection *Customers* is a set of objects of type *customer* where *customer* is defined to be a subtype of type *person*. A customer object therefore has the properties of persons such as *name*, *phone*, *email* and method *send_email* together with those specific to customers, such as *account* and *affiliation*.

Some data models clearly distinguish the concepts of entity representation from that of entity classification by having separate constructs. For example, they may use bulk constructors such as *set* or *collection* to introduce semantic groupings of objects of a given type. In other models, the two notions are fused into a single *class* construct which is both a type definition and an implicit grouping of objects of that type. Other models sit somewhere in between. The problem of fusing the two notions is that it prevents multiple classifications of objects of a given type such as *Males* and *Females* in Figure 1.5. We would have to instead introduce subtypes, possibly with additional properties, to denote these semantic groupings.

A second major difference in the data models of various object-oriented data management systems is the support they give to associations. Some simply represent associations as attribute properties with object references. For example, in Figure 1.6, the attribute *affiliation* of type *customer* is a reference to an object of type *organization*. In turn, an object of type *organization* has an attribute *associates* which is a set of references to objects of type *customer*. If the data model of a system interface provides only this means of representing associations, there is no guarantee of mutual consistency and, further, no special operations or semantics attached to associations. Some systems, such as Objectivity/DB, do recognise two-way associations and also allow special semantics, such as locking or versioning semantics, to be attached to associations. Other systems, for example OMS (17), support a completely separate association construct with its own algebraic operations and also classification structures.

A feature of object-oriented data models that is often used to distinguish them from other data models is their ability to model behavior as well as structure. Objects may have behavioral properties as specified by methods of the associated types. Generally, we find three different uses of methods. First, they may be used to model derived attributes where the values are computed rather than stored. Second, they are used to specify operations or actions associated with an object such as a *send_email* method on a *person* object. Third, they are often used to assist navigation through a database by giving direct access to information associated with an object. In such cases, the methods can be thought of as specifying pre-defined queries on objects. For example, a method associated with *person* objects could be used to directly access the address information of the organizations for which they work.

Methods are usually declared separately from their implementation. Thus, the schema may specify only the method signatures in terms of their arguments and results. The implementations of the methods are given elsewhere—either using a general programming language or possibly a special language of the data management system. In fact, a number of so-called object-oriented models have been proposed which deal only with the declaration of method signatures, but not with their implementation or even a behavioral specification. Doing so would appear to underestimate the significance of adding behavior to the database and the need to have means to model and specify this aspect of an information system.

One major influence of the relational model concerns query languages and the underlying algebraic model. The introduction of an algebra over collections of tuple values can be considered as one of the main contributions of the relational model. Most object-oriented systems also support some form of algebra over collections of values—but in this case the values are objects rather than tuples.

As previously discussed, the ability to model the various roles of application entities and also their associations is central to conceptual modeling. While object data models used for conceptual modeling typically support role modeling (to a greater or lesser extent), it is frequently the case that even the simplest of role models cannot be implemented directly in an object-oriented database system. This arises because their data model is too closely tied to the underlying programming language and, usually, the type system of that language is more restrictive than that of semantic data models. For example, in many object-oriented programming languages, an object could not simultaneously be of type *customer* and *employee* and, further, an object cannot change its types—or may only do so in limited ways.

Thus, the data models offered by most commercial object-oriented database management systems—and also that of the ODMG standard (7)—tend to be pitched below the abstraction level of conceptual modeling and, as a result, some mapping is required between the structures of the initial application model and that of the final application interface. Further, constraints depicted in classification graphs such as those implied by specialisations or those such as the *partition* constraint over *Males* and *Females* are often not supported and must be implemented by the application programmer. Some support for associations and ensuring referential integrity is supported in the ODMG data model and also in some commercial systems such as Objectivity/DB—but in many others there is no specific support for associations other than being able to represent them through reference attributes as described above.

The current situation is therefore that there tends to be two categories of object data models—those developed for conceptual modeling and those developed for data management services as depicted in Figure 1.4. The former focus on semantic expressibility and hence we label them *semantic object* models. The latter focus on operational aspects and are closely related to the object-oriented programming languages and we label them *object-oriented* models.

To attain our ideal of a truly integrated development framework based on a single data model, we need to combine these two categories and develop a new generation of *semantic object-oriented* data models. These models will be semantically expressive and at the same time can support efficient data management in an object-oriented programming environment. While efforts in this direction have been made in the research community, many of these ideas have still to permeate into commercial systems.

1.3   Integrating Databases and Programming

As described above, one of the major research challenges is to develop object-oriented data models which can support the whole of the database development process from conceptual modeling through to implementation. This requires techniques for resolving the conflict that currently arises between the notions of object and type in conceptual modeling and those of object-oriented programming languages. In programming languages, the major concern is to represent computational values and to do so efficiently by performing static type checking whenever possible. This contrasts with the use of types and values to model application entities, their role dependent behavior and evolution—all of which require dynamic type checking together dynamic binding mechanisms.

One solution is to represent object properties associated with roles explicitly rather than through the programming language and variants of this have been proposed for the Smalltalk (11) and Oberon (36) environments. Another solution is to introduce a two-level structure in which database objects are dynamically composed from one of more programming language objects and this is implemented in OMS Java, a data management system and application development framework for the Java environment (35).

The integration of behavior into the database presents new challenges to the designers and developers of information systems as it requires new methodologies and tools which seamlessly integrate concepts and technologies from both the software engineering and database communities.

Within the realm of software engineering, various models and methodologies for object-oriented analysis and design have been proposed and are now in widespread use in the Information Technology sector. Of particular note are the OMT (29) and Booch (5) models and methodologies which have been adapted and integrated within the recent UML proposal (6).

Such methodologies are not intended primarily for database system development, but rather for the development of large systems of which a database may form a part. Thus the emphasis is more on the development of code and application classes and it is often assumed that database functionality will ultimately be provided by a relational storage system which acts as a form of low-level data repository. Rather than providing an integrated solution which exploits object-oriented technologies to the full, the database is a separate component requiring a mapping between the application and storage models. With respect to application programming, this results in the previously described problems of impedance mismatch where the application programmer must deal with fundamentally different models of data.

In the case of information systems, we regard the database as playing a central rather than a subsidiary role. An information architect is responsible for eliciting the information requirements of an enterprise and establishing an information model. These requirements are determined by considering both the structural and dynamic aspects of the information base, application functionality and the characteristics of the information system itself in terms of scope and change. Once this information model has been specified, the development of one or more application systems around it can begin.

At issue is how the software engineering point of view can be merged with this database-centred view. For example, rapid prototyping is advocated in both fields— but the focus differs. In the case of software engineering, rapid prototyping is based on the user interface, while, in database development, it is based on the information model. Is it possible to combine these approaches, or should one be preferred?

Object-oriented technologies have promised benefits in terms of modularity, reusability and extensibility in application development. Further work is required to realise this potential in terms of information system development. We need to reex-amine basic notions such as 'database' and 'schema' and develop improved models and mechanisms for sharing both metadata and data. In terms of extensibility, it has to be recognised that the ability to extend a data management system for specialised application domains managing temporal, spatial or versioned data has to be sup-ported by full *model extensibility*. This means that *all* aspects of a model, and hence of the underlying data management services, have to be extensible. Thus, it should be possible not only to store values of specialised data types, but also to extend the underlying algebra and query language in a natural way.

As can be seen from the contributions in this book, these are challenges that are actively being addressed by the research community. In particular, the first part of the book presents proposals for modeling object behavior. A second important dynamic aspect of object-oriented databases is their ability to cope with and represent change both to individual entities of the application domain and to the application domain itself. This aspect is examined in the third part of the book which considers changes to database states and individual object behavior in terms of temporal and dynamic modeling.

References

1. S. Abiteboul and N. Bidoit. Non First Normal Form Relations to Represent Hierarchically Organized Data. In *Proceedings ACM SIGACT/SIGMOD Symposium on Principles of Database Systems*, pages 191–200. ACM, 1984.

2. S. Abiteboul and C. Beeri. On the Power of Languages for the Manipulation of Complex Objects. (846), 1988.

3. S. Abiteboul and R. Hull. IFO: A formal semantic database model. *ACM Transactions on Database Systems*, 12(4):525–565, 1987.

4. S. Bobrowski. *Oracle8 Architecture*. Oracle Press, 1998.

5. G. Booch. *Object-Oriented Design with Applications*. Benjamin/Cummings, 1991.

6. G. Booch, J. Rumbaugh, and I. Jacobson. *Unified Modelling Language User Guide*. Addison-Wesley, 1998.

7. R.G.G. Cattell, D. Barry, D. Bartels, M. Berler, J. Eastman, S. Gamerman, D. Jordan, A. Springer, H. Strickland, and D. Wade, editors. *The Object Data Standard: ODMG 2.0*. Morgan Kaufmann, 1997.

8. P. P. Chen. The Entity-Relationship Model - Towards a Unified View of Data. *ACM Transactions on Database Systems*, 1(1):9–36, 1976.

9. E. F. Codd. A Relational Model of Data for Large Shared Data Banks. *Communications of the ACM*, 13(6):377–387, 1970.

10. E. F. Codd. Extending the Database Relational Model to Capture More Meaning. *ACM Transactions on Database Systems*, 4(4):397–434, 1979.

11. G. Gardarin, B. Finance, and P. Fankhauser. Federating Object-Oriented and Relational Databases: The IRO-DB Experience. In *Proc. 2nd Intl. Conf. on Cooperative Information Systems CoopIS 97*. IEEE Computer Society Press, 1997.

12. G. Gottlob, M. Schrefl, and B. Röcki. Extending Object-Oriented Systems with Roles. *ACM Transactions on Information Systems*, 14(3), July 1996.

13. R. Hull and R. King. Semantic Data Modeling: Survey, Applications, and Research Issues. *ACM Computing Surveys*, 19(3):201–260, 1987.

14. M. Hammer and D. McLeod. Database Description with SDM: A Semantic Database Model. *ACM Transactions on Database Systems*, 6(3):351–386, September 1981.

15. M. Jarke, R. Gallersdörfer, M. A. Jeusfeld, M. Staudt, and S. Eherer. ConceptBase - A Deductive Object Base for Meta Data Management. *Journal of Intelligent Information Systems*, 4(2):167–192, 1995.

16. G. Jaeschke and H.-J. Schek. Remarks on the algebra of non-first-normal-form relations. In *Proceedings ACM SIGACT/SIGMOD Symp. on Principles of Database Systems*, pages 124–138, 1982.

17. A. Kobler, M. C. Norrie, and A. Würgler. OMS Approach to Database Development through Rapid Prototyping. In *Proc. 8th Workshop on Information Technologies and Systems (WITS'98)*, Helsinki, Finland, December 1998.

18. G. Lakoff. *Women, fire, and dangerous things. What categories reveal about the mind.* University of Chicago Press, 1987.

19. J. Mylopoulos, P. A. Bernstein, and H. K. T. Wong. A Language Facility for Designing Interactive Database-Intensive Systems. *ACM Transactions on Database Systems*, 5(2):185–207, June 1980.

20. M. Missikoff and M. Toiati. MOSAICO – A System for Conceptual Modelling and Rapid Prototyping of Object-Oriented Database Applications. In *Proceedings of the 1994 ACM SIGMOD International Conference on Management of Data*, page 508. ACM, 1994.

21. J. Mylopoulos. Information Modeling in the Time of the Revolution. *Information Systems*, 23(3 & 4), 1998.

22. M. C. Norrie and A. Würgler. OM Framework for Object-Oriented Data Management. *INFORMATIK, Journal of the Swiss Informaticians Society*, (3), June 1997.

23. M. C. Norrie and A. Würgler. OMS Rapid Prototyping System for the Development of Object-Oriented Database Application Systems. In *Proc. Intl. Conf. on Information Systems Analysis and Synthesis*, Orlando, USA, August 1998.

24. J. Peckham and F. Maryanski. Semantic Data Models. *ACM Computing Surveys*, 20(3): 153–189, September 1988.

25. P. Pistor and Traunmuller. A database language for sets, lists, and tables. *Information Systems*, 11(4):323–336, December 1986.

26. H. Putnam. Is Semantics Possible? In P. Schwarz, editor, *Naming, Necessity, and Natural Kinds*. Cornell University Press, 1977.

27. R. Quillian. Semantic Memory. In M. Minsky, editor, *Semantic Information Processing*. MIT Press, 1968.

28. B. Raphael. A computer program for semantic information retrieval. In M. Minsky, editor, *Semantic Information Processing*. MIT Press, 1968.

29. J. Rumbaugh, M. Blaha, W. Premerlani, F. Eddy, and W. Lorensen. *Object-Oriented Modeling and Design*. Prentice Hall, 1991.

30. M. Ryan and A. Doubleday. Evaluating 'Throw Away' Prototyping for Requirements Capture. In *Proc. 3rd World Conference on Integrated Design and Process Technology*, Berlin, Germany, July 1998.

31. M. A. Roth, H. F. Korth, and D. S. Batory. SQL/NF : A Query Language for ¬ 1NF Relational Databases. *Information Systems*, 12(1):99–114, March 1987.

32. M. A. Roth, H. F. Korth, and A. Silberschatz. Extended Algebra and Calculus for Nested Relational Databases. *ACM Transactions on Database Systems*, 13(4):389–417, December 1988.

33. E. Rosch. Cognitive representations of semantic categories. *Journal of Experimental Psychology: General*, 104:192–233, 1975.

34. N. A. Stillings, M. H. Feinstein, J. L. Garfield, E. L. Rissland, D. A. Rosenbaum, S. E. Weisler, and L. Baker-Ward. *Cognitive Science: An Introduction*. MIT Press, 1991.

35. A. Steiner, A. Kobler, and M. C. Norrie. OMS/Java: Model Extensibility of OODBMS for Advanced Application Domains. In *Proc. 10th Conf. on Advanced Information Systems Engineering (CAiSE'98)*, Pisa, Italy, June 1998.

36. J. Supcik and M. C. Norrie. An Object-Oriented Database Programming Environment for Oberon. In *Proc. of the Joint Modular Languages Conference (JMLC'97)*, Linz, Austria, March 1997.

37. A. G. Sutcliffe and M. Ryan. Experience with SCRAM, a SCenario Requirements Analysis Method. In *Proc. 3rd IEEE Intl. Conf. on Requirements Engineering*, Colorado, USA, April 1998.

38. J. M. Smith and D. C. Smith. Database abstractions: Aggregation and generalization. *ACM Transactions on Database Systems*, 2(2):105–133, 1977.

39. H. J. Schek and M. H. Scholl. The Relational Model with Relation-Valued Attributes. *Information Systems*, 11(2):137–147, June 1986.

I   *Behavioral Modeling*

2 *A Behaviorally Driven Approach to Object-Oriented Analysis and Design with Object-Oriented Data Modeling*

Lois M. L. Delcambre
Computer Science & Engineering Department
Oregon Graduate Institute
P.O. Box 91000
Portland, OR 97291-1000
lmd@cse.ogi.edu

Earl F. Ecklund
OBJECTive Technology Group
Beaverton, OR 97008
ecklund@cse.ogi.edu

This paper presents a behavioral approach to object-oriented analysis and design and compares it to a structural approach. The difference between these two approaches is most apparent during the analysis phase of software development when the first object model is selected. Our behavioral approach is use case-driven during analysis: objects are selected and responsibilities are assigned to objects precisely because they are needed to support the behavior of one or more use cases. The contribution of this paper is the detailed description of issues that should be considered and issues that should not be considered during analysis and during design. This paper also discusses several open issues in object-oriented data modeling, regardless of whether a behavioral or structural approach is used.

2.1   Introduction

When software is developed using objects, the software system is modeled as a set of objects with each object an instance of a class. A class[1] defines the messages that can be sent to an object with the corresponding signatures, the attributes to be represented in the object, and the associations between objects of this class

---

1. This is more precisely a type; we use the term class as in OMT.

Table 2.1 Comparison of OMT and our Behavioral Approach to Analysis

	Object Modeling Technique (OMT) (22)	*Disciplined OO Software Engineering (DOOSE)*
Starting point:	Concepts/structure in the real world	Use cases (behavior required by users)
Motivation for objects:	Objects of interest in the real world	Objects to support responsibilities for a use case
Motivation for connecting objects:	Associations of interest in the real world	An object that must invoke a responsibility of another object (a collaboration)
Resulting object structure:	Detailed structure using many structural constructs and constraints	Classes, responsibilities, & collaborations (without explicit attributes or associations)
Results:	Good characterization of how individual objectgs respond to events	Good characterization of how a group of objects collaborate to support a use case

and other objects (of this class or a different class). The software system executes by sending messages to objects. A message to an object invokes the relevant method, which may send messages to other objects, etc. The implementation of objects is encapsulated. That is, the internal data structures and the method bodies are not visible to other objects. The choice of classes, the attributes of classes, and the associations among classes is sometimes called an object-oriented data model.[2]

An object model sets the structure of the software system; at the same time, an object model must include all behavior required of the software system. How can the object model be developed? One popular approach (22) focuses first on the structure of objects based on concepts in the real world of interest to the application. We take a different approach, focusing on the desired behavior of the system as expressed in a set of use cases (17). These two approaches are contrasted in Table 2.1. The difference between these two approaches is most evident during analysis when the first object model is constructed.

The Object Modeling Technique (OMT) (22) recommends that the object model be defined first, with an emphasis on representing objects (and attributes and associations) that correspond to concepts of interest in the real world. The second step is to model each object that has interesting states along with the events that cause state transitions, in a state diagram, based on statecharts (14). Cook and Daniels have described a similar approach more recently (5).

---

2. An object-oriented data model also includes other, more advanced constructs such as aggregation, composition, and generalization among objects as well as more detail such as attribute types, multiplicity of associations, etc.

Our approach focuses first on the desired behavior of the software system by describing use cases[3] (17). Each *use case* describes one interaction with a software system from the point of view of an actor. Each *actor* represents a class of users (such as booking clerk, branch manager, etc. for a car rental application). The scenario of the use case describes how the system must perform, i.e., the desired behaviors of the system to be built. The objects can be discovered using a responsibility-driven approach (26) based on CRC (class-responsibility-collaboration) cards (1). A *responsibility* for an object is something that the object must "do" or must "know." *Collaboration* is when one object sends a message to another object, to receive some assistance to perform the currently invoked responsibility. We refer to our approach as Disciplined Object-Oriented Software Engineering (DOOSE) (6, 7) because of our focus on work products from one step driving the next step and our requirement for traceability among the work products.

These approaches differ in their central focus. OMT produces a richly structured object model that describes objects, attributes and associations that occur in the real world to which methods can be added. Our approach is driven by the desired behaviors of the system. The resulting object model represents a set of responsibilities and collaborations that will support the complete set of use cases.

We focus on a behaviorally driven approach to object-oriented development because we believe that the resulting software is more likely to reflect the needs of the application. We also believe that it is valuable to focus on the responsibilities and collaborations of objects early in the development lifecycle (rather than associations, attributes, and methods) because it provides a more abstract view of objects. However, we must find a way to include the object-oriented data modeling necessary to complete the object model. The contribution of this paper is the identification of which aspects of data modeling should be included (and excluded!) from the analysis step and which aspects of data modeling should be handled during design. This paper also introduces the concept of the shared model to guide the developer as to what should be included and excluded in the use case and analysis models.

Regardless of the object-oriented analysis and design method used, we might wonder whether object-oriented software requires a "database design" step, much like traditional database design, in order to model the persistent data in a way that meets the needs of multiple applications and that provides reasonable performance. Should we take the object model for the software system, perhaps discovered using a behaviorally oriented approach, as the basis for our (object-oriented or other) database schema? One could argue that object-oriented databases set out to eliminate the need for database design. Because they support persistent C++, Java or Smalltalk, it is possible to take classes from the software model and simply make them persistent. We believe that such an approach, although possible, is naive.

---

3. There is, however, a domain glossary developed in conjunction with the use case model to define concepts from the domain.

Database design is a necessary step for several reasons (18). (1) The attributes and data structures of a class required to support the software might not be exactly the attributes and data structures that are to be stored persistently. We may need only a subset of the attributes and data structures to be stored persistently. (2) We may need more than one collection (e.g., set, list, bag, array) of objects of a particular type (class). Thus it is inappropriate to assume that there is a single set of all instances of a given class. (3) Databases typically define a global name space, including such things as table names, attribute names, etc. For objects, we may need persistent "handles" or names for objects that serve as entry points into the persistent data. (4) We may need individual objects that are persistent by themselves, without being in a named collection. Such objects may have the kind of handle mentioned in point (3). (5) Database design requires information about how many instances are likely for each collection, in order to decide about clustering, indices, etc. Such information is typically unavailable in an object model for software.

In the remainder of this paper, we give a brief description of our behavioral approach using an example from the EU Car Rental application in Section 2.2. This is followed by a discussion in Section 2.3 of how to do object-oriented data modeling in this method. Related work is presented in Section 2.4. The paper concludes in Section 2.5 with a brief discussion of open issues with regard to object-oriented data modeling.

2.2   DOOSE Object-oriented Analysis and Design—Example

In this section, we give a quick overview of our approach to object-oriented analysis and design by developing a portion of the Use Case, Analysis, and Design Models for the EU-Rent Rental Car example (23).

We begin by developing the Use Case Model, starting by identifying the scope of the system under development (setting the system boundary), the actors (roles) that interact with the system, and the "original" use cases. For the EU-Rent case study, we identified 11 actors and 46 original use cases, shown in Table 2.2.

For each use case, we develop a scenario, often in the form of a conversation (25) between the actor and the system. The scenario reflects the normal course of execution for the use case (17). We also indicate alternatives, where conditional or exceptional situations require revisions to the scenario. We refine the use case model to eliminate redundant portions of scenarios by factoring them into separate use cases. This brings us to the refined use case model.

A UML use case diagram of the refined use case model for the actor Booking Agent is shown in Figure 2.1. Since a complete refined use case diagram for the system is often quite large, we may draw several use case diagrams where each diagram shows the use cases that pertain to one actor. We see the uses and extends relationships between refined use cases. uses indicates that one use case (the client at the tail end of the arrow) uses the other (at the head end of the arrow) as part of the client's scenario. That is to say that the client's scenario would be incomplete without

Table 2.2   Original Use Cases for EU-Rent Case Study

Branch Offices	**Corporate Head Office**	**Service Depots**
Actor: Booking Clerk	*Actor: Director*	*Actor: Depot Clerk*
1. Accept rental return	21. Maintain car groups	34. Accept service drop off
2. Process late return	22. Set rental tariffs (rates)	
3. Report on late rental returns	23. Set branch purchase budgets	*Actor: Maintenance Foreman*
4. Extend rental for late rental returns	24. Assign branches to service depots	35. Service car
5. Process rental		*Actor: Depot Manager*
6. Take rental reservation		36. Schedule service
7. Cancel rental reservation	*Actor: Clerk*	37. Write off damaged car
	25. Maintain blacklist	38. Contract out service
Actor: Branch Manager	26. Maintain branch information	39. Allocate drivers for next day
8. Extract next day's reservations		40. Maintain service history
9. Transfer cars out	*Actor: Loyalty Incentive Clerk*	41. Report on cars requiring service
10. Cancel transfer out	27. Mail member statements	42. Run report on current week activity summary
11. Transfer cars in	28. Process awards/ vouchers	
12. Manage car pool	29. Maintain membership	**Other**
13. Write off car	30. Compensate branch for award rental	
14. Purchase cars		
15. Sell cars		
16. Report on car conditions		
		Actor: Driver
17. Service cars		43. Pick up car (transfer)
18. Produce booking report	*Actor: Purchasing Agent*	44. Pick up car (service)
19. Run rental report	31. Contact for purchases	45. Deliver car (transfer)
	32. Pay for new cars	46. Deliver car (service)
Actor: Storage Lot Staff	33. Receive payment for used cars	
20. Confirm rental preparation		

the "used" use case's scenario steps. uses links occur when common scenario steps are factored into a separate, shared use case. extends indicates that the extending use case (at the tail end of the arrow) creates an (optional) extended scenario by adding its own scenario steps to the scenario of the extended use case. The extended use case's scenario is complete in its own right and it may also be extended. extends often indicates that the extending use case contains conditional or optional behavior, associated with alternatives of the extended use case.

We use a numbering style for the refined use cases that is intended to hint at the traceability information in the refined use case write-up (e.g., see "Traces to" in Figure 2.2). Original use cases that are un-factored in the refined use case model

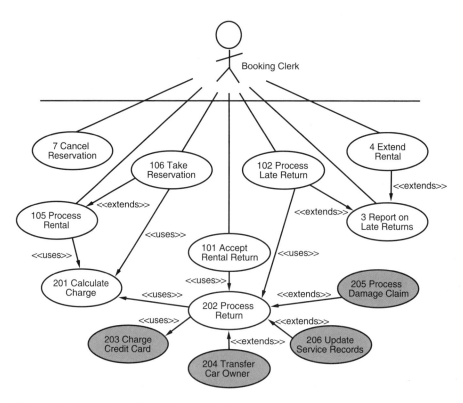

Figure 2.1   Refined Use Cases for Booking Clerk in EU-Rent Case Study

retain their original numbers, such as use cases 3, 4 and 7 in Figure 2.1. Use cases numbered in the 100's are the refined use cases that correspond to original use cases; they are numbered 100 plus the number of the corresponding original use case, e.g., refined use case 106 provides the main actions of use case 6. Refined use cases numbered above 200 are new use cases introduced in the use case refinement process. For example, use case 201 Calculate Charge, is used to estimate the rental charge during the reservation process and the rental process (to pre-authorize the credit card charge), as well as to calculate the actual charge during the rental return process. Refined use cases 106 and 201 comprise the original use case 6. Refined use cases that appear for more than one actor are shown with shaded ovals. For example, use case 204 also appears in the refined use case diagram for the actor Branch Manager, where it is used by use case 111 Transfer Cars In (which refines use case 11).

We advocate incremental and iterative software development. An *increment* is a set of functionality[4] that is to be developed, implemented and tested (and optionally deployed) as a unit. Thus, each increment involves a full *iteration* of the "lifecycle"

---

4. In DOOSE, an increment is defined as the requirements and the set of use cases to be developed in one iteration of the development process.

Use Case 106. Take rental reservation

Actor: Booking Clerk

Purpose: Validate customer and create reservation for specified car group on
                    specified date.

Other Actors:

Traces to: Use Case 6, Use Case 5

Preconditions:

Scenario:

0) Clerk answers phone and receives request for reservation. Clerk obtains customer's
   identification (drivers license number) and age. Clerk enters customer's identification
   (drivers license number).
   1) System determines that customer is not blacklisted.
   2) System displays reservation interface containing customer info, preferred car
      group and car group rate (from customer records and tariff policy), this
      branch as pickup site with tomorrow's date and 8:00 AM as default date
      and time of rental, and this branch as return site with tomorrow's date
      and 6:00 PM as default date and time of return.
3) Clerk enters and edits requested car group, place, date and time of pickup, place,
   date and time of return,
   4) System invokes *Use Case 201* to estimate total cost of rental
5) Clerk verifies all terms, quotes estimated cost to customer, and confirms reservation.
   6) System commits reservation record info and displays confirmation record
      locator number.
7) Clerk reads confirmation record locator number to customer

Postconditions: Reservation record for specified rental date, car group, and branch
                    is created.

Alternatives:

Step 0: Reservation may also be made by mail or by walk-in customer.
         If customer is under 21 years of age, reservation is refused and use case is exited.

Step 1: If customer is blacklisted, reservation is refused, and use case is exited.

Step 5: If customer declines reservation, use case is exited.

Comments:

Figure 2.2   Refined Use Case for Take Reservation in EU-Rent Case Study

of software development activities. Each increment begins with a selection of use
cases from the refined use case model.

   The refined use case model serves as the input to the analysis step; that is, our
object-oriented analysis is use case-driven (16, 17). Each use case in the refined use
case model is written in detail, as shown in Figure 2.2. By following the scenario,
we identify the object instances (and, thus, their classes), the responsibilities, and
the collaborations needed to perform the scenario. For example, from steps 0 and 1
of Use Case 106 (Figure 2.2), we decide that there should be customers (Customer
class), a collection of all customers (Customer Collection class) with the responsibility to lookup customer by drivers license number, and that class Customer should
have the responsibility to "know if blacklisted".

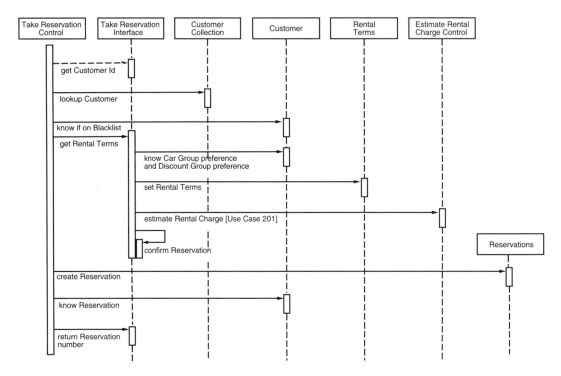

Figure 2.3   Analysis Sequence Diagram for Use Case 106 Take Rental Reservation

Responsibilities are assigned to objects precisely because they are needed to perform the scenario for one (or more) use cases. Thus, although we anticipate that Customer will also have the responsibility to "know drivers license number", we do not need to ask the customer object for this information in this scenario, so we defer adding this responsibility until it is required.

The UML Sequence Diagram is an effective mechanism to record the objects, responsibilities and collaborations required to support a use case. The sequence diagram for Use Case 106 Take rental reservation is shown in Figure 2.3.

As analysis proceeds through successive use cases, we gather, for each class, all the responsibilities and collaborations pertinent to that class. We use the CRC process of discovering objects and responsibilities during analysis (1, 24, 26). The emerging object model can be recorded on the CRC cards.

When the analysis activity is complete, the collected responsibilities of each class are shown in the UML Class Diagram of the Analysis Object Model. A partial class diagram (restricted to only analysis objects) is shown in Figure 2.4; for brevity, we show the class diagram after the Take Reservation and Process Rental use cases have been analyzed. The analysis object classes Take Reservation Control, Take Reservation Interface, Estimate Rental Charge Control, Process Rental Control, and Process Rental Interface are omitted for simplicity. These interface and control objects have straightforward responsibilities and no associations. Note that the dashed lines shown

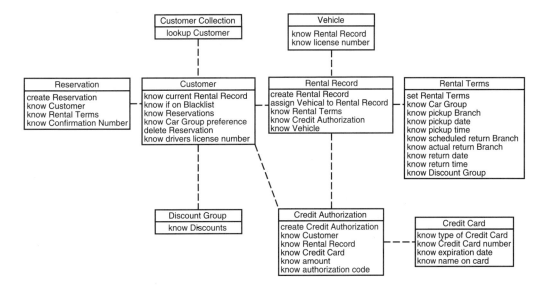

Figure 2.4   Analysis Class Diagram for EU-Rent Case Study after two Use Cases

in Figure 2.4 simply represent the responsibilities to "know" another object in a graphical manner.

Using responsibilities rather than attributes hides the implementation mechanism. For example, Customer has a responsibility to "know if on Blacklist" which could be implemented as a query function against a Blacklist database or data structure, or as a Boolean attribute of Customer. During analysis, these implementation choices are secondary to capturing the behavior that requires a customer to know whether it is or is not blacklisted. Customer also has a responsibility to "know Reservations." We may choose to design a "get Reservations" method that returns a set of Reservations as a collection object, or we may choose to scan the Reservations collection using an Iterator object. Decisions like these are intentionally deferred until design.

We use the analysis model as input to the design phase. Each class must be designed, private data structures selected, method names and signatures set, etc. during the design phase. The design process is responsibility-driven; design proceeds by considering classes, one at a time, and by designing each responsibility for the class. As an example of how we do design, the final design for the RentalRecord class is shown in Table 2.3. Here we assume that C++ is the implementation language. The notation shown uses '-' and '+' as visibility markers on the attributes and operations, to express private and public, respectively. Note that in this example, most of the classes mentioned were introduced in the Analysis Model, however we do find helper objects introduced to support the design, such as the ReturnCode class, which is designed to be an enumerated type. We also see that the responsibility to create Rental Record has been designed as the class constructor and has been overloaded to allow Rental Records to be created with either the vehicle supplied or left null to be assigned later (using the "assignVehicleToRentalRecord" operation).

Table 2.3   Design Class for RentalRecord Class in EU-Rent Case Study

Rental Record

- customer: Customer*
- vehicle: Vehicle*
- rentalTerms: RentalTerms*
- creditAuthorization: CreditAuthorization*
+ RentalRecord(Customer* customer, Vehicle* vehicle,
                    RentalTerms* terms, CreditAuthorization* auth): RentalRecord
+ RentalRecord(Customer* customer, RentalTerms* terms,
                    CreditAuthorization* auth): RentalRecord
+ ~RentalRecord();
+ assignVehicleToRentalRecord(Vehicle* vehicle): ReturnCode
+ getCustomer(): Customer*
+ getRentalTerms(): RentalTerms*
+ getCreditAuthorization*
+ getVehicle(): Vehicle*

2.3   Object-Oriented Data Modeling during Analysis and Design

This section articulates the main goals and activities for the analysis step and the design step of our object-oriented software development method. This section also discusses how object-oriented data modeling fits into this approach. In particular, we describe how object-oriented data modeling is handled during analysis and how it is handled during design.

One question that arises when a development method includes both analysis and design activities is: how do you know when to stop analysis? When is analysis becoming too detailed? Or conversely, how do we keep the use case model as well as the analysis model from becoming too shallow, e.g., by focusing only on the user interface details?

In general we are guided by the principle of the "shared model." The *shared model* (8) is the understanding of the system to be developed that is shared between the actor(s) and the system. The shared model for a use case comprises the actor's understanding of what the system is doing. As an example, the Booking Clerk knows that the system computes the estimated charges for a reservation. Each use case has its own shared model, based on the actor's understanding of the use case processing. The shared model during analysis represents the collective, unified shared model for all use cases. The notion of the shared model helps us articulate what to include and exclude for the use case model and the analysis model. We say that an object or a responsibility belongs in the analysis model precisely when it is in the shared model. In other words, the use case model and the analysis model should include precisely that which is visible and meaningful to the users.

Table 2.4 Analysis: when the implementation and deployment environment is *not* considered.

Activities and Goals	1. Select objects, responsibilities and collaborations.
	2. Be use case-driven.
	3. Be complete. (Analyze all use cases in current increment.)
	4. Recognize UI design as a separate, valuable, perhaps parallel activity.
	5. Use well defined terms, e.g., from a glossary.
Support for Object-Oriented Data Modeling	1. Introduce responsibilities of objects to "know" certain things.
	2. Identify objects that must be remembered. (persistence).
	3. Identify objects that collaborate. (This is a potential navigation path.)
	4. Introduce collection objects (or other information structures) to support searching for objects in the collection, etc.

2.3.1   Analysis—with object-oriented data modeling

The activities and goals of the analysis step are listed in the top portion of Table 2.4. Analysis is when the first object model is discovered through the selection of objects and responsibilities that are understandable to the domain experts or the actors. Our approach to analysis is use case-driven, as shown on the second line of Table 2.4. This means that we require the identification of significant use cases to serve as input for analysis. More than that, it means that we select objects only when they are needed to support one or more use cases. When the first use case is considered, we introduce as many objects as we need. For the second and subsequent use cases, we may introduce new objects; we may introduce new responsibilities for existing objects; or we may reuse existing objects and responsibilities. Similarly, we assign a responsibility to an object only when it is needed to support one (or more) use cases. Thus analysis is literally driven by the behavioral requirements of the system.

We believe that analysis should be complete, with respect to the given set of use cases, as shown in the third line of the top half of Table 2.4. Said another way, we believe that the analysis object model (i.e., the selected objects and responsibilities) represents the cumulative load or cumulative demand on the objects from the complete set of use cases for the current iteration.

It is often the case that the statement of individual responsibilities has been generalized during the course of analysis. The first time a responsibility is conceived, it reflects the needs of a single use case. As the responsibility is used a second or third or n^{th} time, the statement of the responsibility may be more general. This process of generalizing responsibilities (while they are still described simply as a phrase in natural language) is one of the chief advantages of this form of analysis. In a similar vein, we might decide that our choice of objects can be refined or simplified based on what we've learned from the use cases considered so far.

Any software system with human actors will require some form of user interface. We concur with Jacobson (17) that sketching out a user interface can assist with the development of the use case model. However, the actual user interface design, based on aesthetics and other issues, is separate from elaborating the way that the software system must work, as shown in the fourth line of the top portion of Table 2.4.

Because the use case model and the analysis model are both expressed in natural language, it is important to be precise about terms and concepts from the application domain and how they are defined. If standards exist, e.g., through an existing glossary, they can be used directly. The glossary allows us to be precise about concepts from the domain without requiring that the domain concepts appear in the object model. The use of a glossary is listed on line 5 of the top half of Table 2.4.

We believe data structures as well as the detailed structure of the object model should be developed during design. But we need to represent the data required for the application in the analysis model. The bottom half of Table 2.4 describes how we represent data in our analysis model.

If data is present in the system, then it is represented as the responsibility for one object to "know" something as shown in the first line in the bottom half of Table 2.4. As an example, we expect the Customer object in the EU-Rental system to "know driver's license number." Similarly, we might expect a Reservation object to "know customer" who has made the reservation. We intentionally model what might be represented as attributes and what might be represented as associations with this single construct - a responsibility "to know." The duality of values and objects and the associated duality of attributes and associations motivates our choice. A booking clerk can have the responsibility "to know the branch office" whether the branch office is modeled as a value or as an independent object. We can add the branch office object as a separate analysis object, if we need it, without the overhead of transforming all the attributes to associations.

The persistence of data beyond the execution of a program is an issue that will be mainly addressed during design, e.g., influenced by the choice of a database management system or other technology. Should the persistence of data be modeled during analysis? As usual, we answer this question based on the answer to the question "is it in the shared model?". Some persistence is clearly visible to the actors. The booking clerk expects that reservations made yesterday will still be "in the system" today. Such user-visible persistence should be modeled during analysis. See the second line in the bottom half of Table 2.4. There may also be persistent data that is an artifact of the design. For example, we might design a logging process for recovery purposes. The log contents would likely not be user-visible. All classes shown in Figure 2.4 are persistent at the analysis level. (Note that the control objects and interface objects, not shown in Figure 2.4, are not persistent.)

The decision about who to collaborate with and when to collaborate is made during analysis. In fact, decisions about collaboration are at the heart of the analysis process along with the selection of objects and responsibilities. We believe that it is appropriate to decide what collaborations are needed during analysis but *inappropriate* to decide how the collaboration might be supported. In effect, collaboration requires that the collaborator be "known" to this object. But how it comes to be known (e.g., through an association that is persistent or by receiving a parameter that references the other object) is a decision that should be made during design. Thus we see the identification of collaborations during analysis but *no* identification of associations as shown in the third line of the bottom portion of Table 2.4.

Whenever there are multiple objects grouped together, then we may wish to search for objects in the group. Who should have the responsibility to search, e.g., for a customer based on the customer's name? In order to search for an object, we must have a collection or container holding multiple objects. We use the term collection here as an abstract term to represent any container of objects. It might be implemented as a list, a linked list, an array, a B+-tree, a database table, etc. Such implementation choices will be made during design. At this stage during analysis we need only introduce a collection object such as CustomerCollection. It is quite natural then for the collection object to have a responsibility "to lookup customers." The use of collection objects during analysis is shown on the fourth line in the bottom half of Table 2.4.

2.3.2   Design—with object-oriented data modeling

Design begins with the identification of the implementation and deployment environment. The analysis model is characterized by what is visible in the shared model. Design is characterized by how things will be accomplished in the implementation and deployment.

Design is done by considering each class in turn, as shown in the first line in Table 2.5. For each responsibility of a class, we must decide on the data structures needed as shown in the second line of Table 2.5. Data structures are required to support the responsibilities to "know," to hold the arguments for methods, and for any data required for the design. We must also decide on the signature(s) for each method as shown in the third line of Table 2.5. We do so based on the statement of the responsibility from the analysis step and on the other data structures present in this object. The most general signature is generally described first, followed by any overloaded signatures. The overloaded signatures often leave out certain input parameters. These parameters then take on a default value and the more general method is called.

Throughout the design process, we must be systematic. We must make sure that objects exist when they need to exist (that is that all objects are created, as needed), that objects are "known" by some means when collaboration occurs, and that all alternatives and exceptions are handled. These issues are shown on lines 4, 5, and 6 of Table 2.5. These issues were intentionally ignored during analysis, unless they appear in the shared model.[5] The first of these two should be addressed whenever we

---

5. See for example the responsibility to create Rental Record for the Rental Record class in Figure 2.4.

Table 2.5 Design: when the implementation and deployment environment is considered.

Activities and Goals	1. Be class/responsibility-driven.
	2. Design data structures to hold data visible in analysis (with the responsibility to "know" something) plus data needed for the design.
	3. Select method signatures (including overloaded signatures).
	4. Make sure all objects are created as needed.
	5. Make sure that all objects needed for collaboration are "known" to the calling object.
	6. Systematically consider all alternatives and exceptions.
	7. Introduce design objects (i.e., "helper" objects) as needed.
	8. Use patterns (e.g., for "hot spots" that need configurability or flexibility).
	9. Decide on class hierarchy.
Support for Object-Oriented Data Modeling	1. Handle persistence (from analysis plus additional persistence).
	2. Introduce persistent relationships, as needed.
	3. Design the database (with queries/navigation in mind).
	4. Handle transactional aspects including recovery, redundancy.
	5. Design the interface between the object model and the DB.

invoke a responsibility. In order to invoke a responsibility, we must send a message to the appropriate object. And in order to send a message to an object, the object must exist and we must have a reference to that object. The third issue concerns alternatives and exceptions that must be addressed to complete the design of this object. The alternatives may have been identified during the development of the use case model and listed at the bottom of each use case scenario, as in Figure 2.2, or they may be added during design.

Design is when additional objects are introduced to support the implementation as, indicated on line seven of Table 2.5. For example, a complex data structure, such as a list or a binary tree, might introduce one or more objects. Such design objects might be available from a component library (19). Such objects are in the domain of the implementation and are generally not user-visible, i.e., they are not in the shared model.

The use of design patterns (11) may also introduce additional objects into the design, as shown on line eight of Table 2.5. Each design pattern provides flexibility or configurability in one dimension. Wolfgang Pree (20) has introduced the term "hot spot" for any part of your design that is likely to change. It is appropriate to consider using a design pattern for a hot spot provided that the pattern introduces the kind of flexibility or configurability that matches the expected changes.

Once the data structures and method signatures emerge for the design objects, it is appropriate to finalize the class hierarchy. Shared responsibilities, attributes, and associations can be factored out into a superclass. It is also the case that a design pattern may introduce certain class/subclass relationships.

The support for data modeling during object-oriented design is shown in the bottom half of Table 2.5. During design, all of the details about data structure, persistence, associations, external file or database system, queries, and transactions are considered and finalized. It is during design that an appropriate mapping from the object model (that comprises the software system) to the persistent objects or entities must be defined. This mapping is influenced by the choice of the implementation and deployment environment. A recent book by Blaha and Premerlani has a detailed exposition of how a design object model can be mapped to various file systems and database management systems (2).

2.4   Related Work

The current state of object-oriented development methods reflects a synthesis of ideas from a number of methods. Use cases are advocated by many authors beyond their original inventor as evidenced by their appearance in the Unified Modeling Language (UML) (13). State diagrams are widely acknowledged to be useful to describe objects with complex state, particularly where the stimuli to the system can be successfully modeled using events (12). Fusion (4) is a self-proclaimed "second generation" method for object-oriented development precisely because it "fuses" ideas from other methods. Fowler (10) sketches a method (with variations) that includes many of the UML diagrams as work products including use case diagrams, class diagrams, state diagrams, etc.

Approaches to Object-Oriented Analysis can be classified into behaviorally oriented, operationally oriented, and data-oriented. Our approach is behaviorally oriented, as is the Object Behavior Analysis approach of (21) and the Responsibility-Driven Design of (26). We feel that analysis with a behavioral focus, where everything is represented as a responsibility, is at a higher, more abstract level than the other approaches. We also feel that behavioral modeling with a use case-driven approach, is less subject to scope creep, in that objects and responsibilities are discovered as needed, rather than identified in anticipation of being required in some unknown, yet to be identified, future collaboration.

The operationally oriented approach can be characterized as identifying the operations needed to support the application, forming interfaces that collect cohesive sets of operations, and associating each interface with an object class that will own those operations as its responsibilities. Operationally oriented analysis strikes us as a bottom-up approach to modeling behavior, although it may lead to early identification of interfaces useful for reasoning about system architecture. We would describe the Fusion method (4) as operationally oriented.

Data-oriented approaches are, in fact, extending the entity-relationship-style of modeling (3) to object-oriented development. Data-oriented approaches include

OMT (22) and subsequent methods that use a similar approach. Cook and Daniels provide an insightful description of the initial object model describing it as have a "systematic correspondence with the essential model" (5). The essential model describes the relevant portion of the situation that must be represented in the software. This is more specific than simply modeling the "real world". They also acknowledge that there is more in the analysis object model than just the essential model.

Finally, with regard to duality, Embley (9) advocates using only associations (without attributes) during conceptual modeling for many of the same reasons that we recommend using only responsibilities.

2.5   Conclusions and Open Issues for Object-Oriented Data Modeling

Duality is a characteristic of a set of modeling constructs that allows a given item of interest to be acceptably modeled in two distinct ways. Why should we worry about duality? The problem with duality is that the initial choice for the representation of an "object" is often just a guess, a first draft of what it ought to be. As the early model evolves, we need to be aware of the opportunity to promote values into objects or demote objects to values. But an even better approach is to use modeling constructs that minimize duality in the first place.

If we use only responsibilities ("to know x") in place of attributes or associations, then what sort of precautions must we take during analysis?

Naming We must be sure that when we use the same name, we mean the same thing. So if the Customer must "Know-account" and the Meter must "Know-account" and we intend for them both to refer to the same account class, then we must be careful to use the same name "account." This care when naming must be exercised in all aspects of object modeling and in data modeling. When attributes have the same name (in different tables) in relational databases, they will be used to form join conditions when the query expresses the natural join. When two attributes are to take values from the same underlying domain of values or use the same lookup table, we must make sure that we use the same domain or lookup table name in both cases.

For object-oriented analysis, all use of names, as class names, collaborator names, and responsibility names, must be done consistently so that the same name is used precisely when the same concept is intended. Jacobson (17) recommends using a glossary beginning with the use case model (or even during the formulation of requirements (15)) to make the intended semantics clear. Neither style of development method (whether behaviorally or structurally focused) makes the naming problem more difficult nor less important.

Single reference vs. multiple reference One of the reasons for promoting a value to be a class (and changing an attribute into an association) is when the value must be referenced from two or more other objects. Using an attribute/association model, we must promote a value to an object when we discover the second reference to the value. If we only use the responsibility to "know x", then that responsibility can occur once or twice or more, without changing the other "know x" responsibilities.

Unidirectional vs. bi-directional associations There has been considerable debate in the object-oriented modeling world about whether associations should be unidirectional (17) or bi-directional (22). Using responsibilities to represent associations during analysis, we allow uni-directional responsibilities to be discovered according to whether they are needed to support the use cases. We may discover at one point that x needs to know y. At another point, we might discover that y needs to know x. These (inverse) responsibilities can be discovered incrementally, without requiring an update to the existing responsibilities.

We believe that analysis is an important step in the discovery of an object model and we believe that behaviorally driven analysis provides certain advantages. We also believe that the robustness of the object model is improved by separating analysis from design. In this paper we have shown how object-oriented data modeling can be accommodated using our behaviorally driven approach and have articulated how data modeling can be supported in analysis and design.

The focus of object-oriented data modeling is clearly on classes with attributes and associations, because that is precisely what can be stored persistently in a conventional database.[6] We believe that a data-oriented approach is not necessarily the best approach to modeling software because it does not place the focus on behavior, the primary concern of the software. Further, use of attributes and associations, especially early in the development lifecycle, can unnecessarily introduce duality problems, where the model must be changed to reflect new information.

We also believe that a data-oriented approach, much like database modeling, and a behaviorally oriented approach represent two ends of a spectrum. Many other models and methods rightly fall somewhere between the two. Objects encapsulate both data structures and method bodies. Ultimately we need both. Our approach is to use a behaviorally oriented approach early, i.e., during analysis, and make data-oriented decisions during design. Perhaps there are ways to integrate these techniques to capitalize on their respective strengths.

Does a behaviorally oriented approach facilitate or interfere with a database design step? Here we consider the five motivations for an explicit database design step that were presented in Section 2.1 above and provide our analysis.

1. *The attributes and data structures of a class required to support the software might not be exactly the attributes and data structures that are to be stored persistently.* The fact that certain attributes and data structures may not need to be persistent is an issue that must be dealt with, no matter what object-oriented

---

6. Note that it is often necessary to translate associations (and perhaps other modeling constructs) to other model constructs, such as tables and foreign keys for the relational model.

development method is used. We must identify the subset of the attributes and data structures to be stored persistently and factor the object model accordingly.

2. *We may need more than one collection (e.g., set, list, bag, array) of objects of a particular type (class).* OMT does not provide explicit support in the notation nor in the method to describe collections. Blaha and Premerlani even suggest that it is simpler if a "collection" of objects corresponds to the extent of a single class (2). In our behaviorally oriented approach, we explicitly introduce a collection object whenever it is needed and there can be more than one collection of a given kind. This would lead naturally into an implementation with multiple collections (which is often supported in object-oriented programming languages and object-oriented database but not necessarily in conventional databases).

3. *Databases typically define a global name space, including such things as table names, attribute names, etc. For objects, we may need persistent "handles" or names for objects that serve as entry points into the persistent data.* Although our approach doesn't deal explicitly with name spaces, our collection objects do serve as suggestions for named collections in the persistent store.

4. *We may need individual objects that are persistent by themselves, without being in a named collection. Such objects may have the kind of handle mentioned in point (3).* Our approach models individual objects and collection objects at the same level. For any object-oriented development method, persistent names for individual objects must be provided when the database is implemented.

5. *Database design requires information about how many instances are likely for each collection, in order to decide about clustering, indices, etc. Such information is typically unavailable in an object model for software.* All object-oriented approaches (as well as traditional software development approaches) need to gather information about the number of instances likely for a class, etc. for physical database design. Our collection objects, with their associated responsibilities for searching, are obvious candidates for indices in a database.

Note that because our approach is use case-driven (precisely to avoid scope creep), it follows that our approach doesn't necessarily identify widely applicable attributes, associations, and responsibilities nor general purpose queries that might be appropriate for multiple applications. The point is that the analysis and design of one software system results in an object model to suit the needs of the software system. A database to be used by multiple applications requires consideration of the combined persistent data and access needs of multiple software systems.

References

1. K. Beck and W. Cunningham. A laboratory for teaching object-oriented thinking. In *Proc. OOPSLA'89*, pages 1–6. ACM, 1989.

2. M. Blaha and W. Premerlani. *Object-Oriented Modeling and Design for Database Applications*. Prentice Hall, 1998.

3. P. Chen. The entity-relationship model - toward a unified view of data. *ACM Trans. On Database Systems*, 1(1):9–36, 1976.

4. D. Coleman, S. Arnold, D. Bodoff, C. Dollin, H. Gilchrist, F. Hayes, and P. Jeremaes. *Object-Oriented Development: the Fusion Method*. Prentice Hall, 1994.

5. S. Cook and J. Daniels. *Designing Object Systems: Object-Oriented Modeling with Syntropy*. Prentice Hall, 1994.

6. L. Delcambre and E. Ecklund. Class handouts for CSE 504 object-oriented analysis and design. Oregon Graduate Institute of Science and Technology, 1997.

7. L. Delcambre and E. Ecklund. Disciplined object-oriented analysis. In *European Conference on Object-Oriented Programming (ECOOP) Conference*, Brussels, Belgium, July 1998. Tutorial Notes.

8. L. Delcambre and E. Ecklund. The shared model: The key to analysis without paralysis. Technical Report No. CSE-98-011, Oregon Graduate Institute, July 1998. ftp://cse.ogi.edu/pub/tech-reports/.

9. D. Embley. *Object Database Development*. Addison-Wesley, 1998.

10. M. Fowler and K. Scott. *UML Distilled: Applying the Standard Object Modeling Language*. Addison-Wesley, 1997.

11. E. Gamma, R. Helm, R. Johnson, and J. Vlissides. *Design Patterns: Elements of Reusable Object-Oriented Software*. Addison-Wesley, 1995.

12. I. Graham. *Migrating to Object Technology*. Addison-Wesley, 1994.

13. Object Management Group. *UML 1.1*, 1997. http://www.rational.com/uml/.

14. D. Harel. Statecharts: a visual formalism for complex systems. *Science of Computer Programming*, 8:231–274, 1987.

15. M. Jackson. *Software Requirements & Specifications*. Addison-Wesley, 1995.

16. I. Jacobson. Object oriented development in an industrial environment. In *Proc. OOPSLA'87*, pages 183–191. ACM, 1987.

17. I. Jacobson, M. Christerson, P. Jonsson, and G. Övergaard. *Object-Oriented Software Engineering: A Use Case Driven Approach*. ACM Press, 1992.

18. D. Maier. Private communication, August 1998.

19. Rogue Wave Software, Inc. http://www.roguewave.com/products/toolspro/.

20. W. Pree. *Design Patterns for Object-Oriented Development*. Addison-Wesley, 1994.

21. K. Rubin and A. Goldberg. Object behavioral analysis. *CACM*, 35(9):48–62, 1992.

22. J. Rumbaugh, M. Blaha, W. Premerlani, F. Eddy, and W. Lorensen. *Object-Oriented Modeling and Design*. Prentice Hall, 1991.

23. EU-Rent Case Study.

24. N. Wilkinson. *Using CRC Cards*. SIGS Books, 1995.

25. R. Wirfs-Brock. *The Art of Designing Meaningful Conversations*, volume 3. The Small-talk Report, 1994.

26. R. Wirfs-Brock, B. Wilkerson, and L. Wiener. *Designing Object-Oriented Software*. Prentice Hall, 1990.

3 *Objects and Events as Modeling Drivers*

M. Teisseire
Institut des Sciences de l'Ingénieur de Montpellier (ISIM)
161 rue Ada, 34392 Montpellier
Cedex 5 France
Maguelonne.Teisseire@lirmm.fr

P. Poncelet
R. Cicchetti
IUT Aix-en-Provence
Dépt. Informatique
Faculté des Sciences de Luminy, Case 901
163 Avenue de Luminy, 13288 Marseille
Cedex 9 France
Pascal.Ponceletlim.univ-mrs.fr
Rosine.Cicchetti@lim.univ-mrs.fr

In this chapter, we present a conceptual model, IFO_2, intended for modeling classical or advanced applications, encompassing structural and behavioral models. The structural model extends the semantic model IFO defined by S. Abiteboul and R. Hull, and adopts a "whole-object" philosophy. In contrast with related work which offers an object-driven vision of dynamics, behavior is comprehended in a similar way than structure, i.e. by applying the common object-oriented principles. More precisely, the dynamic concepts mirror the structural concepts of the model, and a "whole-event" philosophy is adopted when abstracting behavior. This provides a really uniform representation of the application behavior while offering designers the required conceptual qualities such as the overview of specifications and relevant semantic abstractions for fully capturing reality.

3.1 Introduction

The primary aim of modeling approaches is providing designers with a high-level description for abstracting information systems or software-intensive systems. The takled issue has a twofold aspect since the real universe under examination must be described through its static or structural components and through its dynamics or behavior. With classical approaches (1, 5, 10, 21, 32), emphasis is placed on particular qualities such as an overall vision of representation and its faithfulness to real universe, an easily understood specification valuable for communicating with end-users, and the independance from implementation tools. Modeling approaches complement conceptual descriptions by providing mechanisms for aiding implementation in such or such development environment. Both functionalities are supported by CASE (Computer Aided Software Engineering) tools (3, 25). On the other hand, there is an increased number of development languages or systems, based on different models or paradigms (classical or object programming languages, relational or object-oriented Data Base Management Systems (DBMSs) (16, 6) possibly provided with active capabilities (39)). The object paradigm has influenced modeling approaches not only because new implementation targets must be considered but particularly because it introduces concepts proved to be efficient for increased productivity and improved reliability. From a structural viewpoint, most of current conceptual models (35, 25, 17, 4, 2, 15) attempt to combine advantages of object-oriented models and strenghs of classical semantic approaches (e.g. the Entity/Relationship model (10)). The application structure is described through a diagram of classes, embodding methods, and related by associations or involved in generalization hierarchies. Objects populating classes are provided with an identity, and complex constructions can be handled. Transformation mechanisms are defined for various target languages or systems. They yield, from the structural schema, an inheritance hierarchy of classes or more classical data structures (including relational database schema).

From a behavioral viewpoint, most of modeling approaches describe dynamics of reactive objects using state transition diagrams (4, 15, 17, 35, 28). Actually such diagrams have been extensively used (and proved to be efficient) in specifications for concurrent systems (20, 30, 29, 26, 27). They provide a natural and graphic medium for describing the dynamics of complex systems and verification techniques are proposed to reveal design defects (11, 26, 27). Their philosophy matches well with the object principles, in particular encapsulation. Considering the object life cycle, or more generally object behavior, is somewhat simple and familiar in an object oriented perspective. Each reactive class is provided with a state diagram describing the dynamic pattern for object behavior. Being in given states, objects evolve over time by performing transitions with possible state change. Transitions triggered by events could be constrained by triggering conditions and perform actions.

Additional abstractions are offered for representing more complex mechanisms. Inspired from nested statecharts (20), state generalization in (35, 17) makes it possible to expand a state in a low-level diagram encompassing sub-states and transitions between them. By this way, a dynamic feature can be refined while glossing over the main defect of flat diagrams, i.e. the possible exponential burst of states and transitions when the system grows linearly (20, 35). Moreover, concurrent dynamic patterns can be specified whenever objects play different and non exclusive parts. Aggregation of the highest-level diagrams of reactive classes yields the dynamic schema of the application.

Although this vision of behavior really meets needs of various applications, it has some defects or drawbacks. Primarily, the proposed vision of dynamics focusses on the individual behavior of objects (even if interactions between objects are captured) and it is, by its very nature, instance oriented: states stand for pre and post-conditions constraining reactions of objects populating a class when certain events occur. With this vision, reaction chaining involving objects of various classes are not represented in a clear cut way since they are decomposed in transitions specified in different state diagrams. Moreover, state diagrams are not suitable for modeling set-oriented processing, i.e. global behaviors involving collections of objects. Finally, in particular fields, e.g. when developing transactional applications, representing the global behavior of a set of related objects, even if this behavior is instance-oriented, is critical. Actually, abstracting such a system reaction through a set of individual and interleaved behaviors, is a difficult and errorprone task (individual states of class objects must be exhibited, they could seem artificial to designers and vary from one designer to another, new mecanisms for controlling data consistency are to be defined . . .). Let us notice, that in OMT and UML, additional descriptions are provided for complementing the dynamic models (fonctionnal or activity diagram). They discard some evoked inconveniences but designers must handle a supplementary model.

In this chapter, we present an alternative approach, IFO$_2$, intended for modeling classical or advanced applications, encompassing structural and behavioral models. The structural model extends the semantic model IFO defined by S. Abiteboul and R. Hull (1). When modeling with IFO$_2$, the designer adopts a "whole-object" philosophy: everything is considered as an object (whatever its further implementation (object or value of various and arbitrarily complex type) strongly depending from the chosen target environment). At a conceptual level, apart from the uniformity of description, this style of modeling places much more emphasis on relationships between objects and an additional description granularity is introduced with the concept of fragment. It makes it possible to capture a piece of reality and to handle it as a "whole". This concept provides a formal framework for modularity and reusability of structural components. It offers an intermediary description level between the details of classes and the global description given by the schema. Finally these fragments, each of which offering a particular view point of specifications, could be grouped together for yielding an overall structural schema.

A major and original feature of IFO$_2$ is to offer a uniform framework for both modeling structural and behavioral parts of applications (33, 38). In contrast with related work which offer an object-driven vision of dynamics, behavior is comprehended in a similar way than structure, i.e. by applying the common object-oriented principles. More precisely, the dynamic concepts mirror the structural concepts of the model, and a "whole-event" philosophy is adopted when abstracting behavior. Then any relevant fact is modeled as an event. This provides a really uniform representation of the application behavior while offering designers the required conceptual qualities such as the overview of specifications and relevant semantic abstractions for fully capturing reality. In a similar way than for structure, an intermediary description level is introduced with the concept of behavioral fragment. It supports modularity and reusability of specifications and provides designer with dynamic viewpoints capturing a "macro-reaction" of the system. Application behaviors are then described through IFO$_2$ event schemas built in a modular way from the various defined fragments. These schemas can model object life cycles, as well as global information processing. They capture the expected functionalities of the system, and highlight various relationships between them: chronological, synchronization, but also sharing of common reactions.

An overview of the structural part of IFO$_2$ is given in Section 3.2. The dynamic aspects are defined and illustrated in Section 3.3. Section 3.4 gives an overview of related work and a comparison with our proposal. Finally, as a conclusion, we underline the strong points of the proposed models and evoke additional capabilities offered by our approach.

3.2   Structural Concepts in IFO$_2$

For the structural description of a real universe, IFO$_2$ adopts the fundamental concepts defined in IFO, and extends them for fully meeting object-oriented principles. When abstracting structure, building blocks are *object types*. They could be basic or complex. Relationships between types are captured through functions. An original feature of the model (directly inherited from IFO) is to provide the concept of fragment which groups linked object types for capturing a piece of reality. The various fragments are organized within an IFO$_2$ structural schema.

When modeling using IFO$_2$, the designer adopts a "whole-object" philosophy. This means that anything is modeled as an object which would be an instance of an object type. Three basic object types are proposed:

- The *printable object type* which can be materialized. It is used for application I/O (Input/Output are therefore environment-dependent: String, Integer, Picture, Sound, . . .), and it is comparable to attribute type used in most of conceptual models (from Entity/Relationship model to UML).

- The *abstract object type* reflecting an entity of the real world which is not described by its own structure but rather through its properties (attributes). This type is close to the entity concept of the Entity/Relationship model or the class concept of UML.

- The *represented object type* which stands for another type. By using a represented type, the designer can handle (and thus reuse) any different type without knowing its precise description. The type which is symbolized could be whatever IFO$_2$ object type. Thus a common property, more or less complex, can be shared or an additional role can be assigned to a conceptual entity type.

Example 3.1
When modeling the information system of the car rental company, various object types are defined. Among them, "Name" is a printable type standing for customers' name. "Car" is an abstract type capturing real entities cars of the company and "Assigned-Car" is defined for reusing the previous type.

Printable Object Type   *Abstract Object Type*   *Represented Object Type*

Figure 3.1   Basic Object Type Examples

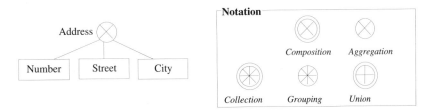

Figure 3.2   Complex Object Type Example

For building complex types, five constructors are proposed with a distinction between exclusive and non-exclusive constructions (C.f. Figure 3.2). These constructors can be recursively applied for building more complex types:

- The *aggregation* and *composition* types represent the aggregation abstraction of semantic models (21) defined by the Cartesian product. It is a composition, if and only if, each object of an aggregated type occurs only once in an object construction.

- The *collection* and *grouping* types stand for the constructor "set-of" used in most of object models (16, 2) with an exclusive constraint for the grouping.

- The *union* type is used for handling, in a similar way, types having different structure. This constructor represents the IS_A generalization link enforced with a disjunction constraint between the generalized types.

Example 3.2

The use of constructors is merely exemplified by considering address of customers. As depicted in Figure 3.2, it is specified as the aggregation of three printable types "Number", "Street" and "City".

Relationships attaching properties to object types are captured through IFO₂ functions. Any type could be provided with additional characteristics for complementing its description. It is then related to appropriate object types by mean of functions. The resulting description can be handle as a whole. It captures a piece of reality, this is why it is called fragment, and focuses on a particular object type, said the fragment heart. Within a fragment, functions express particular semantic constraints since they can combine the following features:

- simple or complex, i.e. the associated property is mono or multivalued;

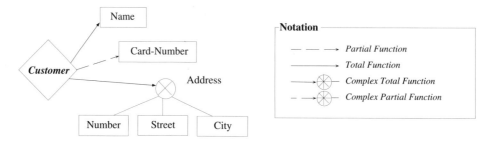

Figure 3.3   The Structural Fragment "Customer"

■ partial or total, for expressing the possible or necessary feature of the property.

Example 3.3

For representing customers of the company, the fragment illustrated in Figure 3.3 is built by associating to the abstract type "Customer" various properties, such as the name, the address (necessary) and the card number (possibly unknown).

A fragment is intended for encapsulating a structure, and it is provided with a set of methods standing for operations performed by the object types involved in the fragment. An operation could be a typical object manipulation (creation, deletion, . . .), a query, or whatever processing (instance or set-oriented). Signature of methods is only required.

The role of fragment is to describe a subset of the modeled application that can then be used as a whole when integrating the various parts of description within a single and overall schema. For reusing fragments, represented types are required. They are related to fragment hearts with IS_A links. By this way, they symbolize within their own fragment the role played by another fragment. Thus, when elaborating conceptual schemas, the designer can delay a type description or entrust it to somebody else, while using a represented type which symbolizes it.

Represented types inherit from their associated fragment heart a structural description as well as manipulation operations. The inherited description could be complemented by attaching additional properties or methods to the represented type. Furthermore, inheritance could be multiple. A represented type can inherit from several fragment hearts.

When modeling, fragments provide an intermediary abstraction level. They capture partial views of the application structure which are organized (by specifying IS_A links) and result in an IFO_2 structural schema.

Example 3.4

The IFO_2 structural schema of the car rental company is partially depicted in Figure 3.4. Only three fragments are described. The first one represents branches of the company, characterized by their location and the set of owned cars. The abstract type "Branch" is merely related to the printable type "Location" and to the represented type "Owned-Car". Let us notice that the latter relationship is captured through a

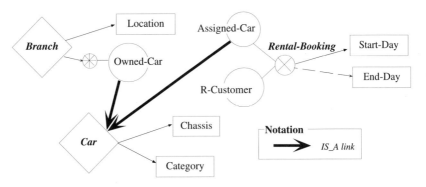

Figure 3.4   Part of the Structural Schema "Car rental"

total and complex function. Cars are described in a second fragment and the represented type "Owned-Car" reuses that description by means of an IS_A link. The abstract type "Car" is provided with properties "Category" and "Chassis". The "Car" description is also reused in the third fragment capturing "Rental-Booking". A rental booking is built up as an aggregation of a single car and a single customer. The former is symbolized by the represented type "Assigned-Car" and the latter is captured through the represented type "R-Customer" which is described in another fragment "Customer" (C.f. Figure 3.3).

A rental booking is characterized by two properties "Start-Day" and "End-Day" giving the booking period.

IFO$_2$ types, fragments and schemas are constrained by building rules guaranteing the description consistency. For instance, rules verify the right number of composants for complex types or control the fragment construction. Constraints applying on structural schemas discard IS_A link cycles and enforce a common inheritance source (somewhere in the fragment hierarchy) in case of multiple inheritance.

3.3   The Dynamic Model of IFO$_2$

For describing dynamics of applications, IFO$_2$ adopts a very similar style of modeling than for capturing the structure, i.e. an object-oriented style. However the dynamic description is not object-driven but instead event-driven.

Building blocks for describing behavior are event types. They could be basic or complex. Relationships expressing causality links between event types are captured through functions having various features. The resulting description is encapsulated in a dynamic fragment provided with the same qualities than structural fragments. Then Dynamic fragments are organized within schemas representing the overall behavior of the application.

Let us examine and illustrate, in the following subsections, these dynamic concepts.

3.3.1 Time and Event Type Definitions

In dynamic approaches (5, 17, 24), events are usually defined as real facts occurring at a particular instant and which vehicule information. IFO_2 adopts a similar vision: events are provided with a time-stamp and vehiculed information is captured through event parameters. They can be objects possibly related by some kind of relationships (aggregation, association, ...), or sets of objets.

Furthermore, an event is identified (exactly like an object in the structural part of the model) and it has a value, depending on the type of the event in question.

Behaviors being modeled enfold within a temporal dimension. For setting this temporal groundwork, time is defined, like in (12), as a set of equidistant instants with an origin and where each point in time can be represented by a non-negative integer. Since spacing of ranges can be ajusted for refining time granularity, we assume that events occurring all along the application life can be ordered according to their time-stamp.

Definition 3.1
Time is an infinite set of symbols and $<_{Time}$ is a total order relation on this set.

Definition 3.2
$\mathcal{TE}$ is an infinite set of event types such that: $\forall te \in \mathcal{TE}$, $Did(te)$ is an infinite set of symbols called the **identifier domain** of te with $Did(te) \subset time$, $Dom(te)$ is an infinite set of symbols, including the empty set, called the **event domain** of te and $Dpara(te)$, the **parameter domain** of te, is included in $\mathcal{P}(S_S)$ (where $\mathcal{P}(S_S)$ is the powerset of the object types of the structural schema[1]).

Definition 3.3
An **event** of type te is a triplet $(id, occ, para)$ such that: $\forall e, e'$ of type te, $\exists (id, id') \in Did(te)^2$, $\exists (occ, occ') \in Dom(te)^2$, $\exists (para, para') \in Dpara(te)^2$ such that: if $e = (id, occ, para)$, $e' = (id', occ', para')$ and $id = id'$ then $e = e'$.

The infinite set of events having type te is called $Evt(te)$.

Example 3.5
 When describing the behavior of our application example, the event type "Reservation" is exhibited. Any event of this type occurs when a car booking is to be created. It concerns a particular customer and a given car (which likely was previously selected) for a renting period. Such an event could be specified as follows: $e_{R_1} = (id_{R_1},$ *create-reservation*, $(_1\_customer, {_3\_car}, {_1\_startday}, {_1\_endday}))$. This means that the event e_{R_1} occurs at the instant id_{R_1}, and concerns a precise customer (identified by $_1\_$ *customer*) a particular car ($_3\_car$) and the period given by a starting day ($_1\_startday$) and an ending day ($_1\_endday$). The *create-reservation* component maps with an oper-

---

1. A structural schema is defined as a directed acyclic graph $G_S = (S_S, L_S)$ where S_S is the set of object types and L_S the link set of the schema (31).

Simple Event Type   Abstract Event Type   Represented Event Type

Figure 3.5   Basic Event Type Examples

ation of the structural schema instanciating the structural fragment "Rental-Booking" (C.f. Figure 3.4).

For each event type *te* of $\mathcal{TE}$, there are two functions: a bijective function *Id* with domain *Evt(te)* and codomain *Did(te)* which associates with each event of type *te* its identifier and an injective function *Para* with domain *Evt(te)* and codomain *Dpara(te)* which associates with each event of type *te* its parameters.

3.3.2   Basic Event Type Definitions

Exactly like object types, IFO$_2$ event types can be provided with a more or less complex structure. The elementary description units are basic types which vehicle various semantics. The proposed basic types (the associated graphic formalism is given in Figure 3.5) are the following:

- The *simple event type* represents the events triggering an operation or method, this operation is considered as the event value. The event parameters must match with the operation signature provided by the concerned structural fragment.

- The *abstract event type* captures external or temporal events, stemmed from the application environment. It is also used to represent internal events which are interesting only through their consequences, i.e. when triggering other events. The value of abstract events is null.

- The *represented event type* symbolizes any other type described elsewhere which can be used without knowing its precise description. Its value depends on the symbolized type.

They are formally defined and then illustrated.

Definition 3.4
Let $\mathcal{TES}$ be an infinite set of **simple** event types and let $\mathcal{TEA}$ be an infinite set of **abstract** event types, two disjoint subsets of $\mathcal{TE}$, such that:

1. $\forall te \in \mathcal{TES}_{Str}$:
   - (a) $\exists op \in OP(F_{Struct}) \mid Dom(te) = op$ where $OP(F_{Struct})$ is the operation set of the structural fragment $F_{Struct} \in G_s$;
   - (b) $Dpara(te) \subseteq \mathcal{P}(V_S)$ where $\mathcal{P}(V_S)$ is the powerset of V_S and V_S is the object type set of the fragment F_{Struct}.
2. $\forall te \in \mathcal{TEA}, Dom(te) = \emptyset$.

Definition 3.5

Let $\mathcal{TER}$ be an infinite set of **represented** event types, subset of $\mathcal{TE}$, such that: $\forall te \in \mathcal{TER}, \exists te_1, te_2, \cdots, te_n \in \mathcal{TE}, n > 0$, called the sources of *te*, such that:

1. $Dom(te) \subseteq Dom(te_1) \cup Dom(te_2) \cup \cdots \cup Dom(te_n)$.

2. $Dpara(te) \subseteq Dpara(te_1) \cup Dpara(te_2) \cup \cdots \cup Dpara(te_n)$.

3. *te* is structurally defined as: $Evt(te) = Evt(te_1) \cup Evt(te_2) \cup \cdots \cup Evt(te_n)$ with $\forall e \in Evt(te), \exists e_i \in Evt(te_i), i \in [1..n]$, such that $e = e_i$.

The definition of represented event types takes into account the multiple inheritance since a represented event type may have several sources.

Example 3.6

Figure 3.5 illustrates the different basic types provided with their parameters. "Reservation" exemplifies simple event type just invokating an operation (C.f. example 3.5).

"Rental-Request" is an abstract event type which represents the external events occurring when customers request a car rental. Finally, "C-Reservation" is a represented event type, introduced in the dynamic description to reuse the type "Reservation". Let us notice that its parameters are a subset of "Reservation" parameters.

3.3.3 Complex Event Type Definitions

For capturing event synchronizations, complex event types can be built. They express different variants of event conjunction and disjunction by using *constructors*. With this approach, we provide not only the required expressive power but also the uniformity with respect to the IFO$_2$ structural modeling. The associated graphic formalism is illustrated in Figure 3.6.

The event constructors, which can be recursively applied, are the following:

- The event *composition* type reflects the conjunction of events of different types.
- The event *sequence* type is defined as the previous one but a chronological constraint is enforced for events of the component types.
- The event *grouping* type expresses conjunctions of events of a common type.
- The event *union* type captures a disjunction of events having different types.

The following definitions explain how composite events are achieved from component events. Their values are obtained by using the value of their components and the structure of tuple (for the two former constructors) or set (for grouping). The associated set of parameters is yielded by the union of component parameters. Finally, an event of the union type is an event of one of its components.

Definition 3.6

Composition and Sequence Event Type

Let $\mathcal{TETC}$ be an infinite set of **composition** event types, and let $\mathcal{TETS}$ be an infinite set of **sequence** event types. $\mathcal{TETC}$ and $\mathcal{TETS}$ are two subsets of $\mathcal{TE}$, such that: $\forall te \in \mathcal{TETC} \cup \mathcal{TETS}, \exists te_1, te_2, \cdots, te_n \in \mathcal{TE}, n > 1$, such that:

1. $Dom(te) \subseteq Evt(te_1) \times Evt(te_2) \times \cdots \times Evt(te_n)$.

2. $Dpara(te) \subseteq Dpara(te_1) \cup Dpara(te_2) \cup \cdots \cup Dpara(te_n)$.

3. te is structurally defined as:

   $\forall e \in Evt(te), \exists e_1 \in Evt(te_1), e_2 \in Evt(te_2), \cdots, e_n \in Evt(te_n)$ such that:

$$e = (id, [e_1, e_2, \cdots, e_n], \bigcup_{i=1}^{n} Para(e_i))$$

   and $\forall e' \in Evt(te)$ with $e \neq e', \exists e'_1 \in Evt(te_1), e'_2 \in Evt(te_2), \cdots, e'_n \in Evt(te_n)$ such that $e' = (id', [e'_1, e'_2, \cdots, e'_n], para')$ with $\forall i \in [1..n], e_i \notin \{e'_1, e'_2, \cdots, e'_n\}$. Furthermore, if $te \in \mathcal{TETS}$, we have: $Id(e_1) <_{Time} Id(e_2) <_{Time} \cdots <_{Time} Id(e_n)$ $<_{Time} Id(e)$.

Definition 3.7
Grouping Event Type

Let $\mathcal{TESG}$ be an infinite set of **grouping** event types, subset of $\mathcal{TE}$, such that: $\forall te \in \mathcal{TESG}, \exists! te' \in \mathcal{TE}$, such that:

1. $Dom(te) \subseteq \mathcal{P}(Evt(te'))$ where $\mathcal{P}(Evt(te'))$ is the powerset of $Evt(te')$.

2. $Dpara(te) \subseteq \mathcal{P}(Dpara(te'))$.

3. te is structurally defined as: $\forall e \in Evt(te), \exists e_1, e_2, \cdots, e_n \in Evt(te')$ such that:

$$e = (id, \{e_1, e_2, \cdots, e_n\}, \bigcup_{i=1}^{n} Para(e_i))$$

   with $\forall i \in [1..n], Id(e_i) <_{Time} Id(e)$ and $\forall e' = (id', [e'_1, e'_2, \cdots, e'_n], para') \in Evt(te)$ with $e \neq e'$ then $\forall i \in [1..n], e_i \notin \{e'_1, e'_2, \cdots, e'_n\}$.

Definition 3.8
Union Event Type

Let $\mathcal{TEUT}$ be an infinite set of **union** event types, subset of $\mathcal{TE}$, such that: $\forall te \in \mathcal{TEUT}, \exists te_1, te_2, \cdots, te_n \in \mathcal{TE}, n > 1$, such that:

1. $Dom(te) \subseteq Dom(te_1) \cup Dom(te_2) \cup \cdots \cup Dom(te_n)$.

2. $Dpara(te) \subseteq Dpara(te_1) \cup Dpara(te_2) \cup \cdots \cup Dpara(te_n)$.

3. te is structurally defined as:
   $\forall i, j \in [1..n]$ if $i \neq j$ then $Evt(te_i) \cap Evt(te_j) = \emptyset$ and
   $Evt(te) = Evt(te_1) \cup Evt(te_2) \cup \cdots \cup Evt(te_n)$
   with $\forall e \in Evt(te), \exists! k \in [1..n]$ such that $e = e_k$ where $e_k \in Evt(te_k)$.

3.3.4   Event Type Definitions

By synchronizing basic types using constructors, arbitrarily complex types can be achieved. In this subsection, we propose general definitions of IFO$_2$ event types. They could be seen as generalizations of the definitions previously given but special attention is payed to event domain, event parameters and type instances.

Definition 3.9

An **event type** $Te \in \mathcal{TE}$ is a directed tree (S_{Te}, E_{Te}) such that:

1. S_{Te}, the set of vertices, is included in the disjoint union of seven sets $\mathcal{TES}$, $\mathcal{TEA}$, $\mathcal{TER}$, $\mathcal{TETC}$, $\mathcal{TETS}$, $\mathcal{TESG}$ and $\mathcal{TEUT}$.

2. E_{Te} is the set of edges called type links.

Definition 3.10

Let Te be an event type and $Evt(Te)$ the infinite set of **events**, instances of Te. Its **event domain**, $Dom(Te)$, and its **parameter domain**, $Dpara(Te)$ are the event domain and parameter domain respectively of its root type.

A **type instance** includes all the events of this type ever occurred.

Definition 3.11

Let Te be an event type, an **instance** J of Te, denoted by J_{Te}, is a finite set of events of type Te, i.e. $J_{Te} \subseteq Evt(Te)$.

The **attached events**, denoted by Evt_att, describe, for each vertex of the type, which events occurred. This concept is particularly useful to specify certain complex constraints (for instance, if an event triggering depends on some other specific events).

Example 3.7

When booking a car rental, it is necessary to check whether the customer is known as a "bad customer" or not. Depending on the result of this "request", two different alternatives can be chosen: actually perform the reservation, or refuse it. In the latter case, the reservation process completes (in a negative way); in the former case, a car must be selected and its reservation is performed for the considered customer and the requested rental period. To model the described twofold reaction of the rental system, an IFO$_2$ complex type, "Rental-Management", is specified as a union type, i.e. the two possible ways for dealing with a reservation. In fact, the reservation can be refused, then the method invoked by the simple type "Refusal" just informs the user of the customer-checking negative result. The second described alternative is itself a composite event type "Rental". This type is a sequence including a simple type "Car-Selection" (the associated method retrieves a car available for the requested period, and perhaps meeting precise customer's expectations), and a represented type "Reserving" which stands for a reservation creation, described elsewhere in specifications.

3.3.5 Fragment Definitions

From a behavioral viewpoint, the relations between events are not only described through synchronization conditions but also through the chaining of events. These causality links are expressed with functions. In fact, the event types are interconnected by functions through the *event fragment* concept, focused on a principal type

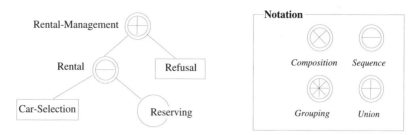

Figure 3.6   Complex Event Type Example

called *heart*. Functions of event fragments express general conditions constraining the event chaining since they can combine the following features:

- *simple* or *complex* (mono or multivalued), i.e. an event of their type origin triggers one or several events of their target;

- *partial* or *total*, i.e. an event of their type origin can or must trigger an event of their target;

- and *deferred* or *immediate*, if there is a delay or not between the occurrences of the origin and target events.

In addition, we make a distinction between *triggering* and *precedence functions*, which roughly express the fact that an event of the fragment heart triggers the occurrence of other events or that it is preceded by the occurrence of other events. In order to emphasize this, let us consider an external or temporal event. By its very nature, it cannot be triggered by another modeled event, therefore it is sometimes necessary to express that its occurrence is necessarily preceded by other events.

Before giving the associated formal definitions, let us examine a couple of examples.

Example 3.8

The fragment in Figure 3.7 describes the reactions of the system when a rental request occurs. The external event type "Rental-Request" is the heart of the fragment, and its events trigger, as soon as they are detected, events of the complex type "Reservation-Taking". Thus the function between the two types is simple, total and immediate. The type "Reservation-Taking" is described as a sequence of simple types. Let us imagine that the method associated to "Form-Filling" just gets, from the user, necessary information (about the customer and the rental period). Then the method invoked by "Customer-Checking" is triggered. The heart of the fragment "Rental-Request" is also related to the union type "Rental-Management", describing how to deal with a rental request. The concerned function is simple, immediate and total.

The second fragment example, in Figure 3.8, describes the system behavior when a customer cancels a reservation. The heart of the fragment is the external event type "Cancellation". When a reservation is cancelled, it must be removed (invocation of a

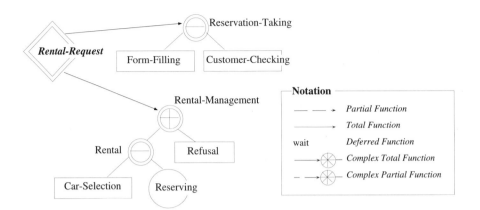

Figure 3.7 The Fragment "Rental-Request"

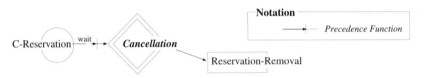

Figure 3.8 The Fragment "Cancellation"

deletion operation through the simple type "Reservation-Removal"). This fragment includes a precedence function between the represented type "C-Reservation" which stands for "Reservation" and the heart "Cancellation". This function captures the existence and chronological constraint between the cancellation of a reservation and its creation. It is deferred to take into consideration a delay which likely elapses between the two events.

Definition 3.12

An **event fragment** is a directed acyclic graph $F_e = (V_{Fe}, L_{Fe})$ with V_{Fe}, subset of $\mathcal{TE}$, the event type set of the fragment and L_{Fe}, the set of fragment links, defined such that:

1. There is a single directed tree $H_e = (V'_{Fe}, L'_{Fe})$, its root is called fragment heart, such that:

   (a) $V'_{Fe} \subseteq V_{Fe}, L'_{Fe} \subseteq L_{Fe}$.

   (b) The source of a triggering edge is either the root of the heart or the root of a type target of a complex edge having the heart root as origin (case of subfragment).

2. $(V_{Fe} - V'_{Fe})$ is either equal to the empty set - and $(L_{Fe} - L'_{Fe})$ too - or it is reduced to a singleton, source of the precedence edge belonging to $(L_{Fe} - L'_{Fe})$ having the fragment heart as target.

The event fragment is called by its heart name.

A fragment instance is a triplet: the generators of heart events, the heart events themselves and events triggered by heart events. It gives an historical view of behavior encapsulated within a fragment, with causality links between events.

Generated events are triggered from heart events. They are achieved by applying the triggering functions to heart type instance.

Definition 3.13

Let F_e be an event fragment with heart T_{e0} having a root r_{e0}, let $a_1 = (r_{e0}, r_{e1})$, $a_2 = (r_{e0}, r_{e2})$, $\cdots a_n = (r_{e0}, r_{en})$ be edges sharing a common source r_{e0}. For each $i \in [1..n]$, let f_{a_i} be the function associated to the edge a_i and let Z_{ei} be the subfragment obtained from the maximal subtree with root r_{ei}. The **set of events generated** from an event e of the heart type of F_e, is achieved by applying the function Ψ_{F_e} which is such that:

$$\Psi_{F_e}(e) = \begin{cases} \varnothing & \text{if the } F_e \text{ fragment encompasses a single type} \\ \bigcup_{i=1}^{n} \left(\bigcup_{k=1}^{q_i} (ei_k, \Psi_{Z_{ei}}(ei_k)) \right) & \text{otherwise} \end{cases}$$

where $\{ei_k; k \in [1..q_i]\}$ is the event set yielded by applying the function f_{a_i} to the event e (q_i is equal to 1 when f_{a_i} is a simple function) and $\Psi_{Z_{ei}}(ei_k)$ is the set of events generated from the event ei_k in the subfragment Z_{ei}.

The set of events triggered from the $J_{T_{e0}}$ instance with m elements, denoted by $\Psi_{F_e}(J_{T_{e0}})$, is then defined by:

$$\Psi_{F_e}(J_{T_{e0}}) = \bigcup_{j=1}^{m} (\Psi_{F_e}(e_j)).$$

Generator events are events having a single image by applying the fragment precedence function.

Definition 3.14

Let F_e be an event fragment having a heart T_{e0} with root r_{e0} and let $a_b = (r_b, r_{e0})$ be the possible edge whose target is r_{e0}. The **set of generator events** of heart events is obtained with the function Υ_{F_e}. Its domain is $J_{T_{e0}}$ - a T_{e0} instance with m elements - and its codomain is either the empty set if a_b does not exist or I_{T_b} an instance of type T_b with root r_b. Υ_{F_e} is defined by:

$$\forall e \in J_{T_{e0}}, \quad \Upsilon_{F_e}(e) = \begin{cases} e_b & \text{if } e_b \in I_{T_b} \text{ exists and is such that } f_{a_b}(e_b) = e \\ \varnothing & \text{where } f_{a_b} \text{ is the function represented by the } a_b \text{ edge.} \end{cases}$$

The set of generator events through the a_b edge of the $J_{T_{e0}}$ instance, denoted by $\Upsilon_{F_e}(J_{T_{e0}})$, is defined by:

$$\Upsilon_{F_e}(J_{T_{e0}}) = \bigcup_{j=1}^{m} \Upsilon_{F_e}(e_j).$$

Fragment Instance

Definition 3.15

Let F_e be an event fragment with heart T_{e0} and let $J_{T_{e0}}$ be an instance of T_{e0} with m elements.

An **instance** of F_e, denoted by I_{F_e}, is defined by:

$$I_{F_e} = (\Upsilon_{F_e}(J_{T_{e0}}), \quad J_{T_{e0}}, \quad \Psi_{F_e}(J_{T_{e0}})).$$

Example 3.9

Let us consider the "Rental-Request" fragment (C.f. Figure 3.7). Since it is devoid of precedence function, any instance is unprovided with generator events. It could be specified through the following triplet: $I_{Rr} = (\emptyset, J_{Rr}, \Psi_{Rr}(J_{Rr}))$.

Let us assume that J_{Rr} merely encompasses the event e_{Rr1}, we have: $\Psi_{Rr}(J_{Rr})$ $= \Psi_{Rr}(e_{Rr1}) = (e_{Rt1}, e_{Re2})$ where e_{Rt1} is an event of type "Reservation-Taking"and e_{Re2} is an instance of "Refusal". This particular fragment instance captures the case of a rental request which is refused.

In a similar way than structural fragments, behavioral fragments are intended for providing designers with an intermediary description level. Event types vehicle details about what could happen. When organized within a fragment and related by appropriate functions, they are involved in the description of a more complex reaction of the modeled application.

3.3.6   Event Schema Definitions

The partial views provided by fragments are grouped together within event schemas which offer an overview of behavior. More precisely represented types are related to heart of fragments by means of IS_A links. These links introduce a behavioral inheritance hierarchy and multiple inheritance is possible: a represented type can inherit from several fragment hearts. Thus the behavior part, modeled through a fragment, can be reused as a whole.

Example 3.10

Apart from the fragments "Rental-Request" and "Cancellation", the schema, illustrated in Figure 3.9, encompasses the fragment "Reservation-Creation" which is merely a simple type. Considering this type in isolation, i.e. creating a separated fragment, makes it possible to reuse it, in the two other fragments, through represented types and IS_A links.

Specialization Link

The specialization link represents either the role of an event type in another fragment or the event subtyping.

Definition 3.16

Let Te be a type of $\mathcal{TER}$ and let $Ts \in \mathcal{TE}$ be a source of Te and heart of frag-

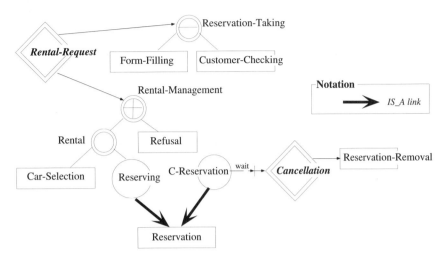

Figure 3.9   Part of the Behavioral Schema "Car Rental"

ment, the link of source Ts and target Te is called an **IS_A** link and is denoted by $L_{IS\_A(Te\rightarrow Ts)}$.

Schema Specification

Definition 3.17
An **event schema** is a directed acyclic graph $G_{Se} = (S_{Se}, L_{Se})$ such that:

1. S_{Se}, the set of schema types, is a subset of $\mathcal{TE}$.

2. L_{Se} is the disjoint union of two sets: L_{Se_A} the fragment link set and L_{Se-IS_A} the IS_A link set.

3. (S_{Se}, L_{Se-A}) is a forest of event fragments.

4. (S_{Se}, L_{Se-IS_A}) follows the two rules: there is no IS_A cycle in the graph and two directed paths of IS_A links sharing the same origin must be extended to a common vertex.

Schema Instance

Definition 3.18
Let G_{Se} be an event schema encompassing by p event fragments F_{e1}, $F_{e2}, \cdots, F_{ep}$ with $p > 0$. An **instance** of G_{Se}, denoted by $I_{G_{Se}}$, is such that:

1.

$$I_{G_{Se}} = \bigcup_{i=1}^{p}(I_{F_{ei}})$$

where $I_{F_{ei}}$ is the instance of the fragment F_{ei}.

2. If $L_{IS\_A_{(T_e'\rightarrow T_e)}} \in L_{Se-IS\_A}$, $T_e \in F_{ei}$ and $T_e' \in F_{ej}$ then:

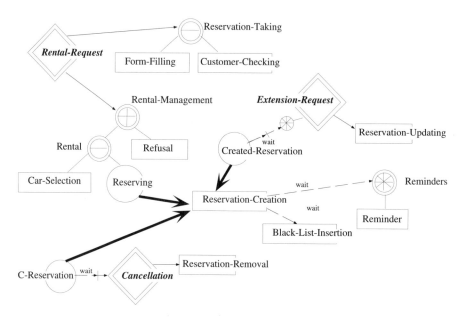

Figure 3.10   Extended Behavioral Schema

$$Evt\_att_{T_e}(I_{F_{ei}}) \subseteq Evt\_att_{T'_e}(I_{F_{ej}}).$$

guaranteed not to run indefinitively.

When activity paths capture iterations within the IFO$_2$ graph, the problem is much more crucial. Such paths encompass a repetitive sequence of event types (denoted by $*$). Authorized repetitive sequence are necessarily constrained by setting a maximal number of iterations or by specifying a termination condition (in fact, iterations are performed as long as the condition holds).

Example 3.11
Let us consider the schema in Figure 3.10. It is a complemented version of our schema example. It extends the "Reservation-Creation" fragment by integrating the system reaction when the customer's payment is not actually registred and a given period completes. We imagine that in such a case the customer is sent a reminder. If he does not react by paying for the rental, a second reminder is sent and finally, after a given number of reminders, he is considered as a bad customer. The associated activity path is the following : < *Rental-Request, Rental-Taking, . . . , Reservation-Creation, (Reminder)∗, Black-List-Insertion* >

We also add, in the schema, the fragment of heart "Extension-Request" which describes the application reaction when a customer requests an extension of the rental period for a given reservation. In fact, we consider a very mere reaction (updating the considered reservation).

When building an activity path, this new fragment can be reached through its precedent type "Created-Reservation", thus only after a reservation creation. But, for a reservation, one or several period extension requests can be considered, each of which triggers an update operation on the concerned reservation. The associated activity path is the following: *< Rental-Request, . . ., Reservation-Creation, Created-Reservation, (Extension-Request, Reservation-Updating)∗ >*.

IFO$_2$ event schemas provide a general specification of behavior, well exhibiting triggering cascades and their possible common points. Nevertheless, they must be complemented to capture much more details about the circumstances in which events can be triggered. The fragment functions express general conditions constraining event triggering (through their features: simple or complex, partial or not, . . .). Nevertheless, they must be refined because they cannot capture very precise details. For instance, it is necessary to describe the conditions under which a period extension request could be satisfied or a reminder is sent to a customer.

In fact, such conditions apply to object values but also to the past behavior of the system. In state-based approaches, these conditions are expressed in a twofold way: through transition conditions or guards and through states. In both cases, conditions are expressed in terms of object properties. Of course, the corresponding attribute and object must exist in the structural representation and if not, some artificial element must be added in the static description.

In IFO$_2$, behavioral conditions can be expressed in terms of existing object values but also in terms of events. Event-based constraints are used everytime the knowledge of the past behavior is necessary to determine the future behavior.

For meeting such a need, IFO$_2$ makes use of the concept of trace, introduced in (23) and used in (14, 36, 40), and proposes an algebraic language, encompassing various operators (37) applying to traces for expressing complex conditions: retrieval of events according to their type, fragment, parameters, or their causality or chronological relationships with other events.

3.4 Related Work: A Comparative Outline

IFO$_2$ adopts, specially for abstracting behavior, a radically different philosophy than current modeling approaches (15, 17, 4, 35). In this section, we propose a comparison between IFO$_2$ and related work, particularly focussing on dynamics. However, before detailing these behavioral features, let us briefly indicate the strenghs of the structural model.

The IFO$_2$ structural model offers an expressive power comparable to the quoted approaches: complex constructions, generalization and specialization, relationships between classes, . . . However, modularity and reusability of specifications are improved by introducing a twofold description granularity with the concepts of object type and fragment. The latter makes it possible to handle as a whole several conceptual entities semantically related.

From a behavioral viewpoint, current approaches make use of state transition diagrams. Although well suitable for capturing the individual behavior of objects, state diagrams have some disavantages. The various states required for representing objet dynamics are not always clear cut and could vary from a designer to another. In some cases, states are artificial: they no longer capture values of intrisic properties and they are only motivated by dynamic considerations. In such cases, the structural schema must be altered for taking into account new attributes or links.

By discarding the concept of state, IFO_2 avoids these disavantages. IFO_2 structural and behavioral schemas are closely related but nevertheless clearly distinct and it is not necessary to complement the structural specifications to take into account dynamic requirements. Actually, the fewer effects on structural representation that the dynamic modeling has, the more likely this static description will stay faithful to the modeled real world.

Let us resume and extend our comparison by considering the concept of event. Essential in modeling approaches (24, 5), events could model external stimuli as well as information communications within the abstracted system. IFO_2 places much more emphasis on this concept than classical and current conceptual approaches. Inspired from active DBMSs, it offers various semantics for basic events and capabilities for handling complex event types. Although addressing a different issue, active DBMSs provide mechanisms, active rules, for specifying automated reactions of the database (39, 19). Such rules are triggered by events and, when some conditions hold, they perform actions. In the context of OODBs, complex events are studied and various constructors are proposed (6, 7, 12, 9). In contrast, resulting from the "whole-event" modeling style, IFO_2 offers similar constructors for synchronizing both events and operations. Thus triggering of actions can be organized. From this viewpoint, the concern is very close to specifying task synchronization when modeling business processes (34, 8, 13, 18). Workflow management approaches, intended for capturing and handling such processes, provide different synchronization capabilities but, in contrast with IFO_2 , they do not consider events.

Although widely improved in nested statecharts, modularity and reusability are limited, in state transition diagrams, to super-states. In (22), the problem is addressed and the difficulty when handling overlapping statechart is underlined. Finally, that the system behavior is seen as the collection of object behaviors can be an additional difficulty when abstracting dynamics. Such a vision does not highlight interactions between objects nor the triggering chaining, over time, of these interactions.

The IFO_2 dynamic model attempts to avoid the evoked difficulties by proposing an alternative vision of behavior. In fact, it applies the very principles of object- oriented paradigm for modeling dynamics. In a similar way than for object types, event types are the elementary units. They could be combined by using event constructors mirroring the structural constructors. Like for the structural part, the concept of fragment introduces an additional granularity, intermediary between event types and event schema, with analogous benefits for modularity and reusability.

Finally, since state-based approaches are by their very nature "object-oriented" or rather "instance-oriented", IFO_2 boosts dynamic representation capabilities by offering the description of both object life cycles and processes (instance or set-oriented). Let us notice that such a concern is also shared by workflow management approaches (34, 13). These approaches as well as functional and activity models (28, 35) could be seen as complementing object dynamics for abstracting various kinds of behavior. IFO_2 attempts to reconcile these two points of view by providing a common formalism suitable for both global and local behaviors.

3.5   Conclusion

In this chapter, we described the IFO_2 conceptual models. Their original aspects are a "whole-object" and "whole-event" approach, the use of constructors to express complex combinations of objects and events and the reusability and modularity of specifications in order to optimize the designer's work.

The IFO_2 approach offers a uniform specification of both structural and behavioral parts of applications. We believe that such a uniformity is particularly important on a conceptual level. In the two frameworks, structural and behavioral, the designer uses the same fundamental concepts, such as reusability, modularity, identification, . . . Types, constructors and fragments are defined by adopting an analogous formalism. A comparable graphic representation is presented and can facilitate dialogue between designers in order to better take advantage of specification modularity.

The presented models of the IFO_2 approach are complemented by additional and original capabilities. Evolution components are defined for updating IFO_2 schemas (31). They offer a minimal set of primitives for performing basic modifications. When combined, these primitives could capture whatever evolution even if it results in an entire reorganization of the schema. Update operations are strictly controlled: applied to a consistent event schema, they yield a new schema still consistent. Enhanced consistency controls are based on the definition of invariants guaranteeing that the schema is well-built. The evolution component provides the basis for aiding designers all along the modeling process, and enforces what we call a first level of controls. Additional verifications are provided for controling behavior. Applied a posteriori, they reveal design defects which could appear even in a well-built schema, such as deadlocks in the triggering chaining, possibly infinite reaction chaining, . . .

Finally, transformation algorithms are proposed for implementing IFO_2 specifications. The considered target systems are relational DBMSs (Oracle) or object-oriented systems (O2) (33). An experimentation has also been performed for C++ and Smalltalk. From behavioral schemas, transformations capabilities are provided. The considered target systems are active DBMSs (39). More precisely, active rules are generated. These rules, similar to Event-Condition-Action rules of HiPAC (7), are chained and when executed, they simulate the behavior of the modeled system (38). IFO_2 approach is supported by a CASE tool encompassing various software components such as graphic interface for an aided construction of schemas (illustrated in Figure 3.11), consistency control algorithms, and translation modules for evoked target systems.

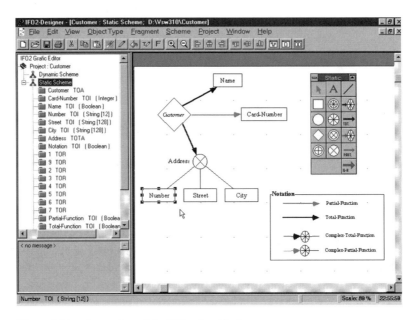

Figure 3.11   A snapshot of the IFO$_2$ Case Tool

References

1. S. Abiteboul and R. Hull. IFO: A Formal Semantic Database Model. *ACM Transactions on Database Systems*, 12(4):525–565, December 1987.

2. M. Bouzeghoub and E. Métais. Semantic Modelling of Object-Oriented Databases. In *Proc. of the 17th Int. Conf. on Very Large Data Bases (VLDB'91)*, pages 3–14, Barcelona, Spain, September 1991.

3. M. Bouzeghoub, E. Métais, and al. A Design Tool for Object Databases. In *Proc. of the 2nd Int. Conf. on Advanced Information System Engineering (CAiSE'90)*, volume 436 of *LNCS*, pages 365–392, June 1990.

4. G. Booch. *Object-Oriented Design with Applications*. Benjamin/Cumming Comp., 1991.

5. M.L. Brodie. On the Development of Data Models. In *On Conceptual Modelling, Perspectives from Artificial Intelligence, Databases, and Programming Languages*, pages 19–48. Springer Verlag, 1984.

6. G.G. Cattel. *Object Management: Object-Oriented and Extended Relational Database Systems*. Addison-Wesley, 1991.

7. S. Chakravarthy, B. Blaustein, A. P. Buchmann, M. Carey, U. Dayal, D. Goldhirsch, M. Hsu, R. Jauhari, and al. HiPAC: A Research Project in Active, Time-Constrained Database Management. Technical report, Xerox Advanced Information Technology, Cambrige, MA, August 1990.

8. F. Casati, S. Ceri, B. Pernici, and G. Pozzi. Conceptual Modeling of Workflows. In *Proc. of the 14th Int. Conf. on O-O and E-R Modeling*, 1995.

9. S. Ceri, P. Fraternali, S. Paraboschi, and L. Tanca. Active Rule Management in Chimera. *Active Database Systems*, pages 151–176, 1996.

10. P. Chen. The Entity-relationship Model-Towards a Unified View of Data. *ACM Transactions on Database Systems*, 1(1):9–36, March 1976.

11. S. C. Cheung and J. Kramer. Tractable Flow Analysis for Anomaly Detection in Distributed Programs. In *Proc. of the 4th European Software Engineering Conf.*, pages 283–300, 1993.

12. S. Chakravarthy and D. Mishra. SNOOP: An Expressive Event Specification Language for Active Databases. *Data and Knowledge Engineering*, 14(1):1–26, 1994.

13. E. Cobb. The Impact of Object Technology on Commercial Transaction Processing. *VLDB Journal*, 6:173–190, 1997.

14. J. Carmo and A. Sernadas. A Temporal Logic Framework for a Layered Approach to Systems Specification and Verification. In *Proc. of the Temporal Aspects in Information Systems Conf. (IFIP 88)*, pages 31–46. Elsevier Science, 1988.

15. P. Coad and E. Yourdon. *Object-Oriented Analysis*. Yourdon Press Computing Series, 1990.

16. O. Deux. The Story of O_2. *IEEE Transactions on Knowledge and Data Engineering*, 2(1):91–108, March 1990.

17. M. Fowler and K. Scott. *UML Distilled: Applying the Standard Object Modelling Language*. Addison-Wesley, 1997.

18. D. Georgakopoulos, M. Hornick, and A. Sheth. An Overview of Workflow Management: From Process Modeling to Workflow Automation Infrastructure. *Distributed and Parallel Databases*, 3:119–153, 1995.

19. N. H. Gehani and H. V. Jagadish. ODE as an Active Database: Constraints and Triggers. In *Proc. of the 17th Int. Conf. on Very Large Data Bases (VLDB'91)*, pages 327–336, Barcelona, Spain, September 1991.

20. D. Harel. On Visual Formalisms. *Communications of the ACM*, 31(5):514–530, 1988.

21. R. Hull and R. King. Semantic Database Modelling: Survey, Applications and Research Issues. *ACM Computing Surveys*, 19(3):201–260, Sept. 1987.

22. D. Harel and C.A. Kahana. On Statechart with Overlapping. *ACM TSEM*, 1(4):399–421, 1992.

23. C.A.R Hoare. *Communicating Sequential Processes*. Prentice-Hall, 1985.

24. J.Y. Lingat, P. Nobecourt, and C. Rolland. Behaviour management in database application. In *Proc. of the 13th Int. Conf. on Very Large Databases (VLDB'87)*, Brighton, UK, September 1987.

25. P. Loucopoulos and R. Zicari. *Conceptual Modeling, Databases and CASE: An Integrated View of Information Systems Development*. Wiley Professional Computing, 1992.

26. Z. Manna and A. Pnueli. Specification and Verification of Concurrent Programs by ∀-Automata. In *Proc. of the Temporal Logic in Specification Conf.*, volume 398 of *LNCS*, pages 124–164, Altrincham, UK, April 1987.

27. Z. Manna and A. Pnueli. A Hierarchy of Temporal Properties. In *Proc. of the 9th Annual ACM Symposium on Principles of Distributed Computing*, pages 377–408, Quebec, CA, August 1990.

28. UML Standard Notation. In *http://www.rational.com/uml/index.jtmpl*, 1999.

29. J.S. Ostroff. *Temporal Logic for Real Time Systems*. Wiley and Sons, 1989.

30. J. S. Ostroff and W. Murray Wonham. A Framework for Real-Time Discrete Event Control. *IEEE TAC*, 35(4):386–397, April 1990.

31. P. Poncelet and L. Lakhal. Consistent Structural Updates for O-O Design. In *Proc. of the 5th Int. Conf. on Advanced Information Systems Engineering (CAiSE'93)*, volume 685 of *LNCS*, pages 1–21, Paris, France, June 1993.

32. J. Peckman and F. Maryanski. Semantic Data Models. *ACM Computing Surveys*, 20(3): 153–189, September 1988.

33. P. Poncelet, M. Teisseire, R. Cicchetti, and L. Lakhal. Towards a Formal Approach for O-O Database Design. In *Proc. of the 19th Int. Conf. on Very Large Data Bases (VLDB'93)*, pages 278–289, Dublin, Ireland, August 1993.

34. J. Puustjarvi, H. Tirri, and J. Veijalainen. Reusability and Modularity in Transactional Workflows. *Information Systems*, 22:101–120, 1997.

35. J. Rumbaugh, M. Blaha, W. Premerlani, F. Eddy, and W. Lorensen. *Object-Oriented Modeling and Design*. Prentice-Hall, 1991.

36. G. Reggio. Event Logic for Specifying Abstract Dynamic Data Types. In *Proc. of 8th Workshop on Specification of Abstract Data Types and the 3rd COMPASS Workshop*, volume 655 of *LNCS*, pages 292–309, Dourdan, France, August 1991.

37. M. Teisseire. Behavioural Constraints: Why using Events instead of States. In *Proc. of the Int. Conf O-O ER'95*, LNCS, pages 123–132, Gold Coast, Australia, December 1995.

38. M. Teisseire, P. Poncelet, and R. Cicchetti. Towards Event-Driven Modelling for Database Design. In *Proc. of the 20th Int. Conf. on Very Large Databases (VLDB'94)*, pages 285–296, Santiago, Chile, September 1994.

39. J. Widom and S. Ceri. *Active Database Systems. Triggers and Rules for Adv anced Database Processing*. Morgan Kaufmann Publishers, 1996.

40. R. J. Wieringa. A Formalization of Objects Using Equational Dynamic Logic. In *Proc. of the 2nd Int. Conf. on Deductive and O-O Databases*, volume 566 of *LNCS*, pages 431–452, Munich, Germany, December 1991.

4

On the Design of Behavior Consistent Specializations of Object Life Cycles in OBD and UML

Michael Schrefl
School of Computer and Information Science
University of South Australia
schrefl@cs.unisa.edu.au

Markus Stumptner
Institut für Informationssysteme
Technische Universität Wien
mst@dbai.tuwien.ac.at

Object-oriented design methods express the behavior an object exhibits over time, i.e., the object life cycle, by notations based on Petri nets or statecharts.

This chapter investigates and compares the specialization of object life cycles in type hierarchies for two design notations: Object Behavior Diagrams (OBD), which have been originally developed for object-oriented database design and are based on Petri nets, and the Unified Modeling Language (UML), which is based on statecharts.

This work treats specialization as a combination of extension and refinement. It uses the notions of observation consistency and invocation consistency to compare the behavior of object life cycles. It presents necessary and sufficient rules to check for behavior consistency in the realm of OBD and outlines how these rules may be applied to UML.

Whereas specialization can always be strictly split into an extension part and a refinement part in OBD, the concurrency restrictions of UML sometimes require using what is technically a refinement in order to represent an intended parallel extension.

4.1 Introduction

Object-oriented systems organize object types in hierarchies in which subtypes inherit and specialize the structure and the behavior of supertypes. These inheritance hierarchies provide a major aid to the designer in structuring the description of an object-oriented system, and they guide the reader who tries to understand the system by pointing out similarities between object types that are so connected. Evidently, object-oriented designs are better to use and to maintain if a subtype does not override the behavior of its supertype arbitrarily. Instead, the behavior of the subtype should specialize the behavior of its supertype according to some clearly defined consistency criteria. This chapter discusses how object-oriented design methodologies can be used to define such criteria and guarantee a given design's adherence to them.

Object-oriented design methodologies such as OMT (26), OOSA (8), OOAD (3), OBD (10), and UML (24) differ from programming languages in that they represent the behavior of an object type not merely by a set of operations, which may be performed on instances of the object type, but instead provide a higher-level, overall picture on how instances of the object type may evolve over their lifetime. For example consider the concept of a reservation (of a hotel room or rental car). A reservation is first requested, then it is either granted (issued) or declined; once a reservation has been issued it may be either used or canceled. The different stages that this reservation passes through during its lifetime correspond to a specification of which sequences of operations are legal to execute on the object. Object-oriented design methodologies typically use notations based on Petri nets or statecharts to express formally how an object may evolve over its lifetime. Such a description is often referred to as "object life cycle". In this chapter, we consider one design notation based on Petri nets, called Object/Behavior diagrams (OBD), and one based on statecharts, the Unified Modeling Language (UML).

Object/Behavior diagrams have been originally developed for the design of object-oriented databases (11, 10, 28, 4). The structure and the behavior of instances of an object type are represented by an object diagram and a corresponding behavior diagram, respectively. We will only consider behavior diagrams in this chapter. A behavior diagram of an object type represents the possible life cycles of its instances by activities, states, and arcs corresponding to transitions, places, and arcs of Petri nets. This approach combines the simple formal semantics and well-understood properties of Petri nets with the clarity and intuitive understanding of an object-centered representation. When mapped to program code, activities are mapped to operations and states to the pre- and postconditions of these operations.

The Unified Modeling Language (UML) has recently emerged as a prominent commercial object-oriented design notation. UML uses the term "object class" in the same sense as the term "object type" is used in OBD, namely, it refers to the description of the structure and behavior of its instances. The behavior of an object class is represented by a statechart, which consists of states and state transitions. When mapped to program code, transitions are mapped to operations and states to pre- and postconditions of these operations.

In type hierarchies, subtypes inherit and may redefine object life cycle of supertypes just as in object-oriented programming languages subtypes inherit and may override operations (or methods) of supertypes. A simple approach to inheritance of object life cycles would be to allow for an arbitrary redefinition just as method implementations may be overridden freely in some object-oriented programming languages, ignoring entirely what the overridden implementation does. Such an approach may seem appealing to increase "code reuse" at the implementation level, but it contradicts the motivation why type hierarchies are used in object-oriented design: as mentioned above, they should increase understandability by exploiting semantic commonality through specialization.

Informally, specialization means for object-life cycles that the object life cycle of a subtype should be a "special case" of the object-life cycle of the supertype. There are two ways in which an object life cycle may be made more special. One way is to add new features, which we call *extension*. For example, a "reservation with payment" extends a "reservation" in that it provides for additional features relevant for payment such as billing, paying, and refunding. The other way is to consider inherited features in more detail, which we call *refinement*. For example, a "reservation with alternative payment" refines a "reservation with payment" in that it provides for special means to pay, such as by cash, by cheque, or by credit card.

Again, extension and refinement should not be employed arbitrarily but according to certain consistency criteria in order to increase understandability and usability. This raises the issue of how such criteria can be formally captured. Ebert and Engels (7) have pointed out that object life cycles can be compared based upon what a user observes (*observation consistency*) and based upon which operations (or activities) a user may invoke on an object (*invocation consistency*). Ebert and Engels saw both consistency notions as conflicting objectives between which "one has to choose". When extending these ideas and distinguishing between two types of invocation consistency (weak and strong), we will see that both objectives are not alternatives but may be achieved in conjunction as well.

Informally, observation consistent specialization guarantees that if features added at a subtype are ignored and features refined at a subtype are considered unrefined, any processing of an object of the subtype can be *observed* as correct processing from the point of view of the supertype. In our example of "reservation with payment", observation consistency is satisfied if the processing of reservations with payment appears (can be observed) as a correct processing of reservations when all features relevant to payment are ignored.

Weak invocation consistency captures the idea that instances of a subtype can be used the same way as instances of the supertype. For example, if one extends a television set by a video text component, one would usually expect that the existing controls of the television set should continue to operate in the same way. An extended property, strong invocation consistency, guarantees that one can continue to use instances of a subtype the same way as instances of a supertype, even after operations (or activities) that have been added at the subtype have been executed. In our television set example, to obey strong invocation consistency means that invoking any video text function should still leave the volume control operative.

In this chapter we discuss inheritance of object life cycles in the realm of Object/Behavior Diagrams (OBD) and in the realm of Unified Modeling Language (UML). We present extensions of earlier results (30, 31) on specialization of OBD and we discuss the applicability of these results to UML. Let us point out beforehand that "refinement" is used in the UML documentation in a wider sense that we do in this chapter, namely, as synonym for "inheritance relationship". But we believe that the term "refinement" should be reserved for the case where existing features are described in more detail. It should not also used to cover the case of newly added features, for which we use the term "extension".

This chapter is structured as follows: In Section 4.2 we present an extended form of behavior diagrams, labeled behavior diagrams. In Section 4.3 we address behavior modelling in UML. In particular, we examine the differences and commonalities between behavior diagrams and UML. In Section 4.4 we treat specialization by extension. We introduce, for behavior diagrams, three different kinds of consistency between a behavior diagram B of a supertype and a behavior diagram B' of a subtype that extends the behavior of the supertype. Next, we present necessary and sufficient rules to check for each kind of consistency. The rules are straightforward and easy to check. Then, we discuss the applicability of these results to UML. In Section 4.5 we treat specialization by refinement. Just as for extension, we discuss behavior consistency and give rules to check for behavior consistency. In Section 4.6 we consider extension and refinement together. We conclude by summarizing the main differences between inheritance in OBD and UML, and by comparing our results to the verbal description of the UML inheritance guidelines (25) as well as to other related work.

4.2   Behavior Diagrams

Object/Behavior diagrams are an object-oriented graphical design notation for the design of object-oriented databases (4, 14, 11, 10).

Object/Behavior Diagrams represent the structure of object types in object diagrams and their behavior in behavior diagrams. For the scope of this chapter we restrict our attention to behavior diagrams.

4.2.1   Behavior Diagrams

A *behavior diagram*, $B_O = (S_O, T_O, F_O, \alpha_O, \Omega_O)$, depicts the behavior of instances of an object type O by a set of states S_O, a set of activities T_O, and a set of directed arcs $F_O \subset ((S_O \times T_O) \cup (T_O \times S_O))$ connecting states with activities and vice versa (the subscripts are omitted if O is understood). Each of the states represents a particular period, each of the activities an event in the life cycle of the instances of the object type. All possible life cycles of instances of an object type have a single start state α, called the *initial state*, and a common set of completion states Ω, called *final states*. The initial state is the only state that has no ingoing arcs. The final states comprise exactly those states with no outgoing arcs. The principal idea behind behavior diagrams stems from Petri Nets (21). States correspond to places of Petri nets, activities to transitions.

Instances of an object type which reside in states correspond to individual tokens of a Petri net. If an activity t is connected by an incoming arc to state s, we say activity t *consumes* from state s and we call s *prestate* of t. If an activity t is connected by an outgoing arc to s, we say activity t *produces* into state s and we call s post state of t.

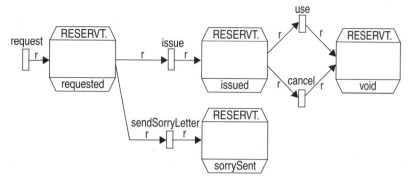

Figure 4.1   Behavior diagram of object type RESERVATION

Due to the underlying Petri net semantics a behavior diagram determines the legal sequences of states and activities, and thus the legal sequences in which activities may be applied: An activity may be applied on an object if the object is contained in every prestate of the activity. If an activity on some object has been executed successfully, the object is contained in every post state of the activity but in no prestate unless that prestate is also a post state. Like Petri nets, alternatives cannot be expressed by "alternative prestates" but must be represented by alternative activities. Unlike Petri nets, where a transition is automatically fired if every prestate contains a token, an activity in a behavior diagram must be explicitly invoked for an object which is in every prestate of the activity. In addition, and unlike Petri nets, activities take time. Therefore, during the execution of an activity on an object, the object resides in an implicit state named after the activity. This state is referred to as *activity state*. Thus, we can say that every instance of an object type is at any point in time in one or several (activity) states of its object type, which are jointly referred to as *life cycle state*.

Example 4.1
Figure 4.1 shows the behavior diagram of object type RESERVATION. Activities are depicted by vertical bars. States are depicted by rectangles which are labeled by the name of the object type they describe at the top and the name of the state at the bottom. For simplicity, the initial state α is not shown; it is also not indicated in subsequent examples. Also, final states are not marked visually. It is assumed that every activity for which no prestate is shown has the initial state as prestate and that every state from which no activity consumes is a final state. The labeling of arcs is explained below.

4.2.2   Labeled Behavior Diagrams

The work described in this chapter is based on an extended form of behavior diagrams, labeled behavior diagrams.

The idea of labeling states and activities is inspired by the way in which in business processes guided by paper work, various carbon copies of a form are given different colors. Each business activity handles one or several copies of a form, it may collect several copies of a form from different input boxes, and it may distribute several copies of a form to different output boxes. A *label* in a labeled behavior diagram corresponds in this analogy to the color given to some copy of a form, an object corresponds to one filled-in form representing a particular business case, and the labels given to an arc identify those copies of a form that are delivered by a business activity to an output box or are taken by a business activity from an input box. We now give a formal definition of this concept. Later, we will use these labels to ensure that if an object leaves a subnet that represents the refinement of an activity or state, it leaves the subnet entirely.

A *labeled behavior diagram (LBD)* $B = (S, T, F, \alpha, \Omega, L, l)$ of an object type O is defined as a behavior diagram $\hat{B} = (S, T, F, \alpha, \Omega)$ with the addition of a non-empty set of labels L and a labeling function l which assigns a *non-empty* set of labels to every arc in F, $l : F \mapsto 2^L \setminus \{\emptyset\}$. Each outgoing arc of the initial state α carries all labels.

Example 4.2

The behavior diagram of object type RESERVATION shown in Figure 4.1 is a labeled behavior diagram. Each arc carries the label r.

We say an activity *consumes* a label, if it has an ingoing arc with that label, and we say an activity *produces* a label, if it has an outgoing arc with that label. Extending the labeling function l from arcs to activities and states, we say that an activity or state *carries* the union of the labels of its incident arcs.

A *labeled life cycle state* $\bar{\sigma}$ is a set of pairs, where the first element is a state or activity and the second element is a label. Thus, the labeled life cycle state indicates in which states or activity state an instance of an object type resides with which label. We denote the initial labeled life cycle state by $\bar{A}$.

Example 4.3

The initial life cycle state of the labeled behavior diagram of object type RESERVATION (cf. Figure 4.1) is $\{(\alpha, r)\}$.

An activity t *can be started* on some life cycle state $\bar{\sigma}$ if that life cycle state contains for each prestate s of t for each label x on the arc between s and t an entry (s, x). The *start of activity* t on some life cycle state $\bar{\sigma}$ yields life cycle state $\bar{\sigma}'$, where for each prestate s of t for each label x on the arc between s and t the pair (s, x) is removed from the life cycle state $\bar{\sigma}$ and the pair (s, t) is added. An activity t *can be completed* on some life cycle state $\bar{\sigma}$ if that life cycle state contains for each post state s of t for each label x on the arc between t and s an entry (t, x). The *completion of activity* t on some life cycle state $\bar{\sigma}$ yields life cycle state $\bar{\sigma}'$, where for each prestate s of t for each label x on the arc between s and t the pair (t, x) is removed from and the pair (s, x) is added to life cycle state $\bar{\sigma}$.

Example 4.4

According to the labeled behavior diagram of object type RESERVATION (cf. Figure 4.1) activity issue can be started on the labeled life cycle state { (requested,r)} yielding LLCS { (issue,r)}, Activity issue can be completed on this LLCS yielding LLCS { (issued,r)}.

As we consider only labeled behavior diagrams in this chapter, we will omit the "labeled" from here on and simply speak of behavior diagrams, life cycle states, and activities.

A behavior diagram of an object type specifies all legal sequences of life cycle states. A particular sequence of life cycle states of an object type is referred to as life cycle occurrence of that object type. More precise, a *life cycle occurrence* (LCO) γ of object type O is a sequence of life cycle states $\sigma_1, \ldots, \sigma_n$, such that $\sigma_1 = \bar{A}$, and for $i = 1 \ldots n - 1$ either $\sigma_i = \sigma_{i+1}$, or there exists an activity $t \in T$ such that either t can be started on σ_i and the start of t yields σ_{i+1} or σ_i contains t and the completion of t yields σ_{i+1}. Any subsequence of γ is called *partial LCO*. A LCO γ is called *complete*, if $\{s \mid (s, x) \in \sigma_n\} \subseteq \Omega$.

Example 4.5

A possible life cycle occurrence of object type RESERVATION is [{(request,r)}, {(requested,r)}, {(issue,r)}, {(issued,r)}, {(cancel,r)}, {(void,r)}] (cf. Figure 4.1).

The set of life cycle states *reachable* from a life cycle state σ, written $R(\sigma)$, contains every life cycle state σ' that can be reached from σ by starting or completing any sequence of activities in T.

Example 4.6

Given the behavior diagram of object type RESERVATION, $R(\{(issued,r)\}) = \{\{(cancel,r)\}, \{(use,r)\}, \{(void,r)\}\}$ (cf. Figure 4.1).

It is often more convenient to denote the sequence of starts and completions of activities that cause a life cycle occurrence than to denote the life cycle states of a life cycle occurrence. An *activation sequence* μ of object type O is a sequence of statements $\tau_1, \ldots \tau_n$ $(n \geq 0)$, where $\tau_i = start(t)$ or $\tau_i = completion(t)$ for some $t \in T$; μ is *valid* on some life cycle state $\sigma_1 \in R(\bar{A})$ if there is some partial life cycle occurrence $\gamma = \sigma_1 \ldots \sigma_{n+1}$ of O where for $i \in \{1 \ldots n\}$ σ_{i+1} results from performing τ_i on σ_i and we say μ yields the *trace* γ. If $n = 0$, the activation sequence is called *empty*. An empty activation sequence can be applied on every life cycle state σ and yields trace σ.

Example 4.7

A possible activation sequence for object type RESERVATION is [s(request), c(request), s(issue), c(issue), s(cancel), c(cancel)], where s stands for start and c for completion. Note: due to lack of parallelism in this example, the completion of every activity immediately succeeds its start. As later examples will show, this need not always be the case.

4.2.3 A meaningful subclass of behavior diagrams

We restrict our discussion of inheritance of object behavior to a meaningful subclass of behavior diagrams, to activity-reduced, safe, and deadlock-free behavior diagrams.

A behavior diagram B is *safe*, if there exists no life cycle state $\sigma \in R(\bar{A})$ such that some activity t can be completed on σ and σ contains already some post state of t. B is *activity-reduced* iff every t is potentially applicable. An activity T is *potentially applicable* if there exists a partial life cycle occurrence $\gamma = \sigma_1 \ldots \sigma_n (n > 0)$ such that t can be started on σ_n. B is *deadlock free* iff for every $\sigma \in R(\bar{A})$ either some $t \in T$ can be started on σ, or $\{s \mid (s, x) \in \sigma\} \subseteq \Omega$.

Again, to restrict the discussion to behavior diagrams satisfying these three criteria is meaningful in practice. First, activities which are not potentially applicable have no influence on object behavior. Such activities correspond to program statements never reached. Second, unsafe nets contradict the intention of behavior diagrams to identify by a state or an activity a single, specific processing state of an object. Third, freedom from deadlocks ensures that, unless processing has finished (i.e., a set of final states has been reached), there is at least one possible way to continue.

Furthermore, we restrict our discussion to a meaningful subclass of labeled behavior diagrams, namely those behavior diagrams which observe the label preservation, the unique label distribution, and the common label distribution property.

A labeled behavior diagram B observes the *label preservation* property if for every t the union of the labels annotated to its incoming arcs equals the union of the labels annotated to its outgoing arcs. B observes the *unique label distribution* property if for every activity the label sets of different incoming arcs are disjoint and the label sets of different outgoing arcs are disjoint. B observes the *common label distribution* property if for every state all arcs incident to the state carry the same set of labels.

To restrict our discussion to behavior diagrams satisfying these properties is meaningful in practice. The label preservation property reflects, in the analogy with business forms, that once an individual form for a business case has been created, each activity in the business process does not consume or produce new copies of the form, the unique label distribution property ensures that some copy of a form is requested by an activity from at most one input box and is delivered by the activity to at most one output box, the common label distribution property ensures that a box holds always the same copies of a form (e.g., the yellow and pink carbon copy).

Example 4.8
Figure 4.2 shows a behavior diagram of object type RESERVATION_WITH_ PAYMENT with the labels r ("registration"), p ("payment"), and f ("refund"). It satisfies the three labeling properties.

As we will see later, using behavior diagrams that satisfy these practically meaningful properties will enable us to check easily for behavior consistency of refinements of behavior diagrams.

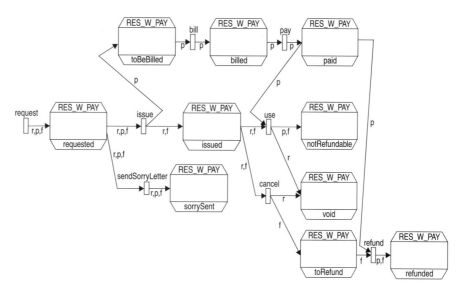

Figure 4.2   Behavior diagram of object type RESERVATION_WITH_PAYMENT

Activities of behavior diagrams can be further described by activity specification diagrams, activity realization diagrams, and activity scripts. These diagrams are not needed in this chapter; the interested reader is referred to (4, 10).

4.3   Behavior Modeling in UML

The Unified Modeling Language (UML) has over the last years become one of the most important notations in object-oriented modeling. It provides notations and diagram types to cover virtually all aspects of object-oriented software development, from analysis to deployment. It is therefore of great interest to examine the UML diagrams that correspond closest to behavior diagrams and discuss the applicability of our results in this related, but somewhat different context.

In UML, the dynamic behavior of a system is modeled by three kinds of diagrams. Sequence diagrams show the interaction of multiple objects over time, displayed by the exchange of messages, signals, and outside events to and from the user. Collaboration diagrams give an overview of a set of message flows between a number of objects, with time being abstracted. Statechart diagrams show "the sequences of states that an object or an interaction goes through during its life in response to received stimuli" ((24), p.103). This diagram type corresponds most closely to behavior diagrams.

UML *statechart diagrams* are derived from Harel's statechart formalism (9), with a number of alternations and restrictions. Basically, an object's life cycle is represented by a set of states and a set of transitions, each connecting usually a single source state with a single sink state. But a statechart may contain next to simple

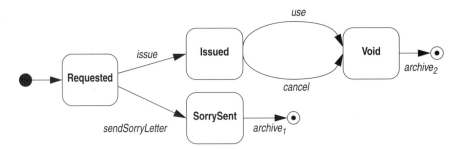

Figure 4.3   UML statechart diagram of object type RESERVATION

states also composite states with either disjoint or concurrent substates. If a statechart contains composite states with concurrent substates, a transition may have several concurrent substates of a composite state as source or target states. Actions may be associated with transitions, entry to or exit from a state. Each UML statechart has an initial state, shown as a small solid filled circle, and one or several final states, shown as solid filled circles.

In object-oriented design, a primary use of UML statecharts is to specify in which order operations, represented by transitions, may be invoked on instances of the object class. Transitions are triggered by call events and their actions invoke the operation at that point (25). Differences to standard statecharts include the property that events are typically considered to correspond directly to operations defined on classes, which means they can carry parameters and model the behavior of specific objects. On the other hand, no processes (activities with temporal extent) are considered to exist.

Example 4.9
Figure 4.3 shows the life cycle of object type RESERVATION as an UML statechart diagram.

The following list describes major distinctions between OBD's and UML notation. For space reasons, we make a few simplifying assumptions, which are also included in the list.[1]

■ Transitions in UML can be annotated by an event trigger, a guard condition, and an action. The action associated with a transition is performed when at the time the specified event occurs all source states of the transition are active (i.e, "contain a token" in Petri net terminology) and the guard condition is satisfied. Thereafter, the sink states of the transitions become active. In OBD, behavior diagrams are complemented by situation/activation diagrams (14) that specify in

---

1. The reader familiar with UML will know that UML provides special forms of states and transitions, such as history states, stubbed transitions, and branch transitions. We do not consider these advanced concepts in this chapter.

which situations other than a direct invocation of the activity, an activity is invoked. Thus, a situation/activation diagram correspond to the event, guard, and action of a transition in UML. We focus in this chapter on the use of UML statecharts to specify in which order operations, represented by transitions, may be executed on instances of an object. Such UML statecharts have a single annotation, the operation, which constitutes the action that is invoked when the call event of the operation occurs. We require that different transitions may carry the same name only if their source states can never be active at the same time. This restriction is meaningful in our context. It ensures that each valid operation call leads to the invocation of exactly one operation (represented by a transition).

- Unlike statecharts, and superficially similar to transitions in OBD, transitions in UML are assumed not to occur in zero time, but to spend time between start and completion. Once an activity has been started in OBD, other activities may be started without waiting for it to complete. In UML, however, transitions may not be interleaved. The timespan of transitions primarily represents the execution time of the code that is called when the transition is executed and is irrelevant for modeling purposes. This restriction implies that if an OBD behavior diagram is mapped to a UML statechart diagram by mapping states to states and activities to transitions[2], then any execution of the UML statechart diagram always corresponds to an OBD life cycle occurrence where the start of an activity is always followed next by the completion of that activity.

- A statechart diagram may contain simple and composite states. A *simple state* cannot be further decomposed. A *composite state* is decomposed either into concurrent substates or into disjoint substates. If a composite state is decomposed into concurrent substates, the graphical region of the state is split into several subregions separated by a dashed line, each representing one concurrent substate. If a composite state is decomposed into disjoint substates, the graphical region of the state contains a nested state diagram.

- Transitions in a statechart are either simple or complex. A *simple transition* has a single source state and a single target state. Simple transitions are not represented by nodes, but simply by directed arcs connecting two states. Complex transitions are used in UML like transitions in Petri nets, to synchronize and/or split control into concurrent threads. A *complex transition* may have multiple source states and target states. It is enabled when all of the source states are occupied. After a complex transition fires, all of its destination states are occupied.[3]

---

2. Notice that not every OBD behavior diagram transformed in this way to an UML statechart diagram will be a valid UML statechart diagram since the resulting statechart diagram might violate the concurrency restrictions of UML (see below).

3. The reader familiar with UML will know that complex transitions are mapped into lower level concepts such as pseudostates with incident fork or join transitions. For the purpose of comparing the behavior of UML statecharts, we consider complex transitions to be atomic.

■ The use of concurrency is rigidly constrained in UML "for practical reasons" ((25), p. 119). The idea is to decompose an UML statechart in a "structured way" such that one can easily check whether all subregions of a concurrent region are always entered and exited jointly. UML requires that the states of an UML statechart can be obtained by decomposing a single complex state recursively into finer states by a kind of *and-or*-tree (cf. (27)), where an *and*-node corresponds to a complex state with concurrent substates and *or*-node to a complex state with sequential substates. Then, a simple transition must connect two states in the same sequential region or two states separated by *or*-levels only. A complex transition entering (or leaving) a concurrent region must enter (or leave, resp.) each subregion of that concurrent region. Two shortcuts are available. First, if a transition enters a concurrent region but omits one or more of the subregions with initial states, the transition enters these initial states. Second, any transition that exits from a state in a concurrent subregion of a composite state by default exits all other concurrent subregions, too.

We will later see that the concurrency restrictions of UML hinder an orthogonal treatment of extension and refinement in UML. In an earlier approach to refinement of behavior diagrams (cf. (28)) we took basically the same approach as proposed in UML, but eventually realized that this approach is too restrictive in practice. This led us to the development of labeled behavior diagrams, which support the flexibility of general refinement on the one hand and an easy check for whether an object leaves a state entirely on the other hand.

■ Transitions may be triggerless. A triggerless transition is activated when an activity associated with the source state of the transition completes, e.g., if the final states of a complex source state are reached. Since we focus on statecharts for modelling sequences of operations performed on an object, we do not consider triggerless transitions. Operations are only executed if invoked by an operation call.

■ Transitions may not only have simple states as sinks and sources, but also composite states. A transition to the boundary of a composite state is a short-hand notation for having the same transition pointing to the initial pseudostate(s) of the composite state. For simplicity, we do not consider short-hand notations herein and assume that all statecharts have nested state diagrams without initial states. Transitions may also emerge from complex states. The activation of such a transition causes the exit from all substates of the composite state. A triggerless transition emerging from a complex state is activated if all final states of the complex state are active. As already stated above, we do consider such triggerless transitions herein.

Example 4.10

Figure 4.4 shows an UML statechart diagram for object type RESERVATION_WITH_ PAYMENT. The statechart diagram illustrates the use of composite states with concurrent substates as well as complex transitions. Not that composite states need not be named in UML.

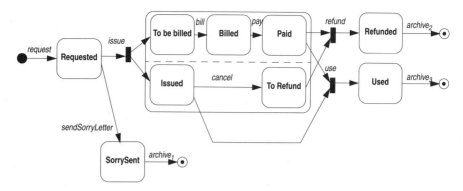

Figure 4.4   UML statechart diagram of object type RESERVATION_WITH_PAYMENT

Finally, we note that UML also supports the notation for a special kind of statechart diagrams called *activity* diagrams. These diagrams allow for the explicit representation of actions and have the potential for a more expressive modeling of object life cycles. However, their purpose is at the moment limited to expressing algorithmic properties of objects instead of modeling the interaction of objects with their environment and the environment outside the application. They, thus, correspond to activity realization diagrams in OBD (10). The influence of activity diagrams on life cycle inheritance is the subject of future research.

4.4   Consistent Extension

In this section, we first introduce three different kinds of consistency between behavior diagrams: observation consistency, weak invocation consistency, and strong invocation consistency. Next, we identify necessary and sufficient rules for checking each kind of consistency for extensions of behavior diagrams. Extension means adding activities, states, labels, and arcs. Then, we discuss behavior consistency and checking behavior consistency in UML.

4.4.1   Kinds of Behavior Consistency

Intuitively, one expects the behavior diagram of a subtype to be "consistent" with the behavior diagram of a supertype. In this section, we define precisely what "consistent" means with respect to extension of behavior diagrams. Similar to inheritance of operations, for which several types of conformance have been defined, several possibilities exist to relate the behavior diagram of a subtype to the behavior diagram of a supertype.

For inheritance of operations, the proposed relations range from no restriction at all, called *arbitrary inheritance*, to allowing no changes to operation interfaces, called *strict inheritance*. The first extreme is too unrestricted in order to be used for building reusable and reliable systems as no general properties about the relationship between operations of a subtype and operations of a supertype are known. The second extreme is too restrictive as it prohibits adding new parameters and redefining inherited ones. In between, two alternative notions of conformance prevail: *covariance* and *contra-variance*. Covariance requires that input and output parameters of operations are restricted to subtypes when operations are redefined at a subtype. Contra-variance requires that input parameters are generalized to supertypes and output parameters are restricted to subtypes. Covariance is favored by object-oriented design methods as it supports the concept of specialization in the tradition of semantic networks of artificial intelligence. Contra-variance is favored by type theoreticians as it supports static type checking in the presence of type substitutability (5, 34), which allows using an instance of a subtype whenever an instance of a supertype is expected.

For inheritance of behavior diagrams, we have, as we will see later, similar choices. If we reject, for the reasons mentioned above, the extremes of allowing arbitrary changes and of allowing no changes, the idea immediately emerges to borrow from Petri nets the notions of "subnet" and "embedding" in order to define the notion of "consistent extension" of behavior diagrams.

Example 4.11
Behavior diagram RESERVATION is embedded in the behavior diagrams RESERVATION_WITH_PAYMENT and FRIENDLY_RESERVATION (cf. Figures 4.1, 4.2, and 4.5).

It is natural to call B' an "extension" of B only if B is a subnet of B' and it is reasonable to call an extension "consistent" only if the identity function on states and activities is an embedding of B in B'. However, as we will see, this is not sufficient to ensure that B and B' exhibit "comparable behavior."

In Petri net literature, two approaches are common for comparing the behavior of two Petri nets (cf. (23) for a comprehensive survey of equivalence notions for net-based systems): (1) Abstracting from actions, one can compare the possible sequences of sets of states in which tokens reside and (2) abstracting from states, one can compare the possible sequences in which transitions can be fired. These approaches are usually followed alternatively (cf. (23)).

Comparing life cycle occurrences of behavior diagrams, both approaches coincide as activities are included next to states in life cycle states, and, thus, we can denote a life cycle occurrence either by the sequence of its life cycle states or by the activation sequence generating it, whichever is more convenient (see above).

We are now ready for describing three kinds of behavior consistency, each pursuing a different reasonable objective.

4.4.1.1   Observation Consistency

It is common in semantic data models and object-oriented systems to consider each instance of a subtype also an instance of the supertype. Then, each instance of a subtype must be observable according to the structure and behavior definition given at the supertype, if features added at the subtype are ignored. We follow this approach, which is in the line of covariant inheritance (see above), when we define observation consistency for life cycle occurrences.

A life cycle occurrence of a subtype can be observed at the level of the supertype, if activities, states, and labels added at the subtype are ignored. This is expressed by the following definitions of the restriction of a life cycle state and the restriction of a life cycle occurrence: The *restriction of a life cycle state* $\bar{\sigma}'$ of an object type O' to object type O, written $\bar{\sigma}'/_O$, is then defined as the set of all pairs (e, x) in $\bar{\sigma}'$ where e is a state or activity in the behavior diagram of O and x is a label in the behavior diagram of O. Put in other words, in the life cycle state $\bar{\sigma}'$ all entries which contain a state, activity, or label that do belong to object type O' are discarded. The *restriction of a life cycle occurrence* $\gamma' = \sigma'_1, \ldots, \sigma'_n$ of object type O' to object type O, written $\gamma'/_O$, is defined as $\sigma_1, \ldots, \sigma_n$, where for $i = 1 \ldots n$: $\sigma_i = \sigma'_i/_O$.

Example 4.12
A possible life cycle occurrence of object type RESERVATION_WITH_PAYMENT (cf. Figure 2) is [{(request,r), (request,p), (request,f)}, {(requested,r), (requested,p), (requested,f)}, {(issue,r), (issue,p), (issue,f)}, {(issued,r), (issued,f), (toBeBilled,p)}, {(issued,r), (issued,f), (bill,p)}, {(issued,r), (issued,f), (billed,p)}, {(issued,r), (issued,f), (pay,p)}, {(issued,r), (issued,f), (paid,p)}, {(cancel,r), (cancel,f), (paid,p)}, {(void,r), (toRefund,f), (paid,p)}, {(void,r), (refund,f), (refund,p)}, {(void,r), (refunded,f), (refunded,p)}]. The restriction of this life cycle occurrence to object type RESERVATION yields [{(request,r)}, {(requested,r)}, {(issue,r)}, {(issued,r)}, {(issued,r)}, {(issued,r)}, {(issued,r)}, {(issued,r)}, {(cancel,r)}, {(void,r)}, {(void,r)}, {(void,r)}]

Observation consistent extension of behavior requires that each possible life cycle occurrence of a subtype is, if we disregard activities and states added at the subtype, also a life cycle occurrence of the supertype. A behavior diagram $B_{O'}$ is an *observation consistent extension* of a behavior diagram B_O if for every life cycle occurrence γ' of object type O', $\gamma'/_O$ is a life cycle occurrence of B.

Example 4.13
The behavior diagram depicted in Figure 4.2 is an observation consistent extension of the behavior diagram depicted in Figure 4.1. Thus every life cycle occurrence of object type RESERVATION_WITH_PAYMENT restricted to object type RESERVATION is also a life cycle occurrence of object type RESERVATION. This is shown for a particular life cycle occurrence in Example 4.12.

Observation consistency ensures that all instances of an object type (including those of its subtypes) evolve only according to its behavior diagram. This property is especially important for modeling workflows, where, for example, the current processing state of an order should always be visible at the manager's abstraction level defined by some higher-level object type. The example below, which violates observation consistency, illustrates this.

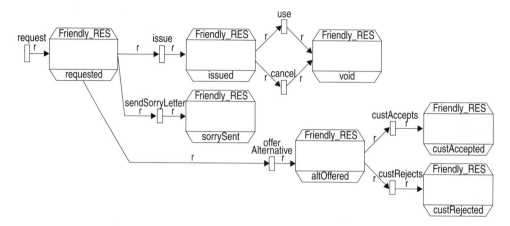

Figure 4.5   Behavior diagram of object type FRIENDLY_RESERVATION

Example 4.14

The behavior diagram of object type FRIENDLY_RESERVATION depicted in Figure 4.5 is no observation consistent extension of the behavior diagram of object type RESERVATION depicted in Figure 4.1. The restriction of life cycle occurrence [{(request,r)}, {(requested,r)}, {(offerAlternative,r)}] of object type FRIENDLY_ RESERVATION to object type RESERVATION yields [{(request,r)}, {(requested,r)}, {}], which is no life cycle occurrence of object type RESERVATION.

4.4.1.2   Weak Invocation Consistency

Type substitutability in object-oriented programming languages allows using an instance of a subtype whenever an instance of a supertype is expected. Thus, any operation invocable on instances of a supertype must under the same precondition also be invocable on instances of any subtype and executing the operation on instances of a subtype meets the postcondition for the operation specified at the supertype. We follow this principle of programming by contract (17), which is supported by contravariant inheritance (see above), when we define invocation consistency for behavior diagrams.

We distinguish two forms of invocation consistency: weak invocation consistency, which corresponds to the notion of "invocable behavior" of Engels and Ebert (7), and strong invocation consistency.

Weak invocation consistency is satisfied, if one can use instances of a subtype in the same way as instances of the supertype: Any sequence of activities that can be performed on instances of a supertype can also be performed on instances of subtypes, producing the effect expected at the supertype. This is expressed by the following definition of weak invocation consistency: A behavior diagram $B_{O'}$ is a *weak invocation consistent specialisation* of a behavior diagram B_O if every activation sequence μ valid on A in B is also valid on A' in B' and for their respective traces γ and γ' it holds that $\gamma = \gamma'/o$.

Example 4.15

The behavior diagram of object type FRIENDLY_RESERVATION depicted in Figure 4.5 is a weak invocation consistent extension of the behavior diagram of object type RESERVATION depicted in Figure 4.1.

Weak invocation consistency ensures that if an object is extended with new features, e.g., a television set with video text, the object is usable the same way as without the extension. This property is violated in the example below.

Example 4.16

The behavior diagram of object type RESERVATION_WITH_PAYMENT depicted in Figure 4.2 is no weak invocation consistent extension of the behavior diagram of object type RESERVATION depicted in Figure 4.1. The activation sequence [s(request), c(request), s(issue), c(issue), s(use)] is valid for object type RESERVATION, but not for object type RESERVATION_WITH_PAYMENT, as s(use) cannot be applied on the LCS {(toBeBilled,p), (issued,r), (issued,f)} reached by executing [s(request), c(request), s(issue), c(issue)].

4.4.1.3   Strong Invocation Consistency

Strong invocation consistency goes beyond weak invocation consistency in that it requires additionally that activities added at a subtype do not interfere with activities inherited from the supertype. Strong invocation consistency is satisfied, if one can use instances of a subtype in the same way as instances of the supertype, despite using or having used new activities of the subtype. This is expressed by the definition of strong invocation consistency: A behavior diagram $B_{O'}$ is a *strong invocation consistent extension* of a behavior diagram B_O if (1) every activation sequence ν valid on $\bar{A}$ in B is valid on $\bar{A}'$ in B', and (2) every activation sequence ν valid in B on $\sigma'/_O$ ($\sigma' \in R(\bar{A}')$) is valid in B' on every life cycle state $\hat{\sigma}'$ that results from performing any activation sequence κ of activities in $T' \setminus T$ on σ', and for the traces γ and γ' generated by performing ν in B on $\sigma'/_O$ and by performing ν in B' on $\hat{\sigma}'$, respectively, it holds that $\gamma = \gamma'/_O$. (Note: ν and κ may be empty).

Strong invocation consistency ensures that if an object is extended with new features, e.g., a television set with video text, the object is usable the same way as without the extension despite new features being used. E.g., using any video text function should not invalidate the volume control of the TV. This property is violated in the example below.

Example 4.17

The behavior diagram of object type FRIENDLY_RESERVATION depicted in Figure 4.5 is no strong invocation consistent extension of the behavior diagram of object type RESERVATION depicted in Figure 4.1: Activity sendSorryLetter can be started for every instance of RESERVATION in life cycle state {(requested,r), (requested,p), (requested,f)}, but it can not be started on an instance of FRIENDLY_RESERVATION if activity offerAlternative has been started before.

4.4.2   Checking Behavior Consistent Extension in OBD

In this subsection we introduce a set of rules for checking whether a given behavior diagram is an observation consistent, a weak invocation consistent, or a strong invocation consistent extension of another behavior diagram. Whereas approaches in the realm of state transition diagrams (e.g., (7)) base such checks on the existence of a homomorphism (for observation consistency) or the existence of an embedding (for weak invocation consistency), we present a set of constructive rules that can be more easily checked by a system designer than the existence of, for example, a homomorphism between two behavior diagrams. It should be mentioned, however, that observation consistency between behavior diagrams could be checked alternatively by a modified version of the net morphism of Winskel (33) that takes into account the notion of "activity state" by splitting each activity into an instantaneous start event, an explicit activity state, and an instantaneous completion event. The existence of an embedding between two behavior diagrams (see above) is a necessary but not a sufficient condition for satisfying weak and strong invocation consistency.

4.4.2.1   *Checking Observation Consistency*

Rules for checking whether a behavior diagram B' is an observation consistent extension of another behavior diagram B are the rule of *partial inheritance*, the rule of *immediate definition of prestates, post states, and labels*, and the rule of *parallel extension and no label deviation* (cf. Figure 4.6).

The rule of *partial inheritance* requires that (a) the initial state of B' is identical to the initial state of B, and the labels of B' are a superset of the labels of B, (b) every activity of B' which is already present in B has at least the prestates and at least the post states that the activity has in B, and (c) each arc inherited by B' from B carries at least the labels that it carries in B.

Notice that although it is meaningful to speak of an "extension" only if all activities of B are also present in B', this is not a necessary condition for observation consistency. While at first unexpected, a more in depth consideration reveals that this result is in line with *covariant inheritance* of operations. Covariance inheritance requires that at subtypes, input parameters of an inherited operation may only be restricted and the precondition of an inherited operation may only be strengthened so that it implies the precondition given for the operation at the supertype. In the extreme, the precondition may be redefined to "false", which implies any other condition. Clearly precondition "false" can never be made true and, thus an operation with precondition "false" can never be invoked. Thus, the operation could be entirely eliminated as well.

The rule of *immediate definition of prestates, post states, and labels* requires that (a) no arc is added in B' between a state and an activity (or between an activity and a state) which belong already to B and are not connected by an arc in B, and (b) no label that belongs already to B is added to an arc inherited by B' from B.

The rule of *parallel extension* requires that an activity added in B' does not consume from or produce into a state already present in B (a1,a2). The rule of *no label deviation* requires that arcs incident to activities added at a subtype carry only new labels (b1,b2). Similarly, arcs incident to states added at a subtype must carry only new labels (b3,b4).[4]

B' is an observation consistent extension of B if and only if rules E1, E2, and E3 of Figure 4.6 are obeyed (cf. (12, 31)).

Example 4.18

Consider the behavior diagrams of object type RESERVATION_WITH_PAYMENT (cf. Figure 4.2) and of object type RESERVATION (cf. Figure 4.1). All activities of RESERVATION are present also in RESERVATION_WITH_PAYMENT. No pre-, post-states, or labels associated with incident arcs of these activities have been omitted. Thus, rules E1 and E4 are satisfied (Note: Rule E4 need not be satisfied for observation consistency). Those arcs added at RESERVATION_WITH_PAYMENT carry only new labels. Hence, rule E2 is satisfied. All arcs incident to activities added at RESERVATION_WITH_PAYMENT, i.e., bill, pay, and refund, consume or produce into states added at RESERVATION_WITH_PAYMENT as well, and they carry only new labels, i.e., labels p and f. Hence, rule E3 is satisfied, too, and RESERVATION_WITH_ PAYMENT is an observation consistent extension of RESERVATION.

4.4.2.2   Checking Weak Invocation Consistency

Rules to check whether a behavior diagram B' is a weak invocation consistent extension of a behavior diagram B are the rule of *partial inheritance*, the rule of *immediate definition of prestates, post states, and labels*, the rule of *full inheritance*, and the rule of *alternative extension* (cf. Figure 4.6). The first two have already been explained.

The rule of *full inheritance* requires that the set of activities of B' is a superset of the set of activities of B. The rule of *alternative extension* requires that an activity in B' which is already present in B consumes in B' at most from those states from which the activity consumes in B.

B' is a weak invocation consistent extension of B if rules E1, E2, E4, and E5 of Figure 4.6 are obeyed (cf. (30, 31)).

We call a behavior diagram B' a *substantial* extension of a behavior diagram B, if a state added in B' is not both prestate of an activity already present in B and post state of an activity already present in B. Adding merely a new state between two old activities is not a substantial extension as an intermediate new activity is missing (For a formal definition, see (30)).

If B' is a substantial extension of B, the rules E1, E2, E4, E5 are not only sufficient, but also necessary to check for weak invocation consistency (cf. (30)).

---

4. Parts (b3) and (b4) are actually redundant. They follow from the other rules and the unique label distribution property

E1. Partial inheritance

(a) $\alpha' = \alpha$, $L \subseteq L'$

(b1) $t \in T' \wedge t \in T \wedge (s,t) \in F \Rightarrow (s,t) \in F'$

(b2) $t \in T' \wedge t \in T \wedge (t,s) \in F \Rightarrow (t,s) \in F'$

(c1) $t \in T' \wedge t \in T \wedge (s,t) \in F \Rightarrow l(s,t) \subseteq l'(s,t)$

(c2) $t \in T' \wedge t \in T \wedge (t,s) \in F \Rightarrow l(t,s) \subseteq l'(t,s)$

E2. Immediate definition of prestates, poststates, and labels

(a1) $(s,t) \in F' \wedge s \in S \wedge t \in T \Rightarrow (s,t) \in F$

(a2) $(t,s) \in F' \wedge s \in S \wedge t \in T \Rightarrow (t,s) \in F$

(b1) $(s,t) \in F' \wedge s \in S \wedge t \in T \wedge x \in L \wedge x \in l'(s,t) \Rightarrow x \in l(s,t)$

(b2) $(t,s) \in F' \wedge s \in S \wedge t \in T \wedge x \in L \wedge x \in l'(t,s) \Rightarrow x \in l(t,s)$

E3. Parallel extension and no label deviation

(a1) $(s,t) \in F' \wedge t \in T' \wedge t \notin T \Rightarrow s \notin S$

(a2) $(t,s) \in F' \wedge t \in T' \wedge t \notin T \Rightarrow s \notin S$

(b1) $(s,t) \in F' \wedge t \in T' \wedge t \notin T \Rightarrow l'(s,t) \cap L = \emptyset$

(b2) $(t,s) \in F' \wedge t \in T' \wedge t \notin T \Rightarrow l'(t,s) \cap L = \emptyset$

(b3) $(s,t) \in F' \wedge s \in S' \wedge s \notin S \Rightarrow l'(s,t) \cap L = \emptyset$

(b4) $(t,s) \in F' \wedge s \in S' \wedge s \notin S \Rightarrow l'(t,s) \cap L = \emptyset$

E4. Full inheritance

$T' \supseteq T$

E5. Alternative extension

$(s,t) \in F' \wedge s \in S' \wedge s \notin S \Rightarrow t \notin T$

Figure 4.6   Rules for checking behavior consistency for extension

Example 4.19

Consider the behavior diagrams of object types FRIENDLY_RESERVATION (cf. Figure 4.5) and of of object type RESERVATION (cf. Figure 4.1). All activities of RESERVATION are present also in FRIENDLY_RESERVATION such that rule E4 is satisfied. No prestates, post states, or labels associated with incident arcs of these activities at RESERVATION have been omitted at FRIENDLY_RESERVATION such that rule E1 is satisfied, too. Also, these activities do not consume from a state added at FRIENDLY_RESERVATION. Hence, rule E5 is also satisfied. Finally, no arcs have been added at FRIENDLY_RESERVATION between states and activities already present at RESERVATION. Hence, rule E2 is also satisfied and FRIENDLY_ RESERVATION is a weak invocation consistent extension of RESERVATION.

4.4.2.3   Checking Strong Invocation Consistency

The rules of Figure 4.6 (rules E1 to E5) are sufficient to check whether a behavior diagram B' is a strong invocation consistent extension of a behavior diagram B (cf. (30, 31)).

Example 4.20

As we have seen already above, the behavior diagram of object type FRIENDLY_ RESERVATION (cf. Figure 4.5) is no strong invocation consistent extension of the behavior diagram of object type RESERVATION (cf. Figure 4.1). The behavior diagram of object type FRIENDLY_RESERVATION introduces an activity offerAlternative which is connected by an arc to prestate requested. Since this state belongs already to RESERVATION, rule E3 is violated. Therefore, FRIENDLY_RESERVATION is neither a strong invocation consistent extension nor an observation consistent extension of RESERVATION.

Strong invocation consistency implies observation consistency and weak invocation consistency. The converse does not hold (cf. (30, 31)).

If B' is a substantial extension of B, rules E1 to E5 are not only sufficient but also necessary for checking strong invocation consistency, and strong invocation consistency is equivalent to observation consistency and weak invocation consistency (cf. (30, 31)).

4.4.3   Behavior Extension in UML

In this subsection, we investigate how, in comparison to behavior diagrams, UML statechart diagrams can be extended by additional states and transitions. In the subsequent subsection, we will discuss the applicability of the consistency rules introduced above for OBD to UML. We restrict our discussion to an informal manner.

As mentioned in Section 4.3, we compare behavior diagrams and statechart diagrams by relating OBD activities and states to UML transitions and states.

We consider a life cycle state of an UML statechart diagram to be a subset of the transitions and states of the statechart diagram, where a life cycle state contains a transition during the time the action associated to the transition is executed and it contains a state when the state is active. If the statechart diagram contains a complex transition that represents a sychronisation of control and/or splitting into concurrent threads (using pseudostates as well as incident join and/or fork transitions), we consider only the complex transition in the life cycle state. I.e., we will compare the behavior of UML statechart diagrams at the level of complex transitions and disregard the mapping of such transitions into lower level concepts (pseudostates and incident transitions).

In a similar manner, we consider a transition sequence of an UML statechart diagram to represent the sequence of start and ends of transitions, (Note: Unlike activities of behavior diagrams, each start of a transition will be succeeded immediately by its completion.) For complex transitions, we consider only the start of its initial transition and the completion of its final transition.

We apply the different notions of behavior consistency to UML in the sense that we defined them formally for OBD. Just as for behavior diagrams, we assume that each state and transition of a statechart diagram has a unique identity on which the comparison of life cycles is based. Two different states or transitions with equal names are not considered identical when life cycles are compared. To get unique identifiers, we differentiate states and transitions with equal names by using different numbers as subscripts.

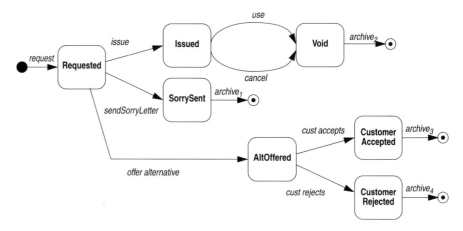

Figure 4.7   UML statechart diagram of object type FRIENDLY_RESERVATION

For UML statechart diagrams, "extension" means adding transitions and states. Simple transitions may become complex transitions and complex transitions may receive additional sink and source states.

Adding an "alternative path" is always easily accomplished in UML.

Example 4.21
Figure 4.7 shows a statechart diagram for object type FRIENDLY_RESERVATION. This statechart diagrams extends the statechart diagram of object type RESERVATION shown in Figure 4.3 and corresponds to the behavior diagram depicted in Figure 4.5.

Adding a "parallel path" is easily achieved in UML if the additional "parallel path" starts in all its alternatives at transitions having the same sink state and, likewise, ends in all its alternatives at transitions having a common source state. Due to the concurrency restrictions of UML (see above), other extensions may not be expressible by adding states and transitions to an existing statechart diagram unless behavior consistency is sacrificed. The semantics of the intended extension must then be alternatively expressed by refinement, i.e., the decomposition of states into so-called substates that provide a more detailed description of the inner workings of that state. This solution may also include the need to "duplicate" transitions and states.

Although we will discuss the refinement of UML statecharts later, we already show here how the example of reservations with payment (which we used to demonstrate extension in OBD), must be mimicked by refinement in UML. We suggest that the reader should try to get an overall impression of the example now and come back to it later.

Example 4.22
The statechart diagram of object type RESERVATION (cf. Figure 4.3) cannot be extended to cover an additional payment process by simply adding transitions and

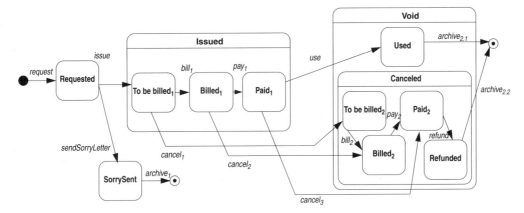

Figure 4.8   UML statechart diagram for object type RESERVATION_WITH_PAYMENT

states. As one can see from the behavior diagram of Figure 4.2, the payment process is either ended by using the reservation or by refunding the payment if the reservation has been canceled before it was used. To express the semantics of the behavior diagram shown in Figure 4.2, the statechart diagram for object type RESERVATION_WITH_PAYMENT (cf. Figure 4.8) is obtained from the statechart diagram for object type RESERVATION by using refinement rather than extension, whereby different transitions from state issued to void for canceling a reservation apply, depending on whether the reservation has still to be billed, has already been billed, or has already been paid. Note that the statechart diagram for object type RESERVATION_WITH_PAYMENT shown in Figure 4.4 is no observation consistent extension of the statechart diagram of object type RESERVATION (see next subsection). However, the statechart diagram shown in Figure 4.8 is an observation consistent specialization of the statechart diagram shown in Figure 4.3. (see Sections 5 and 6.)

4.4.4   Checking Behavior Consistent Extension in UML

We have seen that extending the behavior of an UML statechart diagram cannot always be achieved by merely adding transitions and states. For those cases where it can be, we now verbally rephrase the rules for checking behavior consistency introduced for OBDs for the context of UML statechart diagrams.

  For the purpose of checking behavior consistency, we transform UML statecharts such that they contain only transitions between simple states and such that concurrent substates are always exited explicitly. We apply the following transformation iteratively until no transition that can be transformed is left:

■ For any transition that exits from a concurrent substate s' of a composite state s, but not from the concurrent subregion represented by another substate s'' of that composite state: Add s'' to that transition (If necessary convert the transition from simple to complex).[5]

■ For any transition that emerges from the boundary of a composite state: If the composite state has n disjoint substates, replace the transition by n transitions, each consuming from a different substate. If the composite state has concurrent substates, replace the transition by a complex transition consuming from each concurrent substate.

Since UML concurrency requirements trivially imply that an object always leaves and enters all concurrent substates of a concurrent composite state simultaneously – note that enforcing this was the reason why labeled OBDs were introduced, a topic that will be explored in the next section – no labels are used in UML and we can ignore the rules related to labeling.

Consider two UML statechart diagrams S' and S of an object class O' and its superclass O, where S' extends the statechart diagram of S by additional states and transitions. Then, the rules to check for behavior consistent extension of behavior diagrams are converted to behavior consistent extension of statechart diagrams as follows:

1. The *rule of partial inheritance* specifies that (a) the initial states of the statechart diagrams S' and S must be identical, and (b) every transition of S' which is already in S has at least the same source states and sink states that it has in S.

2. The rule of *immediate definition of prestates, post states, and labels* requires that a transition of S may in S' not receive an additional source state or sink state that is already present in S.

3. The rule of *parallel extension* requires that a transition added in S' does not receive a source state or a sink state that was already present in S.

4. The rule of *full inheritance* requires that the set of transitions of S' is a superset of the set of transitions of S.

5. The rule of *alternative extension* requires that a transition in S' which is already present in S has in S' at most the source states than the transition has in S.

Rules 1, 2, and 3 are sufficient to check whether a statechart diagram S' is an observation consistent extension of another statechart diagram S. They are also necessary, provided that similar assumptions to the ones introduced above for behavior diagrams are taken (e.g., no "dead" transitions, etc.).

Example 4.23

The statechart diagram object type FRIENDLY_RESERVATION in Figure 4.7 is no

---

5. Usually in UML, no arcs are drawn from the boundary of a concurrent substate of a composite state. Note though that such an arc is only temporary and will be replaced in further iteration steps.

observation consistent extension of the statechart diagram for RESERVATION. The rule of parallel extension is violated by transition offerAlternative. Also, object type RESERVATION_WITH_PAYMENT in Figure 4.4 is no observation consistent extension of the statechart diagram for RESERVATION. Transitions cancel and use violate the rule of partial inheritance.

Rules 1, 2, 4 and 5 are sufficient to check whether a statechart diagram S' is a weak invocation consistent extension of another statechart diagram S.

Example 4.24
The statechart diagram for the object type FRIENDLY_RESERVATION in Figure 4.7, is a weak invocation consistent extension of the statechart diagram for RESERVATION.

4.5   Consistent Refinement

In this section, we first introduce – based on observation consistency – the notion of behavior consistent refinement in OBD and we introduce rules to check for behavior consistency. Then we discuss refinement in UML.

4.5.1   Refinement and Behavior Consistency in OBD

Refinement means replacing activities and states by subdiagrams and labels by sub-labels. When activities or states of a behavior diagram are refined into subdiagrams, a major problem is to ensure that if an object leaves one state (or activity state) of a subdiagram and enters a state (or activity state) outside the subdiagram, the object leaves the subdiagram entirely, i.e., it leaves all states and activity states in the subdiagram.

For refinements of Petri nets, a common way to ensure that an object leaves a subnet entirely is to (1) refine a transition into a subnet with an initial transition and a final transition, where the subnet is well-formed in that the final transition consumes all tokens in the subnet, and (2) to refine a place by splitting first the state into an input place, a transition, and an output place, and by refining the transition as under (1) above (cf. (20)). Because this approach (as well as its extensions to multiple, alternative initial transitions and multiple, alternative final transitions, cf. (2)) is not practicable for behavior modeling, where transitions and states have to be refined jointly (cf. (28)), in (28) a set of structured refinement primitives for activities and states was introduced which ensure that an object leaves the refinement of an activity or state always entirely. Here, we follow a more general approach based on the labeling of activities, states, and objects. The labeling is used to explicitly mark parts of an object's life cycle that deal with a particular refined aspect of the original object.

A behavior diagram B_O of a supertype is refined into the behavior diagram B'_O of a subtype by expanding activities and states into subdiagrams. We capture this refinement at the design level by a total refinement function $h_{O' \mapsto O} : S' \cup T' \cup L' \mapsto S \cup T \cup L$. This function is explicitly declared by the designer, just as in many object-oriented systems the position of an object type in a type hierarchy is explicitly declared by a "isSubtypeOf" relationship.

The refinement function h possesses the following properties [6]: (1) It maps each state or activity of a subdiagram to the activity or state that is replaced by the subdiagram. (2) Similarly, a label may be replaced by several sublabels, which corresponds in our business forms analogy to splitting a form into several sections. The refinement function maps a sublabel to the label it replaces. (3) The refinement function is surjective for labels. In the forms analogy, this means that no copy of the form may get lost in the refinement. (4) Activities, states, or labels that are not refined are mapped onto themselves. (5) The initial state of the refined labeled behavior diagram is mapped to the initial state of the unrefined labeled behavior diagram. (6) To preserve compatibility between activities and states, the sources and sinks of subdiagrams that refine an activity must be activities, and, conversely, the sources and sinks of subdiagrams that refine a state must be states.

Example 4.25
Figure 4.9 shows a labeled behavior diagram of object type RESERVATION_WITH_ ALTERNATIVE_PAYMENT that refines the behavior diagram of object type RESER- VATION_WITH_PAYMENT of Figure 4.2. The refinement function h maps activities payCheque and payCash to activity pay, activities claim and receivePayment to state paid, and states chReceived, claimed, and paymentOk to state paid as well. Function h maps each of the remaining activities, states, and labels of RESERVATION_WITH_ ALTERNATIVE_PAYMENT to itself,

We call an activity t' a *source activity* of activity t, if t' is in the refinement of t and consumes from state outside the refinement of t, and we call an activity t' a *sink activity* of activity t, if t' is in the refinement of t and produces into a state outside of t. We call a state s' a *substate* of state s and s a *superstate* of s' if s' is in the refinement of s, i.e., $h(s') = s$.

Example 4.26
In Figure 4.9, which shows a labeled behavior diagram of object type RESERVATION_WITH_ALTERNATIVE_PAYMENT, activity payCheque and payCash are source activities as well as sink activities of activity pay.

Considering a life cycle state of a subtype at the level of the supertype means abstracting from the refinement. For refinements, the abstraction of a life cycle state is the counterpart to the restriction of a life cycle state for extension. The *abstraction of a labeled life cycle state* $\bar{\sigma}'$ of an object type O' to object type O, written $\sigma'/_O$, is defined as $\sigma'/_O = \{(h(e'), h(x')) | (e', x') \in \sigma'\}$.

---

6. We write h instead of $h_{O' \mapsto O}$ of O' and O are understood.

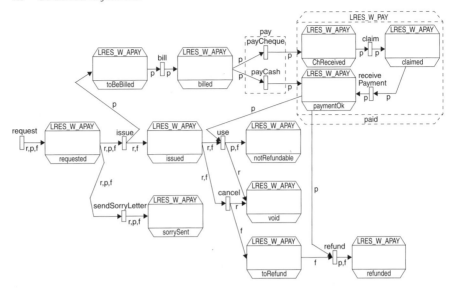

Figure 4.9   Behavior diagram RESERVATION_WITH_ALTERNATIVE_PAYMENT

In Section 4.4.1 we have identified several kinds of behavior consistency. This distinction cannot be applied to refinement the same way as to extension, because an activity which has been refined is "abstract" and, thus, it cannot be invoked on an object (cf. (28)). We define, without further distinction, behavior consistency for refinement in the sense of observation consistency. A behavior diagram $B_{O'}$ with associated refinement function $h_{O' \mapsto O}$ is a *behavior consistent refinement* of behavior diagram B_O if for every life cycle occurrence γ' of object type O', $\gamma'/_O$ is a life cycle occurrence of O.

4.5.2   Checking Behavior Consistent Refinement in OBD

Rules to check whether a behavior diagram $B_{O'}$ consistently refines a behavior diagram B_O are the rules of *Pre- and post state satisfaction* and the rule of *Pre- and post state refinement* (cf. Figure 4.11).

We will explain the rules using a more sophisticated example of refinement than we have seen so far.

Example 4.27
Figure 4.10 shows a labeled behavior diagram of object type CAR_RESERVATION which refines the behavior diagram of object type RESERVATION_WITH_PAYMENT of Figure 4.2. For car reservations, state issued of object type RESERVATION_ WITH_ PAYMENT has been refined into a subnet, in which some time before a customer is expected to use a reservation (which is issued only for a particular model but not for a specific car), a specific car is assigned to him or her (activity assignCar), the car is refueled (activity refuel), and various documents for the rental agreement are

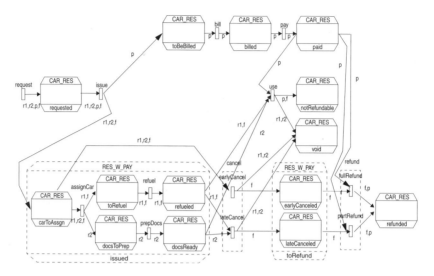

Figure 4.10   Behavior diagram CAR_RESERVATION

prepared (activity prepDocs). Activity cancel of object type RESERVATION_WITH_ PAYMENT is also refined into two alternative activities, earlyCancel and lateCancel. Early cancellations apply to car reservations for which a specific car has not yet been assigned and entitle for a full refund of payments (activity fullRefund), whereas late cancellations entitle only for a partial refund (activity partRefund). The refinement function h for activities and states is visualized in Figure 4.10 by superimposing activities and states of object type RESERVATION_WITH_PAYMENT on the behavior diagram of object type CAR_RESERVATION. The refinement function h maps labels r1 and r2 to r and each of the remaining labels to itself.

The rule of *Pre- and post state satisfaction* requires for unlabeled behavior diagrams (a1) that every source activity t' of an activity t consumes from some substate $\hat{s}'$ in each prestate $\hat{s}$ of t. Note that t or $\hat{s}$ might be actually identical to t or $\hat{s}'$ (if t or $\hat{s}$ has actually not been refined). In this case t and $\hat{s}$ are considered to be trivially refined into t' and $\hat{s}'$.

Example 4.28
Consider activity use of object type CAR_RESERVATION (cf. Figure 4.10) which is a trivial refinement of activity use of object type RESERVATION_WITH_PAYMENT (cf. Figure 4.2). Since activity use of object type RESERVATION_WITH_PAYMENT consumes from states paid and issued, activity use of object type CAR_RESERVA-TION must consume from at least one substate of each of these states. This is actually the case, since activity use of object type CAR_RESERVATION consumes from states refueled and paid.

For labeled behavior diagrams, it must be further ensured (a2) that if activity t' consumes from some substate s' of state s with label x, then the activity t' actually consumes each sublabel x'' of label x from some substate s'' of s. Thus, this rule part ensures that an object either leaves the refinement of a state s with all sublabels or does not leave state s at all. Notice again that t, s, and x might be actually identical to t', s', or x' (if t, s, or x' has not really been refined).

Example 4.29

Consider activity lateCancel of object type CAR_RESERVATION (cf. Figure 4.10). It consumes label r1 from state refueled, which is a substate of state issued of object type RESERVATION_WITH_PAYMENT (cf. Figure 4.2). Since label r1 is a sublabel of label r of object type RESERVATON_WITH_PAYMENT and since label r has another sublabel r2, activity lateCancel must consume label r2 from some substate of issued as well. This is actually the case: Activity lateCancel consumes label r2 from substate docsReady of state issued.

Rule parts (b1) and (b2) are the counterparts to (a1) and (a2) for post states. Rule part (b1) requires that every sink activity t' of an activity t produces into some substate $\hat{s}'$ of each post state $\hat{s}$ of t. For labeled behavior diagrams, it must be further ensured (b2) that if activity t' produces into some substate s' of state s with label x, then the activity t' produces actually each sublabel x'' of label x into some substate s'' of s. Thus, this rule part ensures that an object either enters the refinement of a state s with all sublabels or does not enter state s at all. In the formal definition of this rule in Figure 4.11, $h^{-1}(e) = \{e' \in S' \cup T' \cup L' | h(e') = e\}$.

The rule of *Pre- and post state refinement* requires for unlabeled behavior diagrams that (a1) every source activity t' of an activity t consumes from a state s' only if the activity t already consumed from a superstate s of s'. For labeled behavior diagrams, it must be further ensured (a2) that the arc between state s' and activity t' carries a label x' only if the arc between state s and activity t carries a label x of which x' is a sublabel.

Example 4.30

Consider again the activities lateCancel and cancel from our previous example. Since the arc between state docsReady and activity lateCancel carries label r2, the arc in RESERVATION_WITH_PAYMENT between issued and cancel must, in order to obey the rule of pre- and poststate refinement, carry a label of which r2 is a sublabel. The arc does so with label r.

Conversely, (b1) every sink activity t' of an activity t produces into a state s' only if the activity t already produces into a superstate s of s'. For labeled behavior diagrams, it must be further ensured (b2) that the arc between activity t' and state s' carries a label x' only if the arc between activity t and state s carries a label x of which x' is a sublabel.

A behavior diagram $B_{O'}$ with associated refinement function $h_{O' \mapsto O}$ is a behavior consistent refinement of behavior diagram B_O if and only if rules R1 and R2 of Figure 4.11 are obeyed (cf. (31)). Note that similar to observation consistent extension, it is not a necessary condition for behavior consistent refinement that all activities and states present in B_O are also present in $B_{O'}$.

R1. Pre- and post-state satisfaction

(a1) $t \in T, s \in S, \hat{s} \in S, t' \in T', s' \in S'$:

$$h(t') = t \wedge h(s') = s \wedge (s, t) \in F \wedge (s', t') \in F' \wedge (\hat{s}, t) \in F$$
$$\Rightarrow \exists \hat{s}' \in S' : h(\hat{s}') = \hat{s} \wedge (\hat{s}', t') \in F'$$

(a2) $t \in T, s \in S, t' \in T', s' \in S'$:

$$h(t') = t \wedge h(s') = s \wedge (s, t) \in F \wedge (s', t') \in F' \wedge x \in l(s, t) \wedge x'' \in h^{-1}(x)$$
$$\Rightarrow \exists s'' \in S' : h(s'') = s \wedge (s'', t') \in F' \wedge x'' \in l'(s'', t')$$

(b1) $t \in T, s \in S, \hat{s} \in S, t' \in T', s' \in S'$:

$$h(t') = t \wedge h(s') = s \wedge (t, s) \in F \wedge (t', s') \in F' \wedge (t, \hat{s}) \in F$$
$$\Rightarrow \exists \hat{s}' \in S' : h(\hat{s}') = \hat{s} \wedge (t', \hat{s}') \in F'$$

(b2) $t \in T, s \in S, t' \in T', s' \in S'$:

$$h(t') = t \wedge h(s') = s \wedge (t, s) \in F \wedge (t', s') \in F' \wedge x \in l(t, s) \wedge x'' \in h^{-1}(x)$$
$$\Rightarrow \exists s'' \in S' : h(s'') = s \wedge (t', s'') \in F' \wedge x'' \in l'(t', s'')$$

R2. Pre- and post-state refinement

(a1) $s' \in S' \wedge t' \in T' \wedge (s', t') \in F' \wedge h(s') \neq h(t')$
$$\Rightarrow (h(s'), h(t')) \in F$$

(a2) $s' \in S' \wedge t' \in T' \wedge (s', t') \in F' \wedge h(s') \neq h(t') \wedge x' \in l(s', t')$
$$\Rightarrow h(x') \in l(h(s'), h(t'))$$

(b1) $s' \in S' \wedge t' \in T' \wedge (t', s') \in F' \wedge h(s') \neq h(t')$
$$\Rightarrow (h(t'), h(s')) \in F$$

(b2) $s' \in S' \wedge t' \in T' \wedge (t', s') \in F' \wedge h(s') \neq h(t') \wedge x' \in l(t', s')$
$$\Rightarrow h(x') \in l(h(t'), h(s'))$$

Figure 4.11   Rules for checking behavior consistency of refinements

Example 4.31

The behavior diagram of object type RESERVATION_WITH_ALTERNATIVE_ PAYMENT (cf. Figure 4.9) is a behavior consistent refinement of the labeled behavior diagram of object type RESERVATION_WITH_PAYMENT (cf. Figure 4.2).

4.5.3 Refinement in UML

In UML, "refinement" is used as a synonym for "inheritance relationship". In this chapter, we will continue to use the term refinement in the originally introduced sense, i.e., refinement means replacing a transition or a state in an UML statechart diagram by a subdiagram.

Since transitions in UML correspond to events that are not further decomposable in time, it is only meaningful to replace a transition either by another transition or by several alternative transitions, but it is not meaningful to replace a transition by a statechart diagram. A simple state may be replaced by a composite state, which may be concurrent or not.

Just as for extension, we assume that the statecharts have been transformed such that they contain only transitions between simple states (cf. Section 4.4.4).

The refinement of UML statechart diagrams may be captured by a total refinement function h analogous to the refinement function defined for behavior diagrams. For transitions, similar to the comparison of statechart diagrams for extension, function h is defined upon simple and complex transitions (and not on their lower-level components). For states, function h is defined only on simple states but not on complex states. Then, behavior consistency is defined based on h in a manner analogous to behavior diagrams.

Example 4.32

The statechart diagram of object class RESERVATION_WITH_PAYMENT depicted in Figure 4.8 is a refinement of the statechart diagram of object class RESERVATION shown in Figure 4.3. The refinement function h between RESERVATION_WITH_ PAYMENT and RESERVATION maps each substate of issued to issued, each substate of canceled and used to void, and the remaining simple states of RESERVATION_ WITH_PAYMENT to the same-named states of RESERVATION. In addition, the refinement function h maps transitions shown within composite state issued to issued and transitions shown within composite state void to void, and transitions shown outside of the graphical region of a composite state to the same-named transition, with a possible index being omitted or (in the case of a nested index) truncated one level. The statechart diagram of Figure 4.8 may be refined further to cover alternative payments in a similar manner to the way the behavior diagram of Figure 4.2 has been refined to the behavior diagram of Figure 4.9. However, the de facto duplication of the payment procedure must be taken into account.

4.5.4   Checking Behavior Consistent Refinement in UML

We verbally rephrase the rules for checking behavior consistency introduced for refinements of behavior diagrams in the context of UML statecharts diagrams.

Since UML concurrency requirements trivially imply that an object always leaves and enters all concurrent subregions of a composite state simultaneously, no counterparts for rules R1(a2) and R2(b2) are needed.

Consider two UML statechart diagrams S' and S of an object class O' and its superclass O, where S' refines the statechart diagram of S through refinement function h that maps simple and complex transitions onto simple and complex transitions of S' and simple states of S' onto simple states of S. Then, the rules to check for behavior consistent refinement are:

1. The rule of *pre- and poststate satisfaction* requires that for every transition t' in S': for every source state s of $h(t')$, there exists a state s' in S' such that $h(s') = s$, and for every sink state s of $h(t')$ there exists a sink state s' of t' in S' such that $h(s') = s$.

2. The rule of *pre- and poststate refinement* requires that for every source state s' of a transition t' in S', where s' and t' do not belong to the same refined state (i.e., $h(s') \neq h(t')$), $h(s')$ is a source state of $h(t')$, and for every sink state s' of a transition t' in S', where s' and t' do not belong to the same refined state, $h(s')$ is a sink state of $h(t')$.

Example 4.33

The statechart diagram of Figure 4.8 is an observation consistent refinement of the statechart diagram of Figure 4.3.

4.6   Consistent Specialization

In this section we consider the interaction of extension and refinement, first as applied to OBD, and then in the context of UML.

4.6.1   Specialization in OBD

A behavior diagram B_O of a supertype is specialized into the behavior diagram B_O' of a subtype by expanding activities and states into subdiagrams, by replacing labels through a set of sublabels, by adding states, actvities, and labels, and by removing activities and states.

Example 4.34

The behavior diagram of object type CAR_RESERVATION depicted in Figure 4.10 is a specialization of the behavior diagram of object type RESERVATION depicted in Figure 4.1. When the behavior diagram of Figure 4.10 is considered as a specialization of the behavior diagram of object type RESERVATION, the superimposed state issued is to be considered a state of object type RESERVATION and the superimposed activities cancel and refund as well as the superimposed state toRefund must be ignored. State issued and activity cancel of object type RESERVATION have been expanded, label r of object type RESERVATION has been replaced by labels r1 and r2. Activities bill, pay, fullRefund, partRefund, and states toBeBilled, billed, paid, notRefundable, earlyCanceled, lateCanceled, and Refunded, as well as labels p and f have been added at object type CAR_RESERVATION. Also, activity sendSorryLetter and state sorrySent have been removed.

We capture this specialization at the design level by a total specialization function $h_{O' \mapsto O} : S' \cup T' \cup L' \cup \{\varepsilon\} \mapsto S \cup T \cup L \cup \{\varepsilon\}$, which, like the refinement function, is explicitly declared by the designer.

Inheritance without change, refinement, addition, and elimination are expressed by h as follows:

Inheritance without change: If an activity, state, or label e is not changed, then $h(e) = e$.

Refinement: If an activity or state e in B is refined into a set of activities and states E, then $\forall e' \in E : h(e') = e$. Similarly, if a label x in B is refined into a set of labels E then $\forall x' \in E : h(x') = x$.

Addition: If a set of activities, states, or labels E is added in B', then $\forall e \in E : h(e) = \varepsilon$.

Elimination   : If a set of elements $E \subseteq S \cup T$ is removed from B in B', then $\forall e \in E \nexists e' \in S' \cup T' : h(e') = e$.

Example 4.35

The specialization function h for activities and states in Example 4.34 above is evident from the textual description given in that example and the associated figures. Specialization function h maps labels r1 and r2 to r and labels p and f to ε.

The specialization function h must possess the same properties as the refinement function described in the previous section, with the only exception that states, activities, and labels may be mapped to ϵ.

The specialization of a labeled behavior diagram B_O into another behavior diagram $B_{O'}$ with associated specialization function $h_{O' \mapsto O}$ can be decomposed into a refinement of B_O to an intermediate labeled behavior diagram $B_{\hat{O}}$, which we call *embedded refinement*, and into an extension of $B_{\hat{O}}$ to B_O. The embedded refinement of B_O, $B_{\hat{O}}$, and the associated refinement function $h_{\hat{O} \mapsto O}$ is derived from $B_{O'}$ and $h_{O' \mapsto O}$ as follows:

1. $\hat{S} = \{ s \in S' \mid h'(s) \neq \varepsilon \}$
2. $\hat{T} = \{ t \in T' \mid h'(t) \neq \varepsilon \}$
3. $\hat{L} = \{ x \in L' \mid h'(x) \neq \varepsilon \}$
4. $\hat{F} = \{ (x, y) \in F' \mid x \in (\hat{S} \cup \hat{T}), y \in (\hat{S} \cup \hat{T}) \}$
5. $\hat{\alpha} = \alpha'$
6. $\hat{\Omega} = \Omega' \cap (\hat{S} \cup \hat{T})$
7. $\hat{h} : \hat{S} \cup \hat{T} \cup \hat{L} \mapsto S \cup T \cup L$, where $\hat{h}(e) = h(e)$.

Thus, behavior consistent specialization can be defined in terms of behavior consistent refinement and observation consistent extension. (Remember that it is not meaningful to consider invocation consistency for refinement).

Example 4.36

Figure 4.12 depicts the embedded refinement in the specialization of the behavior diagram of object type RESERVATION (cf. Figure 4.1) into the behavior diagram of object type CAR_RESERVATION (cf. Figure 4.10.)

We now know all concepts needed to characterize consistent specialization. Let behavior diagram $B_{O'}$ be a specialization of another behavior diagram B_O according to some *specialization function $h_{O \mapsto O'}$*. Then B_O is a *behavior consistent specialization* of $B_{O'}$ if

1. the embedded refinement $B_{\hat{O}}$ is a behavior consistent refinement of B_O, and

2. $B_{O'}$ is an observation consistent extension of $B_{\hat{O}}$.

Example 4.37

The behavior diagram of object type CAR_RESERVATION depicted in Figure 4.10 is

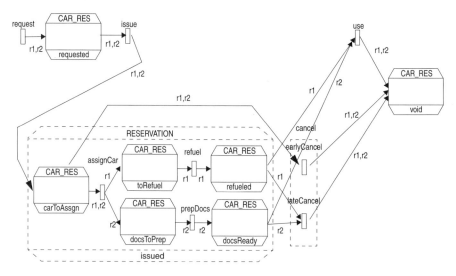

Figure 4.12   Embedded refinement in the specialization of behavior diagram RESERVATION into behavior diagram CAR_RESERVATION

a behavior consistent specialization of the behavior diagram of object type RESER-VATION depicted in Figure 4.1. The embedded refinement (cf. Figure 4.12) is a be-havior consistent refinement of the behavior diagram of object type RESERVATION and the behavior diagram of object type CAR_RESERVATION is an observation con-sistent extension of the embedded refinement.

4.6.2   Specialization in UML

Specialization by concatenating refinement and extension can in principle be applied to UML statechart diagrams. Each specialization of an UML statechart diagram can be technically split into a refinement and an extension. But compared to behavior diagrams, a specialization can – due to the concurrency restrictions of UML – not always be naturally split into an extension part and a refinement part. We have seen in Section 4.4.3 that it is not always possible to produce an intended parallel extension of an UML statechart diagram by merely adding states and transitions. The intended extension is possible, but technically it must be expressed by a refinement. Thus from an application point of view, the clear distinction between extension and refinement is obscured.

Example 4.38
Figure 4.13 depicts UML statechart diagram of object type CAR_RESERVATION which is a specialization of the UML statechart diagram of object type RESERVA-TION (cf. Figure 4.3.). Extension and refinement cannot be clearly separated. The UML statechart diagram of object type CAR_RESERVATION is technically obtained by refinement from the UML statechart diagram of object type RESERVATION. The

refinement function *h* should be evident from the graphical nesting and the names of states and transitions.

4.7 Conclusion

In this chapter we have treated specialization of object life cycles by strictly separating extension and refinement. Such a separation can significantly contribute to understand what actually happens when object types are "specialized".

We have presented necessary and sufficient rules to check for behavior consistency between behavior diagrams and we have outlined how these rules apply to UML.

We summarize them here by giving informal guidelines on how to develop an OBD subtype [UML subclass] that is a behavior consistent specialization of some given OBD object type [UML object class]. In the formulation of these guidelines, we treat simple transitions of UML as complex transitions with an arc leading from the single source state to the transition node and an arc leading from the transition node to the single sink state.

- For *observation consistent extension*:

  (a) Keep all prestates and poststates of inherited activities [transitions].

  (b) Never add an arc between an inherited activity and an inherited state (or vice versa) [inherited state and inherited transition (or vice versa)]

  (c) Never let an added activity [transition] consume from or produce into an inherited state.

- For *weak invocation consistent extension*:

  (a) Keep all prestates and poststates of inherited activities [transitions].

  (b) Never add an arc between an inherited activity and an inherited state (or vice versa) [inherited state and inherited transition (or vice versa)]

  (c) Never add an additional prestate to an inherited activity [transition].

  (d) Keep all activities [transitions] of the supertype [superclass].

- For *strong invocation consistent extension*, obey the guidelines for observation consistent extension and the guidelines for weak invocation consistent extension.

- For *behavior consistent refinement*:

  (a) OBD: For each arc from a state to an activity, where one or both of them have been refined (if only one of them has been actually refined, consider the other one to be refined into itself): Place one or several arcs such that each placed arc connects a state in the refinement of the original state and an activity in the refinement of the original activity. Apply this guideline vice versa for arcs from activities to states. Then verify that, if an activity T' in the refinement of activity T consumes from (or produces into) a state outside of this refinement,

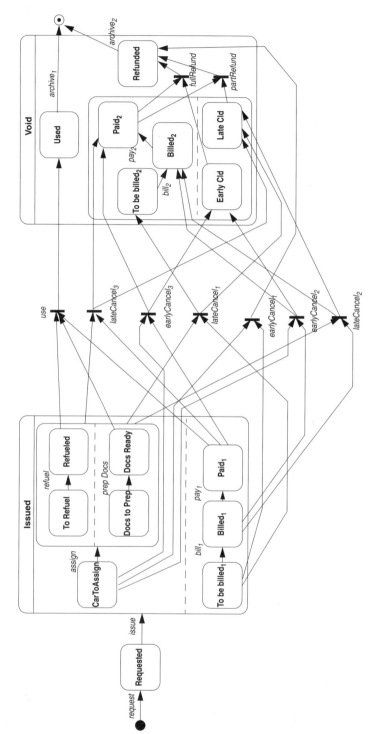

Figure 4.13   UML statechart diagram for object type CAR_RESERVATION

its ingoing (outgoing) arcs possess exactly the labels that are in the refinements of the labels of activity T. If not, add or remove appropriate arcs.

UML: For each arc between a state and a transition where one or both of them have been refined (if only one of them has been refined, consider the other one to be refined into itself): If the state has been refined into concurrent substates, place for each transition in the refinement of the original transition one arc to one state in each concurrent subregion of the original state. If the state has been refined into disjoint substates, place for each transition in the refinement of the original transition an arc to one substate of the original state.

(b) Do not place any other arcs.

- For *behavior consistent specialization*:

  (a) First, develop an intermediate object type [object class] that is a behavior consistent refinement of the given object type [object class].

  (b) Second, develop an object type [object class] that is a behavior consistent extension of the intermediate object type [object class].

Comparing OBD and UML, we have seen that due to the concurrency restrictions in UML, specialization cannot always be naturally split into an extension part and into a refinement part.

Parallel extension of UML statechart diagrams is only possible in a limited manner. Therefore, the intuitive, component-wise interpretation that specialization has in OBD cannot be carried over directly to UML in all cases. If an intended extension is not possible in UML, it must be mimicked by refinement which may result in duplication of subdiagrams.

How do our consistency rules relate to the identified inheritance policies for UML? A number of different inheritance policies are discussed in the context of the UML statechart diagram semantics definition (25). They are referred to as *subtyping, strict inheritance*, and *general refinement*. (Remember that in UML, refinement is a synonym for inheritance.) Of these, the subtyping policy is the one that corresponds most closely to our interests.

The *subtyping policy* requires that a state in the subclass retains all its transitions. Transitions may lead to the same state or a new substate of that state (representing a strengthening of the postcondition of the transition), which is the only way a state (the original superstate of the transition) may lose an incoming transition in the subclass. In addition, guard conditions (i.e., transition preconditions) may be weakened by adding disjunctions. This policy corresponds to weak invocation consistency.

The other two policies provide neither observation nor invocation consistency and are instead geared towards implementation-level and code inheritance issues. *Strict inheritance* is intended to recapture the fact that in many programming languages, features cannot be removed in subclasses once defined in a superclass. The removal of outgoing transitions in subclasses, and the switching of a transition to a different source are forbidden. Guard conditions, transition target states, and incoming transitions may be altered at will. (But strengthening the guard to "false" will practically disable the transition!) Finally, *general refinement* basically places no restrictions on the statechart diagrams of types involved in inheritance relationships.

Other work on inheritance rules for object life cycles includes work by Ebert and Engels (7, 6), as well as Saake et. al. (29). Their approach is based on state diagrams that are related via graph (homo-)morphisms, whereas the work of Paech and Rumpe (22) uses finite automata and McGregor and Dyer likewise use state machines (16). A discussion of life cycles on Petri net basis, but without completeness or sufficiency results, is contained in (32). Most recently Lakos and Lewis have investigated strong substitutability in coloured Petri nets (13). Restrictions on inheritance relationships in concurrent object-oriented languages were examined in (1, 18, 19). Liskov and Wing (15) developed an approach that expresses subtype relations in terms of implications between pre- and postconditions of individual operations plus additional constraints. It provides explicit criteria for individual operations, but is not used for the description of complete object life cycles.

Acknowledgment: We would like to thank Günter Preuner for his help in preparing this paper and Stefano Spaccapietra for his excellent editing comments to improve the presentation of this paper.

References

1. P. America. Designing an object-oriented programming language with behavioural subtyping. In J.W. de Bakker, W.P. de Roever, and G. Rozenberg, editors, *Foundations of Object-Oriented Languages (REX School/Workshop Proceedings)*, Springer LNCS 489, 1990.

2. W. Brauer, R. Gold, and W. Vogler. A survey of behaviour and equivalence preserving refinements of petri nets. In *Proc. 10th Intl. Conf. on Application and Theory of Petri Nets*, Springer LNCS 483, pages 1–46, Bonn, 1991.

3. Grady Booch. *Object-Oriented Analysis and Design with Applications (2nd edition)*. Benjamin Cummings, 1994.

4. P. Bichler and M. Schrefl. Active Object-Oriented Database Design Using Active Object/ Behavior Diagrams. In J. Widom and S. Chakravarthy, editors, *Proceedings of the 4th IEEE International Workshop on Research Issues in Data Engineering (RIDE'94), Houston, Texas*, pages 163–171, 1994.

5. Luca Cardelli. A semantics of multiple inheritance. *Information and Computation*, 76, 1988.

6. J. Ebert and G. Engels. Dynamic models and behavioural views. In *International Symposium on Object-Oriented Methodologies and Systems (ISOOMS)*, LNCS 858. Springer-Verlag, 1994.

7. J. Ebert and G. Engels. Observable or Invocable Behaviour—You Have to Choose. Technical report, Universität Koblenz, 1994.

8. D.W. Embley, B.D. Kurtz, and S.N. Woodfield. *Object-Oriented Systems Analysis: A Model-Driven Approach*. Prentice Hall, 1992.

9. David Harel. Statecharts: A visual formalism for complex systems. *Science of Computer Programming*, 8, 1987.

10. G. Kappel and M. Schrefl. Object/behavior diagrams. In *Proceedings of the 7th International Conference on Data Engineering (ICDE'91)*, pages 530–539, Kobe, Japan, April 1991.

11. G. Kappel and M. Schrefl. Using an object-oriented diagram technique for the design of information systems. In H.G. Sol and K.M. van Hee, editors, *Proceedings of the International Working Conference on Dynamic Modelling of Information Systems*. Elsevier North Holland, 1991.

12. G. Kappel and M. Schrefl. Inheritance of object behavior - consistent extension of object life cycles. In *Proc. East/West Database Workshop*. Springer-Verlag, 1995.

13. Charles Lakos and Glenn Lewis. A practical approach to behavioural inheritance in the context of coloured petri nets. In *Workshop on Semantics of Objects as Processes (SOAP), ECOOP'99*, Lisbon, June 1999.

14. P. Lang, W. Obermair, and M. Schrefl. Modelling business rules using situation/activation diagrams. In *Proceedings of the IEEE International Conference on Data Engineering*, 1997.

15. B. Liskov and J. M. Wing. A behavioral notion of subtyping. *ACM Transactions on Programming Languages and Systems*, 16(6):1811–1841, November 1994.

16. J.D. McGregor and D.M. Dyer. A note on inheritance and state machines. *ACM SIGSOFT Software Engineering Notes*, 18(4), 1993.

17. B. Meyer. Applying "Design by Contract". *IEEE Computer*, 25(10):40–51, October 1992.

18. S. Matsuoka and A. Yonezawa. Analysis of inheritance anomaly in object-oriented concurrent programming languages. In G. Agha, P. Wegner, and A. Yonezawa, editors, *Research Directions in Concurrent Object-Oriented Programming*. ACM Press, 1993.

19. O. Nierstrasz. Regular types for active objects. In *Proc. OOPSLA*, 1993.

20. I. Nierstrasz and T. Murata. A method for stepwise refinement and abstraction of petri nets. *Journal of Computer and Systems Science*, 27, 1983.

21. J. L. Peterson. Petri nets. *ACM Computing Surveys*, 9(3):223–252, September 1977.

22. B. Paech and P. Rumpe. A new concept of refinement used for behaviour modelling with automata. In *Proc. FME'94*, Springer LNCS 873, 1994.

23. L. Pomello, G. Rozenberg, and C. Simone. *A Survey of Equivalence Notions for Net Based Systems*. LNCS 609. Springer-Verlag, 1992.

24. Rational Software Corp. *UML Notation Guide, Version 1.1*, September 1997.

25. Rational Software Corp. *UML Semantics, Version 1.1*, September 1997.

26. J. Rumbaugh, M. Blaha, W. Premerlani, and F. Eddy. *Object-Oriented Modeling and Design*. Prentice Hall, 1991.

27. J. Rumbaugh, I. Jacobson, and G. Booch. *The Unified Modeling Language Reference Manual*. Addison-Wesley Publishing Company, 1999.

28. M. Schrefl. Behavior modeling by stepwise refining behavior diagrams. In H. Kangassalo, editor, *Proc. 9th Int. Conf. Entity-Relationship Approach*, amsterdam, 1991. Elsevier North Holland.

29. G. Saake, P. Hartel, R. Jungclaus, R. Wieringa, and R. Feenstra. Inheritance conditions for object life cycle diagrams. In *Proc. EMISA Workshop*, 1994.

30. M. Schrefl and M. Stumptner. Behavior Consistent Extension of Object Life Cycles. In *Proc. Intl. Conference on Object-Oriented and Entity-Relationship Modeling (OOER '95)*, volume 1021 of *LNCS*. Springer-Verlag, 1995.

31. M. Schrefl and M. Stumptner. Behavior consistent refinement of object life cycles. In *Proc. 16th Intl. Conference on Conceptual Modeling (ER '97)*. Springer-Verlag, 1997.

32. W. M. P. van der Aalst and T. Basten. Life-Cycle Inheritance—A Petri-Net-Based Approach. In *Proc. 18th Intl. Conf. on Application and Theory of Petri Nets*, LNCS. Springer, 1997.

33. G. Winskel. Petri nets, algebras, morphisms, and compositionality. *Information and Computation*, 72, 1987.

34. P. Wegner and S.B. Zdonik. Inheritance as an incremental modification mechanism or what like is and isn't like. In S. Gjessing and K. Nygaard, editors, *Proc. ECOOP'88*, Springer LNCS 322, 1988.

II Transformation and Reverse Engineering

5 Mapping an Extended Entity-Relationship into a Schema of Complex Objects

Rokia Missaoui
Robert Godin
Jean-Marc Gagnon
Université du Québec à Montréal
C.P. 8888, Succursale "Centre-Ville"
Montréal (Québec) H3C 3P8, Canada
{missaoui.rokia/godin.robert}@uqam.ca

This chapter first gives a brief overview of schema transformation and re-engineering of database applications. It then focuses on a methodology for converting an extended entity-relationship (EER) schema into a structurally object-oriented schema. The methodology is based on a semantic clustering technique which produces clustered EER diagrams that are then mapped to object-oriented schemas. Finally, a description of a prototype, called INTERSEM, is given with the purpose to illustrate its main functionalities: semantic modeling, schema manipulation and transformation, complex object formation, and generic schema extraction using a conceptual clustering technique.

5.1 Introduction

Re-engineering is a software engineering process that consists of three steps: reverse engineering, attention to new requirements, and forward engineering (6). The wide use of relational database (DB) management systems (DBMS), the growing interest and development of object-oriented (OO) models and systems, and the high popularity and utilization of the entity-relationship model (10) have lead to the re-engineering of legacy (old conventional) databases to object-oriented ones by first reverse engineering relational schemas using the entity-relationship formalism as a target model. Such a mapping has been extensively studied and handled by many researchers (29, 41, 25, 21).

Our main concern in this chapter is to deal with a part of the issue of re-engineering relational databases to object-oriented ones. More specifically, our objective is to handle the forward engineering task by providing a methodology for converting an extended entity-relationship (EER) schema into a *structurally* OO schema. The methodology is based on a semantic clustering technique which is an adaptation of the technique proposed in (36, 37) to produce clustered EER diagrams which can then be mapped to OO schemas. Our methodology diverges from Teorey's paper in the following way: (i) it aims mainly at complex object formation even though it can be a useful technique for documentation and abstraction, (ii) it leads to an extension to the EER model, called the CEER model, and (iii) it includes additional rules and refinements to handle multiple choices, and preserve the logical sequence of DB schema abstract views.

In the following we will use the UML notation (38) which is an attempt to standardize the notation used for software development artifacts, and a unification effort of the notations used in the OMT, Booch and Objectory methodologies (7).

The chapter is organized as follows. In Section 5.2, research studies related to schema transformations are reviewed and important issues are discussed. Section 5.3 outlines the main features of the clustering technique and presents the process of translating an EER schema into a clustered EER (CEER) diagram. Section 5.4 describes the mapping rules for converting a CEER schema into an object-oriented schema using the object model supported by the ODMG standard (9) as the target model. Section 5.5 gives a brief description of the prototype INTERSEM (28, 15) which includes many interesting functionalities such as semantic modeling based on the EER approach, schema transformation, complex object formation, schema classification and generic schema extraction using a conceptual clustering technique (16, 15). Finally, conclusion is given in the last section.

In the sequel, we assume the familiarity of the reader with the key notions of semantic modeling and object-orientation (20, 24, 23, 9, 6).

5.2   Related Work

The re-engineering of legacy databases and systems to produce object-oriented databases involves at least two main tasks:

- *Reverse engineering*: mapping the existing logical (i.e., relational, hierarchical, or network) schema of the database into a semantic (conceptual) schema,

- *forward engineering*: translating the resulting semantic schema into an OO schema.

In the following, we give a brief overview of studies related to schema transformation, reverse and forward engineering.

5.2.1   Schema Translation

Schema translation is the process that converts a schema in a source data model into a corresponding schema in (most frequently) another model. It happens in situations such as database reverse engineering, view transformation and merging, and integration in multidatabase systems.

There are two types of schema translation that were proposed in the literature: direct mapping and indirect mapping. A direct translation converts the schema of a source model to that of a target model directly by utilizing pair-wise specific transformation procedures. An indirect translation makes use of a common intermediate model (e.g., the entity-relationship formalism) to first convert the original schema into that model, and then to translate the intermediate schema into the target model. The indirect mapping is more frenquently used because it facilitates the re-engineering process and offers higher extensibility.

Atzeni and Torlone (3) take a metamodeling approach for translating schemata from one model to another. In (27), metamodels for the CEER and ODMG models are defined and used in the process of schema transformation.

In order to evaluate the correctness of schema translations, informatio capacity preservation has been exploited in (1, 19, 21, 22, 26). A target schema S_2 has at least the information capacity of the source schema S_1 if every instance of S_1 can be mapped to some occurrence of S_2 without loss of information. The work done by Kosky (22) concentrates on studying the way schema transformations affect the corresponding instances themselves, and proposes metrics for the correctness of transformations. The study also presents a declarative language with a well-defined semantics to express data transformations and integrity constraints.

5.2.2 Database Reverse Engineering

Reverse engineering is a process of software engineering that aims at rebuilding the functional and technical specifications of a software piece by starting mainly from program code. In the context of databases (17, 6), the term is mainly used to mean the process of recovering the logical intent of an existing design expressed by logical (e.g, relational) schemes, and operations (e.g., queries and views).

Most of the work done in the field of database re-engineering focuses on the transformation of the structural aspects of databases using the relational schema (18, 3, 21, 14) or even analyzing a set of relational queries and views (32, 2, 17) or mining database instances (11, 33). However, recent studies tend to investigate the behavioral and data aspects as well (22, 39). Many studies adopt unrealistic assumptions about the quality and completeness of the schema to be transformed. For example, they assume that all integrity constraints are explicitly provided.

Fahrner and Vossen (14) propose a three-step process for directly converting a relational schema into an object-oriented one using the ODMG model as target. The first step consists to complete the original relational schema both structurally (e.g., identify homonyms, synonyms, and inheritance structures) and semantically (e.g., delete redundant inclusion dependencies). The second step translates in a canonical way the completed schema into an ODMG schema. The last step improves the resulting schema with OO features (e.g., eliminate artificial keys, introduce inverse relationships, and create complex structures). Vermeer and Apers (39) present a translation approach that generates not only the OO structure from a relational schema, but also the methods of classes dircty from relational queries and views. For an object schema, the join materialization graph (JMG) is defined. Given an SQL query, a query join graph (QJG) is built where nodes represent the tables involved in the query while the edges reflect natural joins, semijoins and antijoins expressed by the query. A matching object graph (MOG) is a subgraph of the JMG that includes parts of the structural component of the OO schema which match the QJG, and hence allows the definition of methods. By performing such matching between the QJG and the JMG, joins and nested queries are expressed in a more natural way using references and navigational facilities offered by the object model.

Ramanathan and Hodges (33) describe a procedure for directly mapping a relational schema into an OO one. They make use of data mining techniques to discover inheritance hierarchies and aggregations either from data or relational schemes. In (32, 2), it is shown that the procedural part of application programs can be very useful to the discovery of data structures. Join conditions in queries and views are exploited to construct EER schemes, and discover semantics such as inheritance hierarchies and identifying relationships.

In most studies related to the conversion of a relational DB into an EER schema, consistent naming of key attributes and well-designed schemes are assumed. The input consists of relation schemas generally in 3NF, with explicit information on keys, functional and inclusion dependencies. Some approaches enrich the semantics of the initial schema (e.g., (14)) or allow the discovery of class hierarchies and so-called missing entities (8, 21, 39).

5.2.3   Database Forward Engineering

The literature reports at least two kinds of mapping of an ER diagram into an OO schema (35, 13): the first type, *called stable translation*, consists in converting each entity and each relationship into an object as in (30) while the second one, called mapped translation, consists in integrating a relationship into an object class using references, and creating an object class for each ternary relationship. One of the drawbacks and limitations of the OO approach, as pointed out by (12, 24) is the fact that relationships commonly expressed in semantic models are not directly supported in OO models. Instead of being visible, the relationships are expressed indirectly by means of interobject references. This assertion does not hold for the ODMG standard.

As mentioned earlier, some studies (39, 14, 33) handle the DB re-engineering process by omitting the reverse engineering task, and hence by transforming a relational schema directly into an OO one.

The distinctive features of our approach to schema transformation are: (i) the definition of the CEER model as an appropriate intermediate model for a direct and easier translation of a conceptual schema to an OO model, (ii) the fully automated translation process for first converting an EER schema into a schema of complex objects, and then producing an OO schema, and (iii) the design and development of an OO knowledge-based prototype, called INTERSEM, for building, clustering, transforming, classifying and reusing EER diagrams.

5.3   Semantic Clustering

In many real-world applications, designers tend to constitute classes of objects such as concepts, chunks and clusters according to some similarity criteria. The clustering technique proposed in (36, 37) is basically suggested to facilitate the interaction between the designer and the user by presenting the conceptual schema at different levels of detail. It consists in recursively grouping entities and relationships of an initial extended entity-relationship schema, using semantic abstractions such as aggregation, generalization and association. In this chapter, we shall show that some variations of this clustering technique can be useful not only to improve the understanding of the DB conceptual schema and master its complexity, but also to contribute to the construction of complex entities, and therefore could be used as an important step in the mapping process of an initial EER diagram into an object-oriented schema.

We start from an EER schema to produce a set of clustered schemata such that each clustered schema corresponds to a level of abstraction and grouping of the initial schema. As in (36), we use the term grouping to indicate the operation needed to combine entities and their relationships to form a higher-level construct called entity cluster or complex entity. The procedure is performed iteratively in a bottom-up manner by starting from atomic entities and building more complex entities out of them. To ensure a high *semantic cohesion* within complex entities, the grouping operations are done in a priority order. The procedure produces a schema of complex entities by iteratively shrinking portions of an EER diagram into complex entities which hide the details about the components. The user can expand a complex entity through a specified level of clustering to show components at some degree of detail.

Our clustering approach diverges from Teorey's paper in the following way:

- It aims mainly at complex object formation even though it can be a useful technique for documentation and abstraction.
- It leads to an enhancement of the extended ER model as defined below.
- It offers additional rules and refinements to handle multiple choices, and preserve the logical sequence of DB schema abstract views.
- It can suggest a physical clustering scheme for complex objects.

5.3.1   Grouping operations and Priority Order

The four grouping operations and their priority order are slightly different from the ones proposed in (36). The priority order applies as follows: when a given entity E is both involved in a relationship of priority order k and a relationship of priority order $k + 1$, then the grouping of order k is chosen. When a given entity E is candidate to two groupings of a same priority (except for weak entity absorption), then we decide which one to use based on additional rules defined later.

- *Weak entity absorption*

  A strong entity E is collapsed with all its direct dependent entities to form a single complex entity whose label corresponds to the name of the strong entity. The weak relationships as well as any one-to-many relationship and its corresponding related (member) entity associated with E are also absorbed in the complex entity. In the presence of a sequence of weak entities and relationships, our grouping starts with the most dependent entity and assembles entities in cascade as illustrated in (27).

- *Dominance Grouping*

  We define a dominant entity as the one which is in a binary association with at least two entities by a one-to-many relationship. Dominance grouping consists in assembling a dominant entity with its related entities and relationships. The name of the clustered entity is identical to the name of the dominant entity.

- *Generalization and Categorization Grouping*

  The generalization/categorization grouping consists in creating a complex entity whose name is identical to the name of the supertype/category (when there exists only one specialization/categorization of the generalized/category entity) and whose components are the immediate subtypes/supertypes of the generalized entity or category. A category is defined as a subset of the union of some classes (12).

- *Relationship Grouping*

  The n-ary relationships of any degree can be grouped into an entity cluster, reflecting the semantics of the relationship as a whole. As opposed to (37), the name of the entity cluster is not necessarily identical to the name of the relationship. It corresponds to the name of the relationship especially when the association is either a many-to-many binary relationship or n-ary relationship. In the mapping process (see Section 5.4 for more details), the translation of a clustered entity obtained by relationship grouping takes into account the nature of the entities in relationship: key entities, mandatory/optional participation, the existence of attributes associated with relationships, and the number of other associations in which an entity is involved in.

5.3.2   Additional Rules

In order to preserve the logical and natural sequence of viewing a database at different levels of abstraction, to maintain the whole semantics of data, and handle some conflicting situations, we use the following four rules which will be illustrated with an example in Section 5.3.4. We borrow the first two rules from (36) and propose two additional rules.

- *Step-by-step grouping*

  Whenever a new grouping is to be done on a schema C_i (schema with a clustering level i), the output is a schema C_{i+1} as long as at least one grouping operation is achieved on C_i. The initial schema is assigned level 0.

If the n-th clustering operation within level i is achieved around the entity E, then it leads to an entity cluster with a name, and a level expressed by i. The name of the complex entity depends on the kind of clustering: it is the name of the dominant (or strong, or generalized or category, or owner) entity, or the name of the relationship if it is a many-to-many binary relationship, a ternary relationship or any relationship with at least one attribute attached to it.

A grouping operation cannot be achieved at level i if it involves a complex entity recently formed at that same level, and therefore has to be postponed to the next level.

- *Consistency*

    To avoid the possibility of losing the semantics associated with data, and in order to preserve the initial relationships between entities inside and outside a complex entity, we do the following. Whenever a component (or subcomponent) E_i of a complex entity E_j is in a relationship (IS-A, or association) with another entity, the appropriate side of this relationship will be labeled by $E_{j-1}...E_i$ representing the path needed to reach the component E_i inside E_j (see Figure 5.2).

- *Cascading*

    If an entity E_i is both a candidate to a clustering operation of any kind (weak entity absorption, dominance, generalization, categorization, or relationship grouping) as a *slave* entity (i.e. a component of a potential complex entity E), and a candidate to another clustering operation as a master entity (i.e. an entity whose name is identical to the name of a potential cluster such as dominant/strong entities, generalized entities, and one-side entities in a one-to-many relationship), then the inner clustering operation (i.e. the one involving E_i as a master) is applied before the outer grouping (i.e. the one involving E_i as a slave). As a special case, in the presence of a sequence of weak entities with their corresponding relationships, the absorption grouping starts from the most dependent entity and relationship, and then iteratively forms a complex entity until the strong entity is encountered.

- *Visibility/Unvisibility of Entities*

    In any information system, there are some entities that are relevant to many procedures and needs of users. We think that these key entities have to be quite visible at any level of abstraction of the initial schema, and not hidden inside a complex entity. Therefore, any grouping that encapsulates a key entity has to be prohibited.

5.3.3   The Clustered EER

The clustering technique leads to the creation of clustered EER (CEER) diagrams. Like the EER model, the CEER model has entities, relationships, attributes and abstractions such as aggregation, generalization/specialization, derivation and union. However, the CEER model has two main advantages over the EER: (i) it is an additional extension to the EER model, (ii) it allows a more adequate and direct translation to the OO model due to its additional features.

The CEER model has the following concepts and abstractions:

- Attributes in the CEER model can be atomic, multi-valued or derived attributes. As opposed to the EER model, the clustered EER formalism allows attribute values to make reference to a single occurrence or a set of instances of an entity type.

- Entities can be atomic (i.e., no attribute makes reference to instances of entity types) or clustered. A clustered entity is an entity whose attributes can be constructed based on entity types and constructs like sets, tuples and lists.

- The aggregation abstraction is extended to the assembly of entities together with relationships.

- Relationships can serve to link entities of different levels of abstractions: atomic entities (i.e., entities that belong to the initial EER schema), clustered entities or even components of clustered entities.

- Additional information brings more semantic expressiveness to the model. Such information is expressed by the number of grouping operations that lead to a clustered entity, and by the path needed to reach a component of a clustered entity.

  - The depth of the aggregation hierarchy associated to a clustered entity is part of the entity label (see Figure 5.2 and 5.3).

  - Whenever a component entity E_i of the aggregation hierarchy underlying a clustered entity E_j has a link (generalization/specialization, association, or union) with another entity, the appropriate side of this relationship will be labeled by $E_{j-1}...E_i$ representing the path needed to reach the component E_i inside E_j.

We believe that the semantic clustering technique facilitates the mapping process. Moreover, it ensures the information capacity preserving since all the components of the EER structure (e.g., entities, relationships, cardinalities) are systematically converted to a corresponding CEER structure, and each grouping and transformation rule by itself preserves information capacity.

5.3.4   An Illustrative Example

We will use the car rentals case study (40) referenced throughout the book. The diagrams below follow the Unified Modeling Language (UML) standard proposal version 1.1 (38).

The interpretation of the conceptual schema in Figure 5.1 is as follows. Each branch of the car rental company owns cars and offers car sales. Customers make reservations by providing information like the category of cars and the rental period. Customers may have experienced bad situations during their rental (e.g., late return, problems with payment and damage to cars). A blacklist is built to include customers who had frequent bad experiences. The entity *Freq_Trav* describes customers that frequently rent cars. Effective rental occurs once a car is assigned to a *Rental_Booking* record.

Weak entities (*Bad_Exper* and *Repair*) are indicated in Figure 5.1 by qualified associations (*Occurs* and *Subject_to*). Identifiers (primary keys) are specified as

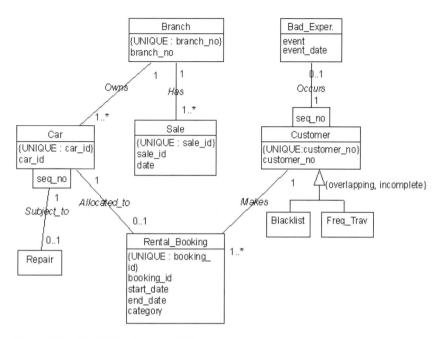

Figure 5.1   The EER schema in UML

constraints in UML. Constraints are noted as text within braces { }. The fact that there is at most one *Repair* object linked to a *Car* for a given *seq_no* (0..1 multiplicity for the role of *Repair* in the *Subject_to* association) implies that the identifier *car_id* of a *Car* plus *seq_no* is an identifier for *Repair*.

Customer is a supertype of the subtypes *Blacklist* (i.e., bad customers) and *Freq_ Trav* (i.e., frequent travellers). The coverage of the generalization is partial (i.e., some clients are neither frequent travellers nor bad customers) and subtypes are allowed to overlap (i.e., some frequent travellers can be bad customers too).

If we assume that *Branch*, *Car*, and *Customer* are key entities, then any grouping in which these entities have to be components of a complex entity is prohibited.

Since the weak entity absorption operation has the highest priority, the weak entities *Bad_Exper* and *Repair* are absorbed by *Customer* and *Car* respectively. At this first stage of grouping, a one-to-many relationship grouping is also allowed between *Branch* and *Sale*. No additional grouping operation is permitted at level 1 because any potential grouping involves either a key entity or complex entities recently clustered at that level (see Figure 5.2).

At the second level of grouping, there are two candidate clustering operations involving the recently clustered entity Customer: one by generalization grouping, and one by one-to-many binary relationship grouping. Since the former has priority over the latter, the generalization grouping is performed at the level 2 to hide the specialized entities *Blacklist* and *Freq_Trav*. Another grouping at the same level is allowed between *Car* and *Rental_Booking*. To maintain the semantic consistency of the clustered schema, relationships (association, ISA, and union) that involve a component of a complex entity must exhibit the path needed to reach that component. For example,

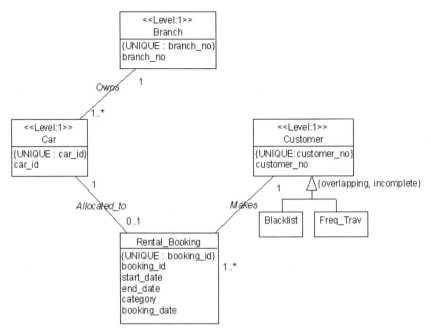

Figure 5.2   A one-level CEER schema

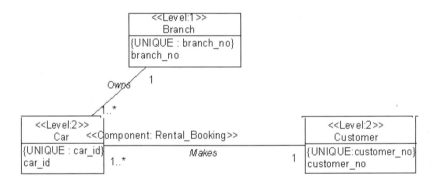

Figure 5.3   A two-level CEER schema

Figure 5.3 shows that the relationship *makes* connects the entity *Customer* to the entity *Rental_Booking* which is a component of the recently clustered entity *Car*. The number attached to clustered entities reflects the number of grouping operations that lead to the construction of these entities. For example, the clustered entity *Car* illustrated in Figure 5.3 is formed using two grouping operations. To express the fact that the relationship *makes* connects *Customer* to *Rental_Booking* which is a component of the clustered entity *Car*, a path to this component is indicated.

To express the grouping level with the UML notation, we make use of the stereotype extensibility mechanism of this language. A <<Level:*n*>> stereotype for a class represents a level *n* of grouping.

In the same way, we define another stereotype on the association role. A $<<$ Component $: C >>$ stereotype on an association role means that the association refers to the C component of the class on the association end. For example, the association role $<<$Component: *Rental_Booking*$>>$ on the *Car* side references the *Rental_Booking* class inside *Car* (see Figure 5.3).

5.4 Mapping a CEER Diagram into an OO Schema

Up to now, we are able to derive a schema of complex entities (CEER) out of an EER schema. This first step aims at facilitating the second step related to the conversion to an object-oriented model by mapping the CEER schema into an object-oriented schema. Below are the transformation rules for such mapping.

5.4.1 Transformation Rules

Definition 5.1
A *structurally* object-oriented database scheme is a couple $(S, \sum)$ consisting of a collection of entity types $E_1... E_m$ closed under references and supertypes, and a set $\sum$ of inter-entity integrity constraints. At the structural level, an entity type E_i can be described by the following properties:

- Supertypes: set of supertypes of E_i,

- Structure: aggregation of (atomic or complex) attributes A_j belonging to either built-in or user-defined types,

- Relationships: set of associations in which E_i participates,

- Specializations: set of specializations where E_i is the generalized entity,

- Category: description of the supertypes that participate to the union (if applicable), and

- Constraints: set of intra-entity constraints.

Definition 5.2
An entity E_j in the initial (i.e, non clustered) schema is a potential candidate to absorption by another entity E_i when one of the following cases occurs:

- E_j is in only one $1:1$ or one $1:N$ relationship with E_j, and E_j has no other associations in the schema under consideration.

- E_j is a weak entity with respect to E_i and participates at most to weak relationships (if any) as a strong entity.

- Each specialized entity E_j of E_i does not have specific properties by its own and does not participate to any relationship.

For example, in the case when *Client_Card* is (i) a non-key entity, (ii) in an optional participation to a one-to-one relationship with the entity *Customer*, and (iii) not related to another association in the schema under consideration, then *Client_ Card* is a candidate to absorption by the entity *Customer*.

Definition 5.3

As opposed to the internal associations which are embedded inside clustered entities, *external relationships* of a CEER diagram are explicitly visible in the corresponding diagram. As illustrated by Figure 5.3, the only external relationships appearing at the clustering level 2 are *owns* and *makes* while associations like *Occurs* are hidden.

The translation process we adopt for transforming a CEER diagram into an ODMG-based schema is a little bit similar to the mapping procedures described in (4, 12):

- Each entity of the clustered EER diagram is mapped into an object type. The structure of the complex object type depends upon the grouping operation used for complex entity formation. Except for entities that are candidates to absorption, each component of the complex object is recursively mapped into an object type. Multivalued attributes are expressed using the set or list constructors. Aggregate attributes are expressed using the tuple constructor.

- Each external relationship of the CEER diagram is mapped into a relationship in the object model. For example, the external relationship *makes* appearing at the clustering level 2 (see Figure 5.3) links the clustered entity *Customer* together with *Car.Rental_Booking* which is a component of the clustered entity Car. It is important to note that while external relationships are translated into the ODMG model as they are (i.e., as abstractions), internal relationships are converted into references (i.e., physical constructs) during the mapping process, as illustrated below.

During the translation process and independently of the way the complex entity E_i has been formed, the reference to an entity E_j inside E_i can take one of the following two forms:

- the actual structure (attributes) of E_j when E_j is a candidate to absorption by E_i,
- a reference attribute (pointer) otherwise.

Weak entity absorption and dominance grouping

For this type of grouping, a complex type is created as an aggregation of the strong/dominant entity and the weak/related entities. Each relationship inside the grouping is mapped to a reference attribute whose name is the label of the relationship, and whose type conforms to the weak/related entity type. Curly braces {} are used whenever there are many occurrences of the weak/related entities for one occurrence of the strong entity.

Relationship grouping

As mentioned earlier, there are two approaches for relationship translations (5, 12): one which explicitly describes the relationship as a class structure (34). The second approach maps the relationship into a pair of direct and inverse references as described in (9). In the last case, reference attributes are used to express the relationships between objects and ensure the navigation in one or both directions. To describe the inverse relationships, inverse reference attributes are used.

We believe that the relationship grouping translation (which is different from external relationship translation) depends on the arity of the relationship and the (minimal and maximal) cardinalities of the associations. Each relationship is mapped onto either new attributes (either references to object types or actual attributes) added to the appropriate entities, or a new entity making reference to the concerned entities. The following cases are considered.

- *One-to-one Relationships.* The translation of one-to-one relationships depends on the kind of the two entities (key or non-key) and their minimal cardinalities in the relationship (optional versus mandatory participation), and on the number of other associations in which each of the two entities is involved in. In the general case, a single reference attribute completes the structure of each entity involved in the relationship.

  As an illustration, let *Client_Card* be (i) a non-key entity, (ii) in an optional participation to a one-to-one relationship with the entity *Customer*, and (iii) not related to another association in the schema under consideration. In such a situation, it may be useful to add the actual attributes of *Client_Card* to the entity *Customer* and destroy the entity *Client_Card*, especially if no new relationships are expected between *Client_Card* and other entities of the schema.

- *One-to-many and Many-to-many Relationships without Attributes.* For one-to-many relationships with no associated attributes, a multi-valued reference attribute is added to the description of the "one side" entity (e.g., a branch) of the link while a single reference attribute completes the structure of the entity on the "many side" part (e.g., a car) of the relationship. For many-to-many links, multi-valued reference attributes are added to the description of each entity involved in the relationship.

- *Other types of relationships.* In the case of either ternary relationships or many-to-many (or even one-to-many) relationships with associated attributes, each entity involved in such relationships is described by means of its own attributes and a new structure is created by aggregating the reference attributes with the participating entities as well as the attributes attached to the relationships.

Generalization/Categorization Grouping

The mapping of such a grouping can be done in different ways (13), and may be based on the type of coverage (e.g., disjoint subtypes with partial cover). In case of disjointness for example, the mapping of a complex entity built from the clustering of a generalized entity with its related specialized entities can be perceived as a mapping of a one-to-one relationship between the generalized entity and each of its subtypes.

Since an object in a category (e.g., *Driver*) appears in only one of its supertypes (e.g., *Customer*, *Employee*), the mapping of a categorization grouping to an OO schema can be handled by adding to the description of the category a reference to the corresponding supertype.

Other Cases

Since there may be many possible transformations of a source schema into a target one, it is crucial to choose the most appropriate one. The choice of a given mapping depends upon:

- The expected usage patterns. For example, if there are queries that ask for cars owned by a given branch as well as requests for branches having some kinds of cars, then it is required to have both direct and inverse reference attributes connecting branches to their cars.

- The expected evolution of the DB schema. For example, if we expect that the entity *Client_Card* can very likely participate to a new relationship with another entity, say *Invoice*, then it may be wise to keep *Client_Card* as an independent object type instead of pushing it inside the *Customer* type.

- The peculiarities of the OODBMS that will be used. In some systems, the database designer is allowed to declare two attributes as inverse of one another. This feature is interesting since it offers a way to maintain the consistency of relationships, as opposed to a need for an explicit declaration of directional relationships.

5.4.2 An Example

Since ODMG is expected to be adopted by many object-oriented DBMS vendors, we will use the ODL syntax to describe a part of the clustered EER diagram illustrated by Figure 5.3.

The object model supported by the Object Database Management Group (ODMG) consortium of OODBMS vendors (9) incorporates a set of primitives and constructs. For simplicity, we will give the most relevant elements:

- The basic primitive is the object.

- Each object has a *unique identifier* and may have one or more user-defined names.

- Similar objects belong to an *Object type* and share structure and behavior.

- Object types are organized into a hierarchy of *subtypes* and *supertypes*.

- The state of objects is expressed by a set of *properties* which can be either attributes or *relationships*.

- The behavior of objects is expressed by a set of *operations* which are defined by *exceptions* and *signatures* (arguments, . . .).

By making the assumption that the entity *Bad_Exper* is the only candidate to real absorption in the schema, the weak entity absorption grouping (with *Customer* as a strong entity) leads to an OO schema (see below) where structures instead of references to *Bad_Exper* are used to describe *Customer*.

interface Branch
// type properties
(**extent** branches
           key branch_no)
// instance properties
{   **attribute** List<Ref<Sale>>sale_records {order_by Sale::date};
           attribute ...
           relationshipSet<Car>owns **inverse** Car::owned_by;
// instance operations
...};
interface Sale
// type properties
(**extent** sales
           key sale_id)
// instance properties
attribute Date date;
           relationship Set<Car> owns **inverse** Car::owned_by;
// instance operations
...};
interface Customer
(**extent** customers
           key customer_no)
{   **attribute** Set<struct<string event, Date event_date>> bad_Exper_info;
           attribute ...
           relationship Set<Car> makes inverse Car.Rental_Booking::made_by;
           ...
};
interface Blacklist: Customer ...};
interface Freq_Trav: Customer ... };
interface Car
{(**extent** cars
           key car_id)
           attribute Set<Ref<Repair>> repair_records;
           attribute Rental_Booking booking_record;
           attribute ...
           relationship Branch owned_by inverse Branch::owns;
           ... };
           interface Rental_Booking
(**extent** rental_Bookings
           key booking_id)
{   **attribute** ...
           relationship Customer made_by inverse Customer::makes;
           ... };

5.5   The INTERSEM Prototype

5.5.1   Overview

In this section we present the main features of the prototype INTERSEM (15), including the semantic clustering and schema transformations. INTERSEM (*Interface sémantique*) is an OO environment from two points of view: (i) it is intended to serve both as an object-oriented semantic modeling tool, and as an interface to an OO database management system, and (ii) it is designed and implemented in an OO way. It aims at reducing the semantic gap between the conceptual modeling of OODBs and the modeling tools by providing a framework and an environment for semantic data modeling, OODB design, reverse engineering, generic model extraction, and DB schema transformation and querying (see Figure 5.4). It provides semantic concepts and abstractions commonly found in the enhanced entity-relationship model (37, 4, 12) such as generalization, classification, derivation, aggregation, categorization, and constraints specification (see Figure 5.5).

INTERSEM can also be seen as a knowledge-based system that represents in a clear and declarative way the clustering process and the various transformations. To that end, the prototype makes use of NéOpus, an extension to Smalltalk with production rules, that integrates a declarative architecture for specifying control (31). For reuse purposes, INTERSEM makes use of a conceptual clustering technique (16) that classifies a set of EER schemas in a lattice structure, and extracts generic parts out of them.

The prototype includes a multi-panel user interface which allows the insertion, deletion, modification and retrieval of semantic concepts (entities, attributes, relationships, types and constraints) related to a given schema. A generic graph editor is also implemented and can be used for EER and CEER diagram representation and manipulation.

INTERSEM has been implemented using the object-oriented paradigm in the environment of ObjectWorks (releases 4.0 and 4.1). The prototype runs both on Unix workstations and MacIntosh micro-computers.

5.5.2   INTERSEM in Action

To illustrate the tasks performed in the environment of the prototype, we provide a set of screen layouts. Figure 5.5 shows the main multi-panel interface where the left-upper side helps describe, view and manipulate conceptual schemes while the left-lower part allows the visualization and description of a given schema in terms of entities under a given view (e.g., class hierarchy, aggregation hierarchy). The right part of the panel exhibits the relationships, integrity constraints, attributes and types associated with a given schema or a given (atomic or complex) entity.

CarRental-1 and *CarRental-2* are produced from the initial schema *CarRental* by applying a one-level and a two-level semantic clustering respectively.

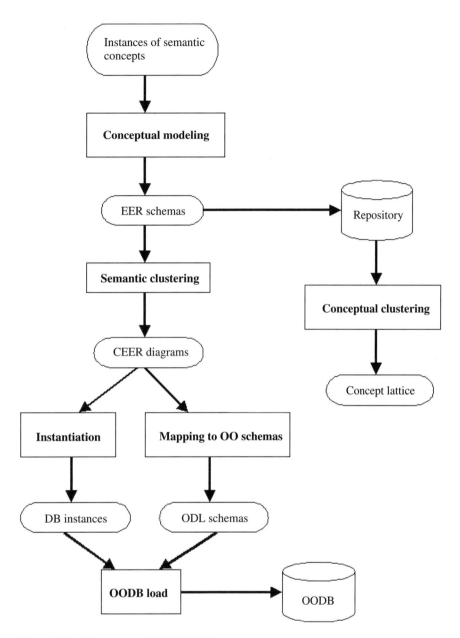

Figure 5.4   Components of INTERSEM

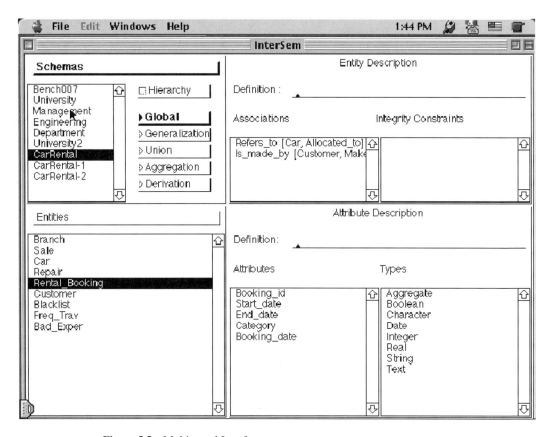

Figure 5.5   Multi-panel Interface

Figure 5.6 highlights the description of the CEER schema of *CarRental-2* by indicating the list of entities, the external relationships associated with the entity Car as well as the attributes of that complex entity. It is important to note that the semantic clustering of the initial schema *CarRental* has lead to the automatic creation of three new types.

The following screen layout shows one of the menus offered by the prototype. The right part of the panel describes the whole set of associations, integrity constraints, attributes and types associated with the schema called *Department*. Integrity constraints are expressed in INTERSEM in a declarative way.

The following illustrates the expression of rules using NéOpus. This rule states that "For any *a*, instance of class *BinaryAssociation*, and any *s* instance of class *Schema*, if the sequence of conditions is satisfied, then the transformation represented by the method *groupManyToManyAssociationWith*" is performed. It is important to note that the rule only describes the process itself. The details of the transformation (as well as the conditions) are hidden in the methods, making the rule easy to understand.

The following screen layout shows a part of the lattice resulting from the conceptual clustering (16) of four schemes (A, B, C and D). Each node of the lattice

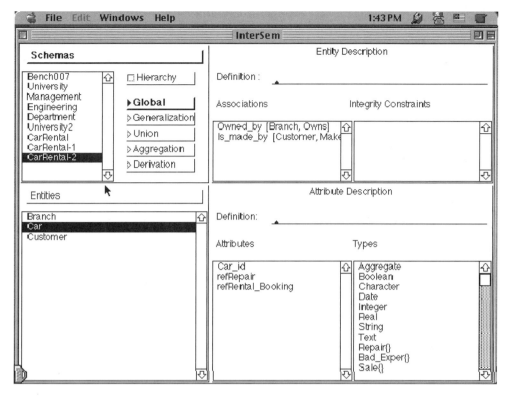

Figure 5.6 Description of a CEER schema

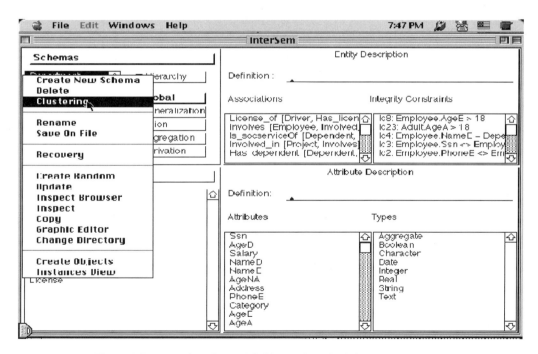

Figure 5.7 Menu for schema definition and manipulation

```
groupAssocNM
    | BinaryAssociation a . Schema s|
        s notNil.
        a sourceEntity isGrouped not .
        a targetEntity isGrouped not .
        a sourceEntity isKey not.
        a targetEntity isKey not.
        a cardMax1 = 'n' .
        a cardMax2 = 'n' .
        a isNeutral.
actions
        a groupManyToManyAssociationWith: s. ''defined in class BinaryAssociation''
        a remove.
        a inverse remove.
        s modified.
        Transcript show: 'Grouping association type N:M ', a printString,'.'; cr.!!
```

Figure 5.8   Example of a rule expressed in Néopus

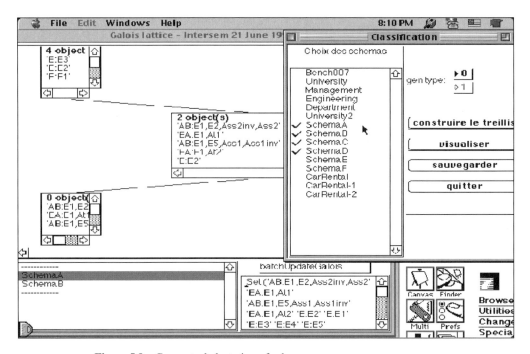

Figure 5.9   Conceptual clustering of schemes

is called a formal concept and is defined in this example by a set of schemes and their corresponding set of common properties (e.g., sharable entities, associations and attributes). For example, the upper node indicates that the four schemes share the entities E_1, E_2 and E_3. The node in the middle shows that schema A and schema B share also some binary relationships (AB) and entity attributes (EA). Background knowledge (e.g., synonyms, generalization hierarchy) can be exploited during the classification process to discover additional formal concepts. This is done by selecting the value 1 for the parameter *gentype* (see the right-upper side) and choosing the appropriate thesaurus.

5.6   Conclusion

In this chapter, we have reviewed studies related to schema transformations, and have presented a semantic clustering methodology as an adaptation of the clustering technique proposed in (36) to produce clustered EER diagrams which can then be mapped to OO schemas. Our methodology diverges from Teorey's paper in the following way:

- It aims mainly at complex object formation even though it can be a useful technique for documentation and abstraction.
- It leads to an extension to the EER model, called the CEER model.
- Additional rules and refinements are proposed to handle multiple choices, and preserve the logical sequence of DB schema abstract views.

The major contributions of our approach to schema transformation are: (i) the definition of the CEER model as an appropriate intermediate model for a direct and easier translation to an OO model, (ii) the fully automated translation process for first converting an EER schema into a schema of complex objects, and then producing an OO schema, and (iii) the design and development of an OO knowledge-based prototype, called INTERSEM, for building, clustering, transforming and reusing EER diagrams.

We have experimented the potential of semantic grouping for physical clustering of complex objects and found that the approach is an economical and efficient alternative, especially when the semantic cohesion between object types holds also in database usage patterns.

Acknowledgments

This work was supported in part by the Natural Sciences and Engineering Research Council of Canada, and by the Ministry of Industry, Commerce, Science and Technology, Quebec, under the IGLOO project organized by the *Centre de Recherche Informatique de Montréal*.

References

1. Abu-Hamdeh R., Cordy J., and Martin P. Schema Translation Using Structural Transformation. In *Proc. Of CASCON'94*, Toronto, 1994, pp. 202-215.

2. Andersson M. Extracting an Entity Relationship Schema from a Relational Database through Reverse Engineering, *Proc. Of the 13th International Conference on the Entity-Relationaship Approach*, Manchester, UK, December 1994, pp. 403-419.

3. Atzeni P. and Torlone R. A Meta Model Approch for the Management of Multiple Models and the Translation of Schemes, *Information Systems* 18, 1993, pp. 349-362.

4. Batini C., Ceri S., and Navathe S.B., *Conceptual Database Design. An Entity-relationship Approach*. The Benjamin/Cummings, New York, 1992.

5. Bertino E. and Martino L., *Object-Oriented Database Systems. Concepts and Architectures*. Addison-Wesley. 1993.

6. Blaha M. and Premerlani W. *Object-Oriented Modeling and Design for Database Applications*. Prentice Hall, 1998.

7. Booch G., Rumbaugh J.E., and Jacobson I. *The Unified Modeling Language User Guide*, Addison-Wesley, 1999.

8. Castellanos M, Saltor F., and Garcia-Solaco M. Semantically Enriching Relational Databases into an Object-Oriented Semantic Model, *Proc. Of the 5th DEXA Conference*, 1994, pp. 125-134.

9. Cattell R.G.G. et al. (Ed.), *The Object Database Standard: ODMG 2.0*, Morgan Kaufmann, San Mateo, 1997.

10. Chen P. The Entity-Relationship Model: Toward a Unified View of Data. *ACM Transactions on Database Systems*, 1, 1 (1976), pp. 9-36.

11. Chiang R.H.L., Baron T.M., and Storey V.C. Reverse Engineering of Relational Databases: Extraction of an EER Model from a Relational Database. *Data & Knowledge Engineering*, 12, 2 (March 1994), pp. 107-142.

12. Elmasri R. and Navathe S.B., *Fundamentals of Database Systems*, Second edition, Benjamin/Cummings, Redwood City, 1994.

13. Elmasri R., James S., and Kouramajian V. Automatic Class and Method Generation for Object-Oriented Databases, *Proc. of the 3th Deductive and Object-Oriented Databases* (DOOD), Phoenix, Arizona, 1993, pp. 395-414.

14. Fahrner C. and Vossen, G. Transforming Relational Database Schemas into Object-Oriented Schemas according to ODMG-93. *Proc. 4th International Conference on Deductive and Object-Oriented Databases* (DOOD), 1995, pp. 429-446.

15. Gagnon, J-M, *Représentation et exploitation de la sémantique dans un modèle orienté objets*. Master's thesis, Université du Québec à Montréal, August 1995.

16. Godin R., Missaoui R., and Alaoui, H., Incremental Concept Formation Algorithms Based on Galois (Concept) Lattices. *Computational Intelligence*. 11, 2 (1994), pp. 246-267.

17. Henrard J., Englebert V., Hick JM, Roland D., and Hainaut J-L. Program Understanding in Databases Reverse Engineering. In *Proceedings of DEXA'98*, Vienna, August 1998, pp. 70-79.

18. Herzig R. and Gogolla M. Transforming Conceptual Data Models into an Object Model. In *Proc. of the 11th International Conference on the Entity-Relationship Approach*, 1992, pp. 280-298.

19. Hull R. Relative Information Capacity of Simple Relational Database Schemata, *SIAM Journal of Computing*, 15, 3 (1986), pp. 856-886.

20. Hull R. and King R., Semantic Database Modeling: Survey, Application, and Research Issues. *ACM Computing Surveys*, 19, 3 (1987), pp. 201-260.

21. Johannesson P. A Method for Transforming Relational Schemas into Conceptual Schemas, *Proc. Tenth International Conference on Data Engineering*, Houston, 1994, pp. 190-201.

22. Kosky A., Davidson S., and Buneman, P. Semantics of database Transformations, *Technical Report* MS-CIS-95-25, Department of Computer and Information Science, University of Pennsylvania, sept. 1995.

23. Lausen G. and Vossen, G. *Models and Languages of Object-Oriented Databases*, Addison-Wesley, 1997.

24. Loomis M.E.S. *Object Databases: Essentials*, Addison-Wesley, 1995.

25. Markowitz V.M. and Makowsky J.A., Identifying Extended Entity-relationship Object Structures in Relational Schemas. *IEEE Transactions on Software Engineering*, 16, 8 (1990), pp. 777-790.

26. Miller R.J., Ioannidis Y.E., and Ramakrishnan R. The use of Information Capacity in Schema Integration and Translation. In *Proc. Of the International Conference on Very Large Data Bases*, Dublin, Ireland, 1993, pp. 120-133.

27. Missaoui R., Godin R., and Sahraoui H.A. Migrating to an Object-Oriented Database Using Semantic Clustering and Transformation Rules. *Data and Knowledge Engineering*, 27, 1, (Aug. 1998) pp. 97-113.

28. Missaoui R., Gagnon J.M. and Godin R. Mapping an Extended Entity-Relationship Schema into a Schema of Complex Objects. In *Proc. of the Fourteenth International Conference on Object-Oriented & Entity Relationship Modelling*, Gold Coast, Australia, December 1995, pp. 204-215.

29. Navathe S.B. and Awong A.M. Abstracting Relational and Hierarchical Data with a Semantic Data Model. In *Proc. of Sixth International Conference on Entity-Relational Approach*, 1987, pp.305-333.

30. Navathe S.B., Pillallamarri M.K. OOER: Toward Making the ER Approach Object Oriented. *Proc. of the 8th International Conference on Entity-Relationship Approach*, 1989, 55-76.

31. Pachet F. On the Embeddability of Production Systems in Object-oriented Languages, *Journal of Object-Oriented Programming*, 8, 4 (1995) pp. 19-24.

32. Petit J-M., Kouloumdjian J., Boulicaut J-F., and Toumani F. Using Queries to Improve Database Reverse Engineering, *Proc. Of the 13th International Conference on the Entity-Relationaship Approach*, Manchester, UK, December 1994, pp. 369-386.

33. Ramanathan S. and Hodges J. Extraction of Object-Oriented Structures from Existing Relational Databases. *ACM Sigmod Record*, 26, 1 (March 1997), pp. 59-64.

34. Rumbaugh J.E. Relations as Semantic Constraints in an Object-Oriented Language. *Proc. of the International Conference on Object-Oriented Programming Systems, Languages, and Applications* (OOPSLA). Orlando, Florida, 1987, pp. 466-481.

35. Song I.Y. A Survey of Object Oriented Database Design Methodologies, *Proc. of the International Conference on Information and Knowledge Management*. Baltimore, MD, 1992, pp. 52-59.

36. Teorey T.J. et al. ER Model Clustering as an Aid for User Communication and Documentation in Database Design, *Communications of the ACM*, 32, 8 (1989), pp. 975-987.

37. Teorey T.J., *Database Modeling and Design. The Entity-Relationship Approach*. Morgan Kaufmann. 1990.

38. OMG. UML, Release 1.1, 1997. (see http://www.rational.com/uml).

39. Vermeer M.W.W. and Apers P.M.G. Enhancing the Semantics of Federated Schemata by Translating SQL-queries into Object Methods. *Technical Report*, University of Twente, Computer Science Department, The Netherlands, 1995.

40. Wilson B. EU-Rent Car Rentals Case Study. *Technical Report*, Model Systems & Brian Wilsons Ass., May 1994.

41. Winans J. and Davis, K.H. Software Reverse Engineering from a Currently Existing IMS Database to an Entity-Relationship Model. In *Proc. Of the 9th international Conference on Entity-Relationship Approach*, Lausanne, 1990, pp. 345-360.

6 Leveraging Relational Data Assets

M. P. Papazoglou
W. J. van den Heuevel
Tilburg University
INFOLAB
GPO Box 90153, Tilburg 5000 LE
The Netherlands
{mikep,wjheuvel}@kub.nl

This chapter articulates an approach to transforming legacy relational databases to semantically equivalent representations accessible via object-oriented interfaces and data languages. In particular, it describes how semantic and syntactic heterogeneity between relational and object-oriented representations can be resolved on the basis of a high-level semantic-oriented protocol employed for inter-model/language mappings. This protocol supports many of the data sharing requirements of database systems such as the need to support a distributed client/server access mode.

6.1 Introduction

Nowadays we experience an increasingly decentralized and communication-focused business climate requires new kinds of applications that can be rapidly deployed and used throughout the business organization and outside the enterprise by its partners, suppliers and customers. Innovative companies with good partner relationships are beginning to share sales data, customer buying patterns and future plans with their suppliers and partners. Although data sharing is key to implementing many of today's business practices, data sharing difficulties within an organization can cause information to be difficult to obtain and expensive to maintain. Typically, the information resources of many organizations consist of a plethora of isolated database systems and applications (viz. its *legacy information systems*) implemented in a variety of technologies which are incapable of functioning together. Legacy information systems are those systems currently operating that incorporate obsolete technology such as closed systems, "stove-pipe" design, and outmoded database management systems. Many of these legacy database systems serve as a defining aspect of business and are mission critical to the ongoing success of an organization, rendering thus conversion or migration a nearly impossible task. However, they constrain the ability of the organization to adapt to changes in business practice due to their poor maintainability, technical obsolescence, and their inherent inability to evolve to meet changing business needs.

In large measure, data problems are due to the diversity of database systems and modeling formalisms, as well as due to diverging data semantics which complicate attempts to transform disparate heterogeneous database systems into a cohesive whole. These are extremely difficult problems to solve. However, as giving up on a legacy system is not feasible for most organizations in the immediate future, the solution to the legacy problem lies in improving the legacy systems so that they become more functional by reconciling them with new technology. Currently, there are two possible solutions to leveraging the legacy database systems:

1. *Legacy system extension:* keeps the system's existing technology and architecture, while incrementally adding new functionality. However, it does not incorporate it into a larger, enterprise wide information architecture. This approach treats each system separately and extends multiple systems independently without allowing for systems to cooperate and share data. Extension does not address realigning technology nor mapping legacy systems to modern business processes and creates poor systems which are very difficult to maintain.

2. *Legacy Access in Place:* these are solutions which attempt to realign legacy systems with modern technology and which decouple and decompose legacy systems into their service-based components. We define a service to be a conceptually coherent set of functions, independent of any implementation. The term access in place is used to imply that modern and legacy systems can share and exchange information, without any modification of the systems themselves, are seamless in terms of operations, and show consistency of representation and behavior (26). Providing access in place requires:

    (a) implementing abstract interfaces that allow the legacy data and contents to be made available for invocation by other database systems;

    (b) understanding the *semantic contents* of the legacy systems.

Several techniques such as reverse engineering have emerged as the basis for restructuring and "re-facing" legacy systems and applications such that they can be used together with newer generation systems. Reverse engineering of a legacy system's data and functionality has proven to be a successful approach to reconstructing the understanding or the physical condition of organizational database systems that have deteriorated or are unable to evolve. Re-engineering of existing database systems improves the quality of the legacy systems at a cost far below that of re-development.

Data re-engineering strives to improve data definitions and in general reconstitute the data assets of a legacy system (1). Data re-engineering of legacy relational data assets is an important field of research nowadays (7). Relational database systems have been very popular due to their conceptual simplicity and because of serving well the needs of business and transactional applications, such as inventory management, payroll, accounting and order processing applications. Relational database systems have been accepted as the dominant solution for managing corporate data. However, they present several drawbacks mainly due to their inherent inability to model closely real world and complex situations and due to their lack of support for data semantics.

In the recent few years object-oriented software development is rapidly becoming the leading database approach, as it copes with the above stated problems and, also because of its ability to build flexible, scalable software systems in client/server environments and spatial distribution/sharing of data and services. Such types of applications have seriously challenged the capabilities of relational systems. These two trends are motivating the need for building object-oriented applications that access relational data and functionality. In fact, object-oriented data models provide a natural approach for facilitating the re-engineering process of legacy relational systems.

In this chapter, we propose an access in place solution for legacy relational data base systems by means of a semantically-oriented protocol. This protocol is based on abstraction formalism that can describe the existing relational data and code, the reverse-engineered semantic intent, and the forward engineered new system. Subsequently, we show how object-oriented data language constructs can access legacy relational data by being converted to semantically equivalent SQL expressions.

6.2   Approaches to Data Re-engineering

Access and integration of legacy applications and data with novel technologies and applications is quite a complex task. Integration of legacy data and applications may come about by "surrounding" them with the technologies that hide their internal information and structure leverages the existing investment in legacy systems and minimizes the cost involved in application conversion. There are two popular strategies in dealing with the conversion of a legacy database system and providing coordinated access to legacy system functionality and data. These are briefly outlined in the following.

6.2.1   Object Wrapping

Object wrapping is the practice of implementing a software architecture given pre-existing heterogeneous components. Object wrapping allows mixing legacy systems with newly developed applications by providing access to the legacy systems. Wrappers provide access to a legacy system through abstract application program interfaces (APIs), regardless of the internal implementation complexity of the legacy system. The legacy API is the software access path to the legacy implementations' supported functions. The advantage of this approach is that it promotes conceptual simplicity and language transparency.

Reverse engineering is inextricably related to wrapping. A key activity associated with reverse engineering is to identify and carefully structure potential reusable assets (in the form of objects) in a way that would enable the application developers to build new applications by reusing legacy data and code in a cost-effective manner. The approaches to object wrapping can be divided into broad categories such as:

- Encapsulated wrapping,
- Mediated wrapping.

6.2.1.1   Encapsulated Wrapping

Object wrapping allows providing access to a legacy system through an encapsulation layer. Encapsulation is the most general form of object wrapping which achieves a separation of interface from implementation. It is used to partition and componentize legacy systems. Encapsulation hides differences in database languages and data structures. Each component can be objectified separately, and then the system can be re-integrated using object-based messaging. When data are wrapped, the legacy system may be accessed via standard object definitions without disrupting the legacy database. The encapsulation layer exposes only the attributes and service definitions desired by the software architect and all access to legacy data and services are performed through interface methods. Using interface methods allows changing implementation details without requiring other changes.

This type of wrapping can be achieved by harnessing the emerging distributed object management technology and by appropriately compartmentalizing existing software and applications. For example, a simple layer of software mapping the legacy APIs to CORBA IDL, provides for broader system interoperation and distribution of legacy system services through CORBA (22). The benefits of this approach is that each component can be reused in place, and system upgrades can happen incrementally.

6.2.1.2   Mediated Wrapping

At the data sharing level, a wrapper needs to provide more functionality than just a simple encapsulation layer. It introduces the additional requirement for mediated services which combine various types of functions such as:

- providing seamless access to disparate legacy data systems,
- facilitating the conversion of data between incompatible formats, and
- employing meta-data to support the above two functions.

Access to legacy systems is provided by means of APIS, as in the case of encapsulated wrappers, which allows the contents of wrappers to be exported and shared by other systems.

Data conversion implies the existence of a variety of data sources with diverse underlying data modeling formalisms, data languages and differing semantics. In order to be able to reuse legacy databases, legacy data formalisms and functionality must be transformed to newer generation data formalisms and functionality and semantic differences between old and newer generation systems must be reconciled. To resolve the heterogeneity mismatches among a diversity of data modeling formalisms, most wrapping techniques involve adding a mapping layer that bridges the new data model and the legacy database. Here, techniques such as meta-modeling (see Section 6.2.2) can prove to be particularly useful for translation purposes.

Perhaps the most effective concept for building adaptable legacy systems is *meta-data*. Meta-data is self-descriptive information that captures the information content of the data in legacy (or other) systems as well information contained in the software architecture and implementation. Meta-data enables the adaptability and discovery of legacy system services and their characteristics. It facilitates clients to integrate with a wider range of object implementation in a cost-effective manner. Since most legacy systems have limited meta-data, meta-data is a key responsibility of the object wrapper. Meta-data allows applications to discover detailed information about the object implementations they wish to utilize. Meta-data can include key information such as supported data formats and the meta-schema of data sources, thus, including descriptions of relations, attribute names and types, length, metric usage, business logic and semantics, constraints and service-specific descriptions. Other key forms of meta-data useful for legacy database system conversion include: white and yellow page directories for discovering service components. The applications can also find out detailed information, such a the methods of communication supported by the implementation, e.g., scripts, and the syntax for this communication.

6.2.2   Meta-Modeling

The issues relating to the coexistence of multiple heterogeneous database systems data model translation have concerned researchers for a number of years (27), (4), (11), (12). Most approaches to data model transparency are based on the adoption of a canonical data model which is able to represent the features of other data models. This approach has been termed *meta-modeling*. The translation process with the meta-modeling typically comprises two steps: first translating from a source (local) data model to a canonical model and then from the canonical model to a target (remote) model. This approach assumes a hierarchy of data models in which the canonical data model is the most expressive and presupposes that it is possible to directly map candidate schemas into the canonical model in an algorithmic (*prescriptive*) fashion. Similarly query/translation algorithms presuppose that a deterministic transformation exists for mapping one query formalism directly into another. Translating a query from a source to a target model is a one-off static process that requires the existence of an entire equivalent canonical schema for both databases.

One of the earliest approaches to meta-modeling was proposed by (27). It illustrated how to construct a global schema on the basis of a simple semantic meta-model and how to map the constructs of local schemas to this meta-model. The thrust of this paper is on integration rather than translation, and on analyzing semantic constraints for the formation of updatable views on the global schema. A different approach is adopted by (4) where a model definition language is used to generate a schema definition for the corresponding model. Translations are specified by means of a programming language and a set of predefined translation-specific functions. In (5) an extensible meta-level system is presented which serves to uniformly represent the syntax and semantics of data models such as the relational and functional data models. The diverse data modeling constructs are mapped to a formal common meta-model. This model focuses on second-order logic-based to provide definitions of meta-types. Emphasis is primarily placed on formalizing aspects of different schemas.

A different approach has been proposed to support the co-existence of applications that combine an object-oriented development method with relational implementation (19). This approach uses a front-end CASE tool that models object diagrams and a back-end compiler that generates relational database schemas. This approach uses a meta-model in the form of a dictionary for multiple relational database systems by providing information about the logical object model from which the schema is mapped.

The concept of a global schema or canonical model has been largely discarded in the multi-database arena, instead the notion of semantic enrichment of component schemas is often used as a basis for facilitating loose interoperability between disparate database systems. Typically semantic enrichment involves the augmentation of the information captured within a database schema with additional, often domain expert-supplied, knowledge about the application domain. By doing this, it is often possible to resolve structural mismatches and semantic heterogeneities which exist between databases. The use of meta-models for resolving schema discrepancies in relational and o-o schema is described in (21) and (23) with particular attention being given to the transformation of data to meta-data and vice-versa in order to resolve certain semantic ambiguities. Finally, the use of meta-data in facilitating transformations between heterogeneous schemas is discussed in detail in (4) and (27) and a number of algorithms are outlined for translating between source model, meta-model and target model.

6.2.3   Re-engineering Tools

The access in place strategy we advocate requires access/integration surround technologies such as the CORBA's IDL and database gateways. Access technologies are used to define the access path between new business applications and legacy systems, whereas the integration technologies are used to provide an uniform interface to shield the access paths. In addition to these enabling technologies, re-engineering requires other tools to support the reverse engineering activity such as: reformatters and restructures, that can be used to enhance the layout of legacy code, source comparators, code analyzers and data/process reverse engineering tools. The actual mapping between the source and target environment lastly, can be (partly) supported by means of several mapping tools.

In this section, we describe state of the art tools to enable the surrounding technologies, e.g., data re-engineering wrappers. We also discuss mapping tools that can be used to (semi-) automatically map relational tables to object schema and back. More extensive descriptions of these tools can be found in (26), (25), and (3).

6.2.4   Integration Technologies

Following (26), we distinguish between two broad types of integration technologies, that make up the two extremes in the spectrum of wrapping: conventional wrappers ("thin" wrappers) and mediating wrappers ("fat" wrappers). Wrappers can be used to reface functions, data, or presentations in such a way that these parts look to the outside world as objects. The thin wrappers correspond to the encapsulating wrappers as discussed in Section 6.2.1.1 and can be used to build facades around individual legacy data components. This category of tools converts the data sources independent from the contents. For example, wrappers that convert SQL-3 queries to SQL-queries. On the other side of the spectrum, we can observe more advanced wrapping tools, the 'mediated wrapping tools', that can handle access to various heterogeneous database or application systems. These advanced wrappers require meta-data repositories in order to redirect remote calls to the right legacy resources. Another term frequently used for thick wrappers is integration gateways (26).

- ■ "Thin" Wrapping Tools
  - • Tools based on the CORBA's Interface Definition Language, such as: Orbix, ObjectBroker, ComponentBroker (IBM). CORBA's IDL is a declarative language to specify a system's API in terms of the services it provides and its required parameters. IDL has language bindings with languages such as Java, C++ and SmallTalk. IDL could for example be used to write an IDL-facade around a C++ legacy application, and let it cooperate with a new Java Business Beans with an IDL-interface (15), (22).
  - • Message Oriented Middleware (MOM): IBM's MQSeries, Digital's DECmessageQ. Message oriented middleware provides brokerage-services such as asynchronous messaging, and message notification services. MOMs tend to be proprietary technologies, whereas CORBA's IDL is standardized.
- ■ "Thick" Wrapping Tools
  - • Integration Gateways
    An integration gateway provides one integral interface that distributes external service calls to several underlying access technologies, such as database or application gateways. To our knowledge fully functioning integration gateways are not (yet) commercially available.

6.2.5   Object Mapping Tools

The object mapping tools can be used to (semi-)automatically map legacy databases to object schemas. Most mapping tools in the market are used to map relation tables to objects and vice-versa on a one to one basis. These tools are built on top of database gateways like the Open Database Connectivity Object Database Connectivity (ODBC) (6) and Java Database Connectivity (JDBC) which provides standard for Java calls to relational database systems (24). These mapping tools promote a direct mapping between the tables and the objects, leaving out a meta-model. An example of such a mapping tool is IBM's San Francisco's Mapping Tool. The San Francisco Schema Mapper is a tool that can be used to map business objects, as supported by the San Francisco run-time environment to relational schemas. The tool consists of two parts: the Default Schema Mapper and the Extended Schema Mapper. The Default Schema Mapper automatically maps one class to one table. The Extended Mapping Tool can be used to perform some more advanced operations like changing the name of the table or column, and change the data type of a column. The schema mapping tool generates (semi-) automatically a Schema Mapping Language file, that is used run-time by the San Francisco programming environment to generate Java code to access the (legacy) database (2).

6.3   Overview of System Functionality

Distributed object technology facilitates the initiation and evolution of a logically uniform environment that provides access to a variety of heterogeneous database systems. Rather than communicating directly, the database systems use common messages via an API—which provides an access path to the database systems' supported functions—through the use of a *publish-and-subscribe* mechanism.

The publish-and-subscribe API is based on the CORBA event services and event channels (22) and uses a single interface to achieve database connectivity. Database systems can be producers and consumers of events. Produces *publish*, viz. export, events to the database network, which then delivers them to those consumers that have *subscribed*, viz. imported, them. Events can be queries or transactions indicating the need for an action to take place or notifications. Notifications normally announce the occurrence of important actions.

An event service object allows database component systems to dynamically register or unregister their interest in specific events. An event channel is a mediating object that connects suppliers and consumers of events. It allows multiple suppliers to communicate with multiple consumers asynchronously and without knowing about each other. Instead of interacting directly with each other, suppliers and consumers obtain proxy objects from the event channel to represent them in future exchanges of events (22). The event channel brokers the exchange of events via these proxy objects. Figure 6.1 shows how objects involved in a car-sales event—e.g., a modify-purchase-order method of the Car_Sales_Order object which invokes a ship event, which in its turn invokes a pick-inventory event—communicate within an ORB environment implementing the publish-and-subscribe service. Through the exchange of request and notification events, objectified producer and consumer database systems can participate in complex interactions while retaining their responsibilities and autonomy. The resulting execution style is highly decoupled and configurable.

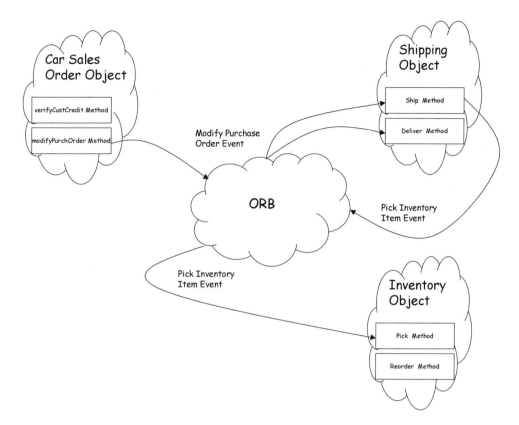

Figure 6.1   Communicating objects using the publish-and-subscribe API.

6.3.1   Summary of the Proposed Approach

Conventional approaches to relational database wrapping involve representing whole tables and files as objects (9). Moreover, most wrapping techniques allow only read access to the database as they bypass integrity rules in application programs to directly access the database tables. A more natural approach to wrapping data within the object-oriented paradigm should break up relations into multiple objects at a finer granularity. This process involves denormalization of relational data and takes into account existing data integrity rules. Moreover, in both cases of wrapping and meta-modeling, little consideration is given to the semantics of the underlying schema and query constructs and as a result both techniques have significant drawbacks when attempting to support interoperation between two applications which differ in the context of their underlying semantics.

In this chapter, we present a protocol for facilitating transformation between heterogeneous data models that addresses many of the problems inherent in the approaches described in Section 6.2. The Semantic Transformation Protocol (STP) – which we have developed to achieve interoperability between relational and object-oriented databases (18), (16) – is a generic transformation framework which utilizes a meta-modeling formalism in conjunction with specialized sets of transformation rules to support data homogenization and data sharing. The translation protocol combines important properties of object wrapping and meta-modeling and enriches the semantic scope of existing database schemas by bringing them up to the lowest level of representation that allows successful data understanding and sharing between heterogeneous database systems. In this chapter we use the STP to show how it guides and controls a semantically-driven translation process involving transforming a legacy relational database system to an equivalent o-o data representation. However, the techniques described are equally applicable for use in integrating systems based on earlier data models (such as the hierarchical or network). The STP is essentially composed of two components:

- an *abstract description model*, known as the ADM, which is specialized according to the characteristics of the data model in question, e.g., relational, and its associated schemas;

- the ADM comprises instantiation and transformation rules for constructing a semantically enriched set of *abstract descriptor classes*, or ADCs, corresponding to a (relational) database schema instantiated through the ADM. The ADCs are used as the basis for schema and query transformation.

The combination of the publish-and-subscribe mechanism with the STP – which employs a point-to-point *descriptive* translation style between heterogeneous data models and data languages – achieves a high degree of flexibility. It allows individual databases to retain complete autonomy and the ADM instances provided for use with the transformation rules, whilst transparent, serve as a kind of enriched export schemas (subscribed API data and functions) for the component databases. These mechanisms ensure that the STP approach will scale effectively where interactions involve a significant number of participant database systems.

6.4   A Semantic-Oriented Translation Protocol

The STP views a data model, e.g., relational, as a collection of high-level abstractions (abstract descriptor classes) describing this model's constructs and ingredients, while it views a database schema as an instantiation of these abstract constructs. This approach is based on the premise that existing models use a rather limited number of constructs which although *conceptually* common to diverse models are represented in different syntactic ways. By virtue of this and the fact that it is not directly based on a specific data model, the STP is capable of ongoing extension as further data models are developed and utilized with it.

The STP assists in guiding and controlling the process of translation between heterogeneous data sources. It achieves this by obtaining the right set of abstract descriptor classes from a set of otherwise independent heterogeneous schemas, potentially with some form of schema enrichment (8), (12). The STP can dynamically map query/transaction constructs – such as classes/relations, attributes, constraints, etc – into an *Intermediate Schema Meta Graph* (ISMG) which comprises all the ADCs instantiated by a given relational schema. It is the ISMG that can then be used as a basis for the semantic translation of, for example, an object-oriented query to an equivalent relational query on a legacy database. This technique extends meta-modeling techniques with semantics-oriented translations on the basis of descriptive abstraction mechanisms alleviating, thus, most of the pitfalls of canonical models. It also allows users to utilize their own local language to access remote databases rather than resorting to a canonical data language. This particular approach to querying re-mote heterogeneous databases is outlined in some detail in (18) and (16).

The major phases of the translation process when converting legacy relational databases to equivalent object-oriented representations are summarized in the fol-lowing:

Enrichment: This phase is supported by an interactive approach to the reverse engi-neering of existing database schemas and expects input from domain experts (19). Relational database schemas are enriched to yield the optimal collection of ADC meta-objects. Schema enrichment information contains for example primary and sec-ondary key information necessary to map onto objects.

Schema Conversion: The enriched relations are converted to the appropriate ADC meta-objects that in conjunction with the transformation rules help transform re-lational constructs to semantically equivalent objects in some object-oriented data model.

Data Language Translation: This phase is employed whenever there is a need to access a legacy relational database system via the data language of an o-o data model. The purpose of this phase is to utilize a class library that generates a relational ISMG corresponding to the portion of the relational schema that is targeted by an o-o query/transaction. In other words, we generate a query graph that describes relational constructs found in the o-o query/transaction. This ISMG is subsequently used to translate the o-o query into a semantically equivalent relational query on the legacy database.

The interrelationship between the three broad phases of the translation process is illustrated in Figure 6.2.

6.4.1   The Abstract Descriptor Classes and their Contents

ADCs are capable of representing concepts such as containment, partitioning, inher-itance, association, dependencies, aggregation and so on. For instance, the relational, and object-oriented data models have several generic, and mostly conceptual, over-lapping properties such as (multi-valued or single-valued) dependencies, associative properties and sub/super typing which are expressed in very different ways. Some properties are represented directly, e.g., dependencies and associations, while others

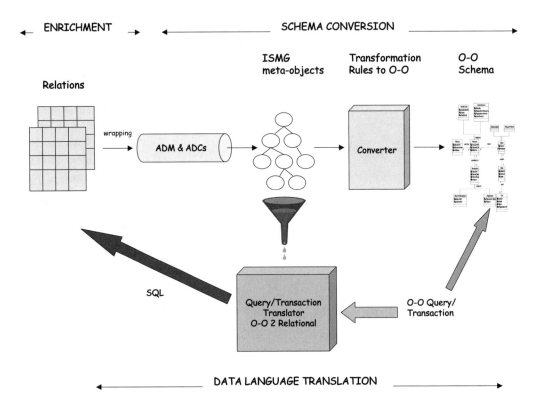

Figure 6.2   The transformation phases of a legacy relational database.

are represented indirectly, e.g., sub/super-typing in the relational model. To represent the direct properties we either use a single meta-level class or a combination of such classes to describe them. Where properties are represented indirectly we use a combination of ADCs and model tailored mapping rules, as a series of methods residing in these ADCs, to achieve the desired results. Both ADCs and mapping rules use rich meta-data descriptions of the database models in use (the relational data model in this publication) and the legacy database schema items to achieve a smooth translation from a legacy to a newer generation data model.

To demonstrate the use of the ISMGs in the process of schema transformation and query execution we assume that we are dealing with a legacy relational database schema based on the EU-rent car rental case study. This sample database schema is described by means of the UML formalism shown in Figure 6.3. This figure illustrates the situation where EU-Rent cars are sold to clients who keep an account with the company. Accounts can be of two types: loan and credit card accounts. Each account can be operated upon by means of one or more transactions. Transactions also comprise two types: branch and adjustment transactions. For reasons of brevity only some illustrative attributes are shown in Figure 6.3. Figure 6.4 illustrates the relational database schema which corresponds to the UML representation in Figure 6.3.

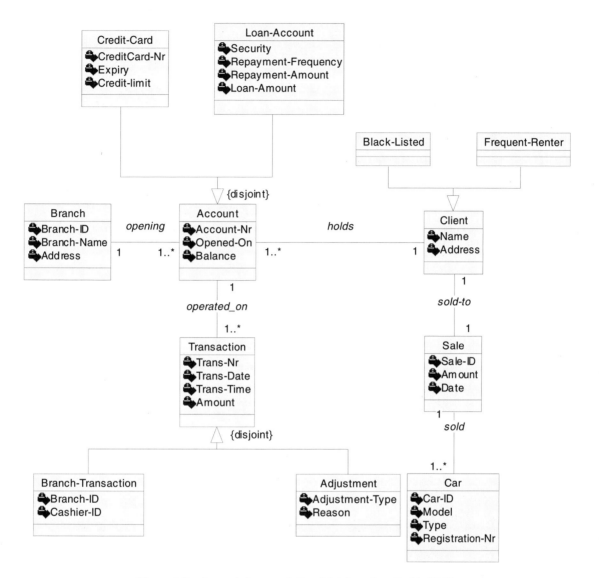

Figure 6.3   A sample legacy relational database described in UML.

For reasons of brevity we depict only that part of the schema that is related to sales accounts.

The elements of the ADCs fall into three broad categories which abstractly define any data model: *DATA-CONSTRUCTS*, *LINKS* and *CONSTRAINTS*. At the conceptual level these elements are independent of the underlying technology with which a database model is implemented and are hence directly applicable to a variety of data models. They constitute the basis for the construction of the description for a given data model.

```
CREATE TABLE CLIENT
(client_id CHAR(10) NOT NULL, name VARCHAR(30) NOT NULL,
 address VARCHAR(30) NOT NULL, city VARCHAR(10),  state VARCHAR(3) NOT NULL,
postcode CHAR(4) NOT NULL, bonus_pts INTEGER NOT NULL,
 work_phone VARCHAR(10), home_phone VARCHAR(10));

CREATE TABLE ACCOUNT
(account_nr CHAR(10) NOT NULL,  account_name VARCHAR(30) NOT NULL,
 opened_on DATE NOT NULL,  type CHAR(6), balance INTEGER);

CREATE TABLE LOAN_ACCOUNT
(account_nr CHAR(10) NOT NULL, security VARCHAR(30) NOT NULL,
 valuation INTEGER NOT NULL, valuation_date DATE NOT NULL,
 repayment_freq CHAR(1) NOT NULL, repayment_amt INTEGER NOT NULL,
 loan_amount INTEGER NOT NULL);

CREATE TABLE CREDIT_CARD_ACCOUNT
(account_nr CHAR(10) NOT NULL, credit_card_nr CHAR(16) NOT NULL,
 expiry DATE NOT NULL, card_name VARCHAR(30) NOT NULL,
 credit_limit INTEGER NOT NULL);

CREATE TABLE BRANCH
(branch_id CHAR(4) NOT NULL, branch_name CHAR(20) NOT NULL,
 address VARCHAR(40) NOT NULL, city VARCHAR(10), state VARCHAR(3) NOT NULL,
         postcode VARCHAR(4) NOT NULL, phone VARCHAR(10), fax VARCHAR(10));

CREATE TABLE OPENING
(account_nr CHAR(10) NOT NULL, branch_id CHAR(4) NOT NULL);

CREATE TABLE TRANSACTION
(transaction_nr CHAR(15) NOT NULL, account_nr CHAR(10) NOT NULL,
 trans_date DATE, trans_time CHAR(6), amount INTEGER);

CREATE TABLE BRANCH_TRANSACTION
(transaction_nr CHAR(15) NOT NULL, branch_id CHAR(4) NOT NULL,
 cashier_id CHAR(8) NOT NULL, workstation_id VARCHAR(10) NOT NULL);

CREATE TABLE ADJUSTMENT
(transaction_nr CHAR(15) NOT NULL, adjustment_type CHAR(3) NOT NULL,
 reason VARCHAR(30) NOT NULL);

CREATE TABLE HOLDS_ACCOUNT
(client_id CHAR(10) NOT NULL, account_nr CHAR(10) NOT NULL);
```

Figure 6.4 Relational legacy database schema.

6.4.1.1   Data Constructs

Data constructs represent discrete primitive types such as string, integer, real or boolean, or a complex type defined by applying (tuple) or (set) constructors on existing fundamental types. We structure these primitive types into *principal* entities which can be of three categories:

Strong Kernel: Strong kernel entities are independent entities with a set of related immediate properties pertinent to a distinct object or concept. For example the entity Account is a strong kernel, see the relational schema in Figure 6.4.

Weak Kernel: An entity is called a weak kernel if its sole purpose is to qualify or further describe a "superior" kernel entity, and it is existence dependent on the entity it qualifies. For example, a Loan-Account may only be identified if an Account is known, hence it is a weak entity.

   Both strong and weak kernel entities may have super/subtype relationships between them.

Association: An association is an entity which defines a relationship between two or more kernel entities. An association is always existence dependent on the kernel entities which it inter-links. For example, consider the entity Holds_Account which associates entities of type Account with entities of type Client.

6.4.1.2   Links

LINKS describe forms of connection between principal entities and are essentially of two types:

inheritance-links: These types of links represent a sub-typing relationship between two constructs. For example, the entities Account and Loan-Account are is-a related.

referential-links: These types of links connect two independent data constructs. They are normally implemented as pointers in the o-o world, and as value-based references in the relational world. For example, the attribute client_id of the entity Holds_Account is a referential link to the entity Client. Referential-links can be further specialized into *existence-links*. This type of link represents an existence reference between a referencing and a referenced data construct.

6.4.1.3   Constraints

The bulk of semantic clarity in the translation process relates to identification and characterization of constraints. Constraints are applied either on attributes or links to enhance the semantic information about the data model elements to which they apply. Constraints can be of various types such as single-valued, multi-valued, mandatory, i.e., non-null, existential, association constraints, i.e., cardinality, inclusion constraints, and enumeration type constraints. Single-valued and multi-valued constraints are conventional forms of constraints that apply equally to both attributes

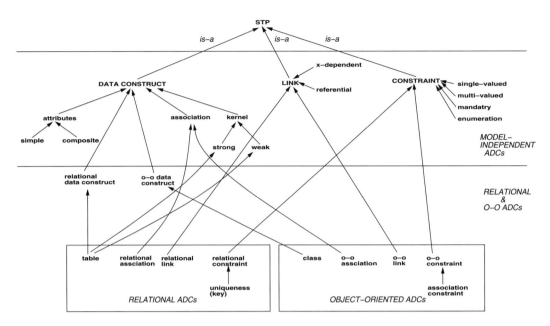

Figure 6.5   The STP abstract descriptor class hierarchy.

as well as data constructs. Mandatory constraints require that an attribute has a non-null value or reference. For example, the attribute name of the entity Client is a single-valued mandatory, non-repeating attribute. Association constraints are related to association data constructs in the o-o data model and require that at least two existence dependency references exist to kernel objects. Finally, enumeration type constraints specify a set of permissible values for a particular data item.

6.4.2   The Abstract Descriptor Class Hierarchy

The three types of constructs outline above, are represented as a collection of meta-level classes in the form of a directed acyclic graph (DAG) Figure 6.5. This graph comprises the abstract data model parts of the STP. More specifically, this figure shows the constructs, viz. ADCs, of two ADMs which capture specific characteristics of the o-o and relational data models. The STP DAG differentiates between constructs which are semantically similar, yet syntactically diverse, in both these models and the ones that are specific to each of them. Thus it can distinguish between a number of typical modeling constructs on a model by model basis. The DAG nodes comprise the ADCs that denote model specific representations of the three broad model-independent categories of *DATA-CONSTRUCTS*, *LINKS* and *CON-STRAINTS*. A schema in the relational model is thus represented as instantiations of the relational ADCs in the DAG. In particular, the relational data model can be represented as an instantiation of a handful of ADCs including: Strong/Weak Kernel and Association Meta-classes; Attribute and Reference Meta-classes; Is-a and Constraint Meta-classes. Behavioral transformations require use of the Meta-Class procedure which is not shown in Figure 6.5.

In the following subsection we concentrate on identifying the o-o constructs derived from relation specifications and determining key and inclusion constraints.

6.4.3   Deriving Abstract Descriptor Classes for a Relational Database

The actual process of ISMG construction is based on a heuristic graph traversal algorithm which maps elements of an enriched relational schema to ISMG meta-objects (ADC instantiations). To produce an ISMG for a relational schema the algorithm takes into account relations, primary key information, foreign-key constraints and sub-classing relationships, determines the type of relationships which exist between constructs, and then instantiates the appropriate ADCs (16). Figure 6.6 illustrates a relational ISMG for the schema in Figure 6.4. Arrows in this figure indicate containment and reference connections between the nodes (constructs) in the ISMG. Figure 6.6 shows only simplified portions of the ADCs generated for the state part of the (enriched) relational schema depicted in Figure 6.4. For example, in Figure 6.6 we have collapsed constraint ADCs within the ADC to which they apply. An example of the behavior part of the relational ISMG is given in Section 6.4.4.2.

The process of generating an ISMG representation for a given relational schema, such as the one depicted in Figure 6.4, is incremental and may require refinements, e.g., in cases where it is difficult to discriminate between associations and subclass relationships. This task is part of the the schema conversion phase in Figure 6.2. ISMG generation is comprised of the following six main steps conducted in sequence:

RI1: *Identify attributes and references:* This step assumes that we have identified all relations in a schema. However, at this stage relations are still not characterized as strong/weak. ADCs are used here to represent various kinds of attributes. A reference node is an attribute node indicating that an attribute is part of some foreign key connection. An existence dependent node is a reference node based on a mandatory attribute such as a primary key, e.g., the reference account_nr of the weak kernel Transaction.

RI2: *Identify primary and foreign key information for each relation:* This is a relatively simple task for most schemas as all of the required information is typically held centrally in the data dictionary for the schema. If this information is not stored with the schema, then it will be necessary either to infer it or request it from a domain expert (17). The existence of a foreign key indicates a reference relationship between the two relations involved. In such a situation, we represent the source attributes involved in the foreign key with a reference meta-object in the ISMG. The reference meta-object links the kernel meta-object representing the source relation to the kernel meta-object representing the target relation and includes details of the constraints

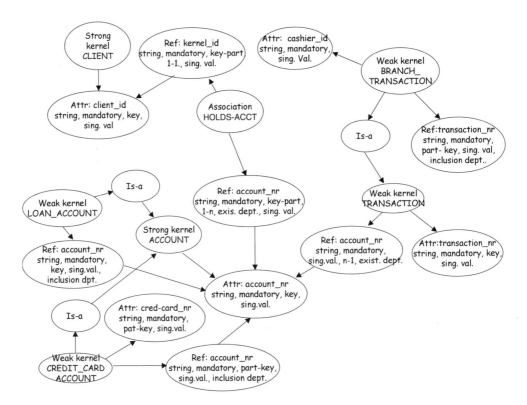

Figure 6.6   Intermediate meta-graph specification for the relational schema in Figure 6.4.

which apply to the reference, see Figure 6.6. Existent dependent links within a relational schema can be identified by non-null (mandatory) foreign key references and are represented in the same manner as references in the ISMG.

RI3: *Determine kernels:* once the primary/foreign key and reference connections have been established the type of relations that we are dealing with can be determined. A strong kernel meta-object is generated in the ISMG for each strong relation in the schema. A strong relation is one which is not existence dependent on another relation via a foreign key connection. A weak kernel meta-object is generated in the ISMG for each weak relation in the schema. A weak relation is one which is existence dependent on another relation via a foreign key connection.

RI4: *Identify inheritance relationships:* Subclass relationships in a relational schema are typically indicated by the existence of foreign key linkages between two relations where the foreign key attributes in each relation operate over the same domain. The foreign key reference is 1-1 and implies an existence dependency between the two relations. This issue involves detection of inclusion dependencies for key attribute values and is discussed at length in (17). Where a subclass relationship is identified, it is represented by an *is-a* meta-object in the ISMG which links the relevant kernels and associations, see Figure 6.6.

RI5: *Identify associations:* All remaining relations which have keys which are not $is - a$ related and include foreign key references to other relations and are existence dependent on these references, represent associations. They are represented by association meta-objects in the ISMG for the schema, see Figure 6.6.

RI6: *Identify procedures:* We assume that the procedure is the behavioral construct within the relational data model. Procedures can be found in application programs that operate on the database schema and data. These may take the form described in the following:

procedure Name ($arg_1 : type_1, arg_2 : type_2, \ldots, arg_n: type_n$): *return-type*

The actual information stored in the corresponding ADC is analogous to that captured by the Procedure meta-class shown below:

metaclass Procedure
    Name : Name
    ReturnType : Domain
    Parameters : $\mathcal{P}$ Argument

The actual process of capturing this information within an ADC is relatively simple where it is available. If the information cannot be directly determined from the schema or application program, then it will need extracted from a domain expert.

6.4.4   Transformation Rules

The transformation rules that follow illustrate the mapping of a relational ISMG to an equivalent o-o database schema. This part follows the ISMG construction sub-phase in the schema conversion phase of Figure 6.2. Their purpose is to support *incremental* relational to o-o schema transformation and subsequent query translation. The actual transformation process is accomplished effectively "through" the ADCs for the source relational schema, as the collection of the relevant semantic information occurs during the initial ISMG construction. The two aspects of the transformation process that are considered are:

1. transformation of structural schema constructs such as attributes, relations and associations to equivalent o-o schema constructs;
2. transformation of behavioral constructs, in the case of the relational model, relational procedures to their o-o equivalents.

6.4.4.1   *Transformation of Structural Relational Schema Constructs*

The transformation process consists of the five following steps:

ROT1: *Identify o-o classes:* This rule results in generating *anchor classes* from strong kernel relations. An anchor class is the outermost class in a configuration of nested classes. First, the anchor class is created directly from its corresponding strong kernel meta-object by including the same types of attributes (see steps $ROT2$ and $ROT3$). Because anchor classes contain dependent classes, e.g., nested classes, we must then identify all classes that are existent dependent on the newly created anchor class. For this purpose we identify all the dependent (weak) relation meta-objects that include the key of the strong kernel relation (represented as an anchor object) as a foreign key. For each such dependent relation we generate a class and establish a reference between the anchor and this class, e.g., Client and Account, (see also $ROT3$). In this case a one to many relationship indicates that the relation on the many side of the relationship is represented as a set of objects nested within another class.

In general, each of the strong kernel meta-objects in the relational ISMG generates an o-o class. However, not all of the weak kernel and association meta-objects will result in the creation of an o-o class. Only weak kernel and association meta-objects which contain attributes that do not participate in a foreign key connection with other meta-objects may result in o-o classes. The algorithms for class identification and for transformation of relational ISMGs to objects, in general, are described in detail in (20).

ROT2: *Identify class attributes:* All of the attribute meta-objects within the ISMG generate attributes in the o-o schema, except for those which are also represented by reference meta-objects. These are mapped to o-o pointer attributes.

ROT3: *Identify references:* Within the relational ISMG, foreign keys are represented by reference meta-objects. These are mapped to pointer attributes in the o-o schema. Association meta-objects within the relational ISMG which do not have any associated attributes and contain precisely two foreign key references can be represented by set-valued pointers within the o-o schema.

The Holds.account_nr attribute is an example of a foreign key which is transformed into a pointer based reference through application of this rule. It retains the same naming structure within the o-o class but its typing changes from that of the Account.account_nr attribute which it references to become a pointer to an Account object, i.e., Account*.

ROT4: *Identify subclass hierarchy:* The hierarchy is easily determined by examination of the *is-a* meta-objects identified in the ISMG for the relational schema. Here one must simply convert the relational *is-a* references to an appropriate object representation. Such meta-objects indicate inclusion dependencies between the keys of two relations. Consider for example the two meta-objects Credit-Card and Account in Figure 6.6. As can be seen from this figure and Figure 6.4, the relation Credit-Card has a composite key comprising the two attributes credit-card_nr and account_nr. The following property holds for the keys of these two meta-objects: $Credit - Card[account\_nr] \subseteq Account[account\_nr]$. This signifies that the key value of every tuple in the Credit-Card relation is included in the Account relation.

The final step within this transformation rule is to deal with the problem alluded to previously, that of removing attributes from class definitions where they are inherited from super-classes. Once the sub-typing relationship has been identified between Credit-Card and Account, it is possible to remove the Credit-Card.account_nr attribute from the class to which Credit-Card is mapped since the account_nr reference is accessible from the superclass Account via inheritance.

In summary, application of each of the aforementioned rules to the schema in Figure 6.4 would yield the o-o schema depicted in Figure 6.7.

6.4.4.2   Transformation of Behavioral Relational Constructs

The behavioral aspects of a schema are not considered as part of the relational model, although most mainstream relational DBMS platforms include the notion of an application program or procedure in order to simplify the interfaces to a relational schema. Instead of of translating application program code and procedures to equivalent query expressions which are attached to new (shadow) classes (28) we concentrate on mapping relational API signatures to o-o method signatures. The use of relational APIs is a common way of fully specifying the behavioral requirements of a relational system. By adopting the API as a generic behavioral construct, we will be able to provide a framework with which to tackle the issues associated with legacy system conversion as the program unit is a construct which is common to all database environments. In addition, by facilitating transformation of behavioral constructs in the form of APIs, we will also be addressing the issues involved in providing dynamic linkages between heterogeneous database systems, a key legacy systems conversion problem.

The transformation of a relational procedure to an o-o method in the STP approach is simplistic in nature as it requires minimal restructuring of the ADC meta-information other than appropriate handling of the binding class. Information about the class where the resulting method is bound requires manual intervention by a database administrator.

Consider the following relational procedure which calculates the amount required to pay-out a loan as at a nominated date:

```
CALCULATE _PAYOUT(account_nr: varchar(8), payout_date: date): integer
```

This procedure would be represented by the simplified ISMG portion (see Figure 6.8) which depicts only behavioral aspect of the relational schema in Figure 6.4. Translation of this procedure would result in the following o-o method signature:

```
class LOAN_ACCOUNT {
  ...
  int CALCULATE _PAYOUT(char payout_date[6]);
  ...
}
```

Essentially, the o-o method signature is identical to the relational procedure signature, except that any attributes in the principal metaclass to which the method is

```
class CLIENT
{
char client_id[10];
char name[30];   char address[30];   char city[10];
char state[3];   char postcode[4]; int bonus_pts;
char work_phone[10];   char home_phone[10];
os_Set<ACCOUNT*> * holds_account;
};


class ACCOUNT
{
char account_nr[10];   char account_name[30];
char opened_on[6];   char type[6];   int balance;
};


class LOAN_ACCOUNT : ACCOUNT
{
char security[30];   int  loan_amount;
char repayment_freq; int repayment_amt;
};


class CREDIT_CARD_ACCOUNT : ACCOUNT
{
char card_nr[16];   char expiry[6];   char card_name[30];   int credit_limit;
}


class BRANCH
{
char branch_id[4];   char branch_name[20]; char address[40];
char city[10];   char state[3];   char postcode[4];
char phone[10];   char fax[10];   os_Set<BRANCH*> * opening_account;
};


class TRANSACTION
{
char transaction_nr[15];
ACCOUNT *account_nr;
char trans_date[6];   char trans_time[6];   int amount;
};


class BRANCH_TRANSACTION : TRANSACTION
{
BRANCH *branch_id;   char cashier_id[8]; char workstation_id[10];
};


class ADJUSTMENT : TRANSACTION
{
char adjustment_type[3];   char reason[30];
};
```

Figure 6.7   O-O schema equivalent of relational schema of Figure 6.4.

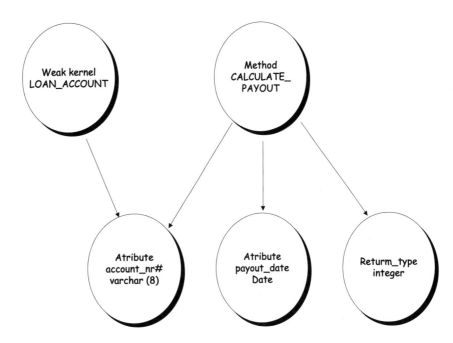

Figure 6.8   Intermediate meta-graph specification for transforming a relational procedure.

bound are omitted. In this case, the method is bound to the Loan_Account class, therefore the account_nr parameter is omitted from the o-o method signature, as it is already accessible to the method upon invocation and does not need to be explicitly passed to it. The other parameter - payout_date - is included in the method signature although its type is modified during the transformation process to one which is supported by the o-o schema. The return type for the method is unchanged.

6.5   Data Language Translation

To access data stored in legacy relational database systems, once they are available in the form of wrapped objects, an object-oriented data language must be utilized. In this chapter, o-o queries are assumed to be framed in a format analogous to the ObjectStore query formalism (14) which essentially takes the form of directed path statements within the o-o schema embedded within procedural source code as required. The actual query statements are assumed to have the following generic format:

query_result = $class_i$[: $condition_1$
    (($\&\&$) | ($\|$)) $condition_2$ . . .
    ($\&\&$) | ($\|$)) $condition_n$)
:];

where *query_result* is the set of elements within *class*$_i$ that satisfy the logical boolean conditions *condition*$_1$ to *condition*$_n$.

The content of *query_result* is determined by evaluating a series of path conditions based on *class*$_i$. Because of the inherent requirement that all properties and restrictions of the query must be based on path connectivity, the power of o-o query formalisms is significantly restricted and many operations which could be handled within frameworks such as relational query languages, e.g., summing the values of a particular attribute for each of the objects within a class, require the introduction of additional procedural code in order to enable the query to be processed. In this section, we only consider the transformation of the o-o query formalism described above.

6.5.1   O-O to Relational Query Translation

The process of o-o to relational query transformation occurs during the data language translation phase as shown in Figure 6.2. More specifically, o-o query transformation occurs in three parts:

1. the source classes in the query are transformed; then
2. the path expressions in the query are transformed; and finally
3. the relational query is constructed.

Each of these steps relates the o-o schema classes to their equivalent ISMG meta-objects and then transforms these to relations. This process is essentially the inverse of what we have presented in sections 6.4.3 and 6.4.4 and is accomplished on the basis of of information stored in the appropriate ISMG meta-objects during the transformation of the relational ISMG meta-objects to o-o schema classes. Subsequently, the remainder of the o-o query is transformed to an equivalent relational expression. To illustrate the transformation process, we utilize the following query and assume the database schema described in Figure 6.7.

os_Set<CLIENT> *selected_clients*;

selected_clients = *CLIENT*[:
    (*city* = 'London') &&
    (*holds_account.type* = 'Loan')&&
    (*holds_account.loan_amount* > 250000) :];

The above query returns selected client objects that are based in London, have a loan account with the EU-rent car rental company, and currently owe the company 250KECUs.

6.5.1.1   *Transforming the Source Classes*

As can be seen from examination of this query three main classes are involved: Client, Account and Loan_Account. These o-o classes have originated from the relational

ISMG classes Client, Account and Loan_Account during the application of the transformation rules, see Section 6.4.4. Mapping these o-o classes back to their relational counter equivalents is a relatively easy process.

6.5.1.2   Transforming the Path Expressions

In order to transform a path expression in an o-o query, it is necessary to find an equivalent path within the relational portion of the ISMG. This ensures that the attributes are accessible from the anchor relation which is implied by the original o-o query (anchor class selection is discussed in Section 6.4.4).

There are three path expressions in the o-o query which must be transformed. These are:

city = 'London'
holds_account.type = 'L'
holds_account.loan_amount > 250000

Each of these path expressions are relative to the anchor class Client in the o-o schema. An equivalent Client relation exists within the relational model for the Client class, therefore it is only necessary to ensure that equivalent attributes exist in the relational ISMG and that they are accessible from the Client relation. To facilitate understanding of this process we illustrate the relational paths identified in the o-o query of Figure 6.9.

Consider the holds_account.type path expression first, the attribute type is attached to the Account class within the o-o schema, see Figure 6.7. An equivalent type attribute exists within the relational schema and is attached to the Account relation. This attribute, however, is not directly accessible from the Client relation, see Figure 6.4. To make it reachable, it is necessary to construct the appropriate relational join conditions to create a path through the relational schema which is equivalent to the original path expression. This is achieved by systematic examination of the paths expressions in the relational ISMG, see Figure 6.9. This figure reveals how the relations in Figure 6.4 need to be joined to generate an equivalent relational expression. The paths indicate that the three relations Client, Account and Hold_Account need to be joined to generate an equivalent expression. The final path expression *holds.loan_amount* > 250000 is slightly more complicated to replicate than the first two expressions. This is a consequence of the fact that the corresponding loan_amount attribute in the o-o schema is relative to the Loan_Account subclass of the Account relation. As we have already explained in Section 6.4.4.1 subtype relations always share a common key with their super-type relation, thus the appropriate equi-join condition for the relational query would be:

ACCOUNT.account_nr = LOAN_ACCOUNT.account_nr

The restriction clause required to replicate this path expression is

LOAN_ACCOUNT.loan_amount > 250000

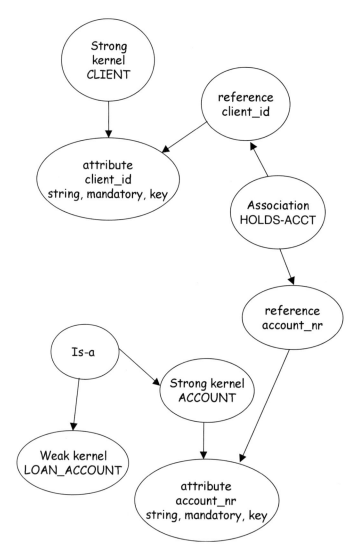

Figure 6.9 Intermediate meta-graph specification for the relational constructs in an o-o query.

6.5.1.3 Constructing the Query

Once the path expressions have been analyzed and transformed, construction of the relational query occurs in three parts:

1. determine the attributes in the select-clause;

2. determine the relations in the from-clause;

3. determine the contents of the where-clause.

As the o-o query is based on a single o-o class, the contents of the select clause are simply a list of the attributes in the relational schema which are equivalent to the attributes in the original o-o class depicted in Figure 6.7. The list of relations in the from clause is constructed from the list of relations to which the classes in the original o-o query map along with any other relations required to create the necessary joins within the relational schema. In this case the list of relations is: Client, Holds_Account, Account, Loan_Account. The conditions contained in the where-clause is simply the conjunction of the conditions identified by traversing the relational ISMG involving the relations and constructs identified in the o-o query posed in Section 6.5.1, see Figure 6.9. Thus the final relational query is:

```
select CLIENT.account_nr,CLIENT.account_name,
    CLIENT.client_id,CLIENT.name, CLIENT.address, CLIENT.city,
    CLIENT.state, CLIENT.postcode, CLIENT.bonus_pts, CLIENT.home_phone
from CLIENT, HOLDS_ACCOUNT, ACCOUNT, LOAN_ACCOUNT,
where   CLIENT.client_id = HOLDS_ACCOUNT.client_id
    and    ACCOUNT.account_nr = HOLDS_ACCOUNT.account_nr
    and ACCOUNT.account_nr = LOAN_ACCOUNT.account_nr
    and LOAN_ACCOUNT.loan_amount > 250000
    and CLIENT.city = 'London'
    and ACCOUNT.type = 'L'
```

6.5.2   Transactions and Statements Involving Methods

Translation statements combine the techniques we employed to translate o-o queries to equivalent relational queries with translation algorithms that address the peculiaritie of deletion/update issues. In the following we consider a simple o-o transaction statement involving updating some of the client details and will show how it translates to an equivalent SQL statement. This statement is similar to deletion statements in ObjectStore. Transforming the ObjectStore procedure into an equivalent SQL statement involves four steps:

1. Determine which relational ISMG meta-object the class in the update statement maps to.

2. Locate the modifier methods for each of the attributes changed within the update statement for this class.

3. Determine how the modifier methods are mapped to equivalent SQL statements by means of the o-o to relational statement transformation rules.

4. Locate all relations which satisfy the condition specified in the ObjectStore statement.

5. Update each of them in turn.

Consider the following ObjectStore update statement:

```
do_transaction() {

    os_Set<CLIENT *> clients;

  clients = (*CLIENT::extent)
      [: !strcmp(name,"Mike Jones") :];

  foreach(CLIENT *client_ptr, clients)
      client_ptr->set_bonus-pts(2000);
}
```

In order to construct an SQL statement which achieves the same function, we first need to locate the relevant modifier methods for the bonus-pts attribute. The o-o attribute has the modifier method set_creditpts associated with it which takes the new rating as a parameter. This indicates that we are dealing with an update statement. The required functionality is thus achieved by the following SQL statement after executing the five steps identified above.

```
update CLIENT
set bonus-pts = 2000
where name = "Mike Jones"
```

6.6   Summary

In this chapter we have described an access in place solution for building object-oriented applications that access legacy relational data and functionality. This approach is based on the use of abstraction mechanisms and a semantically-oriented protocol that provide intermediate abstract constructs supporting the coexistence of diverse data models such as the relational and object-oriented. The mapping process is performed in two steps: first by expressing the structures and semantics underlying the relational model into a series of intermediate meta-classes and then by using these meta-classes in conjunction with a set of translation rules to map relational schemas and queries/transactions to semantically equivalent o-o schemas and data language expressions. These meta-classes are capable of enriching semantically poor data models (such as the relational) so that they can explicitly represent abstractions found in more powerful models.

Currently, extension of the STP approach is underway in the area of behavioral mappings between relational procedure signatures and o-o method signatures. In particular, we concentrate on developing algorithms that will determine the automatic placement (binding) of relational application program API services (procedures) to o-o schema classes on the basis of information provided by the relational ISMGs. Some of the techniques covered in (28) seem to lend themselves for this purpose.

References

1. P.H. Aiken "Reverse Engineering of Data", in IBM Systems journal, vol. 37, no. 2, 1998.

2. S. Abinavam et al. (1998). *San Francisco Concepts & Facilities*. International Technical Support Organization, IBM, February 1998.

3. R.C. Aronica and D.E. Rimel Jr. (1996). *Wrapping your Legacy Systems*. Datamation, vol.42, nr.12 (June 15), pp. 83-88

4. P. Atzeni, R. Torlone. A Mctamodel Approach for the Management of Multiple Models and the Translation of Schemes. *Information Systems*, 18:6, June 1993.

5. T. Barsalou and D. Gangopadhyay, "M(DM): An Open Framework for Interoperation of Multimodel Multidatabase Systems", *Proceedings of the IEEE Data Engineering Conference*, 1992.

6. D. Baum (1993) *Tools for Fast, Easy Access to Legacy Data* Datamation, vol. 39 (1993), nr. 11 (June 01), pp. 75-76

7. O. Bukhres, A. Elmagarmid (eds), "Object-Oriented Multidatabase Systems" *Prentice-Hall Int'l*, 1996.

8. M. Castellanos, "Semantic Enrichment of Interoperable Databases", in Proceedings, RIDE-IMS 1993.

9. D. Diskin "Legacy System Wrapping for DOD Information System Modernization", Defense Information Systems Agency, 1996.

10. J. Hammer, D. McLeod. An Approach to Resolving Semantic Heterogeneity in a Federation of Autonomous, Heterogeneous Database Systems. *Journal of Cooperative Information Systems*, 2:1, March 1993.

11. S. Hong, F. Maryanski. Using a Metamodel to Represent Object-Oriented Data Models. *Proceeding of the Sixth International Conference on Data Engineering*, 1990.

12. P. Johanneson "A Method for Translating Relational Schemas into Conceptual Schemas", *Procs. 10th Int'l Conf. on Data Engineering*, Houston-Texas, February 1994.

13. D.A. Keim, H.P. Kriegel and A. Miethsam, "Integration of Relational Databases in a Multidatabase System based on Schema Enrichment", in RIDE-IMS 1993.

14. ObjectStore Reference Manual, Release 3.0, Object Design, October 1995.

15. Orfali, R. and Harkey, D. and Edwards, J. (1994). *Essential Client/Server Survival Guide*. Van Nostrand Reinhold, New York.

16. M. Papazoglou, N. Russell "A Semantic Meta-Modeling Approach to Schema Transformation" *Int'l Conf. on Information and Knowledge Management CIKM-95*, Baltimore, Maryland, 1995.

17. M. Papazoglou, Z. Tari, N. Russell "Object-oriented Technology for Inter-schema and Language Mappings", in Object-Oriented Multidatabase Systems, A. Elmagarmid, O. Bukhres (eds), *Prentice-Hall*, forthcoming, 1995.

18. M.P.Papazoglou, N. Russell, D. Edmond "A Translation Protocol Achieving Consensus of Semantics between Cooperating Heterogeneous Database System", *1996 Int'l Conf. on Cooperative Information Systems*, Brussels, June 1996.

19. W. Pemerlani, M. Blaha "An Approach for Reverse Engineering of Relational Databases", *CACM*, 37(5), May 1994.

20. N. Russell "Interoperability Protocols for Heterogeneous and Legacy Database Systems", *Master's thesis*, Queensland Univ. of Technology, May 1996.

21. F. Saltor, M.G. Castellanos and M. Garcia-Solaco, "Overcoming Schematic Discrepancies in Interoperable Databases", Proceedings, IFIP WG 2.6, DS5, Semantics of Interoperable Database Systems, Lorne, Victoria, November 1992.

22. J. Siegel (1996). *Corba Fundamentals and Programming*. John Wiley & Sons, New York.

23. M. Siegel and S.E. Madnick, "A Metadata Approach to Resolving Semantic Conflicts", VLDB-17, 1991.

24. A. Taylor *JDBC: Developer's Recourse* Prentice Hall, NJ, 1997

25. M.J. Tucker (1997). *Bridge your Legacy Systems to the Web*. Datamation, vol.43, nr.3 (March), pp. 114-121

26. A. Umar *Object-Oriented Client/Server Internet Environments* Prentice-Hall, Publishing Co. 1997.

27. S. Urban "A Semantic Framework for Heterogeneous Database Environments", *Procs. 1st Int'l Workshop on Interoperability in Multidatabase Systems*, pp. 156-163, April 1991.

28. M. Vermeer "Semantic interoperability for Legacy Databases", PhD thesis, Center for Telematics and Information Technology, Univ. of Twente, Oct. 1997.

III Temporal and Dynamic Modeling

7 Temporally Enhanced Database Design

Christian S. Jensen
Department of Computer Science
Aalborg University
Fredrik Bajers Vej 7E
DK–9220 Aalborg Ø, Denmark
csj@cs.auc.dk

Richard T. Snodgrass
Department of Computer Science
University of Arizona
Tucson, AZ 85721, USA
rts@cs.arizona.edu

The design of appropriate database schemas is critical to the effective use of database technology and the construction of effective information systems that exploit this technology. The temporal aspects of database schemas are often particularly complex and thus difficult and error-prone to design. This chapter focuses on the temporal aspects of database schemas. Its contributions are two-fold. First, a comprehensive set of concepts are presented that capture temporal aspects of schemas. Second, the use of these concepts for database design is explored.

The chapter first generalizes conventional functional dependencies to apply to temporal databases, leading to temporal keys and normal forms. Time patterns identify when attributes change values and when the changes are recorded in the database. Lifespans describe when attributes have values. The temporal support and precision of attributes indicate the temporal aspects that are relevant for the attributes and with what temporal granularity the aspects are to be recorded. And derivation functions describe how the values of an attribute for all times within its lifespan are computed from stored values. The implications of these concepts for database design, of both relational and object-oriented schemas, are explored.

7.1 Introduction

The design of appropriate database schemas is crucial to the effective use of database technology and the construction of information systems that exploit this technology. The process of appropriately capturing the temporal aspects of the modeled reality in the database schema—be it based on, e.g., the relational model or an object-oriented model—is complex and error prone, and the resulting schemas are often overly difficult to understand. With a focus on the temporal aspects of database schemas, this chapter explores the technical foundation for simplifying the conceptual design process.

More than a dozen temporal object-oriented data models have been proposed (38). How to apply database design techniques to schemas in these models is still largely an open problem. The particular data model chosen impacts the manner in which object-oriented schemas are designed. As a natural first approach, this chapter provides a foundation for applying the well-developed relational database design theory to these models. To render the relational design concepts relevant to these various temporal object-oriented data models, this chapter extends these concepts to a temporal relational model, with the application to a particular temporal object-oriented model left as a subsequent task. This application is necessarily highly dependent on the temporal object-oriented model chosen; we exemplify this mapping for a simple object-oriented model, but space limitations prevent more comprehensive coverage. Using the relational model as the basis for this chapter enables the approach to be applicable to the entire spectrum of temporal object-oriented models, while remaining independent of the idiosyncrasies of any particular model.

Specifically, the chapter proposes to separate the design of conceptual database schemas for time-oriented applications into two stages. In the first stage, the underlying temporal aspects are ignored, resulting in the design of simple, single-state (so-called non-temporal) schemas. In the second stage, these initial schemas are annotated with their temporal aspects. These annotations may imply further decomposition of the annotated schemas, leading to the final conceptual schema.

The chapter focuses on the second stage, and begins with a non-temporal database schema. The chapter's contributions are two-fold. First, a comprehensive set of temporal properties that may be used for annotation are defined and illustrated. Second, the use of these properties is explored. Specifically, new guidelines for how the annotations should result in decomposition of the schemas are defined, and their use is explored. The subsequent mapping of annotated, decomposed schemas to implementation platforms is beyond the scope of this chapter.

The chapter is structured as follows. Section 7.2 introduces conceptual temporal relations that may capture the valid time and the transaction time of the stored tuples. These are needed because the non-temporal relation schemas upon annotation may reveal themselves to be temporal. Then, the assumed design process is outlined in order to describe the context of this chapter's topic. At the end, the car rental case that will be used for illustration throughout is introduced.

Section 7.3 reviews how to extend conventional normalization concepts to apply to temporal relations, leading to temporal keys and normal forms. It then argues that the properties of attributes are relative to the objects they describe and thus introduces surrogates for representing real-world objects in the model. The following subsections address in turn different aspects of time-varying attributes, namely lifespans, time patterns, derivation functions, temporal support, and temporal precision. Lifespans describe when attributes have values; time patterns identify when attributes change values and when the changes are recorded in the database; derivation functions describe how the values of an attribute for all times within its lifespan are computed from stored values; and the temporal support and precision of attributes indicate the temporal aspects that are relevant for the attributes and with which temporal granularity the aspects are to be recorded.

Section 7.4, on decomposition guidelines, is devoted to the implications of the temporal properties for conceptual database design. Section 7.5 surveys other approaches to temporally enhanced database design. The final section summarizes and points to opportunities for further research.

7.2   Temporal Database Design—Overview and Context

This section sets the context for discussing temporally enhanced database design. Specifically, we first adopt a particular model of time itself, then add time to conventional relations to yield the conceptual temporal relations employed in the chapter. We also define essential algebraic operators on the temporal relations. A description of the database design process follows, and the section ends with an introduction of the car rental case.

7.2.1   Modeling and Representing Time

Most physicists perceive the *real* time line as being bounded, the lower bound being the Big Bang (which is believed to have occurred approximately 14 billion years ago) and the and upper bound being the Big Crunch. There is no general agreement as to whether the real time line is continuous or discrete, but there is general agreement in the temporal database community that a discrete *model* of time is adequate.

Consequently, our model of the real time line is that of a finite sequence of *chronons* (19). In mathematical terms, this is isomorphic to a finite sequence of natural numbers (20). The sequence of chronons may be thought of as representing a partitioning of the real time line into equal-sized, indivisible segments. Thus, chronons are thought of as representing time segments such as femtoseconds or seconds, depending on the particular data processing needs. Real-world time instants are assumed to be much smaller than chronons and are represented in the model by the chronons during which they occur. We will use c, possibly indexed, to denote a chronon.

A time interval is defined as the time between two instants, a starting and a terminating instant. A time interval is then represented by a sequence of consecutive chronons where each chronon represent all instances that occurred during the chronon. We may also represent a sequence of chronons simply by the pair of the starting and terminating chronon. The restriction that the starting instant must be before the ending instant is necessary for the definition to be meaningful in situations where an interval is represented by, e.g., a pair of identical chronons. Unions of intervals are termed *temporal elements* (14).

7.2.2   Temporal Database Schemas

Two temporal aspects are of general relevance to data recorded in a database. To capture the time-varying nature of data, time values from two orthogonal time domains, namely valid time and transaction time, are associated with the tuples in a bitemporal conceptual relation instance. Valid time captures the time-varying nature of the portion of reality being modeled, and transaction time models the update activity associated with the database.

For both time domains, we employ the model of time outlined in the previous section. The domain of valid times is given as $\mathcal{D}_{VT} = \{c_1^v, c_2^v, \ldots, c_k^v\}$, and the domain of transaction times may be given as $\mathcal{D}_{TT} = \{c_1^t, c_2^t, \ldots, c_j^t\}$. A valid-time chronon c^v is thus a member of $\mathcal{D}_{VT}$, a transaction-time chronon c^t is a member of $\mathcal{D}_{TT}$, and a bitemporal chronon $c^b = (c^t, c^v)$ is an ordered pair of a transaction-time chronon and a valid-time chronon.

Next, we define a set of names, $\mathcal{D}_A = \{A_1, A_2, \ldots, A_{n_A}\}$, for explicit attributes and a set of domains for these attributes, $\mathcal{D}_D = \{D_1, D_2, \ldots, D_{n_D}\}$. For these domains, we use $\perp_i$, $\perp_u$, and $\perp$ as inapplicable, unknown, and inapplicable-or-unknown null values, respectively (see, e.g., (1)). We also assume that a domain of surrogates is included among these domains. Surrogates are system-generated unique identifiers, the values of which cannot be seen, but only compared for identity (17). Surrogate values are used for representing real-world objects. With the preceding definitions, the schema of a bitemporal conceptual relation, R, consists of an arbitrary number, e.g., n, of explicit attributes from $\mathcal{D}_A$ with domains in $\mathcal{D}_D$, and an implicit timestamp attribute, T, with domain $2^{(\mathcal{D}_{TT} \cup \{UC\}) \times \mathcal{D}_{VT}}$. Here, UC ("until changed") is a special transaction-time marker. A value (UC, c^v) in a timestamp for a tuple indicates that the tuple being valid at time c^v is current in the database. The example below elaborates on this.

A set of bitemporal functional (and multivalued) dependencies on the explicit attributes are part of the schema. For now, we ignore these dependencies—they are treated in detail later.

A tuple $x = (a_1, a_2, \ldots, a_n \mid t^b)$, in a bitemporal conceptual relation instance, $r(R)$, consists of a number of attribute values associated with a bitemporal timestamp value. For convenience, we will employ the term "fact" to denote the information recorded or encoded by a tuple.

An arbitrary subset of the domain of valid times is associated with each tuple, meaning that the fact recorded by the tuple is *true in the modeled reality* during each valid-time chronon in the subset. Each individual valid-time chronon of a single tuple has associated a subset of the domain of transaction times, meaning that the fact, valid during the particular chronon, is *current in the relation* during each of the transaction-time chronons in the subset. Any subset of transaction times less than the current time and including the value UC may be associated with a valid time. Notice that while the definition of a bitemporal chronon is symmetric, this explanation is asymmetric. This asymmetry reflects the different semantics of transaction and valid time.

We have thus seen that a tuple has associated a set of so-called *bitemporal chronons* in the two-dimensional space spanned by transaction time and valid time. Such a set is termed a *bitemporal element* (19) and is denoted t^b. Because no two

CuID	Name	Address	Rating	T
007	Leslie	Birch Street	Preferred	$\{(5,5), \ldots, (5,20), \ldots, (9,5), \ldots, (9,20)\}$
007	Leslie	Elm Street	Preferred	$\{(5,21), \ldots, (5,30), \ldots, (25,21), \ldots,$ $(25,30), (UC,21), \ldots, (UC,30)\}$
007	Leslie	Beech Street	Preferred	$\{(10,5), \ldots, (10,20), \ldots, (25,5), \ldots,$ $(25,20), (UC,5), \ldots, (UC,20)\}$

Figure 7.1   A Bitemporal Conceptual Relation

tuples with mutually identical explicit attribute values (termed *value-equivalent*) are allowed in a bitemporal relation instance, the full history of a fact is contained in a single tuple.

Example 7.1

Consider a bitemporal relation recording information about the customers in a rental car company. The schema has these explicit attributes:

```
Customer = (CuID, Name, Address, Rating)
```

Each customer has a unique customer id, CuID, a name, and an address. Also, a rating is maintained that records the value of the customer to the company. This rating is used for preferential customer treatment.

In this example, we assume that the granularity of chronons is one day for both valid time and transaction time, and the period of interest is some given month in a given year, e.g., January 1995. Throughout, we use integers as timestamp components. The reader may informally think of these integers as dates, e.g., the integer 15 in a timestamp represents the date January 15, 1995. The current time is assumed to be 25 (i.e., *now* = 25).

Figure 7.1 shows an instance, customer, of this relation schema. The special value *UC* in the relation signify that the given tuple is still current in the database and that new chronons will be added to the timestamps as time passes and until the tuple is logically deleted.

The relation shows the employment information for Leslie, a preferred customer. On time 5, it is recorded that Leslie's address will be Birch Street, from time 5 to time 20, and Elm Street, from time 21 to time 30. Subsequently, it was discovered that Leslie's address was not Birch Street, but rather Beech Street, from time 5 to time 20. As a result, on time 10, the information about Birch Street was (logically) deleted, and the correct information was inserted.

Depending on the extent of decomposition, a tuple in a bitemporal relation may be thought of as encoding an atomic or a composite fact. We simply use the terminology that a tuple encodes a fact and that a bitemporal relation instance is a collection of (bitemporal) facts.

Valid-time relations and transaction-time relations are special cases of bitemporal relations that support only valid time or transaction time, respectively. Sets of valid-time and transaction-time chronons are termed *valid-time* and *transaction-time elements* and are denoted by t^v and t^t, respectively.

The remainder of the chapter will show how to extend existing normalization and decomposition theory to apply to temporal relations such as that shown in Figure 7.1.

Example 7.2

As an aside, we now exemplify how this approach may be further extended to apply to a temporal object-oriented data model, in this example, a very simple one. We use an object-oriented model in which each tuple of Figure 7.1 is modeled as a separate object, so in this case we have three distinct objects, each with its own identity. This Customer object type has four attributes, CuID, Name, Address, and Rating, as well as an implicit bitemporal element indicating the temporal extent of the object instance. Note that these three objects in the class shown in Figure 7.1 all provide information about the same customer, Leslie.

Now, applying the decomposition approach introduced later in this chapter may replace this object type with new object types, each with a subset of the attributes, and each with an implicit valid-time, transaction-time or bitemporal element. This chapter will give the rules by which these new object types can be configured, to avoid anomalies and redundancy implicit in the original object type.

Note that more complex temporal object-oriented models may also benefit from such decomposition, though the benefits and specifics of applying these decompositions vary from model to model. Hence, the remainder of this chapter will be in terms of the relational model, leaving it to the reader to reformulate these decompositions in terms of the temporal object-oriented model of their choice.

7.2.3 Associated Algebraic Operators

We have so far described the database structures in the bitemporal conceptual data model—relations of tuples timestamped with bitemporal elements. We now define some algebraic operators on these structures that will be used later. A complete algebra is defined elsewhere (36).

Define a relation schema $R = (A_1, \ldots, A_n | T)$, and let r be an instance of this schema. We will use A as a shorthand for all attributes A_i of R. Let D be an arbitrary set of explicit (i.e., non-timestamp) attributes of relation schema R. The projection on D of r, $\pi_D^B(r)$, is defined as follows.

$$\pi_D^B(r) = \{z^{(|D|+1)} \mid \exists x \in r(z[D] = x[D]) \land \forall y \in r(y[D] = z[D] \Rightarrow y[T] \subseteq z[T]) \land$$
$$\forall t \in z[T] \exists y \in r(y[D] = z[D] \land t \in y[T])\}$$

The first line ensures that no chronon in any value-equivalent tuple of r is left unaccounted for, and the second line ensures that no spurious chronons are introduced.

Let P be a predicate defined on A. The selection P on r, $\sigma_P^B(r)$, is defined as follows.

$$\sigma_P^B(r) = \{z \mid z \in r \land P(z[A])\}$$

As can be seen from the definition, $\sigma^B_P(r)$ simply performs the familiar snapshot selection, with the addition that each selected tuple carries along its timestamp T.

Finally, we define two operators that select on valid time and transaction time. Unlike the previous operators, they have no counterparts in the snapshot relational algebra. Let c^v denote an arbitrary valid-time chronon and let c^t denote a transaction-time chronon. The *valid-timeslice* operator (τ^B) yields a transaction-time relation; the *transaction-timeslice* operator (ρ^B) evaluates to a valid-time relation[1].

$$\tau^B c^v(r) = \{z^{(n+1)} \mid \exists x \in r(z[A] = x[A] \land z[T] = \{c^t \mid (c^t, c^v) \in x[T]\} \land z[T] \neq \emptyset)\}$$

$$\rho^B c^t(r) = \{z^{(n+1)} \mid \exists x \in r(z[A] = x[A] \land z[T] = \{c^v \mid (c^t, c^b) \in x[T]\} \land z[T] \neq \emptyset)\}$$

Thus, $\tau^B c^v(r)$ simply returns all tuples in r that were valid during the valid-time chronon c^v. The timestamp of a returned tuple is all transaction-time chronons associated with c^v. Next, $\rho^B c^t(r)$ performs the same operation except the selection is performed on the transaction time c^t.

Example 7.3

Consider the `customer` relation shown in Figure 7.1. The following result is produced by $\tau^B 25(\text{customer})$.

CuID	Name	Address	Rating	T
007	Leslie	Elm Street	Preferred	$\{5, \ldots, 25\}$

This says that at transaction time 5 we stored this information, and this information is still current (at time 25). The valid-timeslice operator selects all tuples with a timestamp that contains a chronon that has the argument chronon as its second component. The timestamp of result tuples contain those transaction-time chronons that were associated with the argument valid-time chronon.

The similar operators for valid-time and transaction-time relations are simpler special cases and are omitted for brevity. We will use superscripts "T" and "V" for the transaction and valid-time counterparts, respectively.

To extract from r the tuples valid at time c^v and current in the database during c^t (termed a *snapshot* of r), either $\tau^V_{c^v}(\rho^B_{c^t}(r))$ or $\rho^T_{c^t}(\tau^B c^v(r))$ may be used; these two expressions evaluate to the same snapshot relation.

7.2.4 Overview of the Design Process

The topics considered in this chapter are displayed in their data modeling context in Figure 7.2 and are discussed in the following.

We assume that an atemporal database schema is initially produced. This database schema consists of atemporal versions of the conceptual-relation schemas described

---

1. Operator ρ was originally termed the *rollback* operator, hence the choice of symbol.

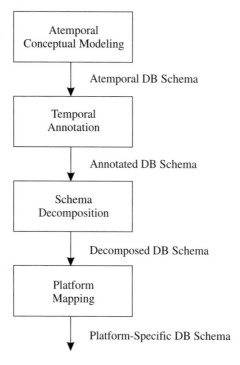

Figure 7.2   Data Modeling Context

earlier in this section. The database schema is atemporal in the sense that all temporal aspects related to valid and transaction time of the relation schemas are simply ignored—or left unspecified. These atemporal relation schemas may also be thought of as primitive object types: Each instance of an object type, i.e., each object (or tuple), has an ID (a surrogate) that is independent of its state, and the state is described solely using single-valued attribute values with domains defined by built-in types.

A wide range of design approaches may be employed to produce the initial atemporal database schema—no assumptions are made.

In the next step, the relation schemas, or primitive object-type schemas, are annotated with temporal properties, to be defined in the next section. Following the annotation, the schema description is complete. The subsequent step is then to apply decomposition guidelines, to be defined in Section 7.4, to the schemas, leading to a decomposed conceptual database schema, with genuine temporal relation schemas as defined earlier. This database schema may subsequently be mapped to various implementation platforms, e.g., SQL–92 (30), SQL3, or TSQL2 (39).

It is an underlying rationale that the database is to be managed by a relational, or temporal-relational, DBMS that employs tuple timestamping. Indeed, increasingly many databases are being managed by relational DBMSs; and these systems, in addition to most temporal relational prototype DBMSs, employ tuple timestamping.

```
Branch = (BrID, Name, Location, Manager, AssistantMgr, Capacity)
Car = (CarID, Branch, Model, Make, Category, Year, Mileage, LastServiced)
Customer = (CuID, Name, Address, Rating)
RentalBooking = (RBID, Branch, Category, Customer, Price, CreditCardNo,
                 CardType)
```

Figure 7.3   Car Rental Schema

Hence, the decomposition that maps the atemporal database schema to a decomposed, tuple-timestamped temporal database schema is an important component of a design framework. Specifically, this decomposed temporal database schema provides an attractive starting point for mapping the database schema to the database schema of a specific DBMS (such as CA Ingres, DB2, Informix, Microsoft, Oracle, or Sybase). It is attractive because the "conceptual distance" to the various DBMS schemas is small.

Throughout, we will use the car rental case for exemplification.

7.2.5   Example—Car Rentals

Figure 7.3 describes the car rental database schema that will be annotated with temporal properties and decomposed in the next two sections. The aspects of the schema that are not self-explanatory are described briefly next. Branches have `Manager` and `Location` attributes. The `Capacity` attribute indicates the maximum number of cars a branch is able to manage. A car belongs to a specific branch, so attribute `Branch` is a foreign key referencing table `Branch`. The `Customer` relation was introduced in Example 7.1. When a car rental is booked, the booking is for a specific branch and car category (e.g., Economy, Compact, Mid-size). It is made by a customer who is quoted a certain price, and the customer made the reservation using a credit card.

7.3   Temporal Properties of Data

The schema just presented is atemporal; there is no mention of time-varying values. The following sections will discuss how this schema is elaborated and decomposed when time is considered. But first we examine conventional functional dependencies, which will be subsequently applied to time-varying relations.

7.3.1   Functional Dependencies

Functional dependencies play a central role in conventional database design and should also do so in our framework. In our framework, we initially design a nontemporal database schema and ignore the issues of valid and transaction time. Thus, different attributes in the same initial schema may have different requirements with respect to temporal support; for example, some attributes may require valid-time support while other attributes do not.

As background for considering temporal functional dependencies, we next state the notion of a functional dependency for conventional (snapshot) relations.

Definition 7.1

Let a relation schema R be defined as $R = (A_1, A_2, \ldots, A_n)$, and let X and Y be sets of attributes of R. The set Y is *functionally dependent* on the set X, denoted $X \rightarrow Y$, if for all meaningful instances r of R,

$$\forall s_1, s_2 \in r (s_1[X] = s_2[X] \Rightarrow s_1[Y] = s_2[Y]).$$

If $X \rightarrow Y$, we say that X *determines* Y.

A functional dependency constrains the set of possible extensions of a relation. Which functional dependencies are applicable to a schema reflects the reality being modeled and the intended use of the database. Determining the relevant functional dependencies is a primary task of the database designer.

7.3.2　Temporal Functional Dependencies

Generalizations of conventional dependencies make it meaningful to apply dependencies to the initial schemas, similarly to how dependencies are applied in conventional normalization. The designer's use of the dependencies is not affected by the attributes' particular levels of temporal support.

7.3.2.1　*Generalizing Functional Dependencies to Temporal Relations*

In database design, functional dependencies are *intensional*, i.e., they apply to every possible extension. This intuitive notion already encompasses time, for a functional dependency may be interpreted as applying at any time in reality and for any stored state of the relation.

To be specific, consider the restricted case of a transaction-time relation r, with schema $R = (A_1, \ldots, A_n | \mathrm{T})$, and a parallel snapshot relation r' with the same schema (but without the implicit timestamp attribute), i.e., $R' = (A_1, \ldots, A_n)$. The current state of r, denoted by $\rho_{now}^{\mathrm{T}}(r)$, where "*now*" denotes the current time, will faithfully track the current state of r'. Past states of r' will be retained in r, and can be extracted via $\rho_t^{\mathrm{T}}(r)$, with "t" being the desired past point in time. A functional dependency on R' will hold for all possible extensions, and hence for all past states of r'. Hence, the same functional dependency must hold for all snapshots of r (this insight first appeared over a decade ago (4)). A similar argument can be applied to valid-time relations and to bitemporal relations, yielding the following characterization (22).

Definition 7.2

Let X and Y be sets of non-timestamp attributes of a bitemporal relation schema R. A *temporal functional dependency*, denoted $X \xrightarrow{\mathrm{T}} Y$, exists on R if for all meaningful instance *r* of *R*,

$$\forall c^v, c^t \forall s_1, s_2 \in \tau^V c^v (\rho^B c^t(r))(s_1[X] = s_2[X] \Rightarrow s_1[Y] = s_2[Y]).$$

In the definition of a temporal functional dependency, a temporal relation is perceived as a collection of snapshot relations. Each such snapshot of any extension must satisfy the corresponding functional dependency.

The parallel between conventional functional dependencies and temporal functional dependencies means that inference rules such as Armstrong's axioms have close temporal counterparts that play the same role in the temporal context as do the non-temporal rules in the non-temporal context. Next, we can also define temporal keys (22). For example, the explicit attributes *X* of a temporal relation schema *R* form a *(temporal) key* if $X \xrightarrow{T} R$. Finally, we can generalize snapshot normal forms in a similar manner.

Example 7.4

These are some of the dependencies that hold in the rental car database schema (this schema was shown in Figure 7.3):

```
In Branch:    Name  ⟶ᵀ  Location Manager AssistantMgr Capacity
In Car:       CarID ⟶ᵀ  Branch Model Make Category Year Mileage
                         LastServiced
In Customer: CuID  ⟶ᵀ  Rating
              CuID Address ⟶ᵀ  Name
```

In table `Customer`, attribute `CuID` determines `Rating`, but because the same customer may have several names and addresses at a time, `CuID` does not determine `Name` and `Address`. Attributes `CuID` and `Address` together determine `Name` because customers have only one `Name` associated with each of their possible several addresses. Note that in table `Branch`, `Name` (and also `BrID`) is a key, as is `CarID` in schema `Car`.

Definition 7.3

A pair (R, F) of a temporal relation schema *R* and a set of associated temporal functional dependencies *F* is in *temporal Boyce-Codd normal form* (TBCNF) if

$$\forall X \xrightarrow{T} Y \in F^+ (Y \subseteq X \vee X \xrightarrow{T} R).$$

Definition 7.4

A pair (R, F) of a temporal relation schema *R* and a set of associated temporal functional dependencies *F* is in *temporal third normal form* (T3NF) if for all non-trivial temporal functional dependencies $X \xrightarrow{T} Y$ in F^+, *X* is a temporal super-key for *R* or each attribute of *Y* is part of a minimal temporal key of *R*.

In a similar fashion, it is possible to devise temporal variants of other well-known dependencies (e.g., multi-valued and join) and normal forms (e.g., fourth and fifth normal forms). Similarly, the notions of lossless-join and dependency-preserving decomposition can be naturally extended to temporal relations. Furthermore, one can define temporal variants of conventional integrity constraints involving uniqueness, referential integrity, and subset and cardinality constraints.

To illustrate, we define foreign key constraints. Let bitemporal schemas R and S have explicit attributes $A_1, A_2, \ldots, A_n$ and $B_1, B_2, \ldots, B_m$, respectively. Attributes X of S is a foreign key referencing attributes Y of R if X and Y have the same number of attributes, if the attributes of X and Y are pair-wise compatible, and if for all meaningful instances r of R and s of S,

$$\forall c^v, c^t (\pi_X^B(\tau_{c^v}^B(\rho_{c^t}^B(s))) \subseteq \pi_Y^B(\tau_{c^v}^B(\rho_{c^t}^B(r)))).$$

If both R and S do not support valid or transaction time, the corresponding timeslice operations are simply omitted in the subset condition above. If only one of R and S supports valid time then the valid-timeslice operation with time argument *NOW* is applied to that relation. The same applies to transaction time. For example, if R supports only transaction time and S supports only valid time, the condition becomes $\pi_X^B(\tau^B NOW(s)) \subseteq \pi_Y^B(\rho^B NOW(r))$.

Example 7.5

In the rental car database schema, all relation schemas are in TBCNF, with the exception of schema `Customer` where non-trivial dependency $\text{CuID} \xrightarrow{\text{T}} \text{Rating}$ violated the requirement that the left-hand side must be a superkey. To bring the database schema to TBCNF, `Customer` is thus decomposed into two schemas.

```
CustomerAddr = (CuID, Name, Address)
CustomerRating = (CuID, Rating)
```

Here, `CuID` of `CustomerRating` would be declared as a foreign key referencing `CuID` of `CustomerAddr`.

7.3.2.2 *Strong Temporal Functional Dependencies*

The temporal dependencies we have seen thus far apply snapshot dependencies to individual snapshots in isolation. Thus, these dependencies are not capable of capturing the relative variation over time of attribute values. So while we were able to capture dependencies such as a salary attribute (at any time) being determined by an employee-name attribute, we cannot capture that a salary of an employee does not change within a month, or never changes. These latter constraints require looking at more than one time point to determine if the constraint is satisfied by a particular relation instance. This distinction has previously been captured more generally with the terms *intrastate* and *interstate* integrity constraints (3).

While a temporal dependency holds if the corresponding conventional dependency holds for each snapshot in isolation, we now "bundle" tuples of certain snapshots and require the corresponding snapshot dependency to hold for each "bundle" in isolation. A "bundle" is defined to contain all tuples in all valid timeslices of the result obtained from applying a single transaction timeslice operation to a meaningful bitemporal database instance of the schema under consideration. This is stated more precisely below.

Definition 7.5
Let X and Y be sets of non-timestamp attributes of a bitemporal relation schema R. A *strong temporal functional dependency*, denoted $X \xrightarrow{\text{Str}} Y$, exists on R if for all meaningful instances r of R,

$$\forall c^t, c^v_x, c^v_y \forall s_1 \in \tau^{\text{B}}_{c^v_x}(\rho^{\text{B}}_{c^t}(r)) \forall s_2 \in \tau^{\text{B}}_{c^v_y}(\rho^{\text{B}}_{c^t}(r))(s_1[X] = s_2[X] \Rightarrow s_1[Y] = s_2[Y]).$$

Strong temporal dependencies are useful in part because they have a practical and intuitive interpretation. Specifically, if $X \xrightarrow{\text{Str}} Y$ holds on a relation schema, this means that Y does not vary with respect to X.

Example 7.6
In the rental car schema, there are several strong dependencies, e.g., the following.

```
In Car:            CarID  ⟶Str  Model Make Category Year
In RentalBooking:  RBID   ⟶Str  Branch Category Customer Price
                                 CreditCardNo CardType
```

Strong temporal normal forms and integrity constraints can be analogously defined.

In the strong temporal dependency $X \xrightarrow{\text{Str}} Y$, attributes X may vary more often than attributes Y, but X must change when Y changes.

Definition 7.6
Let X and Y be sets of non-timestamp attributes of a bitemporal relation schema R. A *strong temporal equivalence*, denoted $X \xleftrightarrow{\text{Str}} Y$, exists on R if $X \xrightarrow{\text{Str}} Y$ and $Y \xrightarrow{\text{Str}} X$.

Intuitively, $X \xleftrightarrow{\text{Str}} Y$ means that the sets of attributes X and Y change values simultaneously, and are thus synchronous. We return to this issue in Section 7.4.4.

It is possible to take these notions of dependencies even further, as has subsequently been done by Wang and his colleagues (45) and by Wijsen (46). Wang et al. generalized strong dependencies to dependencies that were along a spectrum between our temporal functional dependencies, which apply to individual timeslices, and strong functional dependencies, which apply to all timeslices at once. Specifically, they define a functional dependency for each available *granularity* (e.g., second, week, year), and require that the equality holds only during a unit of the granularity. Next, Wijsen has recently developed a normalization theory for valid-time databases that includes three types of temporal dependencies. Two correspond to our temporal dependency and strong temporal dependency. The third dependency is in-between the two. This so-called *dynamic dependency* holds if the corresponding snapshot dependency holds on the unions of all pairs of consecutive snapshots.

7.3.3 Using Surrogates

An attribute is seen in the context of a particular real-world entity. Thus, when we talk about a property, e.g., the frequency of change, of an attribute, that property is only meaningful when the attribute is associated with a particular entity. As an example, the frequency of change of a salary attribute with respect to a specific employee in a company may reasonably be expected to be relatively regular, and there will only be at most one salary for the employee at each point in time. In contrast, if the salary is with respect to a department, a significantly different pattern of change may be expected. There will generally be many salaries associated with a department at a single point in time. Hence, it is essential to identify the reference object when discussing the semantics of an attribute.

We employ surrogates for representing real-world entities in the database. In this regard, we follow the approach adopted in, e.g., the TEER model by Elmasri (11). Surrogates do not vary over time in the sense that two entities identified by identical surrogates are the same entity, and two entities identified by different surrogates are different entities. We assume the presence of surrogate attributes during the design process. Just prior to performing the implementation-platform mapping, surrogate attributes may be either (a) retained, (b) replaced by regular (key) attributes, or (c) eliminated.

Example 7.7
In our database schema, we add a surrogate to each of the (now) six tables. For example, we add a surrogate for branches, BrSur, to table Branch and a surrogate for cars, CarSur, to table Car.

Definition 7.7
Let X be a set of non-timestamp attributes of a bitemporal relation schema R with surrogate attribute S. Then X is said to be *time invariant* if $S \xrightarrow{\text{Str}} X$.

Because it is assumed that different entities are represented by different surrogates and the same entity always is represented by the same surrogate, this is a rather natural definition of *time invariant* attributes. By combining standard temporal dependency and strong temporal dependency, the notion of a time-invariant key (which had previously been used with a different meaning (31)) results.

Definition 7.8
Let X be a set of non-timestamp attributes of a bitemporal relation schema R with surrogate attribute S. Then X is termed a *time-invariant key (TIK)* if $S \xrightarrow{\text{Str}} X$ and $X \xrightarrow{\text{T}} R$.

The first requirement to attributes X is that they be time invariant. The second is that they be a temporal key. In combination, the requirements amount to saying that X is a key with values that do not change (with respect to the surrogate attribute).

Example 7.8

For schema `Branch`, we have seen that `Name` and `BrID` are keys. Because `BrSur` strongly determines only `BrID`, and not `Name`, `BrID` is a time-invariant key. The intuition is that a branch may change name, but not its `BrID` value. In schema `RentalBooking`, we have that $RBSur \xrightarrow{\text{Str}} RBID$, so as we have seen that `RBID` is a key, `RBID` is also a time-invariant key. Surrogates such as `BrSur` and `RBSur` in relations with a time-invariant key are eliminated from the schema.

7.3.4   Lifespans of Individual Time-Varying Attributes

In database design, one is interested in the interactions among the attributes of the relation schemas that make up the database.

Here, we provide a basis for relating the lifespans of attributes. Intuitively, the lifespan of an attribute for a specific object is all the times when the object has a value, distinct from $\perp_i$, inapplicable null, for the attribute. Note that lifespans concern valid time, i.e., are about the times when there exist some valid values.

To more precisely define lifespans, we first define an auxiliary function **vte** that takes as argument a valid-time relation r and returns the valid-time element defined by $\textbf{vte}(r) = \{c^v \mid \exists s(s \in r \land c^v \in s[\text{T}])\}$. The result valid-time element is thus the union of all valid timestamps of the tuples in an argument valid-time relation.

Definition 7.9

Let a relation schema $R = (S, A_1, \ldots, A_n \mid \text{T})$ be given, where S is surrogate valued, and let r be an instance of R. The *lifespan* for an attribute A_i, $i = 1, \ldots, n$, with respect to a value s of S in r is denoted $\textbf{ls}(r, A_i, s)$ and is defined by $\textbf{ls}(r, A_i, s) = \textbf{vte}(\sigma^{\text{B}}_{S=s \land A \neq \perp_i}(r))$.

Lifespans are important because attributes are guaranteed to not have any inapplicable null value during their lifespans.

Inapplicable nulls may occur in a relation schema when two attributes have different lifespans for the same object/surrogate. To identify this type of situation, we introduce the notion of lifespan equal attributes.

Definition 7.10

Let a relation schema $R = (S, A_1, \ldots, A_n \mid \text{T})$ be given where S is surrogate valued. Two attributes A_i and A_j in R are termed *lifespan equal* with respect to surrogate S, denoted $A_i \stackrel{\text{LS}}{=}_S A_j$, if for all meaningful instances r of R, $\forall s \in \text{dom}(S)(\textbf{ls}(r, A_i, s) = \textbf{ls}(r, A_j, s))$.

Example 7.9

In schema `Car`, all attributes are mutually lifespan equal: values exist for all attributes when a car is first registered at a branch, and meaningful values persist for all attributes.

All branches have a manager, but small branches have no assistant manager. Thus, some branches only get a meaningful value for attribute `AssistantMgr` after having reached a certain capacity. This means that `AssistantMgr` is not lifespan equal to the other attributes, e.g., `Manager` and `Capacity`.

The importance of lifespans in temporal databases has been recognized in the context of data models in the past (cf. (6, 5, 11)). Our use of lifespans for database design differs from the use of lifespans in database instances. In particular, using lifespans during database design does not imply any need for storing lifespans in the database.

7.3.5 Time Patterns of Individual Time-Varying Attributes

In order to capture how an attribute varies over time, we introduce the concept of a *time pattern*. Informally, a time pattern is simply a sequence of times.

Definition 7.11
The *time pattern* T is a partial function from the natural numbers $\mathcal{N}$ to a domain $\mathcal{D}_T$ of times: $T : \mathcal{N} \hookrightarrow \mathcal{D}_T$. If $T(i)$ is defined, so is $T(j)$ for all $j < i$. We term $T(i)$ the i'th time point.

In the context of databases, two distinct types of time patterns are of particular interest, namely observation patterns and update patterns. The *observation pattern* O_A^s, for an attribute A relative to a particular surrogate s, is the times when the attribute is given a particular value, perhaps as a result of an observation (e.g., if the attribute is sampled), a prediction, or an estimation. We adopt the convention that $O_A^s(0)$ is the time when it was first meaningful for attribute A to have a value for the surrogate s. Observation patterns concern valid time. The observation pattern may be expected to be closely related to, but distinct from, the actual (possibly unknown) pattern of change of the attribute in the modeled reality. The *update pattern* U_A^s is the times when the value of the attribute is updated in the database. Thus, update patterns concern transaction time.

Note that an attribute may not actually change value at a time point because it may be the case that the existing and new values are the same. The times when changes take place and the resulting values are orthogonal aspects.

We may use time patterns to capture precisely the synchronism of attributes. To this end, define $T|_t$ to be the restriction of time pattern T to the valid-time element t, that is, to include only those times also contained in t.

Definition 7.12
Define relation schema $R = (S, A_1, \ldots, A_n \mid \mathrm{T})$ where S is surrogate valued. Two attributes A_i and A_j in R, with observation patterns $O_{A_i}^S$ and $O_{A_j}^S$, are *synchronous* with respect to S, denoted $A_i \underset{S}{\triangleq} A_j$, if for all meaningful instances r of R and for all surrogates s,

$$O_{A_i}^S|_{\mathsf{ls}(r,A_i,s) \cap \mathsf{ls}(r,A_j,s)} = O_{A_j}^S|_{\mathsf{ls}(r,A_i,s) \cap \mathsf{ls}(r,A_j,s)}.$$

Thus, attributes are synchronous if their lifespans are identical when restricted to the intersection of their lifespans.

Example 7.10
In schema `Car`, attributes `Branch`, `Model`, `Make`, `Category`, and `Year` are synchronous (if ownerships of cars often shift among branches, `Branch` would not be considered synchronous with the four other attributes). Each of attributes `Mileage` and `LastServiced` not synchronous with other attributes in the schema. `Mileage` is updated when a car is returned, and `LastServiced` is updated when a car is serviced (which occurs less frequently!).

In schema `RentalBooking`, values for all attributes are provided when a booking is made and are not subsequently updated. Thus, all attributes in this schema are synchronous.

7.3.6   The Values of Individual Time-Varying Attributes

We proceed by considering how attributes may encode information about the objects they describe. As the encoding of the transaction time of attributes is typically built into the data model, we consider only valid-time relations.

A relation may record directly when a particular attribute value is valid. Alternatively, what value is true at a certain point in time may be computed from the recorded values. In either case, the relation is considered a valid-time relation.

Definition 7.13
A *derivation function* f is a partial function from the domains of valid times $\mathcal{D}_{VT}$ and relation instances r with schema R to a value domain D in the universal set of domains $\mathcal{D}_D$, i.e., $f : \mathcal{D}_{VT} \times r(R) \hookrightarrow D$.

Example 7.11
The `Mileage` attribute of `Car` has associated two derivation functions. One function interpolates recorded mileage values for cars so that a value may be provided for all times. Among other uses, this function is used to project future mileage when scheduling maintenance for the cars. The other derivation function is the discrete derivation function that does not manufacture any information, but only provides mileage values for the times when they are actually recorded.

The importance of derivation functions in data models has previously been argued convincingly by, e.g., Klopprogge and Lockemann (25), Clifford and Crocker (6) and Segev and Shoshani (35).

7.3.7   Temporal Support of Attributes

During database design, a model of a part of reality is created. What aspects of the modeled reality to capture and what to leave out is determined by the functional requirements to the application being created. The application may require any combination of valid-time and transaction-time support, or no temporal support, for each of the time-varying attributes.

Next, attributes may be either state-based or event-based. Values of state-based attributes are valid for durations of time while values of event-based attributes are valid only for instants in time.

Combining these alternatives, there are six possibilities for the temporal support required for a time-varying attribute.

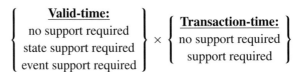

Example 7.12

In schema `CustomerAddr`, support for neither valid nor transaction time is required. In `CustomerRating`, valid-time state support is required for the `Rating` attribute. In schema `RentalBooking`, we require both valid-time-state and transaction-time support for all attributes. The valid time records when the booking is for, and old bookings are to be retained. In schema `Car`, attribute `Mileage` requires valid-time-event support and transaction-time support. The remaining attributes require only transaction-time support.

7.3.8   Temporal Precision of Attributes

Each time-varying attribute has an associated observation pattern, as discussed in Section 7.3.5. A time pattern is a function to a time domain, that has an associated time granularity. The granularity is the precision in which the time-variance is recorded. If a hiring decision occurred sometime during the business day, but it is not known exactly when (i.e., what minute or hour) the decision occurred, then it is inappropriate to store that fact with a timestamp at a minute granularity. The reason is that a particular minute must be chosen, and that minute is probably incorrect, with the implication that the model is incorrect (7).

This property of time-varying attributes is important for database design because temporal relational data models and query languages are frequently based on the (sometimes implicit) assumption that all time-varying attributes of a relation may be recorded with the same precision. For example, in tuple timestamped models, the time-variance of all attribute values is recorded with a single timestamp attribute (or the same set of timestamp attributes).

One approach is to use the minimum granularity of the DBMS at the precision of all relations. As just discussed, this results in a low-fidelity model of reality. A better approach is to choose the most appropriate granularity for each relation. We propose a simple strategy. First, each attribute is associated with a set of granularities. The smallest granularity in this set is the granularity in which the time-variance of the attribute is known. Other, coarser granularities represent granularities which are acceptable to the applications utilizing the relation. Then the relation is decomposed only if there is not a common granularity that is a member of the granularity sets of all attributes.

Example 7.13

In schema `Car`, values for `Mileage` must be recorded with a precision of minutes. The granularity of hours is too coarse because a car may change its mileage within the same hour, which should be possible to record. Bookings of rentals must be recorded by the minute or second. Thus, the attributes of `RentalBooking` have minute and second as their acceptable granularities.

7.3.9   Summary of Attribute Semantics

In summary, the database designer is expected to initially annotate the relation schemas using (regular and strong temporal) dependencies. Then surrogates are used for the modeling of entity types. The notions of lifespans, time patterns, and derivation functions are used for capturing the semantics of attributes, and the temporal support and precision of the attributes are recorded.

Below, we summarize the tasks of the database designer. The designer starts with a set of atemporal conceptual relation schemas in hand. To annotate these schemas with temporal properties, the indicated tasks are performed.

1. *Identify entity types and represent them with surrogate attributes.* The real-world objects (or entities) that the attributes of the database describe are represented with surrogate attributes. Here, time-invariant keys are also identified.

2. *Determine the required temporal support.* For each attribute, indicate the required temporal support for the attribute. Record the interactions (if any) between the valid time and the transaction time implied by the temporal specializations in effect for the attribute.

3. *Describe precisions.* For each time-varying attribute, indicate its set of applicable granularities.

4. *Describe lifespans.* For each relation schema, describe the lifespans of the attributes.

5. *Determine observation and update patterns.* For each relation schema, indicate which attributes are synchronous, i.e., share observation and update patterns.

6. *For each attribute, indicate its appropriate derivation or interpolation function(s).* The functions concern interpolation in valid-time, and there may be several functions per attribute.

7. *Specify temporal functional dependencies on the schemas.* This includes the identification of (primary) keys.

8. *Specify strong temporal functional dependencies.*

7.4   Decomposition Guidelines

In this section, we discuss how the properties of schemas with time-varying attributes as captured in the previous section are used during database design. Emphasis is on the use of the properties for schema decomposition. In addition, issues relevant to the related aspects of view and physical design are touched upon as well.

Database designers are faced with a number of design criteria which are typically conflicting, making database design a challenging task. So, while we discuss certain design criteria in isolation, it is understood that there may be additional criteria that should also be taken into consideration (e.g., good join performance).

Two important goals are to eliminate the use of inapplicable nulls and to avoid the repetition of information. Additionally, the conceptual model employed poses constraints on what attributes that may reside in the same relation schema. We formulate decomposition guidelines that address these concerns.

7.4.1   Normal Form Decomposition

With the introduction of temporal functional dependencies, it is possible to apply conventional normalization theory to our conceptual relations. Thus, dependencies are indicated, satisfaction of normal forms is tested, and relation schemas are decomposed where necessary.

With the introduction of strong temporal functional dependencies and surrogates, it became possible to distinguish between time-varying keys and time-invariant keys, where the latter may serve the purposes of surrogates.

7.4.2   Temporal Support and Precision Decomposition Rules

The characterization of attributes according to the temporal support they require is important for database design because the conceptual data model permits only one type of temporal support in a single relation (as do also temporal implementation data models). We embed this requirement in a simple decomposition rule.

Definition 7.14(Temporal Support Decomposition Rule.)
To achieve the correct temporal support of time-varying attributes, decompose temporal relation schemas to have only attributes with the same temporal support requirements in the same schema, except for the surrogate attribute(s) forming the primary key.

Example 7.14
Schema `Car` must be decomposed. Specifically, attribute `Mileage` is removed from the schema, and a new schema, `CarMileage`, with attributes `CarID` and `Mileage` is introduced.

It may be possible to avoid such decomposition in certain circumstances, but the designer should be aware of the potential drawbacks of doing so. Consider including an attribute S requiring snapshot support together with an attribute T requiring transaction-time support, in a transaction-time relation. Because it is embedded in a transaction-time relation, it is given transaction-time support, and past values are automatically retained. Taking the transaction timeslice at *now* produces the correct values for S, but taking a transaction timeslice at a time in the past, at time $c_t < now$, may retrieve an old value of S, which is inconsistent with the requirement that it be a snapshot attribute. Such queries must take this into account, timeslicing the relation as of *now* to get the value of S, then join this with the timeslice of the relation as of c_t to get the value of T, which is quite awkward.

Including the attribute S along with an attribute V requiring valid-time support is even more problematic. Whereas the system provides the transaction time during modifications, the user must provide the valid time. This raises the issue of what should the valid time be for the snapshot attribute S. All updates have to maintain this semantics, and queries also have to consider the valid time.

Next, the existence of a strict correlation (a type of temporal specialization (18)) between the valid and transaction time of an attribute can reduce the need for decomposition. Consider an attribute D that requires both valid-time and transaction-time support, but which is degenerate, i.e., the valid and transaction times are exactly correlated. Thus whenever a change occurs in the modeled reality, the new data is immediately recorded in the database. This attribute may reside in a valid-time relation with another attribute V requiring only valid-time support. Transaction-time queries can be recast as valid-time queries on the relation, exploiting the correlation between the two kinds of time. Similarly, D may reside in a transaction-time relation with the attribute T.

Moving on to precisions, the conceptual data model, and indeed all temporal relational data models, support only a single precision per relation for each of transaction and valid time. It then becomes necessary to separate attributes that require different, incompatible precisions.

Definition 7.15(Precision Decomposition Rule.)
To accurately reflect the temporal precisions of time-varying attributes, decompose relation schemas so that all attributes in a schema have a compatible temporal precision, that is, a common granularity.

Example 7.15
The Precision Decomposition Rule does not give rise to decomposition in the car rental schema.

A more general approach was recently proposed by Wang and his colleagues, using their temporal functional dependencies based on granularities (45), discussed briefly in Section 7.3.2.2. Their approach is complex and may generate new granularities, of uncertain comprehensibility by the user. The Precision Decomposition Rule above is very simple and does not generate new granularities, but may decompose relations more than Wang's approach.

7.4.3   Lifespan Decomposition Rule

One important design criterion in conventional relational design is to eliminate the need for inapplicable nulls in tuples of database instances. We introduced in Section 7.3.4 the notion of lifespans in order to capture when attributes are defined for the objects they are introduced in order to describe. Briefly, the lifespan for an attribute—with respect to a particular surrogate representing the object described by the attribute—is all the times when a meaningful attribute value, known or unknown, exists for the object.

The following definition uses the concepts from Section 7.3.4 to characterize temporal database schemas with instances that do not contain inapplicable nulls.

Definition 7.16
A relation schema $R = (S, A_1, \ldots, A_n \mid T)$ where S is surrogate valued is *lifespan homogeneous* if $\forall A, B \in R (A \overset{\text{LS}}{\cong}_S B)$.

With this definition, we are in a position to formulate the Lifespan Decomposition Rule, which ties the connection of the notion of lifespans of attributes with the occurrence of inapplicable nulls in instances.

Definition 7.17(Lifespan Decomposition Rule.)
To avoid inapplicable nulls in temporal database instances, decompose temporal relation schemas to ensure lifespan homogeneity.

Example 7.16
In schema `Branch`, attribute `AssistantMgr`'s lifespan deviated from those of the other attributes. Thus, `AssistantMgr` is removed from `Branch`, and a new schema, `Assistant`, with attributes `AssistantMgr` and `BrID` is introduced.

It is appropriate to briefly consider the interaction of this rule with the the existing temporal normal forms that also prescribe decomposition of relation schemas. Specifically, while the decomposition that occurs during normalization does, as a side effect, aid in eliminating the need for inapplicable nulls, a database schema that obeys the temporal normal forms may still require inapplicable nulls in its instances. By adjusting the schema, the lifespan decomposition rule attempts to eliminate remaining inapplicable nulls.

7.4.4   Synchronous Decomposition Rule

The synchronous decomposition rule is based on the notion of observation pattern, and its objective is to eliminate a particular kind of redundancy. In Section 7.3.5, we defined the notion of synchronous attributes, which is here employed to define synchronous schemas and the accompanying decomposition rule. Finally, we view synchronism in a larger context, by relating it to existing concepts, and discuss the decomposition rule's positioning with respect to logical versus physical design.

With this definition, we can characterize relations that avoid the redundancy caused by a lack of synchronism and then state the Synchronous Decomposition Rule.

Definition 7.18
Define relation schema $R = (S, A_1, \ldots, A_n \mid T)$ where S is surrogate valued. Relation R is *synchronous* if $\forall A_i, A_j \in R(A_i \overset{S}{=}_S A_j)$.

Definition 7.19(Synchronous Decomposition Rule.)
To avoid repetition of attribute values in temporal relations, decompose relation schemas until they are synchronous.

Example 7.17
In the current `Car` schema attribute `LastServiced` is not synchronous with the remaining attributes. In consequence, this `LastServiced` is removed from `Car` and the schema `CarService = (CarID, LastServiced)` is included into the car rental database schema.

Alternative notions of synchronism have previously been proposed for database design by Navathe and Ahmed (31), and by Wijsen (46). While these notions are stated with varying degrees of clarity and precision and are defined in different data-model contexts, they all seem to capture the same basic idea, namely that of *value-based synchronism*, which differs from the synchronism used in this chapter.

It is our contention that in this context, the synchronous decomposition rule is only relevant at the level of the schema of the implementation platform, and depending on the actual implementation platform, the rule may be relevant only to physical database design. Surely, the redundancy that may be detected using the synchronism concept is important when *storing* temporal relations. Next, this type of redundancy is of little consequence for the querying of logical-level relations using the TSQL2 query language (21, 39), a particular implementation platform. Indeed, it will often adversely affect the ease of formulating queries if logical-level relations are decomposed solely based on a lack of synchronism.

Finally, the need for synchronism at the logical level has previously been claimed to make normal forms and dependency theory inapplicable (e.g., (13)). The argument is that few attributes are synchronous, meaning that relation schemas must be maximally decomposed, which leaves other normalization concepts irrelevant. This claim does not apply to the framework put forth here.

For completeness, it should be mentioned that while the synchronism concepts presented in this section have concerned valid time, similar concepts that concern transaction time and employ update patterns rather than observation patterns may also be defined.

7.4.5   Implications for View Design

The only concept from Section 7.3 not covered so far is derivation functions. These relate to view design, as outlined next.

For each time-varying attribute, we have captured a set of one or more derivation functions that apply to it. It is often the case that exactly one derivation function applies to an attribute, namely the discrete interpolation function (21), which is a kind of identity function. However, it may also be the case that several nontrivial derivation functions apply to a single attribute.

By using the view mechanism, we maintain the separation between recorded data and data derived via some function. Maintaining this separation makes it possible to later modify existing interpolation functions.

Thus, the database designer first identifies which sets of derivation functions that should be applied simultaneously to the attributes of a logical relation instance and then, subsequently, defines a view for each such set. Although interpolation functions have previously been studied, we believe they have never before been associated with the view mechanism.

Example 7.18

Two derivation functions were associated with attribute `Mileage` of schema `CarMileage`. As the discrete derivation function is the default for event relations, only one view has to be defined, namely one to produce the interpolated `Mileage` values.

7.4.6 Summary

In this section, we have provided a set of guidelines for the decomposition of conceptual relations based on their temporal properties. Here, we briefly review the proposed guidelines.

- With temporal functional dependencies as the formal basis, conventional normalization theory was made applicable to the conceptual relations considered here. In particular, the traditional normal forms, e.g., third normal form, BCNF, and fourth normal form, and their decomposition algorithms are applicable.

- The temporal support decomposition rule ensures that each relation has a temporal support appropriate for the attributes it contains.

- The precision decomposition rule uses the granularity sets to prescribe decomposition of relation schemas and to determine the granularity of the resulting relation schemas.

- The lifespan decomposition rule ensures that inapplicable nulls are not required.

- The synchronous decomposition rule removes redundant attribute values, while being less strict than previous definitions of value synchronism.

- Strong temporal functional dependencies, together with the temporal functional dependencies, allow the designer to identify time-invariant primary keys, which may play the role of surrogates that can then subsequently be eliminated.

- The derivation function associated with attributes induce views computing the derived values.

```
Branch = (BrID, Name, Location, Manager, Capacity)
```
  • valid-time state and transaction-time support is required
  • `BrID` is a time-invariant key and `Name` is a key

```
Assistant = (AssistantMgr, BrID)
```
  • valid-time state and transaction-time support is required
  • `BrID` is a foreign key referencing `BrID` of `Branch`

```
Car = (CarID, Branch, Model, Make, Category, Year)
```
  • transaction-time support is required
  • `CarID` is a time-invariant key

```
CarMileage = (CarID, Mileage)
```
  • valid-time event and transaction-time support is required
  • the precision for valid time is minutes
  • `CarID` is a foreign key referencing `CarID` of `Car`

```
CarMileageView = (CarID, S-C(Mileage))
```
  • view derived from `CarMileage`
  • `S-C` is a step-wise constant derivation function

```
CarService = (CarID, LastServiced)
```
  • transaction-time support is required
  • `CarID` is a foreign key referencing `CarID` of `Car`

```
CustomerAddr = (CuID, Name, Address)
```
  • no temporal support is required
  • (`CuID`, `Name`) is a key

```
CustomerRating = (CuID, Rating)
```
  • valid-time state support is required
  • `CuID` is a foreign key referencing `CuID` of `CustomerAddr`

```
RentalBooking = (RBID, Branch, Category, Customer, Price,
                 CreditCardNo, CardType)
```
  • valid-time state and transaction-time support required
  • the precision for valid time is minutes
  • `RBID` is a time-invariant key
  • `Branch` is a foreign key referencing `BrID` of schema `Branch`
  • `Customer` is a foreign key referencing `CuID` of `CustomerAddr`

Figure 7.4   Final Conceptual Car Rental Schema

Example 7.19
Following the steps described here, the car rental schema in Figure 7.3 now appears as shown in Figure 7.4. Sample annotations are included.

While conceptual design is concerned with adequately modeling the *semantics* of the application, physical design is concerned with performance. The concepts concerning synchronism, i.e., time patterns, including observation and update patterns, are relevant for physical design. Their use was discussed in Section 7.4.4. Physical design may also reverse some of the decomposition that is indicated by logical design.

7.5   Other Approaches to Temporally Enhanced Database Design

This section surveys in turn approaches to temporally enhanced database design based on normalization concepts and approaches based on Entity-Relationship (ER) modeling.

7.5.1   Normalization-Based Approaches

For relational databases, a mature and well-formalized normalization theory exists, complete with different types of dependencies, keys, and normal forms. Over the past two decades, a wealth of temporal relational data models have been proposed. Because these temporal models utilize new types of relations, the existing normalization theory is not readily applicable, prompting a need to revisit the issues of database design.

The proposals for temporal normalization concepts, e.g., dependencies, keys, and normal forms, presented in this chapter are based in part on earlier concepts (surveyed in (22)). Space constraints preclude a detailed coverage of these earlier concepts; instead, we briefly survey but a few dependency and normal form concepts.

Some earlier works involving dependencies, e.g., those by Tansel and Garnett (40) and Lorentzos (28), treat nested relations with temporal information and relations with time interval-valued attributes that are unfoldable into relations with time point attributes as snapshot relations with explicit temporal attributes and apply "temporal" dependencies in these contexts. Other dependencies, specifically Vianu's dynamic dependency (44), Navathe and Ahmed's temporal dependency (31), and Wijsen's dynamic and temporal functional dependencies (46), are inter-state dependencies, and thus are more ambitious than the temporal dependency (an intra-state dependency) considered earlier in this chapter. In fact, these dependencies are more closely related to the notion of synchronism defined in Section 7.3.5 and based on observation patterns.

Now considering earlier normal forms, quite a diverse set of proposals exist. Ben-Zvi (2) bases his time normal form on the notion of a contiguous attribute. Informally, an attribute in a temporal relation is contiguous if there exists a value of that attribute for each point in time and for each real-world entity captured in the relation. Segev and Shoshani define, in their Temporal Data Model, a normal form, 1TNF, for valid-time relations (34). In their data model, it is possible for time-slice operations to result in attributes that have multiple values at a single point in time. The 1TNF normal form ensures that this anomaly is avoided. Navathe and Ahmed (31) base their time normal form (TNF) on their value-based notion of synchronous attributes and define 1TNF to ensure that time-varying attributes are synchronous, i.e., change at the same time. This value-based concepts is related to the identity-based notion of synchronous attributes defined earlier in the chapter. Lorentzos (28) defines a P normal form and a Q normal form. P normal form essentially guarantees the relation to be coalesced (37), and Q normal form appears to have similarities with Navathe and Ahmed's concept of synchronism.

As illustrated by the dependencies and normal forms surveyed above, the early proposals for normalization concepts are typically specific to a particular temporal data model. This specificity is a weakness since a given concept inherits the peculiarities of its data model; it is unsatisfactory to have to define each normalization concept anew for each of the more than two dozen existing temporal data models (33). Furthermore, the existing normal forms often deviate substantially in nature from conventional normal forms.

This chapter represents an attempt at lifting the definition of temporal normalization concepts from a representation-dependent, model-specific basis to a semantic, conceptual basis, in the process making the concepts readily applicable to an entire class of temporal relational data models.

Most recently, proposals that are consistent with and refine the approach adopted in this chapter (and in (21, 22)) have been developed. Specifically, Wang et al. (45) and Wijsen (47) have defined dependencies and associated normal forms that extend the normal forms provided here and that are based on temporal granularities and apply to complex objects. These proposals were discussed in Section 7.3.2.2.

7.5.2   ER-Based Design Approaches

The ER model, using varying notations and with some semantic variations, continues to enjoy a remarkable popularity in the research community, the computer science curriculum, and in industry.

As pointed out earlier, it has been widely recognized that temporal aspects of database schemas are prevalent and difficult to model. Because this also holds true when using the ER model, it is not surprising that enabling the ER model to properly capture time-varying information has been an active area of research for the past decade and a half. About a dozen temporally enhanced ER models have resulted. Reference (15) surveys and compares all such models known to its authors at the time of its writing.

Combined, the temporal ER models represent a rich body of insights into the temporal aspects of database design. Table 7.1 provides an overview of the models and contains references to further readings; the reader is encouraged to study the models.

7.6   Summary and Directions

In order to exploit the full potential of database technology—conventional as well as temporal—guidelines for the design of appropriate database schemas are required.

This chapter has presented concepts for capturing the temporal properties of attributes. These concepts include temporal and strong temporal functional dependencies and time-invariant keys. Also included are surrogates that represent the real-world objects described by the attributes, lifespans of attributes, observation and update patterns for time-varying attributes, and derivation functions that compute

Table 7.1   Overview of Temporal ER Models

Name	Main references	Based on
Temporal Entity-relationship Model	(24, 25)	ER
Relationships, Attributes, Keys, and Entities Model	(12)	ER
Model for Objects with Temporal Attributes and Relationships	(32)	ER & OO
Temporal EER model	(10, 11)	EER
Semantic Temporal EER model	(8, 9)	ER
Entity-Relation-Time model	(42, 43, 29)	ER
Temporal ER model	(41)	ER
Temporal EER model	(27)	EER
Kraft's Model	(26)	ER
TERC+	(48)	ERC+
TimeER	(16)	EER

new attribute values from stored ones. We subsequently showed the important roles these concepts play during database design. We were able to formulate four additional decomposition guidelines that supplement normal-form-based decomposition.

We feel that several aspects merit further study. An integration of all the various existing contributions to temporal relational database design into a complete framework has yet to be attempted. Likewise, a complete design methodology, including conceptual (implementation-data-model independent) design and logical design, for temporal databases should be developed. Finally, a next step is to adopt the concepts provided in this chapter in richer, entity-based (or semantic or object-based) data models.

Finally, the ideas presented here and the methodology that will follow should be transitioned to existing implementation platforms, including non-temporal query languages such as SQL-92 (30). In the short and perhaps even medium term, it is unrealistic to assume that applications will be designed using a temporal data model, implemented using novel temporal query languages, and run on as yet nonexistent temporal DBMSs.

References

1. P. Atzeni and V. De Antonellis. *Relational Database Theory*. Benjamin/Cummings (1993).

2. J. Ben-Zvi. *The Time Relational Model*. Ph.D. thesis, Computer Science Department, UCLA (1982).

3. M. H. Böhlen. Valid Time Integrity Constraints. Technical Report 94-30, Department of Computer Science, University of Arizona, Tucson, AZ (1994).

4. J. Clifford and D. S. Warren. Formal Semantics for Time in Databases. *ACM Transactions on Database Systems*, **8**(2):214–254 (1983).

5. J. Clifford and A. U. Tansel. On an Algebra for Historical Relational Databases: Two Views. In S. Navathe, editor, *ACM SIGMOD International Conference on the Management of Data*, pp. 247–265 (1985).

6. J. Clifford and A. Croker. The Historical Relational Data Model (HRDM) and Algebra Based on Lifespans. In *Proceedings of the International Conference on Data Engineering*, pp. 528–537 (1987).

7. C. E. Dyreson and R. T. Snodgrass. Supporting Valid-time Indeterminacy. *ACM Transactions on Database Systems*, **23**(1), to appear (1998).

8. R. Elmasri, I. El-Assal, and V. Kouramajian. Semantics of Temporal Data in an Extended ER Model. In *Ninth International Conference on the Entity-Relationship Approach*, pp. 239–254 (1990).

9. R. Elmasri and V. Kouramajian. A Temporal Query Language for a Conceptual Model. In N. R. Adam and B. K. Bhargava, editors, *Advanced Database Systems*, Volume 759 of *Lecture Notes in Computer Science*, pp. 175–195, Springer-Verlag (1993).

10. R. Elmasri and G. T. J. Wuu. A Temporal Model and Query Language for ER databases. In *Proceedings of the Sixth International Conference on Data Engineering*, pp. 76–83 (1990).

11. R. Elmasri, G. T. J. Wuu, and V. Kouramajian. *A Temporal Model and Query Language for EER Databases*, Chapter 9, pp. 212–229. In A. Tansel et al., editors, *Temporal Databases,* Benjamin/Cummings (1993).

12. S. Ferg. Modeling the Time Dimension in an Entity-Relationship Diagram. In *Fourth International Conference on the Entity-Relationship Approach*, pp. 280–286 (1985).

13. S. K. Gadia and J. H. Vaishnav. A Query Language for a Homogeneous Temporal Database. In *ACM SIGAct-SIGMOD Principles on Database Systems*, pp. 51–56 (1985).

14. S. K. Gadia. A Homogeneous Relational Model and Query Languages for Temporal Databases. *ACM Transactions on Database Systems*, **13**(4):418–448 (1988).

15. H. Gregersen and C. S. Jensen. Temporal Entity-Relationship Models—a Survey. *IEEE Transactions on Knowledge and Data Engineering*, to appear (1999).

16. H. Gregersen and C. S. Jensen. Conceptual Modeling of Time-Varying Information. TimeCenter TR-35, Department of Computer Science, Aalborg University (1998).

17. P. Hall, J. Owlett, and S. J. P. Todd. Relations and Entities. In G. M. Nijssen, editor, *Modelling in Data Base Management Systems*, pp. 201–220. North-Holland (1976).

18. C. S. Jensen and R. T. Snodgrass. Temporal Specialization and Generalization. *IEEE Transaction on Knowledge and Data Engineering*, **6**(6):954–974 (1994).

19. C. S. Jensen and C. E. Dyreson, editors. A Consensus Glossary of Temporal Database Concepts—February 1998 Version. In O. Etzion, S. Jajodia, and S. Sripada, editors, *Temporal Databases: Research and Practice*, pp. 367–405, LNCS 1399, Springer-Verlag (1998).

20. C. S. Jensen and R. T. Snodgrass. The Surrogate Data Type. Chapter 9, pp. 153–156. In (39).

21. C. S. Jensen and R. T. Snodgrass. Semantics of Time-Varying Attributes and Their Use for Temporal Database Design. In *Fourteenth International Conference on Object-Oriented and Entity Relationship Modeling*, pp. 366–377 (1995).

22. C. S. Jensen, R. T. Snodgrass, and M. D. Soo. Extending Existing Dependency Theory to Temporal Databases. *IEEE Transaction on Knowledge and Data Engineering*, **8**(4):563–582 (1996).

23. C. S. Jensen and R. T. Snodgrass. Semantics of Time-Varying Information. *Information Systems*, **21**(4):311–352 (1996).

24. M. R. Klopprogge. TERM: An Approach to Include the Time Dimension in the Entity-Relationship Model. In *Proceedings of the Second International Conference on the Entity Relationship Approach*, pp. 477–512 (1981).

25. M. R. Klopprogge and P. C. Lockemann. Modelling Information Preserving Databases: Consequences of the Concept of Time. In *International Conference on Very Large Databases*, pp. 399–416 (1983).

26. P. Kraft. Temporal Qualities in ER Models. How? (in Danish) Working paper 93, Department of Information Science, The Aarhus School of Business (1996).

27. V. S. Lai, J-P. Kuilboer, and J. L. Guynes. Temporal Databases: Model Design and Commercialization Prospects. *DATA BASE*, **25**(3):6–18 (1994).

28. N. A. Lorentzos. Management of Intervals and Temporal Data in the Relational Model. TR 49, Agricultural University of Athens (1991).

29. P. McBrien, A. H. Seltveit, and B. Wangler. An Entity-Relationship Model Extended to Describe Historical Information. In *International Conference on Information Systems and Management of Data*, pp. 244–260 (1992).

30. J. Melton and A. R. Simon. *Understanding the New SQL: A Complete Guide*. Morgan Kaufmann Publishers, Inc., San Mateo, CA (1993).

31. S. B. Navathe and R. Ahmed. A Temporal Relational Model and a Query Language. *Information Sciences*, **49**:147–175 (1989).

32. A. Narasimhalu. A Data Model for Object-Oriented Databases With Temporal Attributes and Relationships. Technical report, National University of Singapore (1988).

33. G. Özsoyoğlu and R. T. Snodgrass. Temporal and Real-Time Databases: A Survey. *IEEE Transactions on Knowledge and Data Engineering*, **7**(4):513–532 (1995).

34. A. Segev and A. Shoshani. The Representation of a Temporal Data Model in the Relational Environment. In *Proceeding of the Fourth International Working Conference on Statistical and Scientific Database Management*, Volume 339 of *Lecture Notes in Computer Science*, pp. 39–61, Springer-Verlag (1989).

35. A. Segev and A. Shoshani. A Temporal Data Model Based on Time Sequences, Chapter 11, pp. 248–270. In A. Tansel et al., editors, *Temporal Databases,* Benjamin/Cummings (1993).

36. M. D. Soo, C. S. Jensen, and R. T. Snodgrass. An Algebra for TSQL2, Chapter 27, pp. 505–546. In (39).

37. R. T. Snodgrass. The Temporal Query Language TQuel. *ACM Transactions on Database Systems*, **12**(2):247–298 (1987).

38. R. T. Snodgrass. Temporal Object Oriented Databases: A Critical Comparison, Chapter 19, pp. 386–408. In *Modern Database Systems: The Object Model, Interoperability and Beyond*, W. Kim, editor, Addison-Wesley/ACM Press (1995).

39. R. T. Snodgrass (editor), I. Ahn, G. Ariav, D. Batory, J. Clifford, C. E. Dyreson, R. Elmasri, F. Grandi, C. S. Jensen, W. Käfer, N. Kline, K. Kulkarni, T. Y. C. Leung, N. Lorentzos, J. F. Roddick, A. Segev, M. D. Soo, and S. M. Sripada. *The Temporal Query Language TSQL2*. Kluwer Academic Publishers (1995).

40. A. U. Tansel and L. Garnett. Nested Historical Relations. In *Proceedings of ACM SIGMOD International Conference on Management of Data*, pp. 284–293 (1989).

41. B. Tauzovich. Toward Temporal Extensions to the Entity-Relationship Model. In *The Tenth International Conference on the Entity Relationship Approach*, pp. 163–179 (1991).

42. C. I. Theodoulidis, B. Wangler, and P. Loucopoulos. The Entity Relationship Time Model. In *Conceptual Modelling, Databases, and CASE: An Integrated View of Information Systems Development*, pp. 87–115, Wiley (1992).

43. C. I. Theodoulidis, P. Loucopoulos, and B. Wangler. A Conceptual Modelling Formalism for Temporal Database Applications. *Information Systems*, **16**(4):401–416 (1991).

44. V. Vianu. Dynamic Functional Dependencies and Database Aging. *Journal of the ACM*, **34**(1):28–59 (1987).

45. X. Wang, C. Bettini, A. Brodsky, and S. Jajodia. Logical Design for Temporal Databases with Multiple Granularities. *ACM Transactions on Database Systems*, **22**(2):115–170 (1997).

46. J. Wijsen. Design of Temporal Relational Databases Based on Dynamic and Temporal Functional Dependencies. In J. Clifford and A. Tuzhilin, editors, *Recent Advances in Temporal Databases*, pp. 61–76, Zurich, Switzerland (1995).

47. J. Wijsen. Temporal FDs on Complex Objects. *ACM Transactions on Database Systems*, **23**(4), to appear (1998).

48. E. Zimanyi, C. Parent, S. Spaccapietra, and A. Pirotte. TERC+: A Temporal Conceptual Model. In *Proceedings of the International Symposium on Digital Media Information Base* (1997).

8   *Modeling Object Dynamics*

M. P. Papazoglou
Tilburg University
INFOLAB
GPO Box 90153 , Tilburg 5000 LE
The Netherlands
e-mail: mikep@ikub.nl

B. J. Krämer
FernUniversität Hagen
Data Processing Technology
58084 Hagen
Germany
bernd.kraemer@fernuni-hagen.de

To effectively model complex database applications an object-oriented database must be able to allow the evolution and automatic reconfiguration of individual objects or groups of objects with similar behavior at run-time.

This chapter introduces the role mechanism as an extension of object-oriented databases to support unanticipated behavioral oscillations for objects that may attain many types and yet share a single object identity. A role refers to the ability to seamlessly integrate idiosyncratic behavior, possibly in response to external events, with pre-existing object behavior specified at instance creation-time. In this manner the same object can simultaneously be an instance of different classes which symbolize the different roles that a particular object undertakes.

8.1   Introduction

In object-oriented database systems all domain objects in a particular application are pre-classified and assigned to a single type. All objects of a certain type have exactly the same collection of state variables and methods and are treated strictly uniformly. Once an object is instantiated and populates a class, the only changes permissible are changes to its state variables. This preserves the uniformity of the entire set of objects contained in that specific class. Should the need arise for schema changes, these are applied to the schema types and have to be propagated to all the objects contained in the classes under update. The restructuring of objects in consequence of a schema change is necessary to preserve consistency and conformance between the type associated with each class and the structure and behavior of the class member objects.

During the development phase of a database application the designer can often foresee commonalities between different parts of the application, leading to a desire to share structure and behavior between those similar parts. In several situations it is, however, highly beneficial for a system to have the ability to attach idiosyncratic behavior to an individual object or a set of objects within one or more classes at a later stage. Unfortunately, stating behavior at design time puts severe restrictions on the kinds of unanticipated structural and behavioral nuances that may need to be introduced in an object-oriented database system without reconfiguring database schema classes and all their instances. What is required is the ability to selectively seed new functionality to a distinguishable set of objects within a given class at run-time. *It is often desirable for an object when viewed externally, to appear to oscillate among a set of different behaviors, only some of which can be anticipated when the database schema is designed*. It is therefore necessary to be able to adapt existing objects to new application requirements, while maintaining a single object identity. In this way, it would be possible for members of a class to dynamically acquire different state variables and respond to different messages. Currently this functionality is not supported by conventional object-oriented database systems because it would involve changing the membership of an object from one class to another at run-time. This strictness of traditional object-oriented systems was first pointed out by proponents of prototype-based languages (8), (16). In an object system that does not provide this kind of functionality, an inherent danger lies in the fact that programmers do not have the means to ensure that the object identifier of an evolving object is identical to the object identifier of the object from which it evolved. Programming solutions are not only artificial but also introduce storage and performance overheads as well as adding a high degree of complexity and coupling. Moreover, they are error-prone and may result in corrupting already existing database objects.

From what has been already stated, it follows that we require modeling mechanisms for object-oriented databases to support unanticipated behavioral oscillations for individual objects, or groups of objects, that have different types and yet may be able to share a single object identity. A language facility supports dynamic object properties best if new behavior can be introduced by stating to the system the differences between the existing behavior and the new desired behavior. Such language properties are known to support *object dynamics*.

In this chapter we present a model designed to extend the capabilities of object-oriented database systems so that they can represent object dynamics. Central to our model is the concept of *role*. A role refers to the ability to change the classification of an object dynamically so that the same object can simultaneously be an instance of different classes some of which are created on the fly. Roles designate significant, semantically meaningful shifts in object behavior (obtained dynamically) that are correlated with existing object properties and can be queried exactly like any other conventional class objects. A role is an interface-based specification implemented on the basis of pre-existing objects in a way that allows an existing object to gain (or shed) state and behavior dynamically while retaining its original identity. This chapter introduces the *Object Role-Data Model* (OR-DM), a model which integrates the concept of a role into object-oriented database technology in order to represent object dynamics.

The research presented in this chapter builds on previous work reported in (10), (11), where we illustrated how roles may improve the versatility and modeling power of object-oriented database systems and (12) where we give formal definitions and correctness proofs regarding the role model.

8.2   Basic Concepts and Definitions

The discussion that follows introduces basic concepts and terminology and focuses on objects which have the characteristics described below.

8.2.1   Basic Object Model Characteristics

The basic object model constituents are *types*, *objects*, *classes*, and *relationships* (associations).

In a similar manner to abstract data types in programming languages, types define sets of structured data together with operations to modify such data in a controlled manner. A type consists of a unique type name, a collection of typed attributes and a set of operations (or methods). All types pertinent to a particular application are organized in a *directed acyclic type graph*, or *type DAG*. Figure 8.1 (a) illustrates a schema portion of the car rental object-base in the form of a type DAG. This figure shows that type Customer has as subtypes the two types Company and Person and Customers have HireContracts which refer to RentalCars that belong to a RentalCompany. Type Customer is seen to be related to type HireContract via an association type signs. An association (or relationship) is modeled as a first class object that has its own attributes and is existent dependent on its arguments. The types signs and refers-to in Figure 8.1 (a) are typical examples of such associations. Many object-oriented data models support an explicit relationship construct such as, for instance, COCOON (15).

All objects are instantiated from one type specification defining their structure and behavioral interface. Each object has a unique *object identifier* (oid) and a state. A class is a run-time construct, based on a type specification, which contains a set of objects. A class *extent* denotes the set of all objects that are instances of the class' type at a given point in time. Classes are organized into a *class DAG*, which is isomorphic to the corresponding type DAG. Whenever a new object is created as an instance of a type T, its object identifier is automatically added to the extent of the corresponding class C_T and to the extent of all super-classes of C_T (if any), i.e., $extent(Company) \subseteq extent(Customer)$. Thus an object can be a member of more than one classes at a time (multiple class membership).

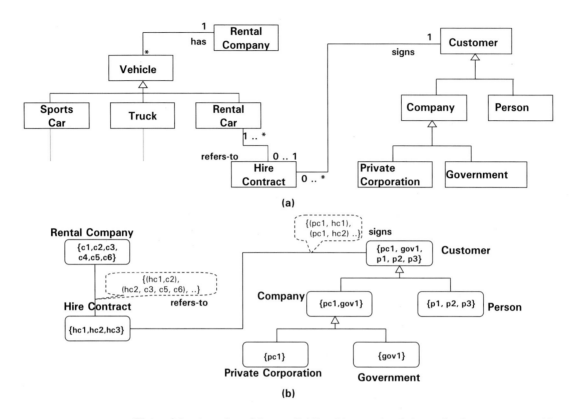

Figure 8.1 A portion of the type DAG and its associated classes for the `car rental` object-base.

Figure 8.1 (b) depicts the class hierarchy derived from the type DAG in Figure 8.1 (a). Rounded rectangles in Figure 8.1 (b) denote class extents, while dashed clouds denote relationship (association) extents. For reasons of brevity we introduced only the `Customer` part of Figure 8.1 (a). To fully understand the context of Figure 8.1 (b) consider an object of type `PrivateCorporation` with the oid `pc1`. When this object is created as an instance of that class, its oid is not only included in the extent of its corresponding class `PrivateCorporation` but also in the extent of its superclass `Company` and `Customer`.

8.2.2 Extending the Basic Model with Roles

A role may be thought of as a typed *abstract channel* providing an alternative perspective on an existing object. A role ascribes properties that may evolve over time and is implemented as an extension of existing objects. The purpose of a role is to model different "active" (application-specific) representation facets for the same object in terms of both structure and behavior. Each role introduces additional attributes and methods to existing objects—through a set of role-specific operations—thereby

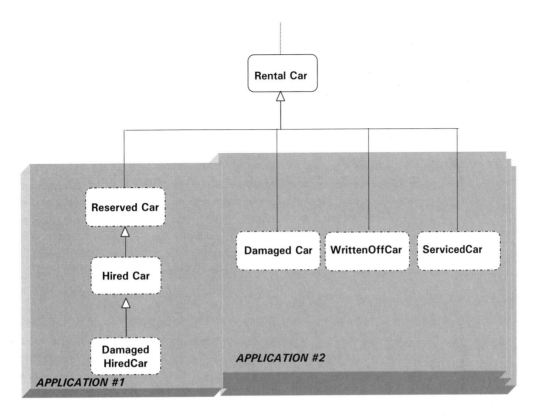

Figure 8.2   The class hierarchy for the type schema in Figure 8.1 evolved with roles.

permitting the representation of behavioral shifts and increments. A particular object may concurrently exhibit many roles which are obtained dynamically throughout its life-span. This type of object dynamism can be achieved by subdividing and grouping together distinguishable (and related) objects contained in the class DAG and by defining subclasses or super-classes dynamically to contain these object groupings. Each of the new classes created in this manner is a *role defining class*.

Figure 8.2 extends the `RentalCar` part in Figure 8.1 (a) with dynamic objects to satisfy the needs of a particular application. The bottom part of Figure 8.2 shows how the class DAG can be privately extended to support role objects. A different application may use the same class DAG and extend (customize) it with different kinds of roles meaningful to its specific context. Roles are transient in nature: they have a finite life-span which may be defined by the application program that has created them, see Section 8.3.4. Roles are created by individual application programs, are stored in an object repository local to the programs that created them, and they have no global scope and effects, i.e., they cannot be "seen" outside the context of the application that created them (or applications built on the basis of these programs). By default, a role is *visible* only within the scope of the specific application that created it. However, in several circumstances it may be useful for a role to be shared (exported) between applications or become permanent, i.e., become a permanent part of the type DAG. This will be explained in some detail in Section 8.3.5.3.

To comprehend how roles relate to object dynamics and how they may impact upon the behavior of objects, consider the case of a RentalCar object with oid c_2 which dynamically obtains the role of an ReservedCar and a HiredCar through a role defining operation (as explained in Section 8.3.1). The dashed rounded rectangles in Figure 8.2 indicate roles which an object may assume or relinquish during its life-span in addition to the properties acquired upon creation. To describe this situation, the class DAG is extended by including two new (role defining) classes, namely ReservedCar and HiredCar that do not correspond directly to the schema types in Figure 8.1. As roles are used to facilitate migration of objects in the class DAG, both roles ReservedCar and HiredCar contain in their extent the RentalCar object with oid c_2. Accordingly, the object with oid c_2 co-exists now in the extent of the classes RentalCar, ReservedCar and HiredCar. As shown in Figure 8.2 another application, e.g, part suppliers or insurers, may choose to customize the base type RentalCar differently by introducing roles such as DamagedCar or ServicedCar.

Roles allow the introduction of new classes into the class DAG without having to modify the definitions of existing classes. As roles redefine behavior defined in their classes of origin, the system may give different answers depending on how a particular object is viewed. For example, assume that we defined a method $current - value$ for RentalCar objects which gives their current value. This method might be redefined when we consider the role of RentalCar object as a WrittenOffCar.

The set of roles played by an object is obviously determined by its position in the class DAG. The existence of all the roles of interest for a given object, its *role-set*, fully characterizes this object. The term role-set, is used here to aggregate information about how an object is evolving, and is determined by the set of role classes in whose extent the object identifier occurs. These classes form a connected subgraph of a given class DAG extended with roles. The role-set is anchored on the *base type* (BT) which is part of the original class DAG and which is used to define roles for some of the objects in its extent. For instance, the role-set $\rho(c_1) =$ {RentalCar, ReservedCar, HiredCar, ServicedCar, DamagedCar, .. } includes all the roles that objects of the base type RentalCar can currently perform. We use the term *ancestor role(s)* to denote all the roles above a given role in the class DAG. The term *parent role(s)* is reserved for the role(s) immediately above a given role, whereas the term *descendant role(s)* is used to denote all the roles below that role in the class DAG. For example, the ancestral roles for HiredCar is ReservedCar and its set of descendant roles consists of DamagedHiredCar, see Figure 8.2. Users can thus access and query objects from any perspective that suits their application, e.g., from the vantage point of an insurance application.

In the first instance, new objects are created only through pre-existing DAG classes and are assigned into roles either eagerly or lazily (4), depending on the case. After these roles have been created new roles may now be created on their basis. The semantics of the OR-DM operations are *object-preserving* in the sense that they return part of the extents of their input classes. More importantly, the extension of the class DAG—due to the introduction of role-classes—does not change the set of objects contained in the class DAGs. These and other virtues of object-preserving operations and transformations have been addressed by (2) and (15).

The main objective of roles in the OR-DM is to customize objects – according to application needs – so that they become equipped with their own idiosyncratic behavior. In this respect roles present some similarity with views, however, unlike views their objective is to cater for dynamic object migration and automatic re-classification – without affecting the database schema. Additional important differences between roles and views relate to semantic preservation (views) vs. semantic upgrades (roles); object generation and updates (views) vs. strict object preservation (roles); and differences in the treatment of object identity.

8.3   Role Class Operations

8.3.1   Elementary Role Operations

The OR-DM provides elementary operations to modify class hierarchies. These include operations to:

1. Modify the class hierarchy by adding and deleting role classes by means of the operations: **addRoleClass** c **asSuperclassOf** $c_1, \ldots, c_k$, **addRoleClass** c **asSubclassOf** $c_1, \ldots, c_k$, and **markDeleteRoleClass** c.

   Addition of new role classes is accomplished by means of *generalization* (or *specialization*) of existing classes. Generalization is useful for adding common behavior to seemingly unrelated classes (which have objects with the same oid in their extents) in a class DAG, as needs arise, by forming a common super-class and associating new behavior with that super-class. Similarly, specialization is used to add common behavior to classes which have a common ancestor (and common oids) in the class DAG by forming a common sub-class and associating new behavior with this sub-class. To prohibit dangling references upon deletion of objects, methods or attributes we provide a specialized *delete* operation which marks as (virtually) deleted all subclasses of a deleted class and all relationships that have any of the marked classes as source or destination. New references to an invalidated role as well as the dispatching of messages to invalidated role objects, result in trapable errors. These classes are garbage collected when no further references to the mark deleted role classes exist.

2. Migrate objects from existing classes to new role classes by means of the operation: **migrateObject** i **fromClass** c_1 **to (Super/Sub)class** c_2.

   Two types of object migration are potentially useful in a class DAG: migration from a class C_T to a subclass or superclass of C_T or to an arbitrary class. The former supports the dynamic specialization or generalization of objects, while the latter models the case where an object changes its structure and behavior arbitrarily.

3. Modify the type definition of a role class by adding attributes and possibly new methods by means of the operations: **addAttribute** $a : t = v$ **to RoleClass** c, and **addMethod** $c.m : t_1 \rightarrow t_2$ **to RoleClass** c'.

Operations for adding new role classes, object migration, method and attribute extension, and deletion marking have been designed to preserve the well-formedness and type-safety of a class DAG. This issue is discussed at some length in (12).

The operations described in the following are implemented on the basis of the elementary role operations described above. It is important to note that the role creation operations described in the following do not only physically create roles but also automatically instantiate their respective role classes and populate them with appropriate objects from their originating classes.

8.3.2   Role Operations Based on the Grouping of Objects

8.3.2.1   *Creation of Roles by Enumeration*

The first and simplest role defining mechanism is *by enumeration*. Here roles can be defined by identifying the role creating objects by means of their object identifiers. The operation

createRoleClass c **asSubclassOf** $c_1, \ldots, c_k$
> **for** $i_1, \ldots, i_n$ **in** c_1:
>> ⟨*roleClassBody*⟩
> **for** $i_1, \ldots, i_n$ **in** c_2:
>> ⟨*roleClassBody*⟩
> ⋮

This operation is the result of applying the command **addRoleClass** c as a common subclass of classes $c_1, \ldots, c_k$ to create a new subclass (role) c and **migrateObject** to migrate *common* oids $i_1, \ldots, i_{n_1}$ from $c_1, \ldots, c_k$ to c. Most typically this operatinis used for the generation of a single subclass.

The statement $roleClassBody$ may include the addition of new attributes and method implementations to capture new behavior for the identified object. The operations in the statement $roleClassBody$ extend the semantics of the high-level operation **createRoleClass** by adding attributes and methods to the new class c. This operation has as effect the creation of an additional facet for an object which retains its original object identifier.

8.3.2.2   *Eager Creation of Roles*

Now consider the classes depicted in Figure 8.3 and assume that a local branch can only hire cars that belong to it although it may have in its pool returned cars that were hired at another branch. Such cars must be transferred back to their original branch at a specific day in the week. In order to distinguish local branch cars from all rental cars in a branch pool we may use the following statement:

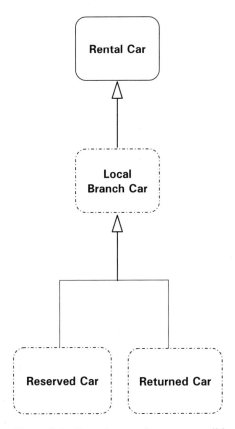

Figure 8.3   Factoring out class commonalities and representing them as roles.

createRoleClass `LocalBranchCar`
  asSuperclassOf `ReservedCar, ReturnedCar;`

As a result of this statement a new subclass relationship is introduced between the smallest common super-class of `ReservedCar`, `ReturnedCar`, namely `Rental-Car`, and the new class `LocalBranchCar`. The semantics of the above operation result in the properties of the class `LocalBranchCar` being the common properties of the classes `ReservedCar`, `ReturnedCar`. This situation is shown in Figure 8.3. The extent of the new role class `LocalBranchCar` is formed by taking the *union* of the extents of the classes `ReservedCar`, `ReturnedCar`. The addition of the role class `LocalBranch` guarantees that all the re-arrangements in the class DAG result in a well-formed DAG as this operation is only defined if all its constituent elementary operations are well defined and, hence, the conjunction of their preconditions is satisfied (12).

This role generating operation is not flexible as it does not permit us to exercise explicit control over groups of objects in specialized classes which we wish to migrate into the more generalized class. To selectively migrate objects from the extent of a specialized to a generalized class we may use a role creating operation, based on generalization, in conjunction with enumeration. To illustrate this concept, consider the following statement in OR-DM:

createRoleClass PopularModel **asGeneralizationOf**
$i_1, \ldots, i_{n_1}$ **in** ReservedCar:
$j_1, \ldots, j_{n_2}$ **in** HiredCar:
with ⟨*roleClassBody*⟩

in conjunction with Figure 8.2.

This operation generates one subclass (role class) named c-c_i, e.g., PopularModel-HiredCar and PopularModel-ReservedCar, for each class of origin c_i, e.g., ReservedCar and HiredCar, and makes the role class c, e.g., PopularModel, become their common parent class. More specifically, the above OR-DM statement creates a new role, namely PopularModel for objects that belong to different classes, namely the classes ReservedCar, HiredCar. The semantics of this operatin is that we assume that the objects with oid $i_1, \ldots, i_{n_1}$ in ReservedCar and the objects with $j_1, \ldots, j_{n_2}$ in HiredCar constitute PopularModels. Notice that after the execution of this statement the new role class PopularModel is generated for the enumerated objects, contained in the role creation statement, as a direct subclass of RentalCar. This is due to the fact that RentalCar is the common (direct) superclass of all these three classes. The new role PopularModel includes in its extent all the objects enumerated in the role creation statement. Further specializations of this new role class are also automatically generated by employing multiple-inheritance to represent the roles PopularModel-HiredCar and PopularModel-ReservedCar. PopularModel is a role assumed by some and not all the objects in the classes ReservedCar, HiredCar, accordingly only the enumerated objects in these classes will appear in the extents of the specialized classes. This situation is depicted in Figure 8.4.

8.3.2.3 Creation of Roles by Value or Predicate

Value-based roles may be defined using an expression based on the values of attributes of the object in question. The semantics of value-based role class operations are defined in a similar manner as enumeration-based operations on the basis of the elementary operations. Value-based roles can be defined according to the following syntax.

createRoleClass c **asSubclassOf** | **asGeneralizationOf** c' **grouped by** e:
⟨*roleClassBody*⟩

where e denotes an expression referring to attribute values of particular at tributes.

For example, if we wish to introduce a new role for cars that the EU-Rental wishes to sell after they have traveled 20000 kms or they are over a year old, we could declare a role class as follows:

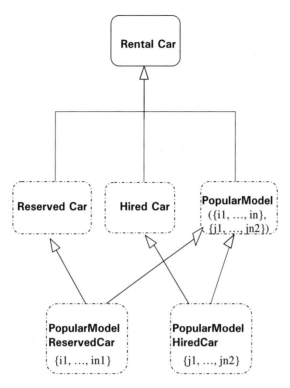

Figure 8.4   Automatic role generation by means of generalization statements.

createRoleClass SaleableCar **asSubclassOf** Car
    grouped by Car.Mileage >= 20000 or Car.Age >= 12:
      ⟨*roleClassBody*⟩

The statement *roleClassBody* includes the definition of attributes and methods and is treated in the same manner as previously explained.

Roles can be also be created by means of predicates which must be satisfied by all the members of a role class. This distinguishing property of OR-DM is usually found in classification languages such as KL-ONE (3). Predicate-based roles are defined according to some predicate P satisfied by all members of any particular role class as specified by the following statement:

createRoleClass asSubclassOf | asGeneralizationOf c
grouped by $case_1, \ldots, case_k$:
    ⟨*roleClassBody*⟩

where each role is individually defined through a case-like statement $case_i$. Each case statement has the structure c_i **is** P_i where c_i are the new role classes and the predicates P_i refer to particular properties of the given class of origin c. The condition of the last case may be the keyword **other**, which applies only if all other cases failed. Note that if the cases are not logically disjoint, the sequence of cases determines the role in which those objects matching multiple conditions are placed. Again the semantics of this operation correspond to a sequence of **addRoleClass** c_i **asSubclassOf** c and **migrateObject** elementary operations such that only those objects that satisfy the condition P_i migrate to the new role class.

For example, in case that we wish to divide EU-Rental customers according to their rental history, we could declare the following role classes:

createRoleClassasSubclassOfCustomer **grouped by**
> OneOffCustomer   **is** Customer.RentalPerYear == 1:
>> ⟨*roleClassBody*⟩
> InfrequentRenter   **is** Customer.RentalPerYear <= 5:
>> ⟨*roleClassBody*⟩
> FrequentRenter   **is other**:
>> ⟨*roleClassBody*⟩

The above role generating conditions are applied to and affect the extents of the classes mentioned in the role creation statement, e.g., Customer, at the time of execution of this statement. After the execution of this statement the role generating conditions act as demons on an *if-instantiated* basis and are evaluated "lazily" whenever a new object is instantiated and inserted into the extent of their associated role class, e.g., Customer. This leads to an automatic classification of newly created Customer objects into one of the three role classes OneOffRenter, InfrequentRenetr, and FrequentRenter.

8.3.3   Role Operations based on Inter-Object Relationships

The following role creating operations allow one group of objects to be defined in terms of another in some other class in the DAG. The role creating operations permit dynamic control over the patterns of inter-object linking. The semantics of role operations based on inter-object relationships correspond to a sequence of **addRoleClass** c_i **asSubclassOf** c and **migrateObject** elementary operations.

8.3.3.1   *Reference Induced Roles*

Roles can be created by inter-relating object classes. The role operations described in this subsection exhibit the general form: $< object\text{-}group_1 > references < object\text{-}group_2 >$. The semantics of the reference induced role creation operation are reminiscent of the division operation of the relational algebra and require that the operation returns a subset of objects from the $object - group_1$, where all the members of that subset are associated with all the members of $object - group_2$. The $object - group_1$ signifies a subset of the class extent of class c whereas the $object - group_2$ corresponds to the oids $i_1, \ldots, i_k$ in the following operation:

createRoleClass c **as asSubclassOf** c_1
reference ⟨*link − name*⟩
for $i_1, \ldots, i_k$ **in** c_2:
> ⟨*roleClassBody*⟩

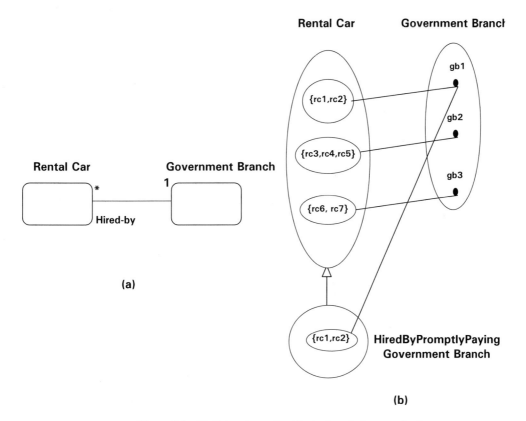

Figure 8.5   Defining dynamic object roles via the use of references.

The reference can be in the form of a link reference such as an attribute of a particular class which may have its domain in another class, e.g., the class `RentalCar` may have an attribute called `hired-by` that connects one or more rental car objects to a single object of type `GovernmentBranch`, see Figure 8.5(a). Consider the following example where a new role is created for the class `RentalCar` named `HiredTo-PromptlyPayingGvtBranch` in association with Figure 8.5(a).

createRoleClass HiredToPromptlyPayingGvtBranch **asSubclassOf** RentalCar
   reference RentalCar.Hired-to **for** gb1 **in** GovernmentBranch:
     ⟨*roleClassBody*⟩

Figure 8.5(b) shows some sample data for the above situation. From the context of this figure it can be seen that the `RentalCar` objects $\{rc_1, rc_2\}$, $\{rc_3, rc_4, rc_5\}$ and $\{rc_6, rc_7\}$ are `hired-to` the `GovernmentBranch` objects gb_1, gb_2 and gb_3, respectively. As a result the role `HiredToPromptlyPayingGvtBranch` is generated for the `RentalCar` objects rc_1, rc_2.

Alternatively, the reference may be substituted by a method in the body of c_1 which returns a set of objects of the type of objects belonging to the group ⟨*object-group$_2$*⟩. For example, instead of having a reference to objects of type `GovernmentBranch` we may have a method which returns these objects. The method must obviously be declared in the body of the class which contains in its extent the object group *object-group$_1$*, i.e., RentalCar.

8.3.3.2 *Creation of Roles through Explicit Linkages*

There are roles which can be specified through explicit inter-object linkages which resemble dynamic role-relationships in KL-ONE (3). In the OR-DM a relationship may be used to act as a predicate and capture the commonality among a set of individual role playing objects. Therefore, relationships which associate two classes of objects may be used to generate a new role for a subset of the objects which are contained in the extent of the class at their point of destination. This operation can be exemplified by the following situation. Consider the relationship type signs(Customer, setOf HireContract) between the types Customer and HireContract (see Figure 8.1 (a)). This relationship type accepts Customer and HireContract class objects as its parameters and imposes the constraint that a single Customer object may be related to a set of HireContract objects[1].

The following statement:

createRoleClass CompanyHiredContract_pc$_1$
    from signs(pc1, **setOf** HireContract):
        ⟨*roleClassBody*⟩

generates a new role called CompanyHiredContract_pc$_1$ and populates it with the HireContract objects that are associated with the particular RentalCar identified by the object identifier pc$_1$. The new role is a subclass of the class HireContract. The oids hc$_1$ and hc$_2$ in the extent of class HireContract, see Figure 8.1 (b), are the only ones that also occur in the pairs of the extent of the relationship (association) signs.

8.3.4 Roles with a Temporal Dimension

The OR-DM can capture another aspect of application semantics, the temporal aspect. Operations that involve a temporal dimension are illustrated in this section.

8.3.4.1 *Role Lifespans*

Most object-oriented applications are developed under the assumption that the object-base contains only the current "snapshot" of the object data. This may prove to be too restrictive in many situations where it is desirable to maintain temporal

---

1. In fact this relationship is a polymorphic one since according to the principle of argument contravariance its argument domains may be expanded by subclasses of either its origin and/or its destination.

information regarding roles. In order to address such temporal issues in OR-DM we use the notion of *role-lifespan* for currently active roles. For instance, the lifespan of a `RentalCar` would include a history of the roles that this object has performed, e.g., `ReservedCar, HiredCar, ServicedCar`, together with the *transaction time* that a specific role was assumed or deleted. In this way we can store and query a set of historical data regarding the role activities of a certain object. Role-lifespans are useful as they allow applications to "infer" about the behavior of role objects. For example, how many times a particular car was hired, how often it was serviced and so on.

We use the function $lifespan(RC_{oid})$ to denote the life span of an object as a member of the extent of a role class RC. For a pair of superclass RC_1 and subclass RC_2, the following constraint must hold (17): $lifespan(RC_{2_{oid}}) \subseteq lifespan(RC_{1_{oid}})$. For instance for the rental car hierarchy the following constraints will hold:

$$lifespan(Vehicle_{oid}) = lifespan(RentalCar_{oid}) \supseteq$$
$$lifespan(ReservedCar_{oid}) \supseteq lifespan(HiredCar_{oid})$$

Lifespans of non-role objects which have a subclass-superclass relationship, with a counterpart in the type DAG (see Figure 8.1 (a)), are perpetual rather than temporal. This means that an object of type `RentalCar` will always be in the extent of its own role class as well as its superclass `Vehicle` for an equal amount of time. However, this is not true for role objects of type `ReservedCar` which may spend much less time in the extent of the class `ReservedCar` in comparison to the extent of `RentalCar`. This allows us to define a *temporal extent* which returns all the objects with roles RC at a particular point in time t.

The combination of roles and temporal data leads to the formulation of interesting queries regarding historical role data. For this purpose we use the `when` operator which is the valid-time analogue of the `where` clause in SQL. This clause specifies a predicate on the event or interval time stamps of role objects that must hold for those objects which satisfy a query. For example, consider the following query which specifies the times and duration during which a particular `RentalCar` with object identifier rc_1 was damaged.

select *Time, Time.interval*
    when rc_1 **in** *extent(DamagedCar)*;

The above query statement returns the (transaction) time(s) when a specific object with role `DamagedCar` entered the extent of this role class. It also calculates the duration of time that this car object spent in the `DamagedCar` role extent as the difference between the role extent exit and entry transaction times in each occasion.

8.3.4.2   Controlling Role Changes

The following operations control how objects may change the current role that they are playing. The simplest operation is to relinquish a current role, for an object or a set of objects, in favor of some other specified role. The following statement illustrates how an object may relinquish a role.

relinquish *RoleClass* **for**
    $i_1, \ldots, i_n$ | ⟨*ValueBasedExpression*⟩ | ⟨*PredicateBasedExpression*⟩
    [**resume** *RoleClass*] | [**resume** *RoleClass* **when**⟨*event*⟩];

An object may relinquish its current role and assume either: its immediate parent role (default case if the *resume* statement is missing); or a specified role in its role-set by means of the *resume* statement; or finally, revert to the class were it originated from. The operation relinquish is implemented by invoking the elementary operation **removeObject** for objects that satisfy the relinquish criterion. Consider the BlackListCustomer object with oid c_3 and the following statement:

relinquish BlackListCustomer **for** c_3;

this statement results in relinquishing the role BlackListCustomer for the object c_3. This object then is deleted from the extent of this role class and all of its subclasses.

In the following, we will explain the use of a simple *resume* statement in conjunction with the *relinquish* operation. The use of an event-triggered resumption of a role will be explained when we consider role suspension. The statement:

relinquish *ValuedCustomer* **for** c_3
    resume *InfrequentCustomer*;

results in the object with oid c_3 being removed from all class extents between Customer (its base type) and ValuedCustomer and reverts to the InfrequentCustomer role. Role relinquishing (and suspension, see below) are governed by invariants which apply automatic coercion of relinquished roles with existing role objects in the DAG and, in general, control how an object can change a role it currently plays (12).

8.3.4.3 *Delaying Operations and Role Transformation*

The most common mechanism for the transformation of roles in OR-DM is provided by means of triggers. A trigger in OR-DM is thought of as a monitor on a data item (which may change value) or as a logical condition-action pair. When the condition is fulfilled, the action is executed. Consider the following example.

trigger
when this (FrequentRenter.status == "member"
    and FrequentRenter.revenue $>= 10000$)
    this FrequentRenter **becomes** ValuedCustomer
end trigger

The previous example shows how an object with FrequentRenter role may become an ValuedCustomer. This trigger, like a method, is defined in the body of the class

FrequentRenter. This may involve deleting and adding properties and behavior, removing objects from the extents of a class and placing it in that of another class.

The trigger conditions are not only applied to the current extents of the classes involved in the condition part of the trigger, they are also applied lazily to any objects joining the extents of these classes at a later stage.

The following operation is used for synchronization purposes, mainly in conjunction with a trigger-like event specification. It results in suspending further actions of an object (under a particular role) until a certain event occurs.

suspend *RoleClass* **for**
  $i_1, \ldots, i_n$ | *ValueBasedExpression* | *PredicateBasedExpression*
resume *RoleClass* **when** ⟨*event*⟩;

This operation is a further specialization of the operation *relinquish*. The main difference between these two operations is that objects specified by the operation suspend may remain suspended or "frozen" for an indefinite period of time, as the application demands, and then resume their previous role by means of the operator *resume* only when a pre-specified event has occurred.

Consider the following example.

suspend ValuedCustomer **for** ValuedCustomer.NotActiveMember ≥ 12
resume ValuedCustomer **when this** (Customer.revenue $>= 5000$
  or CustomerNrOfHires $>= 5$)

The above statement specifies that an object of type ValuedCustomer may lose its valued customer status for an indefinite period of time and resumes its parent, i.e., FrequentRenter, role until an event occurs, i.e., a condition is fulfilled, which makes it possible for this object to revert to its suspended role.

8.3.5 Additional Role Operations

Additional OR-DM operations on role classes are defined below. In contrast to the operations covered previously, these operations accept already existing roles as input. The operations either operate on the extents of role classes or on an entire role class. In the former case the role operations assume a role class as input and add/remove or migrate objects to/from it, whereas in the latter case they accept a role class as input and operate on its entire extent as a whole.

The set of role operations described in the following is representative of the possible operations on roles. There are other simpler operations which traverse the class DAG and compute role transitive closures such as *find-roleSet*, *find-Class-of-origin*, *find-parent*, *find-descendants* of a role and so on, which together with elementary operations help construct the operations that follow.

8.3.5.1 Assuming a Role

The following statement illustrates how an object may assume a new role.

assume *RoleClass* **for**

$i_1, \ldots, i_n \mid \langle ValueBasedExpression \rangle \mid E \, \varepsilon \, la \, PredicateBasedExpression \rangle$;

An object may assume an already existing role by using this operation. The convention is that an object cannot assume a role unless a role defining class for this role already exists.

8.3.5.2   Constraining Roles

Role interaction is taken to mean how objects in one role class extents may interact with objects in another role class. Role interaction is mainly exemplified by the concept of mutual exclusion which leads to role blocking. Two roles having a common ancestor are *mutually exclusive* if an object is prohibited from joining both of these roles and is forced to select either one.

Consider, for example, the Customer objects which may need to assume the additional roles of ValuedCustomer and BlackListCustomer. It is desirable to block objects of type ValuedCustomer from being BlackListCustomer objects at the same time. Thus, we designate their respective role classes as being mutually exclusive, i.e., objects which appear in the extents of the classes ValuedCustomer are not allowed to appear in the extent of class BlackListCustomer, and vice-versa.

constrainRoleClass ValuedCustomer, BlackListCustomer **for** Customer
    with ValuedCustomer **mutex** BlackListCustomer

If two or more role defining classes are mutually exclusive, then all of their subclasses are also mutually exclusive. This invariant guarantees that descendants of the ValuedCustomer role objects, do not become members of the class BlackList-Customer, and vice-versa.

8.3.5.3   Sharing and Solidifying Roles

Normally, there is no need for roles to become globally persistent and hence visible by all other application programs and users. However, in several situations there are some roles which might be useful for a large number of users and application programs. To provide for additional modeling flexibility the OR-DM allows roles (and individual role objects in their extent) to be shared between applications or to be promoted to persistent types and objects, respectively.

To allow roles to be shared between applications, we use the following operation:

share *RoleClass* **with** $ap_1, \ldots, ap_m$
[**for** $i_1, \ldots, i_n \mid ValueBasedExpression \mid PredicateBasedExpression$]

This operation extends the visibility of *RoleClass* from its local application context to other applications ap_i (for $i = 1 \ldots m \geq 1$).

Role classes and selected objects in their extent may be made persistent by invoking the operator *solidify*. Solidified role classes have their definitions become automatically part of the type DAG and thus can no longer be distinguished from other database classes. In other words, this operation results in the evolution of the object-base as it automatically adds new types and their respective instances. The syntax of this operation is as follows:

solidify *RoleClass*
[**for** $i_1, ..., i_n$ | *ValueBasedExpression* | *PredicateBasedExpression*]

When making a role class persistent other role classes may also be solidified transparently. If a role is solidified all objects included in its extent must also become permanent. This process is governed by the following invariant. To solidify (share) a role, we must also solidify (share) all roles appearing in all reachable paths between the role's class of origin and the defining class for that role. Moreover, all role defining classes referred to in the method signatures and in the role's definition statements must also be made permanent (sharable).

8.4   Application of Roles

Roles can be useful for several type of applications based on the use of object-oriented technology. They can for example represent separation of duties and associate them with particular individuals performing activities within an organizational context. In the following we will concentrate on two broad types of applications that call for role support: *security* and *workflows*.

8.4.1   Role-based Security and Separation of Duty

Roles are useful for business security applications as they ease the task of managing large numbers of users or user groups by assigning different privilege to users (office workers). Security applications based on object-orientation and roles can effectively deal with managing the authentication, authorization and auditing of relationships between users, data and processes. Roles in particular can prescribe how specific personnel (or groups) are authorized to access data.

Separation of duty is found in business security applications where processes acting on behalf of office personnel are required to perform a given task. Such a task would be broken into subparts which are assigned to different people. Every individual is then required to perform (possibly) more than one subtask. A role-based approach to security and protection uses differentiated access to realize protection for organizational activities. A privilege, in the organizational context, determines an office worker's access rights with respect to a data item, e.g., a document, spreadsheet, etc. For example, during processing a car rental request an office worker who has participated in some tasks (roles) in the activity, e.g., obtaining customer information, reserving a car, filling out insurance forms, etc, is barred from executing further steps (roles) in the process, e.g., financial transactions. By authorizing different users to assume different roles, we can enforce both the order of execution on the objects and separation of duty constraints on method execution (9).

8.4.2 Workflow Applications

A workflow is concerned with the coordination and streamlining of business activities where documents, information or tasks are passed between participants according to a defined set of rules to achieve an overall business goal. The workflow application specifies the individual activity steps, the order and the conditions under which the activities must be executed, the flow of data between the activities and the users responsible for the execution of activities. Workflow applications are also characterized by personnel's defined organizational roles in the routing process, such as the originator, reviewer, editor and approval authority. A workflow application may also allocate read/write privileges based on the recipient's workgroup or position in the organization (6). For example, in the car rental application individual recipients may have different views of the same document, e.g., estimation of benefits, handling of complaints, billing, etc, and may be allowed to input or modify different data items.

The attributes that may apply to an organizational role may include the authorization field, organizational entities, and capabilities (7). The authentication field may include role-specific passwords or pointers to a user's public-key certificate. The organizational units describe the relevant project, workgroup department, e.g., marketing, administration and so on, or company branch associated with a participant's role in the workflow. The capabilities describe a person's authorized capabilities along three dimensions: process definitions, work items, and workflow. Process definitions determine whether a user is authorized to originate, revise, approve/disapprove, or delete process definitions. Work items determine whether a user is authorized to originate, revise, approve/disapprove, or delete work items. The workflow capability determines whether a user may be authorized to monitor or suspend a workflow in progress.

8.5 Related Work

In the following we summarize research activities which share some concern about the evolution of objects and outline their differences from roles.

The notion of role has also been used in expressing potential object states and behavior in the context of office information systems (13). Roles in this model are static: they are specified in their totality at the schema level and are not created dynamically on demand. In this model the behavior of an object can be derived by means of an abstract state which defines all of its active roles and roles instantiations.

Aspects (14) is another approach to dynamic object modeling. Aspects are used in a strongly typed object-oriented environment, which introduces sharp dichotomy between abstract data types and implementations, to support multiple independent object views. Type implementations and type interfaces are defined separately without any explicit relationship. This model has an incomplete notion of conformance and does not support re-usability and specialization of roles by means of inheritance.

A different approach to roles is taken by the the object-oriented database programming language Fibonacci (1) where the role concept is an integral part of complete new programming environment. Fibonacci focuses mainly on implementation issues such as the use of delegation for implementing inheritance and message passing. It introduces a relatively restrictive approach to method dispatching in that messages that cannot be handled by a current role are delegated down the role hierarchy. This leads to undesirable semantic behavior and undesirable side effects as no provisions are made for methods available at a specialized role level to handle a wider domain of arguments, viz. *contravariance* and *type safeness*, for roles defined at higher levels in the role hierarchy.

A more recent approach to role modeling at the instance level rather than at the type level is reported in (5) where the authors represent an extension of Smalltalk to illustrate how roles can be supported without changing the semantics of the base language. This approach is based on the same premise with the role model presented herein in that they both advocate extending an existing object-oriented database system by combining class and role hierarchies. A major difference of the model in this chapter is that roles can be customized and used in the context of different applications as they can inherit (and refine) both structure and behavior whereas the model presented in (5) uses the notion of delegation and does not allow the redefinition of inherited structure or operations. Another important difference is that our role model builds on the notion of behavioral compatibility, and operation safeness, and thus allows objects to change roles dynamically and migrate to a new role context by having their environment re-evaluated dynamically.

8.6   Summary

To effectively model complex object-oriented applications in which constantly changing situations can be represented, a system must be able to support the evolution and reconfiguration of individual objects. The strict uniformity of objects contained in a class is unreasonable: run-time structural and behavioral nuances should be specifiable for objects on an individual basis without restructuring the database schema or reorganizing the database contents. This inability of contemporary object-oriented database systems to represent evolution and reconfiguration of individual objects may lead to a loss of modeling assumptions and inter-object dependencies. This limitation makes the maintenance of consistency of dynamic objects almost impossible.

In this chapter we have presented an extension to the object-oriented paradigm which supports a natural way of representing object dynamics and addresses such shortcomings. More specifically, we introduced the Object Role-Data Model (OR-DM) as an extension of object-oriented databases to support unanticipated behavioral oscillations for individual objects, or groups of objects, that have many types and share a single object identity. Upgrowths of behavior in the OR-DM are known as roles that objects play which can be assumed and relinquished dynamically to reflect shifting modeling requirements.

The purpose of the OR-DM is to add more modeling power and flexibility to the object-oriented approach by capturing different aspects of object dynamics. OR-DM offers the possibilities for a variety of object-oriented data models to provide the following features:

- Support for objects with changing type: objects which dynamically change the current roles that they play – by gaining or retracting behavior;
- control of such forms of object evolution in accordance with application semantics by allowing objects to react to external events in order to modify their behavior;
- respect of the structural and behavioral consistency of typed objects.

When treating roles as classes, as in the approach taken herein, one gains all the benefits of the object-oriented paradigm but also one faces a fundamental problem: the dynamic change of the type of an object can lead to type inconsistencies and integrity problems. The fundamental problem is to ascertain that the behavioral upgrowths that an object assumes dynamically conform to its pre-defined behavior and lead to type safe systems and consistent computations. In the OR-DM we have taken a rather conservative approach in that respect by introducing some stringent safety criteria which limit modeling flexibility. For example, we can add role objects only as sub/super-classes of existing objects. We are currently researching safety criteria that restrain the dynamic nature of roles and guarantee that safety considerations are met and efficient implementations are possible when retrofitting new object code into existing objects anywhere in the DAG axis.

References

1. A. Albano, *et al.* "An Object Data Model with Roles", *Procs. 19 VLDB Conf.*, Sept. 1993, pp. 39- 51.

2. P. Bergstein "Object-Preserving Class Transformations", *Procs. OOPSLA'91 Conference*, pp. 299-313.

3. R. Brachman, J. Schmolze "An Overview of the KL-ONE Representation System", *Cognitive Science*, 9(2):171–216, April 1985.

4. F. Ferrandina, T. Meyer, R. Zikari "Implementing Lazy Database Updates for an Object Database System", *Procs. 20th VLDB Conf.*, Santiago, 1994, pp. 261-272.

5. G.Gottlob, M. Schrefl, B. Röck, "Extending Object-Oriented Systems with Roles", *ACM Transactions on Information Systems*, vol. 14, no. 3, July 1996, pp. 268-296.

6. D. Hollinsworth. "The Workflow Reference Model" *Technical report*, Workflow Management Coalition, Brussels, Belgium, November 1994, http://www.aiai.ed.ac.uk/WfMC/DOCS/refmodel/rmv1-16.html.

7. J. Kobielus "Workflow Strategies", *IDG Books*, 1997.

8. H. Lieberman "Using Prototypical Objects to Implement Shared Behavior in Object-Oriented Systems", *Procs. OOPSLA'87 Conference*, pp. 214-223.

9. M. Nyanchama, S. Osborn "Role-based Security, Object-Oriented Databases and Separation of Duty", *SIGMOD Record*, vol. 22, no. 4, Dec 1993, pp. 45-51.

10. M.P. Papazoglou "Roles: A Methodology for Representing Multifaceted Objects", *Procs. DEXA-91: Database & Expert Systems Applications Conf.*, Berlin 1991.

11. M.P.Papazoglou, B.J. Krämer, A. Bouguettaya "On the Representation of Objects with Polymorphic Shape and Behavior", *13th Int'l Conf. on The Entity-Relationship Approach*, Manchester, Dec. 1994, pp. 223-240.

12. M.P.Papazoglou, B. Kråmer "Representing Transient Object Behavior", *VLDB Journal*, vol. 6, no. 2, pp. 73-96, May 1997.

13. B. Pernici "Objects with Roles", in *Procs ACM Conf. on Office Information Systems*, April 1990, pp. 205–215.

14. J. Richardson and P. Schwartz, "Aspects: Extending Objects to Support Multiple, Independent Roles", Proc. 1991 ACM SIGMOD Int'l. Conf. on Management of Data, ACM, New York, 1991.

15. M. Scholl, *et. al* "The COCOON Object Model", *technical report ETH Zürich*, 1992.

16. L.A. Stein, H. Lieberman, D. Ungar "A Shared View of Sharing", *in Object-Oriented, Concepts, Databases & Applications*, W. Kim, F. Lochovsky (eds), Academic-Press, 1989.

17. A. Tansel et. al "Temporal Databases: Theory, Design and Implementation", *Addison Wesley*, 1993.

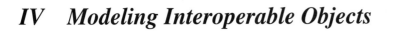

IV Modeling Interoperable Objects

9   *Database Integration: The Key to Data Interoperability*

Christine Parent
University of Lausanne
HEC-INFORGE
CH-1015 Lausanne
Switzerland

Stefano Spaccapietra
Swiss Federal Institute of Technology
Database Laboratory
CH-1015 Lausanne
Swizterland

Most of new databases are no more built from scratch, but re-use existing data from several autonomous data stores. To facilitate application development, the data to be re-used should preferably be redefined as a virtual database, providing for the logical unification of the underlying data sets. This unification process is called database integration. This chapter provides a global picture of the issues raised and the approaches that have been proposed to tackle the problem.

9.1   Introduction

Information systems for large organizations today are most frequently implemented on a distributed architecture, using a number of different computers interconnected via Intranet or Internet. Information is usually stored in various databases, managed by heterogeneous database management systems (DBMSs), or in files, spreadsheets, etc. Disadvantages of using multiple independent databases within the same organization are well known, including: high potential for incompleteness, inaccuracy and inconsistencies in data acquisition and data processing, lack of coordination resulting in duplication of efforts and of resources, and eventually conflicts in the allocation of responsibilities for data maintenance. Still, such situations are very common. For instance, different databases in different departments support applications specific to each department. Interoperability is the magic word that is expected to solve these problems, allowing heterogeneous systems to talk to each other and exchange information in a meaningful way.

Two levels of complexity may be separated in addressing interoperability. The more complex case is when information involves data sources that are not in a database format, typically local files and spreadsheet data or external data reached through Internet. In this case, understanding of unstructured (e.g., free text) or semi-structured (e.g., a web page with html incrustation) data calls for sophisticated mechanisms for extraction of semantics. Moreover, the global information system has to be able to dynamically evolve according to changes in configuration of the available data sources (new data or new sources become available or available ones temporarily or definitely disappear). The relevant sources may even not be defined a priori, but may have to be determined on the fly through one or more web searches. To implement interoperability in such a context many diverse functionalities are needed. They include (47):

■ a communication kernel enforcing information exchange standards for data representation and exchange requests,

■ a set of knowledge discovery tools supporting various forms of intelligent data browsing, semantic extraction, and learning.

■ a set of tools for semantic interoperability: wrappers, to adapt local sources to specifications of the global system (typically performing schema, data and query language translations) and mediators, performing integration of data or services from the various local sources,

■ a global distributed data management system extending traditional DBMS operations to the federated context: query decomposition and optimization, transaction management, concurrency and recovery.

The simpler case is when the scope of information exchange is limited to databases within the organization (e.g., a typical Intranet environment). Here existing database schemas provide basic knowledge about the semantics of data, which may be easily enhanced into data dictionaries or data warehouse formats through interviews of current users and data administrators or analysis of the documentation. Exchange standards become easier to define and enforce as part of some general policy for information technology within the organization. Hence the challenge in the design of an integrated information system is on the mediators in charge of solving discrepancies among the component systems.

Interoperability among database systems may basically be achieved in three ways, supporting different levels of integration:

■ at the lowest level, i.e. no integration, the goal is nothing but to enable one DBMS to request and obtain data from another DBMS, in a typical client/server mode. Gateways, i.e. dedicated packages, support this limited functionality and are currently marketed for a number of existing DBMSs. Most well known gateways are ODBC-compliant tools, where ODBC (Open DataBase Connectivity) is an SQL-based emerging standard from Microsoft.

■ at an intermediate level, the goal is to support user-driven access and/or integration of data from multiple databases. The term user-driven refers to the fact that users are given the possibility to simultaneously manipulate data from several sources in some uniform way. However, it is also user's responsibility to access and manipulate the local databases consistently. The system is not in charge of guaranteeing consistency across database boundaries. To implement such a framework, a software layer is developed, whose functionality may range from:

  • a multidatabase query language, e.g. OEM-QL (47), providing a single SQL-like syntax that is understood by a set of translators, each one of these mapping the query to an underlying DBMS. The benefit for users is the capability to address many systems through a single language.

  • to a multidatabase system, where users are provided with a language that has full data definition and manipulation capabilities. In particular, the system supports view definition, which allows users to define their own external schema through a mapping to relations (or classes) from the different sources. MSQL (36) is a well-known reference is this domain for relational database environments. An extension of MSQL functionality to include some conflict resolution strategies is reported in (43). Based on user's explicit description of semantic relationships among data domains, these strategies are intended to solve, during query processing, some of the inconsistencies that may arise among related data from different databases. Similar proposals for multidatabase systems based on some object-oriented model also exist (e.g., (25)).

■ at a higher level, the goal is to develop a global system, sitting on top of the existing systems, to provide the desired level of integration of the data sources.

  • Total integration is implied in distributed data base (DDB) management systems (9). All existing data are integrated into a logically unique database (the DDB), and henceforth managed in a consistent way under a single global control authority. This approach has proved not to be suited for many enterprises where the need for accessing several data sources should not interfere with the actual control of these sources by their respective owners.

  • To provide more flexible integration, researchers have lately developed specifications for federated database (FDB) systems (55). FDB systems aim at scalable integration, supporting a harmonious coexistence of data integration and site autonomy requirements. Site autonomy is guaranteed as local usage of the local data is preserved, schema and data evolution remains under local control, and data sharing is on a volunteer basis. Each database administrator (DBA) defines the subset of the local data, if any, which is to be made available to distant users of the federated system. The defined subset is called the local export schema. Local export schemas define the data available for integration into one (or more) virtual database, called the FDB. Virtual, here, stands for a database that is logically defined (its schema exists) but is not directly materialized. The data described by the federated schema resides in the local databases. There is not one physical FDB somewhere, but only parts of the FDB which belong to the source databases. The FDB thus provides an integrated access without any need for data duplication. Integration, as well as import/export of data into/from the FDB, is managed by the federated system (FDBMS). The FDBMS role is to enforce cooperation agreements as established by the participating DBAs (in terms of semantics of data, access rules, copy maintenance, etc.), to perform integration of data and services, as well as the traditional operations of a distributed DBMS (e.g., query processing).

While gateways and multidatabase systems do not attempt to unify the semantics of data from the various sources, distributed and federated database systems base their services on an integrated view of the data they manage. Users access the DDB or FDB like a centralized database, without having to worry about the actual physical location of data, the way the data is locally represented, or the syntax of the languages of the local DBMS. These advantages easily explain why the federated approach, in particular, is so popular today. However, before FDB systems come to reality, a number of issues have to be solved (see (28, 55) for comprehensive overviews). These include design issues, related to the establishment of a common understanding of shared data, as well as operational issues, related to adapting database techniques to the new challenges of distributed environments. The former focus on either human-centered aspects (e.g., cooperative work, autonomy enforcement, negotiation procedures) or database centered aspects (e.g., database integration, schema or database evolution). The latter investigate system interoperability mainly in terms of support of new transaction types (long transactions, nested transactions, . . .), new query processing algorithms, security concerns, and so on.

The kernel of design issues, and the most relevant for the topic of this book, is the database integration problem. Simply stated, database integration is the process which:

- takes as input a set of databases (schema and population), and

- produces as output a single unified description of the input schemas (the integrated schema) and the associated mapping information supporting integrated access to existing data through the integrated schema.

Database integration is a complex problem. Quite a large number of papers have investigated various facets of it, resulting in many technical contributions, a few methodologies and a few prototypes. As it is impossible to meaningfully synthesize all existing material, we apologize for incompleteness. This chapter provides a survey of the most significant trends. Our primary goal has been to draw a clear picture of what are the approaches, how far we can go with the current solutions and what remains to be achieved. The focus is on the concepts, the alternatives and the fundamentals of the solutions, not on detailed technical discussions, for which further readings are listed in the references. The presentation is organized according to the temporal sequence of actions that compose the database integration process. We identify three major steps in this process (see Figure 9.1):

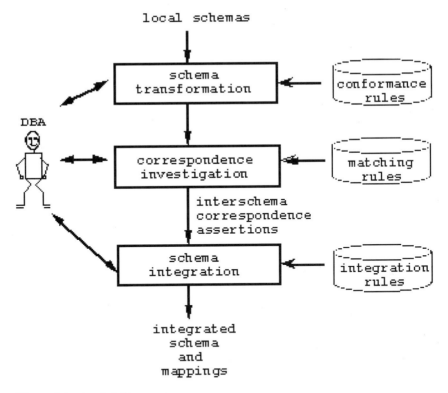

Figure 9.1   the global integration process

- pre-integration, a step in which input schemas are re-arranged in various ways to make them more homogeneous (both syntactically and semantically);

- correspondence identification, a step devoted to the identification of related items in the input schemas and the precise description of these inter-schemas relationships;

- and integration, the final step which actually unifies corresponding items into an integrated schema and produces the associated mappings.

The last sections discuss methodological aspects and conclude on further directions of work.

9.2   The Example

Discussions in the sequel will mostly be illustrated referring to the car rental example, the common case study used throughout this book. To put the example into an interoperability framework it suffices to assume that the branches of the car rental company have independently developed different databases. A company level decision to set up an integrated information system on top of existing data would lead to the database integration problem. Equivalently if we assume that different car rental companies, each one equipped with its own database, decide to merge businesses, which include merging of the information systems.

Let us consider that the databases to be integrated are described by the schemas that illustrate various chapters in this book. Having a common case study perfectly illustrates the diversity in schema designs due to different perceptions by each designer (in this case the authors of the chapters) of the same real world (the document describing the case study). Such a situation is representative of what happens in real applications.

Some differences simply stem from terminological choices. The key to identify a car, for instance, is either named "CarId", or "car_id", "Chassis#", or "Chassis". Terminological tools will easily identify the first two and the last two as being equivalent terms. But finding the equivalence between "CarId" and "Chassis#" requires a database perspective, i.e. consideration that both serve as unique key in equivalent structures (the Car relation, the Car object type, the Car entity type) and both have the same value domain.

More differences come from the fact that designers have chosen different properties for the same object type. Car has properties (Chassis#, category) in the chapter by Gogolla and has properties (CarId, Branch, Model, Make, Category, Year, Mileage, LastServiced) in the chapter by Jensen and Snodgrass.

Structural differences may be illustrated considering customer information. Jensen and Snodgrass propose a Customer relation which includes a "Rating" property (with value domain: "Preferred", . . .) to discriminate various categories of customers. Missaoui et al. materialize the same idea adding two subtypes (Blacklist, Freq_ Trav) to the Customer supertype. This difference between the two representations is mainly due to heterogeneity of the underlying data models (i.e. the model used by Jensen and Snodgrass does not support the generalization concept). Papazoglou and Kramer also use a data model with is-a links, but propose a different hierarchy: Customer has subtypes Person and Company, the latter with subtypes PrivateCorporation and Government. These two hierarchies are based on different specialization criteria.

Different classifications scheme, not involving is-a links, are visible when comparing the design by Missaoui et al., with the one by Gogolla. The latter includes two object types for bookings: one for current bookings (those where a specific car has been assigned), another for non-current bookings (where only a car category is specified). Missaoui's design has all bookings in a unique Rental-Booking type. Current bookings are found by restricting Rental-Booking objects to those that are linked to a car object by the Allocate-to link.

These differences give an idea of the complexity inherent to the database integration process, which will have to sort out differences to build a consistent representation of the data. They also point at the benefit expected from the integration. In a federated car rental information system it will be possible for a user at Gogolla's site to query the model of a car, an information that is not present at that site but can be found at Jensen and Snodgrass' site if the latter stores the requested car. Also, it becomes possible for a user at Papazoglou and Kramer site to know if a given customer is blacklisted or not, by looking at the related information in Missaoui's database.

9.3   Preparing for Integration

Generally, the databases to be integrated have been developed independently and are heterogeneous in several respects. A worthwhile first step is therefore to attempt to reduce or eliminate such discrepancies. The path from heterogeneity to homogeneity may take three complementary routes:

- syntactic rewriting. The most visible heterogeneity is when existing databases have been installed on DBMSs based on different data models (relational, CODASYL, object-oriented, . . .). Efficient interoperation calls for the adoption of a common data model serving as information exchange standard among participating locations. Dedicated wrappers have to be developed to enforce data model transformations between the local model and the common model (21).

- semantic enrichment. Data model heterogeneity also induces semantic heterogeneity, in the sense that constructs in one model may provide a more accurate description of data than constructs in another model. For instance, an entity-relationship schema has different constructs for entities and associations, while some equivalent relational schema may describe the same data without making an explicit distinction between entities and associations. To compare the two schemas, one should be able to identify, in the relational schema, which relations describe entities and which relations describe associations. This is a very primitive form of semantic enrichment, i.e. the process that aims at augmenting the knowledge about the semantics of data. A more elaborate one aims at describing the semantics of the data by building semantic ontologies.

- representational normalization. One more cause of heterogeneity is the non-determinism of the modeling process. Two designers representing the same real world situation with the same data model will inevitably end up with two different schemas. Enforcing modeling rules will reduce the heterogeneity of representations. This is referred to as representational normalization.

We discuss hereinafter how to cope with these three issues.

9.3.1   Data model heterogeneity

The issue here is how to map data structures and operations from one DBMS into data structures and operations conforming to a different DBMS. Most papers on database integration simply assume that the input schemas are all expressed in the same data model, i.e. the so-called "common" data model, on which the integrated system is built. A data model mapping step is assumed as a pre-requisite to integration and is dealt with as a separate problem. The needed mappings are those between any local data model and the common data model. Unfortunately, the state of the art in data model mapping is poor in tools for automatic mapping (except for many CASE tools for database design, supporting entity-relationship to relational mapping). Latest developments focus on mapping between object-oriented and relational models, as part of a major effort to develop the new object-relational DBMSs, which are supposed to support both paradigms. Typically, the way the problem is addressed nowadays is by splitting the mapping task into: 1/ a series of transformations (i.e. data structure modifications within a given data model), and 2/ a translation, i.e. the rewriting of the transformed schema using the syntax of the target model. The goal of transformations is to remove from the source schema the constructs in the source data model that do not exist in the target data model. Removal is performed using alternative design strategies in the source data model (38). The benefit of the decomposition is to allow for the implementation of a library of schema restructuring operations (the transformations) that can be reused in different mappings (63).

Beyond data structure transformations, some researchers have also considered the complementary problem of how to translate operations from one DBMS to another one. This is needed for a fully multilingual system, i.e. a system in which users from participating systems use the languages of the local DBMS to access the federated system. Because of their additional complexity, multilingual federations are rarely advocated in the literature. Still they offer users the substantial benefit of not having to learn new languages to interact with the FDBS.

One of the unresolved debates is the choice of the common data model. Basically, two directions have supporters. The majority favors the object-oriented approach. The argument is that it has all the semantic concepts of the other models and that methods can be used to implement specific mapping rules. An open issue is to agree on which one of the many existing object-oriented models is best in this role. A second problem is that the richest the model is in modeling concepts, the more likely it is that different designers will model the same reality using different constructs, based on their own perception of the relative importance of things. Known as semantic relativism, this flexibility makes integration more complex, as it will have to solve the many possible discrepancies dues to different modeling choices. To make integration simpler, the alternative is to adopt a data model with minimal semantics embedded, such that there is little chance of conflicts in data representation. Data representations in semantically poor models are brought down to elementary facts for which there is no modeling alternative. Binary-relationships models compete in this role with functional models (51).

A stream of more basic research investigates the possibility of developing a generic wrapper, capable of performing mapping between any two data models (5, 45, 49). In a traditional federated system, algorithms to map schemas in the local data models into schemas in the common data model CDM (and vice versa) are explicitly implemented by the local wrappers. Adding a new data model Mj to the federation requires the development of a new wrapper supporting the two mappings: Mj to CDM, CDM to Mj. It is possible to avoid such a burden by moving from the procedural approach (defining and implementing algorithms) to a declarative approach. The latter relies on the definition of a meta-model (i.e. a data model suited for the description of data models) (65). The meta-model includes a number of basic modeling concepts and knows how to map each concepts into another one (for instance, how to nest flat tuples to obtain a nested tuple). Once the definitions of the local data models, in terms of the meta-model, are fed into the generic mapping tool, the tool is capable to map any source schema into any target schema. First, the source schema is mapped into the meta-model concepts. Second, restructuring rules are applied within the meta-model database to turn source concepts into target concepts, third the result is mapped into the target model. In this context, adding a new data model Mj to the federation simply calls for the definition of the Mj concepts in terms of the meta-model. Beyond data structures, (12) extends the mapping task to include processing of some associated non-standard constraints.

9.3.2   Semantic enrichment

Whatever the approach, translations raise a number of difficult problems and it is unlikely that they can be fully automated. Interactions with database administrators are needed to solve ambiguities that rise because schemas only convey incomplete information on the semantics of data. On the one hand, however powerful, data models cannot express all the semantics of the real world. Limitations in the modeling concepts cannot be avoided, as the required exhaustiveness would lead to a model of unmanageable complexity. On the other hand, even augmented with integrity constraints, a schema usually relies on many implicit assumptions that form the cultural background of the organization. Implicit business rules are supposed to be known to all users, hence they need no description. But when the database enters a federation, it becomes open to users who know nothing about its implicit rules.

Semantic enrichment is basically a human decision process, used to provide more information either on how a schema maps to the real world, or on the schema itself. An example of the former is adding a definition of "Employee" as "those persons who have an employment contract with the enterprise". An example of the latter is specifying that the attribute "boss" in the "Department" relation is an external key to the "Employee" relation. Semantic enrichment is not specific to poor data models. Object-oriented schemas may also need to be augmented with information on cardinalities or on dependencies (which are not represented but are necessary, for instance, for a correct translation of multivalued attributes). As another example, reformulating an object-oriented schema may call for turning an attribute into an object: the question immediately arises whether two identical values of this attribute should be translated into only one or two objects. No automatic decision is possible, as the answer depends on the real world semantics.

Some techniques aid in acquiring additional information about the semantics of a schema. Poor data structures may be turned into richer conceptual structures using reverse engineering techniques. Such poor structures exist, for instance, in old relational systems, which only stored the description of the relations and their attributes, with no notice of primary keys, candidate keys, foreign keys, or dependencies. More-over, relations in existing databases are not necessarily normalized, thus obscuring the underlying semantics. Reverse engineering relies on the analysis of whatever information is available: schema specifications, index definitions, the data in the database, queries in existing application programs. Combining inferences from these analyses (in particular, about keys and dependencies) makes it possible to recom-pose complex object types from flat relations, and to identify association structures and generalization hierarchies. The result still needs confirmation by the DBA. For instance, join conditions in queries may indicate, but not assert, the existence of a foreign key; the usage of a "distinct" clause in an SQL statement may lead to the conclusion that the retrieved attribute is not a primary key (22, 62), and so on. Simi-lar but more complex techniques are used to reengineer existing files (4).

Beyond data structures, when it comes to understanding the semantics of data, knowledge discovery, or knowledge elicitation, techniques are appropriate. The ba-sic goal is to build an integrated semantic dictionary whose scope spans over all databases in the federation. Integrating ontologies, building concept hierarchies or context integration are alternative denotations for this process. Description logic is a well-known theoretical support for developing vocabulary sharing based on syn-onym relationships (39). Statistical analysis of combined term occurrences may help in determining relationships among concepts (24). A global organization of the lo-cal knowledge is thus achieved (8). For more enrichment, contextual information is gathered to make explicit the rules and interpretations not stated in the local schemas (33). For instance, a salary item may be complemented with the information on the local monetary unit, not otherwise described. When the inference cannot be done using some automatic reasoning, interaction with the DBAs is necessary (46).

Semantic enrichment becomes an even more challenging issue when application data has to be collected dynamically from non-predefined sources available at the moment the application is run. This is the case in particular when the data is collected over the Web. Web data is typically semi-structured, and comes with little descrip-tions attached. Many ongoing projects address the issue of extracting semantics from a Web site data, whether on the fly during execution of a query or in a more static setting through exploration of designated Web sites (e.g., (6, 13)).

9.3.3   Representational normalization

Modeling choices are guided by the perception of the designer and by the usage the data is for. The same real world data may thus be described using different data struc-tures, which represent modeling alternatives supported by most data models. Support for such alternatives is known as semantic relativism. The richest a data model is in semantic expressiveness, the more it opens up to modeling alternatives. Seman-tic relativism is often criticized as a weakness of a model, because the designer is confronted with a non-trivial choice among alternatives. In our opinion, it should rather be considered as an advantage, as it offers flexibility to closely adjust the representation of data to the intended usage of the data. However, undesirable discrepancies may be reduced through enforcement of rules that constrain designers to certain choices. This could be at the organizational level, by enforcing corporate modeling policies (including terminology), and/or at the technical level, by applying normalization rules. Organizational rules may range from defining the terminology to be used (i.e., names of data items) to adopting design patterns (i.e., pre-defined representation schemes) or even a complete pre-established design for the whole organization (e.g., when using the SAP product). Normalization rules are well known in the context of relational databases, but still have to be elaborated for object-oriented databases. Two types of normalization rules can be defined. First, they may enforce design rules that command the use of a representation instead of another one. Examples are:

- if a property of an object type is only relevant for a subset of its instances (e.g., maiden name for persons), represent this using a supertype/subtype structure (e.g., a supertype Person with a subtype Wife), where the subtype bears this attribute as mandatory; do not represent this as an object type with an optional attribute. This rule allows having schemas without optional attributes.

- if a property of an object type may hold many values within the same instance (e.g., telephone number for persons), represent the property as a separate object type and a reference to it from the original type (e.g., a type Telephone and a reference to Telephone in Person); do not represent the property as a multivalued attribute in the original type. This rule allows having schemas without multivalued attributes.

- a type with an enumerated property (e.g., Person and the sex property whose domain has two predefined values) should be replaced by a supertype/subtypes structure (e.g., a Person supertype with Man and Woman subtypes).

This type of rules enforces syntactic normalization, independently of the semantics of data. Another set of normalization rules aims at conforming the schemas to the underlying dependencies. An example of a possible rule of this type is: if there is a dependency between attributes A and B of an object type, and A is not a key, replace these attributes by a composite (tuple) attribute with A and B as component attributes. This may resemble relational normalization, but differs from it on the intended purpose. Relational normal forms aim at reducing data duplication to avoid update anomalies. The object-type normal form we used as example is intended to enhance the semantics of the schema. More work on normalization is needed before normal rules for objects are agreed upon (61).

9.4   Identifying Interdatabase Correspondences

Once the input data sources have been rewritten and enriched into whatever level of conformance is achievable, the next step is the identification of overlapping or complementary information in different sources. Indeed, providing users with an integrated view of the available data implies that:

- at the schema level, the descriptions of related information from different sources are somehow merged to form a unique and consistent description within the integrated schema, and

- at the instance level, a mechanism is set up to link a representation within a source to related representations within the other sources. These links support integrated data access at query time.

Interdatabase correspondences are frequently found by looking for similarities in the input schemas. However, similarity between representations is not the ultimate criterion. Similarity evaluation may be misled by terminological ambiguities (homonyms and synonyms) and, more generally, by differences in the implicit contexts. Also, representations of the same data (whether real world objects, links or properties) may be completely different from one source to the other. Hence, database integration has to go beyond representations to consider what is represented rather than how it is represented. For instance, we want to know if Hans Schmidt, represented in database A, is also represented in database B, even if the two instances have completely different sets of attributes. Two databases are said to have something in common if the real world subsets they represent have some common elements (i.e. a non-empty intersection) or have some elements related to each other in a way that is of interest to future applications. An example of the latter is the case where a car rental company has a database of cars in each branch, recording cars of that branch, and it is worthwhile for the company to form an integrated database showing a single object type Car that represents all cars belonging to the company.

At the instance level, two elements (occurrence, value, tuple, link, ...) from two databases are said to correspond to each other if they describe the same real world element (object, link or property). As an example, let us assume that an object type Employee, holding a Salary attribute, exists in both an Austrian database and a German database, and an employee Hans Schmidt belongs to the two databases. If Hans Schmidt in Austria is the same person than Hans Schmidt in Germany, the two database objects correspond to each other. If this correspondence is not stated, the system will assume that two persons are just sharing the same name. If there is only one person Hans Schmidt and he has only one salary, represented in marks in the German database and in shillings in the Austrian database, the two salary values correspond to each other (there exist a mapping that deduces one from the other). If the two salary values are not stated as corresponding to each other, it means that Hans Schmidt gets two salaries, independent of each other even if by chance they happen to represent the same amount.

If a correspondence can be defined such that it holds for every element in an identifiable set (e.g., the population of a type), the correspondence is stated at the schema level. This intensional definition of a correspondence is called an interdatabase correspondence assertion (ICA). The complete integration of existing databases requires an exhaustive identification and processing of all relevant ICAs. In an exhaustive approach, the integration process consists in finding all interdatabase correspondences and for each correspondence adding to the integrated schema an integrated description of the related elements (supporting the mapping at the instance level). Local elements with no counterpart elsewhere are directly integrated in the global schema. At the end of the process the integrated schema provides a complete and non-redundant description of all data in the FDB. The mappings between the integrated schema and the local schemas support integrated data access for users of the FDB.

Such a complete and static integration is not always possible, not even desirable. This is the case when, for instance, the number of local databases is too high, or the schemas contain too many items, or in evolvable environments where input databases may dynamically be connected and disconnected. In these cases, partial, dynamic or incremental integration strategies are advisable. Strategy issues are discussed in Section 9.6. Whatever the strategy, ICAs will have to be found, made explicit and processed: they are a cornerstone for data interoperability. Techniques for these activities do not depend on the strategy.

The precise definition of an interdatabase correspondence assertion calls for the specification of:

- what are the related elements, both at the schema level and in terms of the population subsets that are involved in the correspondence. This information is used to build the data structure in the integrated schema;

- how to identify, for each instance involved in a correspondence, which are the corresponding instances in the other sources. This information is used for integrated access to data;

- how the representations of corresponding instances are related. This information is used to build non-redundant descriptions in the integrated schema.

We discuss below the specifications in detail.

9.4.1   Relating corresponding elements

To declare a correspondence between two databases, it is desirable to identify as precisely as possible the elements that are being related. Assume, for instance, that two car rental companies decide to join their efforts and build an integrated service, hence an integrated database. Each company has its own database, say A and B, which include an object type CarModel to describe models of cars being rented. Both companies rent cars from the same manufacturers and, in particular, the same car models. They agree to keep this as a rule for future evolution of their business. In other words, they agree that updates of the available car models made by one company are also effective for the other company. In database terms, the populations of the two object types A.CarModel and B.CarModel are kept equivalent at any point in time: each object in A.CarModel always has a corresponding object in B.CarModel. Equivalence means that the car models represented in A and B are the same in the real world, although their representation in the two databases may differ (e.g., they may include different attributes). These assumptions lead to the assertion of the following ICA:

$$A.CarModel \equiv B.CarModel.$$

If the two companies prefer a more flexible integration, and in particular one which supports update autonomy, i.e. each company performs its own updates and no update is mandated by the other company, integration will be based on an intersection relationship:

$$A.CarModel \frown B.CarModel.$$

This instructs the system that at any time there may be in A a subset of CarModel objects which have an equivalent in the population of B.CarModel, and vice versa. Updates do not need anymore to be propagated. The correspondence rule at the instance level (see next subsection) determines which objects belong to the corresponding subsets. Assume that A.CarModel and B.CarModel are merged into a single object type I-CarModel in the integrated schema. At data access, objects in the (virtual) population of I-CarModel will show more or less information, depending on their existence in A only, in B only, or in both. In other words, attributes that exist in only one database will appear as optional attributes to the integrated user.

It may be the case that the subsets involved in the intersection are known in advance. For instance, the two car rental companies may be sharing models but only for a specific manufacturer, say BMW, for which exactly the same models are offered. In this case the ICA is stated as:

$$\sigma\,[manufacturer = \text{``BMW''}]A.CarModel$$
$$\equiv \sigma\,[manufacturer = \text{``BMW''}]B.CarModel$$

where σ denotes the selection operator. It is possible, in particular, to split the population of a type into subsets corresponding to populations of different types in the other database. Assume a database D1 with a type Person and another database D2 with two types, Man and Woman, which represent the same set of real world persons. It is then correct to state:

$$\text{case } 1{:}\sigma\,[sex = \text{``male''}]D1.Person \equiv D2.Man$$
$$\sigma\,[sex = \text{``female''}]D1.Person \equiv D2.Woman$$

This is more precise, hence preferable, than the single ICA:

$$\text{case } 2{:}\quad D1.Person \equiv D2.Man \smile D2.Woman$$

or the two ICAs:

$$\text{case } 3{:}D1.Person \frown D2.Man$$
$$D1.Person \frown D2.Woman$$

The explicit statement defining the selection criteria (case 1) allows to build more precise mappings between the integrated schema and the input schemas. For instance, if it is only known that Person is equivalent to the union of Man and Woman (case 2), a query from a federated user asking for women will be directed to D2, which knows about women. The specification of the selection criterion allows, instead, the system to either direct the query to the object type Woman in D2 or to the object type Person restricted to women in D1. This gives more power in terms of query optimization strategies. Moreover, update propagation can be supported from D1 to D2 and vice-versa, while in case 2 updates can only be propagated from D2 to D1. Allowing D1 users to update the set of persons would imply bothering the user to determine whether the person is a man or a woman.

Related sets of elements may be denoted by algebraic expressions of any complexity on each side of the correspondence. In the examples we have seen so far, the mapping at the instance level is 1:1: one person corresponds to either a man or a woman. That is not always the case. For example, a CarModel type may describe car models in one database, while in another database only parts of a car model (e.g., motor, chassis) are described in a Part type. There is a correspondence between each instance of CarModel and the set of Part instances describing this car model. This situation is referred to as a fragmentation conflict, first introduced in (16). Fragmentation conflicts are frequent in spatial databases, when databases at different resolution levels are interrelated (14).

Relating schema elements is not sufficient to precisely capture all interrelationships among databases. Relating intra-database links is also important. For instance, assume two databases A and B, each one showing object types Car and Customer linked by a CC relationship. The fact that correspondences are stated between A.Car and B.Car and between A.Customer and B.Customer does not imply a correspondence between the two relationships (A.CC and B.CC). One could imagine that in database A the CC path between Car and Customer expresses the fact that a customer holds a booking for the car, while in database B CC is used to express that a customer has already rented this car in the past. In this case, assuming the integrated schema keeps the Car and Customer object types, Car and Customer will be linked by two separate relationships, images of A.CC and B.CC, each one with its specific original semantics. If in both databases the CC relationships have the same semantics, this has to be explicitly stated as a valid ICA, so that integration results in only one relationship in the integrated schema. The ICA reads, for instance:

$$A.Car - CC - Customer \equiv B.Car - CC - Customer$$

This is interpreted as the assertion that any time in database A car x is related via A.CC to customer y, in database B car x' (corresponding to x) is related via B.CC to customer y' (corresponding to y). Paths in an ICA are denoted by enumerating the elements they traverse. Path integration, first discussed in (60), has been investigated in detail in (29).

The above examples have shown relevance of the equivalence ($\equiv$) and intersection ($\cap$) relationships in the definition of an ICA. Inclusion ($\supseteq$), or disjointedness ($\neq$) relationships may also be used. Inclusion states that the set denoted for one database is included in the set denoted for the other database. Assume a car rental branch B only rents small or medium size cars, while another branch A from the same company rents all types of cars. A relevant ICA may be:

$$A.CarModel \supseteq B.CarModel$$

Finally, disjointedness relates sets that have no common elements, but whose integration is desired. For instance, assuming each rental branch has its own cars, the ICA

$$A.Car \neq B.Car$$

directs the integration process to merge the two car object types in the integrated schema, despite the fact that the two populations are disjoint. The virtual population of the integrated type is the union of the source populations.

9.4.2   How corresponding instances are identified

When federated users request a data element via the integrated schema, the federated system may find that some properties of the element exist in one database, while other properties exist in another database. To provide users with all available data, the system has to know how to find in one database the object (instance or value) corresponding to a given instance/value in another database. Assume, for instance, that CarModel in A has attributes (name, manufacturer, number of seats, trunk capacity) and corresponding CarModel in B has attributes (code, manufacturer, year, available colors). To answer a user query asking for Ford models with trunk capacity greater than 800cm3 and available in blue or black, the federated system knows that it has to perform a join between objects in A (which hold the trunk capacity criterion) and corresponding objects in B (holding the color criterion). How does the federated system know which join criterion applies?

To solve the issue, each ICA has to include the specification of the corresponding mapping between the instances: we call this the "matching criterion" (MC) clause. If we assume that code in B is nothing but the name in A, the ICA:

$$A.CarModel \supseteq B.CarModel \quad MC \quad A.name = B.code$$

specifies that corresponding car model objects from the two databases share a common identifying value, value of name in A and value of code in B. The join condition discussed above is nothing but A.name = B.code.

The general MC clause involves for each database a (possibly complex) predicate specifying the corresponding instances/values. Most often value-based identifiers (e.g. primary keys in relational models) can be used to match corresponding instances. This, however, does not have to be the case, and any 1:1 mapping function is acceptable, including user-defined functions, historical conditions, complex heuristics, and look-up tables. Materialization of matching data has been suggested as a way to reduce the cost of matching when very complex criteria have to be evaluated (68). This induces a maintenance problem, which also arises when updates to real world objects are captured asynchronously in the source databases. A complex probabilistic approach, using historical information in transaction logs, has been proposed to solve this update heterogeneity problem (58). A matching technique for semi-structured data has been proposed in (48), where object identification is generated by extraction of semantics when objects are imported by the mediator. In some approaches, import of objects by the mediator comes with a virtual object identity generation mechanism (26), where virtual identities are used to denote objects at the federated level. In such a setting, the federated system has to check for the transitivity of object matching: if o1 matches o2 and o2 matches o3, then o1 matches o3. Indeed, such transitivity is not necessarily guaranteed by the object identity generation mechanism (3).

Spatial databases offer a specific alternative for identification of correlated objects: by location, i.e. through their position in space. This allows to assert that two instances are related if they are located in the same point (line, area, or volume) in space. Notice that sometimes in spatial databases there is no thematic attribute to serve as an object identifier, hence no alternative to a spatial matching (14).

9.4.3   How representations are related

Back at the schema level, let us now consider representations of related elements, i.e. the set of properties attached to the corresponding elements. Properties include both attributes and methods. In order to avoid duplication of properties in the integrated schema, it is important that shared properties, beyond those used for identification (denoted in the MC clause), be identified and the mappings in between specified. To this extent a "corresponding properties" (CP) clause is added to the ICA. For instance, if the two related CarModel types both include a "maker" attribute and all other properties are different, the ICA stated in 9.4.2 becomes

$$
\begin{aligned}
A.CarModel \quad &\supseteq B.CarModel \\
MC \quad A.name &= B.code \\
CP \quad A.maker &= B.maker
\end{aligned}
$$

The general format for a correspondence between properties X and Y is: f(X)rel g(Y), where rel is equality (=), if X or Y is monovalued, or a set relationship ($\equiv, \supseteq, \frown, \neq$) if X and Y are multivalued; f and g are two functions used, whenever needed, to solve a representation conflict. The semantics of the CP clause is that, if E and F are the database elements related by the ICA, the sets of values E.X and F.Y (possibly converted through functions f and g respectively) are related by the given set relationship. Attribute matching has been extensively analyzed in the literature (32). Method matching is a recent issue raised by object orientation (40).

9.4.4   Consistency of correspondences

Given a set of ICAs between two databases, the ICAs can be checked for consistency and minimality. Assume one schema has a A is-a B construct and the other schema has a C is-a D construct. An example of inconsistent ICA specification is: $A \equiv D$, $B \equiv C$. Both cannot be true because of the acyclity property of is-a graphs.

Some ICAs are derivable from others: if $A \equiv C$ is asserted, $B \supseteq C$ and $D \supseteq A$ may be inferred. Hence, only ICAs bearing non-derivable correspondences need to be explicitly stated.

(29) analyzed the consistency issue for path correspondences. The authors defined two sets of rules:

- rules that specify which kind of paths cannot correspond to each other, e.g. a reference link cannot be equivalent to an is-a link,
- rules that check consistency of path correspondences, e.g. if two correspondences contain the same sub-path, they are either redundant or inconsistent.

9.4.5   Investigation of correspondences

With real, large schemas to be integrated, the task of identifying all relevant ICAs is far from trivial. A significant amount of research has been and is being invested into tools for automated identification of plausible correspondences. Traditional approaches (20, 40) measure the similarity between two schema elements by looking for identical or similar characteristics: names, identifiers, components, properties, attributes (name, domain, constraints), methods. Computing the ratio of similarities versus dissimilarities gives an evaluation of how plausible the correspondence is. The idea has been put to an extreme in (10), where metadata is dumped to unformatted text on which information retrieval tools evaluate string similarity. (18) takes the opposite direction and proposes to enrich the schemas before comparison by extracting semantics from an analysis of data instances. In a similar attempt to limit erroneous inferences due to synonyms and homonyms, (17) recommends terminological knowledge bases to explain the terms used in the application domain and the semantic links in between.

Unconventional approaches include (34) and (37). The former uses neural networks to match equivalent attributes. The latter uses knowledge discovery tools borrowed from the data mining community. (54) advocates the use of machine learning techniques for settling correspondences in spatial database integration. The complexity of spatial matching criteria makes it difficult for a designer to specify correspondences without errors or approximations. It is easier to point at specific correspondences at the instance level and let the system learn from these examples until the system can propose a general expression.

Whatever the technique, it is recommended that the final step be an interaction with the DBA for validation/invalidation of the findings and provision of additional information on the ICAs (e.g., the relationship between extents).

9.5   Solving Conflicts

Except if data sets to be integrated originate from a previous decision to duplicate data, at least partially, (e.g., for performance reasons), it is unlikely that related elements from different databases will perfectly match. Different but related databases have rather something than all in common, i.e. they represent overlapping subsets of the real world. Discrepancies may arise on various respects. The common set of real world objects or links may be organized into different classification schemes. The set of properties attached to objects and links may differ. Each of these differences is seen as a conflict among existing representations (interschema conflict), due to different design choices. A different type of conflict (interdata conflict) has its source in data acquisition errors or inaccuracies: this is when the same data in different databases has different values.

Conflicts have to be solved to provide federated users with an integrated view of conflicting data. Solving an interschema conflict means: 1) deciding how the related conflicting elements are going to be described in the integrated schema, and 2) defining the mappings between the chosen integrated representation and the local ones. These mappings are used by the query processor component of the FDBS to transform each federated global query into the corresponding set of local queries, which are executed by the local DBMSs to retrieve and recompose all bits and pieces of data that are needed to provide the requested data. Solutions to interdata conflicts are discussed in Section 9.5.4.

The existence of alternatives in conflict resolution strategies has received little attention (16). Authors usually propose specific solutions for each conflict type, with no concern about consistency of integration choices. However, different organizational goals are possible and lead to different technical solutions (cf. Figure 9.2):

- the goal may be simplicity (i.e. readability) of the integrated schema: the appropriate technique then is to produce a minimal number of schema elements (object types, attributes and links). Related representations will be merged into an integrated representation, which will hide existing differences. For instance, if one object type in one database is asserted to intersect an object type in the other database, only the union type will be described in the integrated schema. The selection criterion that defines the input types will show up in the mapping between the integrated schema and the local database. Mappings in this merging technique need to be sophisticated enough to cope with the schema conflicts. The advantage of readability is of course in human communication and understanding;

- the goal may be completeness, in the sense that every element of an input schema appears in the integrated schema. In this case, if one object type in one database is asserted to intersect an object type in the other database, both types and their common intersection subtype will be described and linked by is-a links in the integrated schema. The advantage of completeness is that elements of input schemas can be readily identified within the integrated schema, thus helping in maintaining the integrated schema when input databases evolve. Also, mappings get close to identity functions, which simplifies query processing;

- the goal may also be exhaustiveness, i.e. having in the integrated schema all possible elements, including those who are not in input schemas but complement what

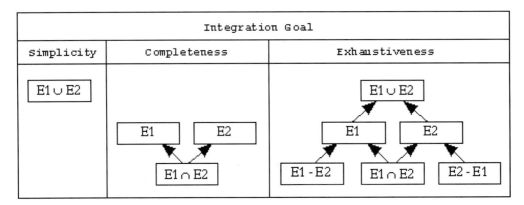

Figure 9.2   Alternative integrated schemas for the ICA E1 ∩ E2

is there. For the running example, this principle leads to the inclusion in the integrated schema of both input types, together with their union (common supertype), their intersection (common subtype) and the complements of the intersection (two subtypes). In some sense, this is intended to ease future integration with new databases, as chances are higher that types found in a newly considered input schema will already be present in the IS.

For a rigorous, systematic approach to database integration, it is important that the involved DBAs agree on the integration goal. Moreover, an explicit choice allows defining the rules that mediators need to automatically perform integration. Otherwise, specific rules have to be defined in each mediator for each conflict type or conflict instance.

Taxonomies of conflicts abound in the literature, from very detailed ones (56) to simpler ones (59). Some examples of well-known conflict categories are:

- heterogeneity conflicts: different data models support the input schemas;

- generalization/specialization conflicts: related databases represent different viewpoints on the same set of objects, resulting in different generalization/ specialization hierarchies, with objects distributed according to different classification abstractions (32, 20, 27);

- description conflicts: the related types have different sets of properties and/or their corresponding properties are described in different ways (27);

- structural conflicts: the constructs used for describing the related types are different (60);

- fragmentation conflicts: the same real world objects are described through different decompositions into different component elements (16, 14);

- metadata conflicts: the correspondence relates a type to a meta-type (50);

- data conflicts: corresponding instances have different values for corresponding properties (57, 1).

In most cases, conflicts from different categories will combine to form a given correspondence. An open issue is to demonstrate if the resulting integrated schema is the same irrespectively of the order in which conflict types are addressed in a mediator. If not, the next issue is to find the best order, either in terms of quality of the result or in terms of processing time.

Detailed, and different, proposals on how to solve the above conflicts can easily be found in the literature. Despite the differences, some general principles supporting conflict resolution and integration rules may be highlighted:

- preservation of local schemas and databases: input databases should be kept as they are to preserve the investment in existing data and programs. If modifications are needed to solve conflicts and conform each input database to the integrated schema, they are only virtually performed, i.e. modifications are implemented as part of the mappings between the integrated schema and the existing input schemas. These mappings may rely on a view mechanism;

- production of both an integrated schema and the mappings to input schemas: mappings are necessary to make integration operational;

- subsumption of input schemas by the integrated schema: the integrated schema must describe all data made available in the input databases. Hence integrated types must subsume the corresponding input types: subsume their capacity to describe information (adopting the least upper bound) and subsume the constraints which are inherent to or attached to them (adopting the greatest lower bound). Capacity denotes which combination of identity/value/links is modeled by a given construct (60). For instance, an attribute in OO and relational approaches models either a value or a link, while in ER approaches it models only a value. A relational relation models a value and possibly links (through foreign keys), not identity. Therefore, if an ICA between relational schemas identifies a relation (value+links) as corresponding to an attribute (value or link), the integrated schema will retain the relation. The same principle dictates that every type with no counterpart elsewhere should be added to the integrated schema as it is. The least upper bound of its capacity and the greatest lower bound of its constraints define the type itself. Finally, this principle also directs the way to integrate integrity constraints: keep their greatest lower bound.

The next subsection discusses general principles that apply whenever a correspondence relates one instance in one database to one instance in the other database, i.e. there is a 1:1 mapping at the instance level. The following subsection similarly discusses n:m mappings. Third we discuss structural conflicts. Finally, interdata conflicts are considered.

9.5.1   One to one matching

We discuss here the situation where it is possible to identify a one to one mapping between two sets of objects of two databases. In other words, for each object from a given set in database A, there is a corresponding object in database B, and vice versa. The major conflict in this case is when objects have been classified using different schemes (generalization/specialization conflict). For instance, in database A there may be an object type Customer, with subtypes GoodCustomer and BadCustomer, while in database B there is an object type Customer with subtypes ExternalCustomer and LocalCustomer. Let us assume Hans Schmidt is a customer in both databases. He will be represented as an instance of some object type on both sides, but not the same. If the membership predicate for each object type is known, the hierarchy of customer object types in A can be mapped onto the hierarchy of customer object types in B.

Because of the 1:1 mapping at the instance level, predicates expressing the inter-database correspondence assertions will use object-preserving operations. Algebraic expressions in the ICAs will thus include selections, unions or intersections, to re-compose the distribution of objects, but no join or aggregation. They may also include projections in order to reduce the sets of properties to the common set (i.e. properties present in both databases). As an example, ICAs for the related customer hierarchies may be:

$$A.GoodCustomer = (\text{SELECT } B.ExternalCustomer$$
$$\text{WHERE } type = \text{``good''})$$
$$\text{UNION}(\text{SELECT } B.LocalCustomer$$
$$\text{WHERE } type = \text{``good''})$$
$$A.BadCustomer = (\text{SELECT } B.ExternalCustomer$$
$$\text{WHERE } type = \text{``bad''})$$
$$\text{UNION}(\text{SELECT } B.LocalCustomer$$
$$\text{WHERE } type = \text{``bad''})$$
$$B.LocalCustomer = (\text{SELECT } A.GoodCustomer$$
$$\text{WHERE } state = \text{``CH''})$$
$$\text{UNION}(\text{SELECT } A.BadCustomer$$
$$\text{WHERE } state = \text{``CH''})$$
$$B.ExternalCustomer = (\text{SELECT } A.GoodCustomer$$
$$\text{WHERE } state \neq \text{``CH''})$$
$$\text{UNION}(\text{SELECT } A.BadCustomer$$
$$\text{WHERE } state \neq \text{``CH''})$$

A strategy for integration of generalization hierarchies related by multiple ICAs is presented in (52). The main problem stems from the twofold semantics of generalization/specialization links: extent inclusion and property inheritance. The two semantics tend to diverge when two somehow interrelated hierarchies with populated types are merged. When inserting a type from one hierarchy into the other hierarchy, the place determined according to the extent inclusion may differ from the place determined according to property inheritance. The algorithm in (52) complies with both

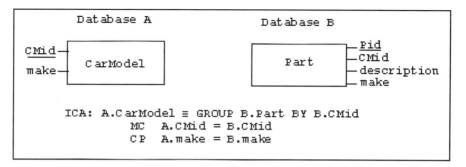

Figure 9.3   a fragmentation conflict

semantics in merging two hierarchies, but to achieve this it has to split the input types so that, for each pair of corresponding types, their extents are distributed into three sets: the common extent (objects in a 1:1 correspondence) and the extents that belong to only one database (objects with no correspondence). The type of each partial extent receives all attributes of both schemas which are meaningful (i.e. valued) for the extent. In general, the integrated schema will contain new types, with smaller extents than the input ones. A refinement phase allows suppressing abstract types or types without own attributes. The approach assumes that the distribution of objects is known, i.e. specialization criteria are explicitly defined.

9.5.2   Many to many matching

Many to many correspondences relate a set of objects in one database to a set of objects in another database, such that there is no one to one mapping between the objects of the two sets. As mentioned in section 4.1, these have been called fragmentation conflicts, which expresses that the conflict stems from a different decomposition of the real world thing being represented in the two databases. Let us recall the example we used (cf. Figure 9.3): a CarModel type may describe car models in one database, while in another database only parts of a car model (e.g., motor, chassis) are described in a Part type. In this specific example the correspondence is 1:n, between one object (a CarModel instance) and a set of objects (the corresponding instances of the Part type).

   To illustrate a generic n:m correspondence let us consider two cartographic databases that include representations of buildings for map production purposes. Let us assume the two databases have different resolutions (i.e. they contain information to produce maps at different scales), and there is a set of buildings, e.g. a university campus, which needs to be represented using some abstraction because the scale does not allow precise representation of each individual building. This abstraction mechanism is known as cartographic generalization. It may be the case that generalization in database A resulted in representing the campus as 8 fictitious buildings, while generalization for less precise database B resulted in representing the same campus as a set of 5 other fictitious buildings. Assuming there is no correspondence

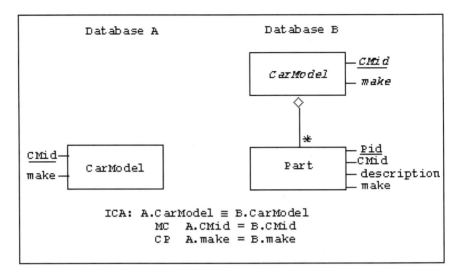

Figure 9.4   Transformation of a 1:n correspondence into a 1:1 correspondence

between the individual fictitious buildings, the only ICA relating these fictitious buildings states that the set of 8 fictitious buildings corresponds to the set of 5 fictitious buildings.

There is no easy, meaningful operation to map a set of objects into another set of objects. However, fragmentation conflicts may be solved by transformation of the n:m matching into an equivalent 1:1 matching. This is done through schema enhancement and object-generating operations. Whenever a configuration of objects (i.e. a set of objects and links in between) in a database is collectively involved in a correspondence, a new type is created, whose instances represent those configurations. The new types will be linked to the existing ones by an aggregation link or by any kind of link of the data model which is able to express an aggregation (composition link, association, external key, etc.). Once the new types are established by means of object generating expressions, the correspondence may be restated as a 1:1 correspondence between the new types (14). In the previous CarModel versus Part example, a derived CarModel object type is defined for B, such that a CarModel object is the aggregation of the Part objects that share the same value for the Cmid property (cf. Figure 9.4). The aggregated object has derived properties Cmid and maker, derived from the related Part objects. At this point, the correspondence between A and B can be stated as a 1:1 correspondence between the CarModel type in A and the derived CarModel type in B.

9.5.3   Structural conflicts

The schema restructuring principle is also used to solve structural conflicts. These arise whenever something in the real world has been represented by different constructs, which have different representational power or different constraints: a car model, for instance, may be represented as an object class in one database and as an attribute in another database. Similarly for object types and a relationship types.

The solution of structural conflicts obeys the rule that the integrated schema must describe the populations of the two conflicting types. Hence, as stated at the beginning of Section 9.5, the integrated type must subsume both input types in terms of information capacity and constraints. Typical constraints to be considered are cardinality constraints and existence dependencies. For instance, an attribute is existence dependent on its owner, while an object is generally not constrained by existence dependencies. If an ICA relates an object type to an attribute, the integrated schema will retain the object type (the greatest lower bound in this case is: no constraint). More about the solution of structural conflicts may be found in (60).

An extreme case of structural conflict is the so-called data/metadata conflict. Here, the decision choices that generate the conflict are the representation of the same thing as a value for some data on one hand, and as a name of some schema element on the other hand. For instance, the car model ZY-roadster may be represented by a value of an attribute car-model in a Car object type, or by an object type ZY-roadster whose instances represent such cars. Again, schema transformation operations are needed to solve the conflict, such as partitioning a class into subclasses according to the value of a specialization attribute, or creating a common superclass, with a new classifying attribute, over a set of given classes. Different variants of this solution may be found in (50), (30) or (41).

9.5.4   Interdata conflicts

This type of conflict occurs at the instance level if corresponding occurrences have conflicting values for corresponding attributes. For instance, the same car is stored in two databases with different car model values. Sources for interdata conflicts include typing errors, variety of information providers, different versioning, deferred updates. Spatial databases have an even richer set of possible conflicts (nine kinds are identified in (1)).

These conflicts are normally found during query processing. The system may just report the conflict to the user, or might apply some heuristic to determine the appropriate value. Common heuristics are choosing the value from the database known as "the most reliable", or uniting conflicting values in some way (through union for sets of values, though aggregation for single values). Another possibility is to provide users with a manipulation language with facilities to manipulate sets of possible values; such a set is built as an answer to a query whenever a data conflict occurs (64). Similarly, (2) and (15) propose a flexible relational data model and algebra, which adapt the relational paradigm to inconsistent data management by making visible the inconsistency, if any, among tuples of an integrated relation (i.e. tuples with the same value for the key and different values for the same attribute).

9.6   Integration Strategies

Beyond the technical issues that we have surveyed, a very important open question relates to the strategy to be used to face database integration in real, quite complex environments. Complexity may be due to a huge number (hundreds or more) of databases to be integrated, as it is the case in some telecommunications businesses, or to very large schemas with hundreds of object or relationship types, or to the heterogeneity of the sources, ranging from purely unstructured to fully structured data, coupled with very little information available on the semantics of the existing data (which is the case, in particular, for data gathered via Internet).

In real applications, achieving full integration may be a very long process, which needs to be carefully planned for a step by step implementation possibly over several years. This idea of incremental integration has become very popular and most contributions today aim at providing a way to smoothly install integrated services while existing systems stay in operation. In fact, being incremental is orthogonal to the methodology, as all integration methodologies can be revisited and reformulated so that they can be applied in a stepwise way.

Incrementality may be database driven: each time an interdatabase correspondence is identified, the corresponding elements (instances or types) are integrated, either by adding the integrated element to an evolving integrated schema, or by adding logical interdatabase references at the instance level. The latter provides a direct way to navigate from an element in one database to the corresponding element in the other database (53, 29, 66). Another database driven technique is clustering of existing databases by areas of interest (42).

Alternatively, incrementality may be user driven: each time a query is formulated (or a class of similar queries is identified) which calls for accessing related data in several databases, a multidatabase view is explicitly defined and implemented in an ad hoc mediator (23, 35). While the database driven approach aims at ultimately building a global federated system, the user driven approach trades the benefits of integration for the simplicity of multidatabase operations. It is our feeling that the user driven approach is more rewarding in the short term, as ad hoc services are easily implemented, but may in the long term result in a chaotic system with no global view of the information system and no global consistency. Notice that whatever the approach, the issues that we discussed (identification of correspondences, conflict resolution, integration rules) are relevant.

It is worthwhile mentioning that there is a basic split in the philosophy behind integration methodologies that characterizes methodologies as manual or semi-automatic. Manual strategies build on the fact that necessary knowledge of data semantics is with the DBA, not in the databases. Hence they choose to let the DBA lead the integration process. They just provide a language for schema manipulation, that the DBA uses to build (if the language is procedural) or to define (if the language is declarative) the integrated schema. Procedural languages offer schema transformation primitives which allow to restructure input schemas up to the point where they can be merged by a mere union operation into a unified schema. The system automatically maintains the mappings between input schemas and the current integrated schema (44). Declarative, logical languages are easier to use, as the DBA or user only has to define the rules inferring the integrated schema from the input schemas (35). Manual strategies are easier to implement, but they can only be operational if the DBA knows which integrated schema is to be installed. This may not be the case, resulting in many iterations (try and go) before a correct result is achieved. Conversely, semi-automatic strategies aim at building a tool, which automatically performs integration once the ICAs are defined. The tool also defines the mappings. The DBA keeps responsibility for the identification of the ICAs and for the choice among integration alternatives.

The issue likely to be tackled next is the heterogeneity in existing data models and DBMS. Integration methodologies generally assume that all input schemas have been translated into a common model. In fact, they only integrate schemas that are expressed in their own data model. In current terms, each participating DBMS is equipped with a wrapper that ensures this homogenization task. A different approach has been proposed in (60). It advocates that problems and solutions for each type of conflicts are basically the same ones, irrespectively of data models. It is therefore feasible to identify the set of fundamental integration rules that are needed and to define, for any specific data model, how each rule can be applied by reformulating the rule according to the peculiarities of the model under consideration. A tool can then be built, capable of supporting direct integration of heterogeneous schemas and of producing an integrated schema in any known data model. Higher order logic has also been suggested as a formalism capable of solving all types of conflicts, including heterogeneity (30, 31). Such a language allows users to directly define the integrated schema over heterogeneous input schemas.

Most approaches today recommend building a common ontology before integration starts, i.e. a repository of all current knowledge in the organization or beyond (33, 7). To some extent this is similar to the data warehouse approach. The ontology describes the semantics of all concepts and the relationships in between, and is therefore capable of correctly identifying interdatabase correspondences. If a new database joins the existing federation, its schema is used to enrich the ontology with the additional knowledge it may contain. In case of conflicts, the ontology dominates the new schemas (11). The content of an ontology is not limited to existing schemas. It includes the description of the contextual knowledge that is necessary to support proper interpretation of the specific semantics of each database. For instance, it will contain a definition of a car as seen in the different databases, to make sure there is no confusion: a Car type in one database may classify a van as a car, while another database may have a specific Van type such that a van is not a car.

9.7   Conclusion

Integrating existing databases is a very difficult task. Still, it is something that enterprises face today and cannot avoid if they want to launch new applications or to reorganize the existing information system for better profitability.

We have discussed basic issues and solutions. We focused on the fundamental concepts and techniques, insisting on the alternatives and on criteria for choice. More details are easily found in an over-abundant literature. To the best of our knowledge, no integration tool has yet been developed as a commercial product. Some research projects have produced significant prototypes, e.g. (29, 33, 6, 19, 67, 35). One commercial product, dbMain, intended for schema maintenance and engineering, and database reverse engineering, is being extended with capabilities for schema integration (63).

Despite research has been active for nearly twenty years, with a significant increase in the very last years, several important problems remain to be investigated, at least to some extent. Examples of these are: integration of complex objects (as commonly found in object-oriented databases), complex correspondences (fragmentation conflicts), consideration of integrity constraints and methods, direct integration of heterogeneous databases. Theoretical work is still needed to assess integration rules and their properties (commutativity, associativity, . . .), as well as heuristics in using the rules. It is therefore important that the effort to solve integration issues be continued and that proposed methodologies are evaluated through experiments with real applications.

References

1. Abdelmoty A., Jones C.B. Towards Maintaining Consistency of Spatial Databases. In *Proceedings of the ACM International Conference on Information and Knowledge Management*, CIKM'97 (November 10-14, Las Vegas, USA), 1997, pp. 293-300

2. Agarwal S., Keller A.M., Wiederhold G., Saraswat S. Flexible Relation: An Approach for Integrating Data from Multiple, Possibly Inconsistent Databases. In *Proceedings of the 11th International Conference on Data Engineering* (March 6-10, Taipei, Taiwan), 1995, IEEE CS Press, pp. 495-504

3. Albert J. Data Integration in the RODIN Multidatabase System. In *Proceedings First IFCIS International Conference on Cooperative Information Systems* (June 19-21, Brussels, Belgium), 1996, IEEE CS Press, pp. 48-57

4. Andersson M. Searching for semantics in COBOL legacy applications. In *Data Mining and Reverse Engineering*, Spaccapietra S., Maryanski F. (Eds.), Chapman & Hall, 1998, pp. 162-183

5. Atzeni P., Torlone R. MDM: a Multiple-Data-Model Tool for the Management of Heterogeneous Database Schemes. In *Proceedings of ACM SIGMOD International Conference* (May 13-15, Tucson, AZ, USA), 1997, pp. 528-531

6. Bayardo R.J. et al. Infosleuth: Agent-Based Semantic Integration of Information in Open and Dynamic Environments. *In Proceedings of ACM SIGMOD International Conference* (May 13-15, Tucson, AZ, USA), 1997, pp. 195-206

7. Bressan S. et al. The Context Interchange Mediator Prototype. In *Proceedings of ACM SIGMOD International Conference* (May 13-15, Tucson, AZ, USA), 1997, pp. 525-527

8. Castano S., De Antonellis V. Semantic Dictionary Design for Database Interoperability. In *Proceedings of the 13th International Conference on Data Engineering* (April 7-11, Birmingham, UK), 1997, IEEE CS Press, pp. 43-54

9. Ceri S., Pelagatti G. Distributed databases: principles & systems. McGraw-Hill, 1987

10. Clifton C., Housman E., Rosenthal A. Experience with a Combined Approach to Attributed-Matching Across Heterogeneous Databases. In *Data Mining and Reverse Engineering*, Spaccapietra S., Maryanski F. (Eds.), Chapman & Hall, 1998, pp. 428-450

11. Collet C., Huhns M.N., Shen W.-M. Resource Integration Using a Large Knowledge Base in Carnot. *Computer, 24, 12* (December 1991), pp. 55-62

12. Davidson S.B., Kosky A.S. WOL: A Language for Database Transformations and Constraints. In *Proceedings of the 13th International Conference on Data Engineering* (April 7-11, Birmingham, UK), 1995, IEEE CS Press, pp. 55-65

13. De Rosa M., Catarci T., Iocchi L., Nardi D., Santucci G. Materializing the Web. *In Proceedings Third IFCIS International Conference on Cooperative Information Systems* (August 20-22, New York, USA), 1998, IEEE CS Press, pp.24-31

14. Devogele T., Parent C., Spaccapietra S. On Spatial Database Integration. *International Journal of Geographic Information Systems, Special Issue on System Integration, 12, 4*, (June 1998), pp. 315-352

15. Dung P.M. Integrating Data from Possibly Inconsistent Databases. *In Proceedings First IFCIS International Conference on Cooperative Information Systems* (June 19-21, Brussels, Belgium), 1996, IEEE CS Press, pp.58-65

16. Dupont Y. Resolving Fragmentation Conflicts in Schema Integration. In *Entity-Relationship Approach - ER'94*, P. Loucopoulos Ed., LNCS 881, Springer-Verlag, 1994, pp. 513-532

17. Fankhauser P., Neuhold E.J. Knowledge based integration of heterogeneous databases. In *Proceedings of IFIP DS-5 Conference on Semantics of Interoperable Database Systems* (November 16-20, Lorne, Australia), 1992, pp. 150-170

18. Garcia-Solaco M., Saltor F., Castellanos M. A Structure Based Schema Integration Methodology. In *Proceedings of the 11th International Conference on Data Engineering* (March 6-10, Taipei, Taiwan), 1995, IEEE CS Press, pp. 505-512

19. Genesereth M.R., Keller A.M., Duschka O.M. Informaster: An Information Integration System. In *Proceedings of ACM SIGMOD International Conference* (May 13-15, Tucson, AZ, USA), 1997, pp. 539-542

20. Gotthard W., Lockemann P.C., Neufeld A. System-Guided View Integration for Object-Oriented Databases. *IEEE Transactions on Knowledge and Data Engineering*, 4, 1 (February 1992), pp. 1-22

21. Hammer J. et al. Template-Based Wrappers in the TSIMMIS System. In *Proceedings of ACM SIGMOD International Conference* (May 13-15, Tucson, AZ, USA), 1997, pp. 532-535

22. Hainaut J.-L., Englebert V., Hick J.-M., Henrard J., Roland R. Contribution to the reverse engineering of OO applications: methodology and case study. In *Data Mining and Reverse Engineering*, Spaccapietra S., Maryanski F. (Eds.), Chapman & Hall, 1998, pp. 131-161

23. Hohenstein U., Plesser V. A Generative Approach to Database Federation. In Conceptual Modeling - ER'97, Embley D.W., Goldstein R.C. (Eds.), LNCS 1331, Springer, 1997, pp. 422-435

24. Kahng J., McLeod D. Dynamic Classificational Ontologies for Discovery in Cooperative Federated Databases. In *Proceedings First IFCIS International Conference on Cooperative Information Systems* (June 19-21, Brussels, Belgium), 1996, IEEE CS Press, pp. 26-35

25. Kaul M., Drosten K., Neuhold E.J. ViewSystem: Integrating Heterogeneous Information Bases by Object-Oriented Views. In *Proceedings of the 6th International Conference on Data Engineering* (February 5-9, Los Angeles, USA), 1990, IEEE CS Press, pp. 2-10

26. Kent W., Ahmed R., Albert J., Ketabchi M., Shan M.-C. Object Identification in Multidatabase Systems. In *Proceedings of IFIP DS-5 Conference on Semantics of Interoperable Database Systems* (November 16-20, Lorne, Australia), 1992

27. Kim W., Choi I., Gala S., Scheevel M. On Resolving Schematic Heterogeneity in *Multidatabase Systems. Distributed and Parallel Databases, 1, 3*, (July 1993), pp. 251-279

28. Kim W. (Ed.) Modern Database Systems: The Object Model, Interoperability and Beyond, ACM Press and Addison Wesley, 1995

29. Klas W., Fankhauser P., Muth P., Rakow T.C., Neuhold E.J. Database Integration using the Open Object-Oriented Database System VODAK. In *Object Oriented Multidatabase Systems: A Solution for Advanced Applications*, Bukhres O., Elmagarmid A.K. (Eds.), Prentice Hall, 1995

30. Lakshmanan L.V.S., Sadri F., Subramanian I.N. On the Logical Foundation of Schema Integration and Evolution in Heterogeneous Database Systems. *In Deductive and Object-Oriented Databases*, Ceri S., Tanaka K., Tsur S. (Eds.), LNCS 760, Springer-Verlag, 1993, pp. 81-100

31. Lakshmanan L.V.S., Sadri F., Subramanian I. SchemaSQL A Language for Interoperability In Relational Multi-database Systems. In *Proceedings of the 22nd VLDB Conference* (September 3-6, Mumbai, India), 1996, pp. 239-250

32. Larson J.A., Navathe S.B., Elmasri R. A Theory of Attribute Equivalence in Databases with Application to Schema Integration. *IEEE Transactions On Software Engineering, 15, 4*, (April 1989), pp. 449-463

33. Lee J., Madnick S.E., Siegel M.D. Conceptualizing Semantic Interoperability: A Perspective from the Knowledge Level. *International Journal of Cooperative Information Systems, 5, 4*, (December 1996), pp.367-393

34. Li W.S., Clifton C. Semantic Integration in Heterogeneous Databases Using NeuralNetworks.In *Proceedings of the 20th VLDB Conference* (Santiago, Chile), 1994, pp. 1-12

35. Li C. et al. Capability Based Mediation in TSIMMIS. In *Proceedings of the 1998 ACM SIGMOD Conference*, (June 1-4, Seattle, USA), *ACM SIGMOD Record, 27, 2*, (June 1998), pp.564-566

36. Litwin W., Mark L., Roussopoulos N. Interoperability of multiple autonomous databases. *ACM Computer Surveys, 22, 3* (Sept. 1990), pp. 267-293

37. Lu H., Fan W., Goh C.H., Madnick S.E., Cheung D.W. Discovering and Reconciling Semantic Conflicts: A Data Mining Perspective. In *Data Mining and Reverse Engineering*, Spaccapietra S., Maryanski F. (Eds.), Chapman & Hall, 1998, pp. 409-426

38. McBrien P., Poulovassilis A. A Formal Framework for ER Schema Transformation. In *Conceptual Modeling - ER'97*, Embley D.W., Goldstein R.C. (Eds.), LNCS 1331, Springer, 1997, pp. 408-421

39. Mena E., Kashyap V., Sheth A., Illarramendi A. OBSERVER: An Approach for Query Processing in Global Information Systems based on Interoperation across Pre-existing Ontologies. *In Proceedings First International Conference on Cooperative Information Systems* (June 19-21, Brussels, Belgium), 1996, IEEE CS Press, pp. 14-25

40. Metais E., Kedad Z., Comyn-Wattiau I., Bouzeghoub M. Using Linguistic Knowledge in View Integration: Toward a Third Generation of Tools. *Data and Knowledge Engineering, Vol. 23, No. +*, June 1997, pp. 59-78

41. Miller R.J., Ioannidis Y.E., Ramakrishnan R. Understanding Schemas. In *Proceedings of RIDE-IMS'93 Interoperability in Multidatabase Systems* (April 19-20, Vienna, Austria), 1993, pp. 170-173

42. Milliner S., Bouguettaya A., Papazoglou M. A Scalable Architecture for Autonomous Heterogeneous Database Interactions. In *Proceedings of the 21st VLDB Conference* (Zurich, Switzerland), 1995, pp. 515-526

43. Missier P., Rusinkiewicz M. Extending a Multidatabase Manipulation Language to Resolve Schema and Data Conflicts. In *Database Application Semantics*, Meersamn R. and Mark L. eds., Chapman & Hall, 1997, pp. 93-115

44. Motro A. Superviews: Virtual integration of multiple databases. *IEEE Transactions On Software Engineering, 13, 7*, (July 1987), pp. 785-798

45. Nicolle C., Benslimane D., Yetongnon K. Multi-Data Models Translations In Interoperable Information Systems. In *Advanced Information Systems Engineering*, Constantopoulos P., Mylopoulos J., Vassiliou Y. (Eds.), LNCS 1080, Springer, 1996, pp. 176-192

46. Ouksel A.M., Ahmed I. Coordinating Knowledge Elicitation to Support Context Construction in Cooperative Information Systems. *In Proceedings First IFCIS International Conference on Cooperative Information Systems* (June 19-21, Brussels, Belgium), 1996, IEEE CS Press, pp. 4-13

47. Papakonstantinou Y., Garcia-Molina H., Widom J. Object Exchange Across Heterogeneous Information Sources. In *Proceedings of the 11th International Conference on Data Engineering* (March 6-10, Taipei, Taiwan), 1995, IEEE CS Press, pp. 251-260

48. Papakonstantinou Y., Abiteboul S. Garcia-Molina H. Object Fusion in Mediator Systems. In *Proceedings of the 22nd VLDB Conference* (September 3-6, Mumbai, India), 1996, pp. 413-424

49. Papazoglou M., Russell N., Edmond D. A Translation Protocol Achieving Consensus of Semantics between Cooperating Heterogeneous Database Systems. In *Proceedings First International Conference on Cooperative Information Systems* (June 19-21, Brussels, Belgium), 1996, IEEE CS Press, pp. 78-89

50. Saltor F., Castellanos M.G., Garcia-Solaco M. Overcoming Schematic Discrepancies in Interoperable Databases. In *Proceedings of IFIP DS-5 Conference on Semantics of Interoperable Databases Systems*, (Nov. 16-20, Lorne, Australia), 1992, pp. 184-198

51. Schmitt I., Saake G. Integration of Inheritance Trees as Part of View Generation for Database Federations. In *Conceptual Modeling ER'96*, Thalheim B. (Ed.), LNCS 1157, Springer, 1996, pp. 195-210

52. Schmitt I., Saake G. Merging Inheritance Hierachies for Database Integration. In *Proceedings Third IFCIS International Conference on Cooperative Information Systems* (August 20-22, New York, USA), 1998, IEEE CS Press, pp.322-331

53. Scholl M.H., Schek H.-J., Tresch M. Object Algebra and Views for Multi-Objectbases. In *Distributed Object Management*, Ozsu T., Dayal U., Valduriez P. (Eds.), Morgan Kaufmann, 1994, pp. 353-374

54. Sester M. Interpretation of Spatial Data Bases using Machine Learning Techniques. In *Proceedings 8th International Symposium on Spatial Data Handling*, (July 11-15, Vancouver, Canada), 1998, IGU, pp. 88-97

55. Sheth A., Larson J. Federated database systems for managing distributed, heterogeneous, and autonomous databases. *ACM Computer Surveys, 22, 3* (Sept. 1990), pp. 183-236

56. Sheth A., Kashyap V. So Far (Schematically) yet So Near (Semantically). In *Proceedings of IFIP DS-5 Conference on Semantics of Interoperable Databases Systems*, (Nov. 16-20, Lorne, Australia), 1992, pp. 272-301

57. Sheuermann P., Chong E.I. Role-Based Query Processing in Multidatabase Systems. In *Advances in Database Technology - EDBT'94*, Jarke M., Bubenko J., Jeffery K. (Eds.), LNCS 779, Springer-Verlag, 1994, pp. 95-108

58. Si A., Ying C., McLeod D. On Using Historical Update Information for Instance Identification in Federated Databases. In *Proceedings First IFCIS International Conference on Cooperative Information Systems* (June 19-21, Brussels, Belgium), 1996, IEEE CS Press, pp. 68-77

59. Spaccapietra S., Parent C. Conflicts and Correspondence Assertions in Interoperable Databases, *ACM SIGMOD Record, 20, 4*, (December 1991), pp. 49-54

60. Spaccapietra S., Parent C., Dupont Y. Model Independent Assertions for Integration of Heterogeneous Schemas. *VLDB Journal, 1, 1* (July 1992), pp. 81-126

61. Tari Z., Stokes J., Spaccapietra S. Object Normal Forms and Dependency Constraints for Object-Oriented Schemata. *ACM Transactions On Database Systems, 22, 4*, (December 1997), pp. 513-569

62. Tari Z., Bukhres O., Stokes J., Hammoudi S. The reengineering of relational databases based on key and data correlation. *In Data Mining and Reverse Engineering*, Spaccapietra S., Maryanski F. (Eds.), Chapman & Hall, 1998, pp. 184-215

63. Thiran Ph., Hainaut J.-L., Bodart S., Deflorenne A., Hick J.-M. Interoperation of Independent, Heterogeneous and Distributed Databases. Methodology and CASE Support: the InterDB Approach. in *Proceedings Third IFCIS International Conference on Cooperative Information Systems* (August 20-22, New York, USA), 1998, IEEE CS Press, pp. 54-63

64. Tseng F.S.C., Chen A.L.P., Yang W.-P. Answering Heterogeneous Database Queries with Degrees of Uncertainty. *Distributed and Parallel Databases, 1*, (1993), pp. 281-302

65. Urban S.D. A Semantic Framework for Heterogeneous Database Environments. In *Proceedings of RIDE-IMS'91 Interoperability in Multidatabase Systems* (April 7-9, Kyoto, Japan), 1991, pp. 156-163

66. Vermeer M., Apers P. On the Applicability of Schema Integration Techniques to Database Interoperation. in *Conceptual Modeling ER'96*, Thalheim B. (Ed.), LNCS 1157, Springer, 1996, pp.

67. Yan L.L., Otsu M.T., Liu L. Accessing Heterogeneous Data Through Homogenization and Integration Mediators. In *Proceedings Second IFCIS International Conference on Cooperative Information Systems* (June 24-27, Kiawah Island, SC, USA), 1997, IEEE CS Press, pp.130-139

68. Zhou G., Hull R., King R., Franchitti J.-C. Using Object Matching and Materialization to Integrate Heterogeneous Databases. In *Proceedings of the Third International Conference on Cooperative Information Systems* (May 9-12, Vienna, Austria), 1995, pp. 4-18

10   *Identifying Objects by Declarative Queries*

M. Gogolla
Dept. for Mathematics and Computer Science
University of Bremen
PO Box 330440
D-28334 Bremen
Germany
gogolla@informatik.uni-bremen.de

Object identification in data models, especially in semantic, Entity-Relationship, and Object-Oriented data models is studied. Various known approaches to object identification are shown, and an alternative proposal to the topic is put forward. The main new idea is to attach to each object type an arbitrary query, a so-called observation term, in order to observe a unique, identifying property of objects of the corresponding type.

10.1   Introduction

Conceptual modeling of information systems means to fix the static and dynamic characteristics of the system to be developed before going into implementation details. One of the main tasks in conceptual modeling is to identify the type of objects to be handled with the system under development: The objects are of central interest. Our approach concentrates on the question how to refer to single objects and identify them in a global system context.

One very often used approach for object identification is to refer to objects by a single, unique number like a document number or a personal identification number. The drawback of this approach is however that such a number is frequently not a natural property of the object is question. Such an identification number is something which comes from outside the object and which is only used to distinguish one object from another object, often in an unnatural way. Therefore one may argue that such artificial identification mechanisms do not have to do with conceptual modeling because they already bring efficiency and implementation issues into consideration.

In contrast, our proposal here is to refer to objects by some of their natural, inherent properties. These properties are explicitly declared as contributing to the object identification (or reference) mechanism. The main new idea of our proposal is to attach to each object type an arbitrary query, a so-called observation term, in order to observe a unique, identifying property of objects of the corresponding type. The advantages of our so-called observation term approach are that

- it is possible to retrieve abstract objects by concrete data values,

- the approach allows not only a single identification mechanism but multiple observation terms are allowed,

- observations terms can be used in a variety of data models like Object-Oriented or Entity-Relationship data models,

- observation terms can be introduced dynamically during the lifetime of an information system as they are needed,

- it is possible to make even updates on the attributes contributing to the observation terms, and

- the approach is completely formally defined.

Our paper is organized as follows. In Section 10.2 we explain the basic idea of our approach and introduce an example schema which will be used throughout the paper. In Section 10.3 the interpretation of object schemas is sketched in an informal way. Several known and our new proposal (the so-called observation term approach) to object identification are studied in Section 10.4. The advantages of our new proposal are discussed in Section 10.5, and its formal definition is presented in Section 10.6. Our approach is put into the context of papers from the literature in Section 10.7. Section 10.8 concludes the paper.

10.2　The Basic Idea

As the starting point we consider in Figure 10.1 a simple fraction of a car rentals case study (42). We take into account car rental company branches providing services like rental bookings and car deliveries. Branches are characterized in a simplified way by their street address and their location in a town. Towns, in which also the customers live, lie in countries. Towns and countries are recorded with their names and population. Branches own a set of cars characterized by a chasis number and an equipment category. Customers, which are described by their names, ask for bookings of cars in a certain category and for a certain time period in form of a start and end day. Such bookings are recorded together with the current date as the order date and a running booking number. After the start day bookings are associated with the car which has been delivered to the customer. A graphical description for a corresponding object schema following the UML notation (7) but neglecting the data types of attributes is given in Figure 10.1.

We shortly mention the UML class diagram features employed in our example: Object types (classes) are pictured as rectangles containing the attributes. Relationships (in UML terminology associations) are shown as lines together with the relationship name and an optional indication for the read-direction of the name: The black triangle indicates that, for example, towns lie in countries. Cardinalities are shown as integer intervals, in which a star * may indicate that no upper bound is specified. The intervals express the minimal and maximal number of associated ob-

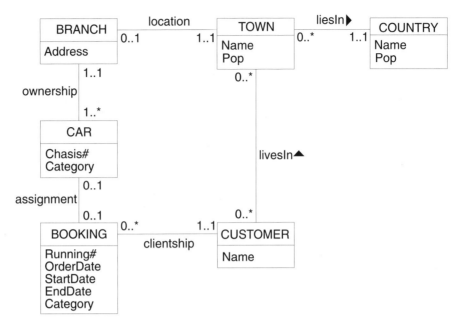

Figure 10.1   Graphical UML description of the car rentals case study schema

jects on the other side of the relationship: For example, each booking is related via the association 'clientship' with exactly one customer, but a customer may have zero or more bookings.

In Figure 10.2 we make the diagram more precise by stating which data types the attributes have. Relationships are expressed as object-valued attributes, which are either single- or set-valued depending on the upper bound of the cardinality specification: An upper bound 1 indicates a single-valued, an upper bound ∗ a multi-valued attribute (interval 0..1 for optional, 1..1 for mandatory, 0..∗ for empty set allowed, 1..∗ for empty set not allowed). Inverse object-valued attributes are indicated in comments. The textual formulation of the diagram is given in an O_2-like style (10) employing type constructors like `tuple` and `set`. We use the UML convention that role names for opposite object types in relationships are given by the name of the object type written with only lower case letters. Thus, for example, the relationship 'assignment' between 'BOOKING' and 'CAR' induces (through the role names) the object-valued attributes 'booking: CAR → BOOKING' and 'car: BOOKING → CAR'.

After having clarified the syntactic situation we can proceed to explain the basic idea of our proposal. As said before, the plan is to attach to each object type a query term which observes the identity of the corresponding objects. We show such query terms for some of the object types of the schema.

Object type 'CAR': We have a simple situation for cars because they possess a natural identification number. By natural we mean that such an identification number already is present in the problem domain and must not be introduced in an artificial

```
define type BRANCH:
  tuple( Address:   string,
         car:       set(CAR),        -- inverse of CAR.branch
         town:      TOWN );          -- inverse of TOWN.branch
define type CAR:
  tuple( Chasis#:   string,
         Category:  string,
         branch:    BRANCH,          -- inverse of BRANCH.car
         booking:   BOOKING );       -- inverse of BOOKING.car
define type BOOKING:
  tuple( Running#:  nat,
         OrderDate: string.
         StartDate: string,
         EndDate:   string,
         Category:  string,
         car:       CAR,             -- inverse of CAR.booking
         customer:  CUSTOMER );      -- inverse of CUSTOMER.booking
define type CUSTOMER:
  tuple( Name:      string,
         booking:   set(BOOKING),    -- inverse of BOOKING.customer
         town:      set(TOWN) );     -- inverse of TOWN.customer
define type TOWN:
  tuple( Name:      string,
         Pop:       int,
         branch:    BRANCH,          -- inverse of BRANCH.town
         customer:  set(CUSTOMER),   -- inverse of CUSTOMER.town
         country:   COUNTRY );       -- inverse of COUNTRY.town
define type COUNTRY:
  tuple( Name:      string,
         Pop:       int,
         town:      set(TOWN) );     -- inverse of TOWN.country
```

Figure 10.2   Textual O_2-like description of the car rentals case study schema

way by the information system to be developed. Cars are identified by their chasis number which is a simple data-valued attribute. Thus the following integrity constraint has to be respected in all information system states.

$$\forall(c_1, c_2 : CAR)(Chasis\#(c_1) = Chasis\#(c_2)) \Rightarrow (c_1 = c_2)$$

We can also formulate this constraint equivalently by taking $(c_1 \neq c_2)$ as the premise.

$$\forall(c_1, c_2 : CAR)(c_1 \neq c_2) \Rightarrow (Chasis\#(c_1) \neq Chasis\#(c_2))$$

This formulation clearly points out that different cars can be observed by their different chasis numbers. Thus the string-valued chasis number constitutes the observation term τ for cars.

$$\tau(c : CAR) \equiv Chasis\#(c)$$

Object type 'BRANCH': The situation is more involved for branches because we cannot avoid that two branches have the same street address, for example, both are located on "700 Main Street". Our solution is to take into account that branches lie in towns which again lie in countries.

$$\tau(b : BRANCH) \equiv tuple(Name(mvtown(b)), Name(country(town(b))))$$

This observation term induces a constraint like the above one for cars which will be respected in all information system states. Again, this observation term is data-valued. The term has the sort *tuple(string, string)*.

Object type 'CUSTOMER': As the last example at this point we take into account customers. They may be identified, for demonstration purposes, by their own names together with the set of names of towns they live in.

$$\tau(c : CUSTOMER) \equiv tuple(Name(c), (select\ Name(t)$$
$$from\&(t : TOWN)$$
$$where\ t\ in\ town(c)))$$

As this last example shows, observation terms can have a complex structure because they may even include queries. They are however in any case data-valued. The sort of the last term is *tuple(string, bag(string))*.

The ideas underlying these examples will be explained and justified in more detail in the sections to follow.

10.3   Interpretation of Database Schemas

Before going into the details how exactly single elements of the given object domains are identified, we have to clarify how we formally interpret schemas like the above ones. Looking at the textual version of the schema in Figure 10.2 we recognize that the following items must have an interpretation: Data sorts and data operations, object sorts, data-valued attributes, type constructors, and object-valued attributes. We explain the interpretation of these notions by examples from the above schema.

Data sorts: Each data sort like `string` is associated with a corresponding set of values denoted by $I(\texttt{string})$.[1]

Data operations: Each data operation like the string concatenation operation `concat : string string -> string` is associated with a function with respective source and target like $I(concat) : I(string) \times I(string) \rightarrow I(string)$.

---

1. Here, we give formal semantics to syntactic items by applying the function I which returns for the parameter the corresponding interpretation. The convention throughout the paper is that I denotes the interpretation of a syntactic item.

Object sorts: Each object sort is connected with an infinite universe of object identities[2] for this object sort, like $U(\texttt{TOWN}) = \{\texttt{twn}_n \mid n \in \mathbb{N}\}$ for the object sort TOWN. In each database state there is an "active" finite subset of object identities like $I(\texttt{TOWN}) = \{\texttt{twn}_2, \texttt{twn}_4, \texttt{twn}_8\}$ representing the objects in the current state.

Data-valued attributes: In each database state, a data-valued attribute is seen as a function from the appropriate active object domain into the associated set of values like $I(\texttt{Name}) : I(\texttt{TOWN}) \rightarrow I(\texttt{string})$ for the attribute Name : TOWN -> string.

Type constructors: Each type constructor takes its argument and builds a new collection of items corresponding to its task while assuming that the active domain is fixed. For example, for set(TOWN) with $I(\texttt{TOWN})$ as above we have $I(\texttt{set})(I(\texttt{TOWN}))$ = $\{\ \emptyset, \{\texttt{twn}_2\}, \{\texttt{twn}_4\}, ..., \{\texttt{twn}_2, \texttt{twn}_4\}, ..., \{\texttt{twn}_2, \texttt{twn}_4, \texttt{twn}_8\}\ \}$. Thus set(TOWN) is consisting of all sets which have elements of the active domain for TOWN.

Object-valued attributes: In each database state an object-valued attribute is connected with a function from the respective active object domain into the appropriate target. For example, for the attribute country : TOWN -> COUNTRY we have $I(\texttt{country}) : I(\texttt{TOWN}) \rightarrow I(\texttt{COUNTRY})$, and for the attribute town : COUNTRY -> set(TOWN) we have $I(\texttt{town}) : I(\texttt{COUNTRY}) \rightarrow I(\texttt{set})(I(\texttt{TOWN}))$. Thus, in a concrete state we could have for instance $I(\texttt{country}) : \texttt{twn}_2 \mapsto \{\texttt{cty}_{42}, \texttt{twn}_8\}$ and $I(\texttt{town}) : \texttt{cty}_{42} \mapsto \{\texttt{twn}_2, \texttt{twn}_8\}$.

A more general description for the presented items will be given later in Section 10.6.

10.4   Approaches to Object Identification

After we saw how to interpret schemas like the above one, in particular how to interpret object sorts by object identities, we can now proceed and discuss the topic of object identification. In principle, all occurring questions originate from the freedom and flexibility offered by the above interpretation for object sorts and, in consequence of this, from the freedom for the interpretation of attributes. The following situation can occur: There may be objects which have different identities, say country objects $\texttt{cty}_2$ and $\texttt{cty}_4$, but for which the interpretation of all attributes $I(\texttt{Name})$ and $I(\texttt{Pop})$ coincides. Thus we cannot distinguish between the objects $\texttt{cty}_2$ and $\texttt{cty}_4$ with respect to their characteristics, but assume we would like to do so, because we argue that formally different objects must somehow be formally different to the outside. The internal object identities are of no help in this case because both identities $\texttt{cty}_2$ and $\texttt{cty}_4$ do not tell us anything about the properties of the objects. Therefore, there

---

2. Object identities have appeared under the name surrogates in (9), l-values in (28), and object identifiers in (4).

must be some other means to distinguish them. In the following we discuss several approaches to achieve this distinction, namely

- data-valued key attributes,
- data- and object-valued key attributes,
- data- and object-valued key attributes with additional contributions from other attributes having the respective object sort as target sort,
- identity observing formulas, and
- identity observing terms and queries.

Data-valued keys: In the relational data model it is usual to mark some of the attributes of a relation as keys. This means that tuples in the relation are already uniquely identified by the values of the key attributes. This is also possible in our object model. For example, we could require that the attribute 'Name' is the key for the object type 'COUNTRY'. By doing this, we state a restriction on the interpretation of 'Name' and 'Pop' saying that the value of 'Name' already determines the rest of the object. However, we have to be careful with the formalization of this requirement. At least two different possibilities exist:

$$(1)\forall(c_1, c_2 : COUNTRY)$$
$$(Name(c_1) = Name(c_2)) \Rightarrow (Pop(c_1) = Pop(c_2))$$
$$(2)\forall(c_1, c_2 : COUNTRY)$$
$$(Name(c_1) = Name(c_2)) \Rightarrow (c_1 = c_2)$$

The first formula (1) requires that whenever two COUNTRY objects coincide in their 'Name' attribute, then they must also have equal values for the 'Pop' attribute. The second formula (2) states that under the same precondition as in (1) the two *objects* must be identical not only their 'Pop' *data values*. Data values are printable and meaningful to users while pure objects (not their attributes) are not meaningful to users and therefore not printable.[3] The difference between formulas (1) and (2) can be explained best by the sample state mentioned above where two different COUNTRY objects exist which have identical values for their 'Name' and 'Pop' attributes: This state is accepted as valid by formula (1) but not by formula (2). Following the arguments from above stating that different objects with indistinguishable properties have to be avoided we cannot accept (1) as a proper solution but must prefer the stronger[4] formula (2) as the right formulation for the problem. Let us explain how the above formulas contribute to object identification. We first re-formulate formula (2) equivalently by employing the simple logical law $(\alpha \Rightarrow \beta) \Leftrightarrow (\neg\beta \Rightarrow \neg\alpha)$.

$$(2')\forall(c_1, c_2 : COUNTRY)(c_1 \neq c_2) \Rightarrow (Name(c_1) \neq Name(c_2))$$

---

3. The distinction between values and objects is discussed, for instance, in (6).
4. 'Stronger' in the sense that (2) implies (1).

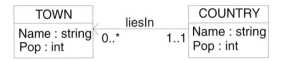

Figure 10.3 Part of modified car rental schema

This formulation now clearly states that two different countries must have different names.

Data- and object-valued keys: What we have done for data-valued attributes above can also be done for object-valued attributes. For example, we can require that 'Name' and 'country' constitute the key for TOWN allowing that different towns in different countries can have the same name. The restricting formula then reads as follows:

$$(3)\forall(t_1, t_2 : TOWN)$$
$$(Name(t_1) = Name(t_2) \wedge country(t_1) = country(t_2)) \Rightarrow (t_1 = t_2)$$
$$(3')\forall(t_1, t_2 : TOWN)$$
$$(t_1 \neq t_2) \Rightarrow (Name(t_1) \neq Name(t_2) \vee country(t_1) \neq country(t_2))$$

Data- and object-valued keys plus other attributes: The above achievement can even be extended by allowing not only attributes of the considered object type to contribute to object identity but also attributes of other object types which have the considered object sort as their target sort. Consider the slight modification of Figure 10.1 presented in Figure 10.3. As indicated by the arrow pointing to 'TOWN' we have replaced the bi-directional association 'liesIn' between 'TOWN' and 'COUNTRY' by a uni-directional association traversable only from 'COUNTRY' to 'TOWN'. Uni-directional associations are another language feature in UML and are different from the read-direction indication. This change means that we do not have the function 'country : TOWN → COUNTRY' available anymore. Now consider the same requirement for towns as above, namely that different towns in different countries with the same name are allowed to exist. Expressing this requires to refer to an attribute not belonging to the object type 'TOWN'. The respective formula reads as follows:[5]

$$(4)\forall(t_1, t_2 : TOWN)$$
$$(Name(t_1) = Name(t_2) \wedge$$
$$\forall(c : COUNTRY)(t_1 \text{ in } town(c) \Leftrightarrow t_2 \text{ in } town(c)))$$
$$\Rightarrow (t_1 = t_2)$$

---

5. Requirements (2) and (3) look like requirements for well-known functional dependencies from relational database theory, however, this requirement (4) and the ones to follow cannot be expressed in this way.

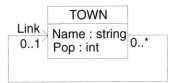

Figure 10.4   Schema for towns linked to nearest neighbours

Again, it will be instructive to re-formulate the formula equivalently by employing the logical law $(\alpha \Rightarrow \beta) \Leftrightarrow (\neg\beta \Rightarrow \neg\alpha)$. Then the requirement, in which $\oplus$ denotes the exclusive or, looks as follows:

$$(4')\forall(t_1, t_2 : TOWN)$$
$$(t_1 \neq t_2) \Rightarrow$$
$$(Name(t_1) \neq Name(t_2) \vee$$
$$\exists(c : COUNTRY)(t_1 \; in \; town(c) \oplus t_2 \; in \; town(c)))$$

The formula states that, if two towns are different, then their names are different or there is a country such that one town lies in the country and the other not. Thus inequality of towns can be observed by 'Name' or 'town' (or both).

Identity observing formulas: All above axioms had a very particular form. Speaking in general terms, they were instances of the following axiom schema where the item *os* refers to an object sort and ϕ is a formula with two free variables o_1 and o_2.

$$(5)\forall(o_1, o_2 : os) \; \phi(o_1, o_2) \Rightarrow (o_1 = o_2)$$

For instance in the case of formula (3) we had $\phi(t_1, t_2) \equiv (Name(t_1) = Name(t_2) \wedge country(t_1) = country(t_2))$ which is a precondition analogously to the precondition of key constraints in the relational model. But if we take a broader view and allow not only these special key constraints, the formula $\phi(o_1, o_2)$ can be any formula (with free variables o_1 and o_2) which then serves as an object identification mechanism. One such alternative choice is for instance $\phi(t_1, t_2) \equiv (Name(t_1) = Name(t_2) \vee country(t_1) = country(t_2))$ which requires that two different towns must have different names *and* must lie in different countries. Although such general preconditions offer a great amount of flexibility and look attractive, there are some difficulties which can arise when we employ such formulas for observing the identity of objects. Consider the schema in Figure 10.4 in which each town (apart from having a 'Name') has a direct 'Link' to its nearest neighbour town. Here, the association in the UML schema does not possess a name but only a role name is specified. Assume that different towns must have different names or must be linked to different towns, which could be tried to be formulated as follows:

$$(6)\forall(t_1, t_2 : TOWN)$$
$$(t_1 \neq t_2) \Rightarrow (Name(t_1) \neq Name(t_2) \vee Link(t_1) \neq Link(t_2))$$

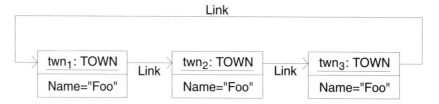

Figure 10.5   Database state with cyclic links

We re-formulate the formal requirement equivalently and obtain the equation $t_1 = t_2$ as the conclusion.

$$(6')\forall(t_1, t_2 : TOWN)$$

$$(Name(t_1) = Name(t_2) \wedge Link(t_1) = Link(t_2)) \Rightarrow (t_1 = t_2)$$

Although this seems to be some kind of observable inequality there is a problem with this formula. Consider the state in Figure 10.5 with three different TOWN objects twn_1, twn_2 and twn_3 which have identical 'Name' attribute values and are linked as depicted. The formulas (6) and (6') accept the state in Figure 10.5 as a valid state but due to the cyclic 'Link' structure there is no possibility to distinguish between, say, the TOWN objects twn_1 and twn_2, by taking data observations only. Therefore the towns in the state cannot be observed to be different although the formula is valid. Thus we need something stronger and more informative than just truth values of formulas: We take data-valued queries.

Identity observing terms and queries: The above deficiency will be removed when one employs not only formulas for identification purposes but data terms which can be looked at and which can really generate object identities. Therefore the general idea for identity observing terms and queries is to have axiom schemas of the following form where τ is a term with a sort built over data sorts and type constructors and with one free variable of object sort os.

$$(7)\forall(o_1, o_2 : os)(\tau(o_1) = \tau(o_2)) \Rightarrow (o_1 = o_2)$$

Let us examine the above examples again in the light of this new perspective. We specify the observation terms τ which have to be substituted in the above axiom schema in order to yield the desired constraints.

- The formula (2) can be achieved if we actualize the above axiom schema with the term $\tau(c : COUNTRY) \equiv Name(c)$ which has the free variable $(c : COUNTRY)$ and is of sort *string*. Of course, we obtain a formula equivalent to formula (2') from above.

- Requirement (3) from above is gained by substituting the term $\tau(t : TOWN) \equiv tuple(Name(t), Name(country(t)))$ with free variable $(t : TOWN)$. The term has the sort *tuple(string, string)*. *tuple* is assumed to be a type constructor which takes a collection of single values and returns the tuple value which consists of the given values.[6]

- Constraint (4) may be seen as an instantiation of the above schema with the following observation term:

$$(8)\tau(t : TOWN) \equiv tuple(Name(t), \ (selectName(c)$$
$$from \ (c : COUNTRY)$$
$$where \ t \ in \ town(c)))$$

This query term has exactly one free variable ($t : TOWN$) and is of sort $tuple(string, bag(string))$. It employs a query term which is evaluated for the free variable ($t : TOWN$) as a kind of parameter. The query follows the well-known select-from-where structure proposed in SQL. In our approach, the result of a query is a bag of values retaining duplicates; sets can also be obtained by applying an operator eliminating the duplicates (for details, see (17)). The 'where' part is a formula which returns true if the parameter town t is an element of the set $town(c)$. The 'select' terms are only evaluated and returned for those countries for which the 'where' part yields true. Although we expect the query to return exactly one string value, we must formulate it as a multi-valued term because in the syntactic situation described in Figure 10.3 the association is traversable in only one direction and the term 'Name(country(t))' is syntactically not allowed.

- The most complex situation was given in formula (6) where a cyclic 'Link' structure was specified in the schema, and also a cyclic state structure was given in the counter example state in Figure 10.5.

$$(9)\tau(t : TOWN) \equiv tuple(Name(t), Name(Link(t)), Name(Link(Link(t))))$$

This term is again a tuple term and has one free variable ($t : TOWN$). It is of sort $tuple(string, string, string)$ and selects the name of the 'parameter' town and the names of the first and second towns linked to the parameter town. Thus the above state (with three towns named 'Foo') is not accepted by the constraint generated by the axiom schema if we actualize it by this observation term.

Let now us focus on the most important point of identity observing terms and queries. We assume that each object sort os in the database schema is attached to such an observation term τ_{os} of sort s_{τ} and that this attachment induces the constraint given hereafter. The sort s_{τ} may be a simple data sort or a complex sort expression, but a sort expression built only over data sorts with no object sorts in it.

---

6. If want we to very precise we have to distinguish syntactically between the type constructor *tuple* (for example to construct the sort $tuple(string, int)$) and an operation mk_{tuple} constructing an appropriate value (for example $mk_{tuple} : string \times int \rightarrow tuple(string, int)$). However, we use the notation *tuple* in both positions.

$$\tau_{os} \text{ injective}$$

$$\tau_{os} : os \rightarrow s_\tau$$

$$os \leftarrow s_\tau \quad : f_{\tau_{os}}$$

$$f_{\tau_{os}} \text{bijective on } \tau_{os}(os)$$

Figure 10.6   Overview on observation term τ_{os} and induced function $f_{\tau_{os}}$

TEAM	Members	PLAYER
Nationality : string 0..*		0..* Name : string

Figure 10.7   Teams and players

$$(10)(\forall o_1, o_2 : os)(o_1 \neq o_2) \Rightarrow (\tau_{os}(o_1) \neq \tau_{os}(o_2))$$

We assume further that this constraint is enforced during the lifetime of the database. This means that two different os objects with the same τ_{os} value of sort s_τ cannot exist. This value can be computed for an os object by applying the term τ_{os} to the object and the other way round: An os object can be computed from an s_τ value. Or, to say it in other words, we have described the concept of a partial function $f_{\tau_{os}} : s_\tau \rightarrow os$ which will be *bijective* in all database states (on the part where it yields defined values). The function can therefore serve for object identification purposes. The function will be given an s_τ value as a parameter. It will respond by either returning a uniquely determined object with that s_τ value, or it will say that there is no object in the current database state with the respective property. Because of the possibility of this negative answer, the function will be partial. An overview of the situation is given in Figure 10.6. In the total, we achieve with observation terms an approach which seems to be more general than and thus can be refined to the well-known "deep equality".[7]

Let us finally give an example for an observation term where queries are really necessary. As pictured in Figure 10.7 we consider teams of sportswomen and sportsmen who play, for instance, the Daviscup. Because there may be many teams for one nationality, one has to take into account the names of the team members for identifying single teams.

$$(11)\tau(t : TEAM) \equiv tuple(Nationality(t), (select\ Name(p)$$
$$from\&(p : PLAYER)$$
$$where\&p\ in\ Members(t)))$$

---

7. "Deep equality" again refines to "shallow equality" and the "identity predicate" as pointed out in (24).

The observation term above has one free variable ($t : TEAM$) and has the sort *tuple*(*string*, *bag*(*string*)). In general, the 'select' term will return a proper multivalued result because teams usually consist of more than one player.

10.5 Advantages of the Observation Term Approach

Our observation term approach to object identification embodies a number of features that distinguishes it from other ways to handle the problem and offers a greater amount of flexibility. We explain how to retrieve objects, how to treat multiple observation terms, how to apply the approach to other data models, how to dynamically use observation terms, how to handle updates on the attributes involved in observation terms, and how to define the approach formally.

Retrieving abstract objects by concrete values: Within the observation term approach it is possible to retrieve abstract objects, which are internally identified by surrogates, with the help of concrete data values. After retrieving an object in this way one can access other properties which are different from the identifying ones.

Multiple observation terms: It is also possible to have more than one observation term for a single object sort. Consider the case that we have for COUNTRY objects in addition to a 'Name' observation (i.e., 'Name' is a key for COUNTRY) also an attribute for the country's geometry. In order to keep things simple we assume this geometry is given by the country's border represented by a polygon: 'Geo : COUNTRY $\rightarrow$ polygon'. Now clearly two different countries will have different geometries, i.e., different polygons, and therefore the attribute 'Geo' can serve as a second observation structure for a COUNTRY object ($c : COUNTRY$): $\tau(c : COUNTRY) \equiv Geo(c)$. Such multiple observation terms and their implementation by some sort of index are helpful from the conceptual point of view, because different identification mechanisms for one object sort are supported. Such multiple observation terms are also useful from the implementation point of view in terms of query optimization, because these 'query' indexes can be employed for faster query evaluation and constraint enforcement.

Observation terms for other data models: Clearly, the applicatibility of the observation term approach is not restricted to the object-oriented world. The underlying idea originated from keys in the relational model, and therefore, this approach is applicable to the relational model per se. Another candidate for application are Entity-Relationship schemas.

Dynamic observation terms: Yet another distinguishing feature of the observation term approach is that it can be employed dynamically during the lifetime of a database. It is not necessary to specify all observation terms at the time when the database schema is fixed. Initially, only one such term may be given. Afterwards, other such observations may be added and dropped as it is needed. This is analogously to the relational model where indexes on different attributes for a relation may be created and deleted dynamically.

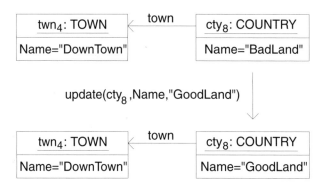

Figure 10.8   Update on an observation contributing attribute

Updates on observation contributing attributes: The observation term approach generalizes key attributes of the relational model, and there has been a debate in the database field whether to allow for updates on key attributes or not. Formally, we do not have key attributes but we can coin the notion of an *observation contributing attribute* for an attribute which is needed for calculating the τ_{os} value for an object o of sort os. And then we can ask the same question as in the relational model, namely, whether to allow updates on these attributes or not. Our answer to this is very simple: Yes, we allow for such updates as long as the integrity of the database is respected. Take for example the observation term (4) from above and the situation depicted in Figure 10.8. The attribute 'Name' of 'COUNTRY' is an observation contributing attribute for 'TOWN' in the above sense of the word, and it is updated in the example in Figure 10.8. This update presents no difficulty as long as the follow-up state obeys the specified constraints. In the new state we use $tuple("DownTown", \{"GoodLand"\})$ to identify the object twn_4 instead of $tuple("DownTown", \{"BadLand"\})$ in the old state. If one does not want the effect that an object is identified by data term t_1 in one state and data term t_2 in the other one, then one can exclude this behavior by additional transitional (or even temporal) constraints. For the general case, we prefer to have the freedom to change observation contributing attributes, because additional requirements in this respect are really a restriction which can be formulated explicitly.

Formal definition: As will be pointed out in the following Section 10.6, our approach is defined on a formal mathematical basis. Thus, comprehension and implementation is supported without any ambiguities.

10.6   Formal Definition

This section gives (in a very condensed way) the formal definitions neccessary for the well-definedness of our approach. A more elaborate treatment is given for example in (17, 22). Readers with no or little mathematical background are invited to inspect those papers first. We start with some preliminary notations.

Notation: Let sets $S, S_1, \ldots, S_n$ be given. Then $\mathcal{F}(S)$ denotes the restriction of the powerset of S to finite sets, $\mathcal{B}(S)$ the set of finite multisets (bags) over S, and $S_1 \times \ldots \times S_n$ the Cartesian product of the sets $S_1, \ldots, S_n$. Finite sets are written as $\{c_1, \ldots, c_n\}$, bags as $\{\!\{c_1, \ldots, c_n\}\!\}$, lists as $< c_1, \ldots, c_n >$, and elements of the Cartesian product as $(c_1, \ldots, c_n)$.

The basis of our framework assumes a data signature and a corresponding interpretation to be given. Such an interpretation is mainly an algebra in the sense of abstract data type theory.

Definition 1: Data signature

A data signature is given by a triple $\Sigma = (S, \Omega, \Pi)$ in which S denotes a set of sorts, $\Omega = \{\Omega_s\}_{s \in S^* \times S}$ an $S^* \times S$-indexed family of operation symbols and $\Pi = \{\Pi_s\}_{s \in S^*}$ an S^*-indexed family of predicate symbols.

$\omega_{s_1 \ldots s_n, s} \in \Omega$ is also written as $\omega : s_1 \times \ldots \times s_n \to s$ and $\pi_{s_1 \ldots s_n} \in \Pi$ as $\pi : s_1 \times \ldots \times s_n$.

For a given data signature Σ an interpretation structure is defined as a triple $I(\Sigma) = (I(S), I(\Omega), I(\Pi))$.

- $I(S)$ associates each sort $s \in S$ with a set $I(s)$ such that $\bot_s \in I(s)$.

- $I(\Omega)$ associates each operation symbol $\omega : s_1 \times \ldots \times s_n \to s \in \Omega$ with a total function $I(\omega) : I(s_1) \times \ldots \times I(s_n) \to I(s)$.

- $I(\Pi)$ associates each predicate symbol $\pi : s_1 \times \ldots \times s_n \in \Pi$ with a relation $I(\pi) \subseteq I(s_1) \times \ldots \times I(s_n)$.

The interpretation of some standard data sorts may be fixed as follows.

$I(\text{nat}) = \mathbb{N}_0 \cup \{\bot_{\text{nat}}\}$, $I(\text{int}) = \mathbb{Z} \cup \{\bot_{\text{int}}\}$, $I(\text{real}) = \mathbb{Q} \cup \{\bot_{\text{real}}\}$,
$I(\text{bool}) = \{true, \ false\} \cup \{\bot_{\text{bool}}\}$,
$I(\text{char}) = A \cup \{\bot_{\text{char}}\}$, $I(\text{string}) = A^* \cup \{\bot_{\text{string}}\}$,

Here, A denotes a finite set of characters. Standard operations and predicates have the usual meaning. Formally, we have a bottom value $\bot_s$ representing undefined for every sort s. When no confusion can occur we drop the additional index.

Examples:

i.   string $\in S$

ii. concat : string string $\to$ string $\in \Omega$

iii. = : string string $\in \Pi$

Definition 2: Sort expressions

Let a set S with $S = S_D \cup S_O$, S_D a set of data sorts according to Def. 1 and S_O a set of object sorts be given. Then the set $S - Expr(S)$ of sort expressions (or type constructor applications) over S is defined as follows.

i.   If $s \in S$, then $\mathbf{s} \in S - Expr(S)$.

ii. If $s \in S - Expr(S)$, then $\mathbf{set}(s), \mathbf{bag}(s), \mathbf{list}(s) \in S - Expr(S)$.

iii. If $s_1, \ldots, s_n \in S - Expr(S)$, then **tuple**$(s_1, \ldots, s_n) \in S - Expr(S)$.

Let us assume that there is a fixed interpretation I of S_D according to Def. 1. Then the interpretation of sort expressions is defined as follows.

i. $I(ds)$ is given as in Def. 1 for data sorts $ds \in S_D$. For each object sort $os \in S_O$ we have an infinite universe of object identifiers $U(os) = \{os_n \mid n \in \mathbb{N}\} \cup \{\bot\}$. In each database state we have an "active" finite subset $I(os) \subseteq_{finite} U(os)$ of the universe representing the objects in the current state with $\bot \in I(os)$.

ii. $I(\text{set}(s)) := \mathcal{F}(I(s)) \cup \{\bot\}$. $I(\text{bag}(s)) := \mathcal{B}(I(s)) \cup \{\bot\}$. $I(\text{list}(s)) := I(s)^* \cup \{\bot\}$.

iii. $I(\text{tuple}(s_1, \ldots, s_n)) := (I(s_1) \times \ldots \times I(s_n)) \cup \{\bot\}$.

Sort expressions are usually associated with a large number of *generic* (or overloaded) functions. There are operations and predicates that

- *compose* structured values from simpler ones. For instance, $\{ \ldots \}$ is used as a constructor for set values and *tuple*$(\ldots)$ is used as a constructor for tuple values.

- *decompose* structured values into simpler ones. For instance, the operation $PRJ_i : \text{tuple}(s_1, \ldots, s_n) \to s_i$ selects the ith component of a tuple.

- *convert* structured values. For instance, $\text{BTS}_{\text{bag}(s)} : \text{bag}(s) \to \text{set}(s)$ converts a bag into a set by duplicate elimination.

- *exploit* the distinct properties of certain kinds of structured values. For instance, $\text{CNT}_{\text{set}(s)} : \text{set}(s) \to \text{nat}$ counts the elements in a finite set (also defined for bags and lists), $\text{OCC}_{\text{bag}(s)} : \text{bag}(s) \times s \to \text{nat}$ counts the occurrences of a given item in a bag, $\text{IN}_{\text{set}(s)} : \text{set}(s) \times s$ denotes the membership predicate (also defined for bags and lists).

There are many other generic operations (for details see (15, 17)) All operations induced by sort expressions and the operations induced by the database schema are summarized in $\Omega_E(S - Expr(S))$. Analogously all predicates are combined in $\Pi_E(S - Expr(S))$.

Examples:

i.   TOWN $\in S_O$

ii. bag(tuple(CUSTOMER,tuple(int,set(string)))) $\in S - Expr(S_D \cup S_O)$

iii. Name : CUSTOMER $\to$ string $\in \Omega$

iv. town : COUNTRY $\to$ set(TOWN) $\in \Omega$

From now on let $\Sigma_D = (S_D, \Omega_D, \Pi_D)$ denote a data signature according to Def. 1 so that $\Sigma = (S, \Omega, \Pi)$ denotes an extended signature given by $S = S - Expr(S_D \cup S_O)$, $\Omega = \Omega_D \cup \Omega_E(S - Expr(S_D \cup S_O))$, and $\Pi = \Pi_D \cup \Pi_E(S - Expr(S_D \cup S_O))$. Furthermore, all following syntactic items (variables, terms, formulas, declarations, queries, constraints) are interpreted in a given database state. Such a database state allows only a finite number of current objects (according to the definition of sort expression).

Definition 3: Variables and variable assignments

Let an S-indexed family $Var = \{Var_s\}_{s \in S}$ of sets of variables be given. The set of variable assignments B is defined by $B := \{\alpha \mid \alpha : Var_s \to I(s) \text{ for all } s \in S\}$. The special assignment $\epsilon : Var \to \{\bot\}$ is called the *empty assignment*.

The index of a set of variables denotes the sort of the respective variables.

Examples:

i. $s \in V_{string}$

ii. $t \in V_{TOWN}$

Definition 4: Terms

The syntax of terms is given by an S-indexed family $Term = \{Term_s\}_{s \in S}$ and a function free : $Term \to \mathcal{F}(Var)$ defined by the following rules.

i. If $v \in Var_s$, then $\mathbf{v} \in Term_s$ with free$(v) := \{v\}$.

ii. If $\omega : s_1 \times \ldots \times s_n \to s \in \Omega$ and $\tau_i \in Term_{s_i}$ $(i = 1 \ldots n)$, then $\omega(\tau_1, \ldots, \tau_n)$ $\in Term_s$ with free$(\omega(\tau_1, \ldots, \tau_n)) := $ free$(\tau_1) \cup \ldots \cup$ free(τ_n).

iii. If $\tau \in Term_s$, $\delta \in Decl$ and $\varphi \in Form$, then $\{\!\!\{\tau \mid \delta, \varphi\}\!\!\} \in Term_{bag(s)}$ with free$(\{\!\!\{\tau \mid \delta, \varphi\}\!\!\}) := ($free$(\tau) \cup$ free$(\delta) \cup$ free$(\varphi)) \setminus$ decl(δ).

For a fixed interpretation I and a variable assignment $\alpha \in B$ the evaluation of terms is defined as follows.

i. $(I, \alpha)[\![v]\!] = \alpha(v)$.

ii. $(I, \alpha)[\![\omega(\tau_1, \ldots, \tau_n)]\!] = I(\omega)((I, \alpha)[\![\tau_1]\!], \ldots, (I, \alpha)[\![\tau_n]\!])$.

iii. $(I, \alpha)[\![\{\!\!\{\tau \mid \delta, \varphi\}\!\!\}]\!] = \{\!\!\{(I, \alpha')[\![\tau]\!] \mid \alpha' \in B \text{ with } \alpha'(v) = \alpha(v) \text{ for all } v \in Var \setminus $ decl(δ) and $(I, \alpha') \models \delta$ and $(I, \alpha') \models \varphi\}\!\!\}$.

Examples:

i. $c \in TERM_{COUNTRY}$

ii. town$(c) \in TERM_{set(TOWN)}$

iii. $\{\!\!\{$ Name(c), Name$(t) \mid (c:COUNTRY; (t:TOWN)), t \text{ in town}(c) \}\!\!\}$
$\in TERM_{bag(tuple(string,string))}$

Definition 5: Formulas

The syntax of formulas is defined by a set *Form* and a function free : $Form \to \mathcal{F}(Var)$ defined by the following rules.

i. If $\pi : s_1 \times \ldots \times s_n \in \Pi$ and $\tau_i \in Term_{s_i}$ $(i = 1 \ldots n)$, then $\pi(\tau_1, \ldots, \tau_n) \in Form$ with free$(\pi(\tau_1, \ldots, \tau_n)) := $ free$(\tau_1) \cup \ldots \cup$ free(τ_n).

ii. If $\tau_1, \tau_2 \in Term_s$, then $\tau_1 = \tau_2 \in Form$ with free$(\tau_1 = \tau_2) := $ free$(\tau_1) \cup$ free(τ_2).

iii. If $\varphi \in$ *Form*, then $\neg(\varphi) \in$ *Form* with free($\neg(\varphi)$) := free(φ).

iv. If $\varphi_1, \varphi_2 \in$ *Form*, then $(\varphi_1 \vee \varphi_2) \in$ *Form* with free($(\varphi_1 \vee \varphi_2)$) := free($\varphi_1$) $\cup$ free(φ_2).

v. If $\delta \in$ *Decl* and $\varphi \in$ *Form*, then $\exists \delta(\varphi) \in$ *Form* with free($\exists \delta(\varphi)$) := (free(δ) $\cup$ free(φ)) \ decl(δ).

For a fixed interpretation I and a variable assignment $\alpha \in B$ the validity of formulas is defined as follows.

i. $(I, \alpha) \models \pi(\tau_1, \ldots, \tau_n)$ iff $((I, \alpha)[\![\tau_1]\!], \ldots, (I, \alpha)[\![\tau_n]\!]) \in I(\pi)$.

ii. $(I, \alpha) \models \tau_1 = \tau_2$ iff $(I, \alpha)[\![\tau_1]\!] = (I, \alpha)[\![\tau_2]\!]$.

iii. $(I, \alpha) \models \neg(\varphi)$ iff not $(I, \alpha) \models \varphi$.

iv. $(I, \alpha) \models (\varphi_1 \vee \varphi_2)$ iff $(I, \alpha) \models \varphi_1$ or $(I, \alpha) \models \varphi_2$.

v. $(I, \alpha) \models (\exists \delta(\varphi))$ iff there is a variable assignment $\alpha' \in B$ with $\alpha'(v) = \alpha(v)$ for all $v \in Var \setminus$ decl(δ) and $(I, \alpha') \models \varphi$ and $(I, \alpha') \models \delta$.

The other logical connectives $\wedge$, $\Rightarrow$, $\Leftrightarrow$, and the quantifier $\forall$ can be defined by the given material.

Examples:

i. Name(c)="Greece" $\vee$ t in town(c) $\in$ *Form*

ii. clientship(b,c) $\Rightarrow$ StartDate(b) $\leq$ EndDate(b) $\in$ *Form*

Definition 6: Declarations

The syntax of declarations is given by a set *Decl* and the functions free, decl : *Decl* $\rightarrow$ $\mathcal{F}(Var)$ defined by the following rules.

i. If $v \in Var_s$, $\tau \in Term_{\text{set}(s)}$ and $v \notin$ free(τ), then $(v : \tau) \in$ *Decl*, free($(v : \tau)$) := free(τ) and decl($(v : \tau)$) := $\{v\}$.

ii. If $v \in Var_s$, $\tau \in Term_{\text{set}(s)}$, $\delta \in$ *Decl* and $v \notin$ free(τ) $\cup$ free(δ) $\cup$ decl(δ), then $(v : \tau; \delta) \in$ *Decl*, free($(v : \tau; \delta)$) := (free(τ) \ decl(δ)) $\cup$ free(δ) and decl($(v : \tau; \delta)$) := $\{v\} \cup$ decl(δ).

For a fixed interpretation I and a variable assignment $\alpha \in B$ the validity of declarations is defined as follows.

i. $(I, \alpha) \models (v : \tau)$ iff $\alpha(v) \in (I, \alpha)[\![\tau]\!]$.

ii. $(I, \alpha) \models (v : \tau; \delta)$ iff $\alpha(v) \in (I, \alpha)[\![\tau]\!]$ and $(I, \alpha) \models \delta$.

For a declaration δ the function free returns the free variables of δ and the function decl gives the set of variables declared within δ. For a declaration sequence $(x_1:\tau_1; (x_2:\tau_2; \ldots ; (x_n:\tau_n)))$ this is $\{x_1, \ldots, x_n\}$. In such a declaration sequence a variable x_i must not be declared twice and is not allowed to be free to the right, i.e., to be free in τ_j with $j \geq i$.

Examples:

i.   (c:COUNTRY; (t:TOWN)) ∈ *Decl*

ii. (c:COUNTRY; (t:town(c))) ∈ *Decl*

The concrete syntax of terms, formulas, and declarations may vary from the concise notation above. For example, instead of ⫨τ | δ, φ⫨ we have used the more familiar (*select τ from δ where φ*). Furthermore, because object sorts are interpreted by finite sets (of object identities), we allow them as set-valued terms in declarations. For example, (*t : T O W N*) is a valid declaration.

Definition 7: Queries and constraints

1. Every term $\tau \in$ *Term* with free(τ) $= \emptyset$ defines a query. The evaluation of queries is determined by $(I, \epsilon)[\![\tau]\!]$.

2. Every formula $\varphi \in$ *Form* with free(φ) $= \emptyset$ defines a constraint. The validity of constraints is determined by $(I, \epsilon) \models \varphi$.

Examples:

i.   Query: (select Name(c), (select Name(t) from (t:town(c))) from (c:COUNTRY))

ii. Constraint: ∀ (b:BOOKING) StartDate(b) ≤ EndDate(b)

10.7   Comparison with Other Approaches

Our approach is unique in comparison to related work because the general concept of observation term has not been introduced before. Observation terms are not even found in the literature under a different label. The degree of formality of our approach also seems to distinguish it from others. Nevertheless object identity has been studied intensively in recent literature. The approaches can be categorized into programming and specification language-oriented and database-oriented ones.

Database-oriented approaches: In (5) the significance of object identity w.r.t. data base query languages is pointed out. The proposed query language IQL employs object identities to represent data structures with sharing and cycles, to manipulate sets, and to express any computable database query. (35) discusses object identity with special emphasis on query optimization, and (36) extends the relational key concept. Object identities from the deductive databases point of view are treated in (23). Logic databases are also considered in (26) with special emphasis on updates, a topic which seems to be one of the mayor problems in this field (2). For the special purpose of databases, a functional language incorporating parametrized set types is introduced. Different kinds of (not necessarily formal) object equality definitions are studied in (32). The implementation of the proposed concepts in the database management system OMEGA is also discussed there. In (41), algebraic query processing was the main motivation for given a set-theoretic semantics for object identities in the presence of multiple-inheritance. The paper also discusses implementation issues in the context of the EXTRA/EXCESS system. A similar framework like ours but with emphasis on integrating different databases and with attention to the instance level has been put forward in (13). (40) studies object identity in connection with federated databases.

Programming or specification language-oriented approaches: A proposal to object identity from the functional programming perspective by the use of categorical monad structures is given in (34). (25) treats object identity from the data type point of view by providing a special identifier data type for this purpose. The approach in (30) is motivated from the declarative programming language implementation point of view. Our approach differs from the cited ones because we establish a connection between abstract object identities and concrete data values in order to identify objects. Our proposal to object identification can be implemented our the object specification language TROLL *light* (14, 38) which has been used recently in connection with the Unified Modeling Language (18, 20, 21).

10.8   Conclusion

We have studied object identification in the context of Entity-Relationship and Object-Oriented data models. The new idea of our proposal, the so-called observation term approach, was to associate with each object type a query in order to observe an identifying property of objects. This proposal seems to be more general than the well-known "deep equality" approach (24). We have argued that the advantages of our approach are the possibility of multiple observation terms, dynamic observation terms, updates on observation contributing attributes, and its formal definition.

We have not taken into account implementation issues, for example index and clustering techniques. Such techniques are advantageous in terms of query optimization, because 'query' indexes induced by observation terms can be employed for faster query evaluation and constraint enforcement.

References

1. M. Atkinson, F. Bancilhon, D. DeWitt, K. Dittrich, D. Maier, and S. Zdonik. The Object-Oriented Database System Manifesto. In W. Kim, J.-M. Nicolas, and S. Nishio, editors, *Deductive and Object-Oriented Databases*, pages 223–240. Elsevier (North-Holland), 1990.

2. S. Abiteboul. Updates, a New Frontier. In M. Gyssens, J. Paredaens, and D. Van Gucht, editors, 2nd Int. Conf. on Data Theory (ICDT), pages 1–18. Springer, Berlin, LNCS 326, 1988.

3. A. Auddino, Y. Dennebouy, Y. Dupont, E. Fontana, S. Spaccapietra, and Z. Tari. SUPER-Visual Interaction with an Object-Based ER Model. In G. Pernul and A.M. Tjoa, editors, *Proc. 11th Int. Conf. on Entity-Relationship Approach (ER'92)*, pages 340–356. Springer, Berlin, LNCS 645, 1992.

4. S. Abiteboul and R. Hull. IFO—A Formal Semantic Database Model. *ACM Trans. on Database Systems*, 12(4):525–565, 1987.

5. S. Abiteboul and P. Kanellakis. Object Identity as a Query Language Primitive. *ACM SIGMOD Record*, 18(2):159–173, 1989. Proc. ACM SIGMOD Conf. on Management of Data.

6. C. Beeri. A Formal Approach to Object-Oriented Databases. *Data & Knowledge Engineering*, 5(4):353–382, 1990.

7. G. Booch, I. Jacobson, and J. Rumbaugh, editors. *UML Summary (Version 1.1)*. Rational Corporation, Santa Clara, 1997. http://www.rational.com.

8. P.P. Chen. The Entity-Relationship Model—Towards a Unified View of Data. *ACM Trans. on Database Systems*, 1(1):9–36, 1976.

9. E.F. Codd. Extending the Database Relational Model to Capture More Meaning. *ACM Trans. on Database Systems*, 4(4):397–434, 1979.

10. O. Deux et. al. The O2 System. *Communications of the ACM*, 34(10):34–48, 1991.

11. K.R. Dittrich. Object-Oriented Database Systems: A Workshop Report. In S. Spaccapietra, editor, *Proc. 5th Int. Conf. on Entity-Relationship Approach (ER'86)*, pages 51–66. North Holland, Amsterdam, 1987.

12. G. Engels, M. Gogolla, U. Hohenstein, K. Hülsmann, P. Löhr-Richter, G. Saake, and H.-D. Ehrich. Conceptual Modelling of Database Applications using an Extended ER Model. *Data & Knowledge Engineering, North-Holland*, 9(2):157–204, 1992.

13. S. Prabhakar E.-P. Lim, J. Srivastava and J. Richardson. Entity Identification in Database Integration. In IEEE, editor, *Proc. 9th Int. Conf. Data Engineering (ICDE'93)*, pages 294–301, 1993.

14. M. Gogolla, S. Conrad, and R. Herzig. Sketching Concepts and Computational Model of TROLL light. In A. Miola, editor, *Proc. 3rd Int. Symposium Design and Implementation of Symbolic Computation Systems (DISCO'93)*, pages 17–32. Springer, Berlin, LNCS 722, 1993.

15. M. Gogolla and U. Hohenstein. Towards a Semantic View of an Extended Entity-Relationship Model. *ACM Trans. on Database Systems*, 16(3):369–416, 1991.

16. M. Gogolla, R. Herzig, S. Conrad, G. Denker, and N. Vlachantonis. Integrating the ER Approach in an OO Environment. In R. Elmasi and V. Kouramajian, editors, *Proc. 12th Int. Conf. on Entity-Relationship Approach (ER'93)*, pages 373–384. ER Institute, Pittsburgh (CA), Participants' Proceedings, 1993.

17. M. Gogolla. *An Extended Entity-Relationship Model—Fundamentals and Pragmatics*. Springer, Berlin, LNCS 767, 1994 (Also http://www.db.informatik. uni-bremen.de).

18. M. Gogolla and F. Parisi-Presicce. State Diagrams in UML - A Formal Semantics using Graph Transformation. In M. Broy, D. Coleman, T. Maibaum, and B. Rumpe, editors,

Proc. ICSE'98 Workshop on Precise Semantics of Modeling Techniques (PSMT'98), pages 55–72. Technical University of Munich, Technical Report TUM-I9803, 1998.

19. M. Gogolla and M. Richters. On Constraints and Queries in UML. In M. Schader and A. Korthaus, editors, *Proc. UML'97 Workshop 'The Unified Modeling Language - Technical Aspects and Applications'*, pages 109–121. Physica-Verlag, Heidelberg, 1997.

20. M. Gogolla and M. Richters. Equivalence Rules for UML Class Diagrams. In P.-A. Muller and J. Bezivin, editors, *Proc. UML'98 Workshop 'Beyond the Notation'*, pages 86–97. Universite de Haute-Alsace, Mulhouse, 1998.

21. M. Gogolla and M. Richters. On Combing Semi-Formal and Formal Object Specification Techniques. In F. Parisi-Presicce, editor, *Proc. 12th Int. Workshop Abstract Data Types (WADT'97)*. Springer, LNCS, 1998.

22. R. Herzig and M. Gogolla. A SQL-like Query Calculus for Object-Oriented Database Systems. In E. Bertino and S. Urban, editors, *Proc. Int. Symp. on Object-Oriented Methodologies and Systems (ISOOMS'94)*, pages 20–39. Springer, Berlin, LNCS 858, 1994 (Also http://www.db.informatik.uni-bremen.de).

23. R. Hull and M. Yoshikawa. ILOG: Declarative Creation and Manipulation of Object Identifiers. In R. Sacks-Davis D. McLeod and H.-J. Schek, editors, *Proc. Int. Conf. Very Large Data Bases (VLDB'90)*, pages 455–468. Morgan Kaufmann, 1990.

24. S.N. Khoshafian and G.P. Copeland. Object Identity. *ACM SIGPLAN Notices*, 21(11): 406–416, 1986. Proc. OOPSLA.

25. J.W. Schmidt K.-D. Schewe and I. Wetzel. Identification, Genericity and Consistency in Object-Oriented Databases. In J. Biskup and R. Hull, editors, *Proc. 4th Int. Conf. on Database Theory (ICDT'92)*, pages 341–356. Springer, Berlin, LNCS 646, 1992.

26. M. Kramer, G. Lausen, and G. Saake. Updates in a Rule-Based Language for Objects. In Li-Yan Yuan, editor, *Proc. 18th Int. Conf. on Very Large Databases, Vancouver*, pages 251—262, 1992.

27. G. Kappel and M. Schrefl. A Behaviour Integrated Entity-Relationship Approach for the Design of Object-Oriented Databases. In C. Batini, editor, *Proc. 7th Int. Conf. on Entity-Relationship Approach (ER'88)*, pages 175–192. ER Institute, Pittsburgh (CA), Participants' Proceedings, 1988.

28. G.M. Kuper and M.Y. Vardi. A New Approach to Database Logic. In *Proc. 3th ACM Symp. Principles of Database Systems (PODS)*, pages 86–96, 1984.

29. K.J. Lieberherr, P. Bergstein, and I. Silva-Lepe. Abstraction of Object-Oriented Data Models. In H. Kangassalo, editor, *Proc. 9th Int. Conf. on Entity-Relationship Approach (ER'90)*, pages 81–94. ER Institute, Pittsburgh (CA), Participants' Proceedings, 1990.

30. G. Lopez, B.N. Freeman-Benson, and A. Borning. Constraints and Object Identity. In M. Tokoro and R. Pareschi, editors, *Proc. 8th European Conf. Object-Oriented Programming (ECOOP'94)*, pages 260–279. Springer, Berlin, LNCS 821, 1994.

31. T.W. Ling and P.K. Teo. A Normal Form Object-Oriented Entity Relationship Diagram. In P. Loucopoulos, editor, *Proc. Int. Conf. on Entity-Relationship Approach (ER'94)*, pages 241–258. Springer, Berlin, LNCS 881, 1994.

32. Y. Masunaga. Object Identity, Equality and Relational Concept. In J.-M. Nicolas W. Kim and S. Nishio, editors, *Proc. 1st Int. Conf. on Deductive and Object-Oriented Databases (DOOD'89)*, pages 185–202. North-Holland, Amsterdam, 1990.

33. S.B. Navathe and M.K. Pillalamarri. OOER: Toward Making the E-R Approach Object-Oriented. In C. Batini, editor, *Proc. 7th Int. Conf. on Entity-Relationship Approach (ER'88)*, pages 55–76. ER Institute, Pittsburgh (CA), Participants' Proceedings, 1988.

34. A. Ohori. Representing Object Identity in a Pure Functional Language. In S. Abiteboul and P.C. Kanellakis, editors, *Proc. 3rd Int. Conf. on Database Theory (ICDT'90)*, pages 41–55. Springer, Berlin, LNCS 470, 1990.

35. S.L. Osborn. Identity, Equality, and Query Optimization. In K. Dittrich, editor, *Proc. 2nd Int. Workshop on Object-Oriented Database Systems*, pages 346–351. Springer, Berlin, LNCS 334, 1988.

36. N.W. Paton and P.W.D. Gray. Identification of Database Objects by Key. In K. Dittrich, editor, *Proc. 2nd Int. Workshop on Object-Oriented Database Systems*, pages 280–285. Springer, Berlin, LNCS 334, 1988.

37. M.P. Papazoglou, B.J. Kraemer, and A. Bouguettaya. On the Representation of Objects with Polymorphic Shape and Behaviour. In P. Loucopoulos, editor, *Proc. 13th Int. Conf. on Entity-Relationship Approach (ER'94)*, pages 223–240. Springer, Berlin, LNCS 881, 1994.

38. M. Richters and M. Gogolla. A Web-based Animator for Validating Object Specifications. In B.C. Desai and B. Eaglestone, editors, *Proc. Int. Database Engineering and Applications Symposium (IDEAS'97)*, pages 211–219. IEEE, Los Alamitos, 1997.

39. E. Rose and A. Segev. TOODM - A Temporal Object-Oriented Data Model with Temporal Constraints. In T.J. Teorey, editor, *Proc. 10th Int. Conf. on Entity-Relationship Approach (ER'91)*, pages 205–230. ER Institute, Pittsburgh (CA), Participants' Proceedings, 1991.

40. I. Schmitt and G. Saake. Managing Object Identity in Federated Database Systems. In M.P. Papazoglou, editor, *Proc. Int. Conf. Object-Oriented and Entity-Relationship Modelling (ER'95)*, pages 400–411. Springer, Berlin, LNCS 1021, 1995.

41. S.L. Vandenberg and D.J. DeWitt. Algebraic Support for Complex Objects with Arrays, Identity, and Inheritance. In *Proc. ACM SIGMOD Conf. on Management of Data (SIGMOD'91), SIGMOD Record, 20(2)*, pages 158–167, 1991.

42. B. Wilson. EU-Rent Car Rentals Case Study. Technical report, Model Systems & Brian Wilson Associates, 1994.

43. R. Wieringa and W. de Jonge. The Identification of Objects and Roles—Object Identifiers Revisited. Technical Report IR-267, Faculty of Mathematics and Computer Science, Vrije Universiteit Amsterdam, 1991.

V Modeling Object Collaborations

11 *Conceptual Modeling of Workflows*

Fabio Casati
Stefano Ceri
Barbara Pernici
Giuseppe Pozzi
Dipartimento di Elettronica e Informazione
Politecnico di Milano
Via Ponzio 34/5, I-20133 Milano, Italy

Workflow management is emerging as a challenging area for databases, stressing database technology beyond its current capabilities. Workflow management systems need to be more integrated with data management technology, in particular as it concerns the access to external databases. Thus, a convergence between workflow management and databases is occurring.

In order to make such convergence effective, however, it is required to improve and strengthen the specification of workflows at the conceptual level, by formalizing within a unique model their "internal behavior" (e.g. interaction and cooperation between tasks), their relationship to the environment (e.g. the assignment of work task to agents) and the access to external databases.

The conceptual model presented in this chapter is a basis for achieving convergence of workflows and databases; the workflow description language being used combines the specification of workflows with accesses to external databases. We briefly indicate how the conceptual model presented in this chapter is suitable for being supported by means of active rules on workflow-specific data structures. We foresee an immediate application of this conceptual model to workflow interoperability.

11.1 Introduction

Workflows are activities involving the coordinated execution of multiple tasks performed by different processing entities that work jointly towards accomplishing a common business goal. A task defines some work to be done by a person, by a software system or by both of them. Specification of a workflow (**WF**) involves describing those aspects of its component tasks (and the processing entities that execute them) that are relevant to control and coordinate their execution, as well as the relations between the tasks themselves.

Information in a WF mainly concerns when a certain work task (**WT**, or simply *task*) has to start, the criteria for assigning the task to agents, and which tasks it activates after its end; therefore, less emphasis is placed on the specification of the task itself (which may be informally described and only partially automated), while the focus is on the tasks' coordination. Connections among tasks can be rather complex, and some of them may be run-time dependent. A workflow management system (**WFMS**) permits both to specify WFs and to control their execution. During a WF execution, a WFMS has to schedule tasks (including their assignment to users) on the basis of the (static) WF specifications and of the (dynamic) sequence of events signaling the completion of tasks and of generic events produced within the execution environment (including exceptions).

The first descriptions of WFs have been proposed by *office modeling*, as a way of describing office procedures (4). Such descriptions were based on extensions of classical formal models (such as Petri Nets, production rules and flowcharts); a number of modeling support tools were proposed. The need of a closer relationship between modeling techniques and enactment of processes has been particularly developed within the *process modeling* area in software engineering. This research has produced several methodological contributions and WF specification languages (13, 15). Several tools for process modeling, generally based on Petri Nets, are focused on the ability of "animating" WFs, thereby understanding their dynamic behavior (2).

Recently, a growing interest has concentrated on connecting WF systems to existing information systems. In particular, the desire of interconnecting to existing data and of coping with large volumes of WF information has provided impetus to the bridging of WF and database technologies. The challenge posed by WF management pushes towards removing some of the classical limitations of databases in the context of concurrency and transactional models (22). Object-oriented techniques applied to databases and novel features of databases, such as active rules, are seen as particularly promising in the context of WFs (12, 28).

In this context, we are proposing a new conceptual model and language specifically focused on modeling WF interaction with external sources of information. The conceptual model and languages described in this chapter are the starting point of a wider research project aiming at the integrated management of different WFs (*semantic workflow interoperability*)[1] (7), at the implementation of a WFMS on the basis of an active DBMS (6), and at the management of evolution of WFs due to changes in the application domain (8, 14, 21). Several WF models (e.g., (1, 13, 18, 23, 26, 27, 29)) as well as programming and distribution support for workflow applications (3, 25) have been proposed in the literature, and a standardization effort is undergoing by the WF Management Coalition (WfMC) (17); we extend current approaches by presenting a model that is a basis for achieving convergence between workflows and databases; in particular, we allow the definition of task's preconditions evaluated over the state of an external database, of a procedural specification of a task's semantics (specified by defining modifications to workflow variable or to data in external databases), and we provide a flexible exception handling mechanism,

---

1. *semantic* workflow interoperability is related to the integration of two or more workflows, specified in the same model, that have to cooperate (e.g., in a producer-consumer application). This is an orthogonal issue with respect to WFMS interoperability, which deals instead with the exchange of process definitions and work activities between different WFMSs.

enabling the definition of a variety of exceptional behaviors as well as reactions to them. The proposed model is suited for being supported by active rules, following the approaches proposed in (6, 12, 16, 19, 20).

The chapter is structured as follows: Section 11.2 presents the main concepts of the proposed WF model and language; we illustrate the graphical symbols used for describing WFs. Section 11.3 describes the architecture of the proposed WFMS and informally illustrates the operational semantics of task executions and of WF execution. We also briefly indicate how active rules may be used to implement and support such operational semantics; a full description of the semantics, however, falls outside the scope of this chapter. Section 11.4 presents a classical WF example by giving both its linguistic and its graphical description.

11.2   Workflow Concepts

We define a *WF schema* as a structure describing relations among the tasks that are part of a WF. In the schema, we describe which tasks should be executed, in which order, who may be in charge of them, which operations should be performed on objects of external databases. WF schemas are described by means of *WF Description Languages* (**WFDL**).

A *WF instance* (or *case*) is a particular execution of a schema. For example, a WF schema may describe the process of booking a car and then picking it up; a WF instance of that schema is created whenever a customer makes a phone call for the reservation of a car. Thus, normally, several WF instances of the same WF schema (one case per one reservation) may be active at the same time.

11.2.1   Workflow Description Language

A Workflow Description Language describes tasks to be performed during the WF executions and the mechanisms which are used for their activation and termination, both in normal and in exceptional situations. task coordination is supported in a restricted number of alternative ways, thereby providing classical constructs for parallelism, such as *split* (or *fork*) and *join*. In addition, the behavior of tasks is formally described by listing their preconditions, their actions, and their exceptional conditions during their execution. The peculiar feature of the proposed WFDL is to enable, within tasks' conditions, actions, and exception sections, the manipulation of external databases. This section presents a "bird eye's view" on WFDL features; Appendix presents the most relevant features of the syntax of the WF description language while Appendix includes the textual language for the car rental example.

11.2.1.1   Definition Sections

A WF schema is composed of descriptions of flows, supertasks, and tasks; each of the above sections starts with definitions of constants, types, variables, and functions.

Definitions in the context of flow descriptions are global (visible to every task in the WF); definitions in the context of supertasks or tasks are local (visible in a supertask or task). In both cases, variables are not persistent: they exist only during an execution of the WF or task instance. Therefore, variables cannot be used within WF instances in order to link to other WF instances.

The flow declaration may also include the definition of persistent data (**DB**) which are shared by all WF agents and possibly by agents of other WFs. These data can normally be externally defined (i.e. their existence can be independent of the particular WF application being modeled). In our approach, data manipulation and retrieval is the only way of exchanging structured data with other WFs, thus following a blackboard approach. Data manipulation and retrieval primitives are executed upon an object-oriented schema, and are expressed in the object-oriented database language Chimera (9, 10). Other external databases which are independently accessed by agents during the execution of their tasks do not need to be explicitly defined. In the following, we do not deal with issues related to database design (which is typically outside the scope of workflow management): rather, we assume that data in external databases are either pre-existent (this is the typical case) or they are designed by means of existing (object-oriented) design techniques.

11.2.1.2   *Tasks*

Tasks are the elementary work units that collectively achieve the WF goal. The WFMS takes care of determining when a certain task must start being executed and of assigning it to an executing agent, according to some assignment polices.

Each task has five major characteristics:

- *Name*: a mandatory string identifying the task.
- *Description*: few lines in natural language, describing the task.
- *Preconditions*: a boolean expression of simple conditions which must yield a truth value before the action can be executed. Simple conditions may either contain (conventional) boolean expressions in WFDL, or be based on the (boolean) result of a method `exists` applied to a Chimera query, returning `true` if the result of the query is not empty.
- *Actions*: an action is a sequence of statements in WFDL which define how both temporary and persistent WF data are manipulated by the task. Inputs from the agent who executes the task are collected by the `get` statement; the `select_one` method extracts one single object randomly selected from the query result; database actions are performed by means of Chimera `create` and `modify` statement. Note that the specification of actions in the task is concerned with a fraction of the task's semantics; in general, the user executing the task has full freedom on the way the task itself should be executed, provided that eventually the actions which are listed in its action part are performed. Therefore, the action specification is somehow equivalent to giving the tasks' postcondition, however with a procedural description.

- *Exceptions*: in every task it is possible to specify a set of pairs <Exception, Reaction> to handle abnormal events: every time an exception is raised, the corresponding reaction is performed. An exception is a WFDL predicate, which may include predicates related to time and to the state of the OODBMS. All exceptions are monitored by the WFMS; when they become true (possibly at the start of the task), the exception is raised. A reaction is next performed by the WFMS to handle the exception. Reactions can be selected among a restricted set of options that includes END (imposes the termination of the task), CANCEL (the task is canceled), NOTIFY (a message is escalated to the person responsible for the task) and a few others; a brief description of available reactions can be found in (5). A typical exception is raised when a task is not completed within a specified deadline.

The definition of preconditions, actions, and exceptions based on the state of an external database are key features for the integration of workflows and databases. In particular, they enable database support for synchronizing WF execution and for monitoring exceptional situations.

11.2.1.3   Connections among Tasks

Connections describe the *flow structure*, i.e., the interactions among tasks; connections have both a linguistic description (in WFDL) and a graphical description. A task can have only one input connection and only one output connection. Two tasks A and B can be directly connected, in which case they are linked by an edge; the intuitive meaning is that, as soon as A ends, B is ready for execution. In all other cases, connections among tasks are performed by *connectors*. Each connector can be a *split*, for initiating concurrent task executions, or a *join*, for synchronizing tasks after concurrent execution.

Splits are preceded by one task, called its *predecessor*, and followed by many tasks, called *successors*. They are classified as:

- *Total*: after the predecessor ends, all successors are ready for execution (also called *and-split*).

- *Non deterministic*: the fork is associated with a value k; after the predecessor ends, k successors nondeterministically selected are ready for execution.

- *Conditional*: each successor is associated with a condition; after the predecessor ends, conditions are instantaneously evaluated and only successor tasks with a true condition are ready for execution.

- *Conditional with mutual exclusion*: it adds to the previous case the constraint that only one condition can be true; thus, after the predecessor ends, if no condition or more than one conditions are true an exception is risen, otherwise one of the successors is ready for execution.

Joins are preceded by many tasks, called its *predecessors*, and followed by one task, called *successor*. They are classified as:

- *Total*: the successor becomes ready only after the end of all predecessors (also called *and-join*).

- *Partial*: the join is associated with a value k; the successor becomes ready after the completion of k predecessor tasks. Subsequent completions of predecessor tasks have no effect, and are disregarded.

- *Iterative*: the join is associated with a value k; the successor becomes ready whenever k predecessor tasks are completed. Iterative joins are implemented by counting terminated predecessor tasks and resetting that counter to zero whenever the successor task becomes ready. Unlike partial joins, sebsequent completions of predecessor tasks are not disregarded, but cause the increment of counter k. Iterative join with $k = 1$ is used to describe *or-joins*.

The above values k may be associated with constants, variables, or functions expressed in WFDL; in the last two cases, their value becomes known at execution time.

11.2.1.4 Start and Stop Symbols

Start and stop symbols enable the creation and completion of WF instances (cases). Each WF schema has one start symbol and several stop symbols; the start symbol has one successor task (possibly a connection task) and each stop symbol has several predecessor symbols. After the WF instance creation, the successor of the start symbol becomes ready for execution; when any stop symbol becomes ready, the WF is completed. tasks which are still active are canceled.

11.2.1.5 Supertasks

It is often useful to group several related tasks, so as to introduce a notion of modularization and to define common preconditions and exceptions for a set of tasks. This is possible by a particular type of task, called *supertask* (**ST**).

STs have features of both WFs and tasks. Like WFs, they are internally decomposed into tasks (and possibly other STs); each ST has one start symbol and several stop symbols. Like tasks, STs have name, description, preconditions and exceptions. The action part of a ST is instead missing, as the job the ST performs is in effect decomposed into smaller jobs performed by the component tasks. STs have constant, types, variables and functions definitions, whose scope is restricted to the component tasks.

When a ST is ready, the successors of its start symbol becomes ready; when any stop symbol becomes ready, the ST is completed. The meanings of preconditions and exceptions in a ST are as follows:

- When a ST is ready, its precondition is evaluated; if it is `false`, then the successors of its start symbol become *inhibited* (see Section 11.3).

- Reactions to exceptions specified for a ST are propagated to the component tasks which are active at the time the exception is raised. For example, if the reaction is

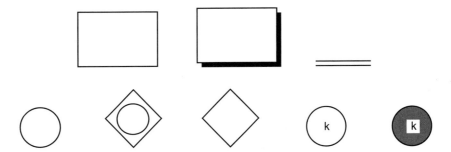

Figure 11.1   Graphical symbology for tasks and RTs. Tasks (left to right, first line): WT, ST, start/stop symbols; RTs (second line): total fork, conditional fork, conditional fork with mutual exclusion, non deterministic fork, iterative join. A total join has the same symbol as a total fork; a partial join has the same symbol as a non deterministic fork.

SUSPEND, all component tasks are suspended; only a RESUME at the ST level will enable the continuation of the tasks.

Figure 11.1 represents the adopted graphical symbology for tasks and RTs.

11.2.1.6   Multitasks

In many WFs it is necessary to define a set of tasks that perform exactly the same job in parallel, but are assigned to different agents. In order to do so, we introduce a *multitask* (**MT**); each MT has a *component* which can be either a task or a ST; the MT acts as a "multiplier" that generates several instances of its component, and assigns them for execution to several agents.

Each MT is associated with a value j indicating the number of task instances that becomes ready when the MT's predecessor ends. It is also possible to specify when a MT must be considered finished, by associating it to a threshold value called *quorum*. When the number of components which have ended reaches the quorum, the MT is also ended, and the MT's successor becomes ready. Subsequent ending of components has no effects.

Note that the semantics of MTs can be expressed by means of nondeterministic forks and partial joins. For example, consider a WF with tasks A, B, and C, where j instances of B become ready at the end of A and C becomes ready after the end of k instances of B. Two equivalent representations of this WF are given in Figure 11.2: on the left, the WF is represented by using a non deterministic fork and a partial join with multiple copies of task B, while on the right a MT is used.

11.2.2   Agents

A WF is populated by tasks, types, variables, and also by persons. These are called the *workflow agents*.

Each WF is defined by a "workflow administrator" (**WFA**) who is responsible of generating and compiling the WF schema. The WFA is notified of certain exceptions

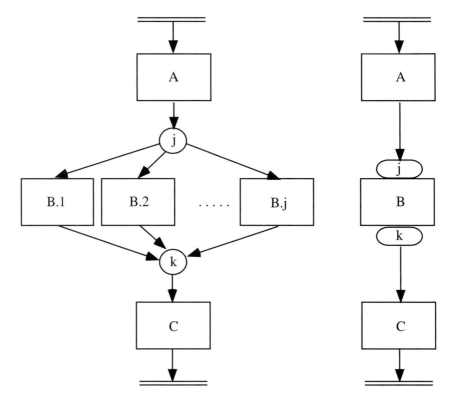

Figure 11.2 Two equivalent WF representations by means of non deterministic fork and partial join (on the left) and by means of a MT (on the right).

that may occur in the WF execution. Then, WF execution is performed by assigning tasks to agents. In general, agents have also the privilege of initiating the execution of a WF. This agent is known to the WFMS, and is normally notified of exceptional behaviors; the WF creator is also informed when the WF is terminated.

Each task may be fully automated or be assigned to one agent. If the task is fully automated, i.e. an external system like a software program or a machine can perform the task, then this feature must be specified adding the qualification `auto` to the task name. If instead the task is manual, then it has to be assigned to an agent. Note that we required each task execution to be under control of one specific agent; this is a requirement that should be taken into account in designing task granularity.

The assignment of a task to an agent can be predefined in the WF description, or can be selected by the WFMS. In this latter case, which is most interesting and also most frequent in practice, the WFMS performs the selection by means of application-specific rules (such as: equalization of load, use of "experienced" agents for "critical tasks", and so on). Agents are in this case described by suitable dictionary information in the WFMS.

A ST is not assigned to any agent; however, some agents (or the WFA) may be in charge of managing the ST's exceptions.

11.3   WorkFlow Execution

In this section, we first give a brief description of the WFMS architecture, and then describe task evolution by means of a state-transition diagram. Finally, we explain the operational semantics of WF instances whose schema is written in WFDL.

11.3.1   Architecture

We assume a WFMS architecture composed of two cooperative environments, one dedicated to WF coordination and one to task execution.

WF coordination is performed by a *workflow engine*, which is responsible of the execution of WF instances. The WF engine makes access to stored data describing agents and active tasks; it is driven by the information in the WF schema. The behavior of a WF engine is *event-driven*: the engine is sensible to events, such as `start-case` (generated by the agent who initiates a case), `end`, `cancel`, `suspend`, `refuse` (generated by tasks at the end of their execution; see the next section), time-related events (generated by a clock), and manipulation of shared databases (insert, delete, or update operations on specific objects). The WF engine reacts to events by activating tasks, assigning them to agents, compiling historical information, and sending warning messages to agents. The WF management environment supports also tools for editing and compiling WF schemas (specified in WFDL) and administration tools (for agent management and for reporting the WF history).

The task management environment is organized with a client-server architecture, where the client environment of an agent is application-specific; the task server is created by the WF engine and is responsible of managing WT evolution, according to the schema that will be presented in the next section. In particular, a WT server communicates WT termination to the WF engine (through the `end`, `cancel`, `suspend`, and `refuse` events) and can update shared databases, thereby generating events for WTs of other WFs.

Figure 11.3 depicts the WFMS architecture.

11.3.2   Task Execution

The execution of a task is initiated by the WF engine and next controlled by the agent in the context of the WT management environment. Two state diagrams, represented in Figure 11.4, define WT execution in the two environments.

In the engine environment, a task becomes *ready* for execution only due to the completion of some predecessors. If the task has no precondition or if the preconditions are `true`, then the task becomes *active* on the agent's environment by creating a unit of execution within the agent's task server. If instead the task's precondition is `false`, then the task's state becomes *inhibited* and the WF engine waits for some external event which changes the truth value of the precondition; after such an event occurs, the task becomes *active*. However, exceptional conditions may cause the task

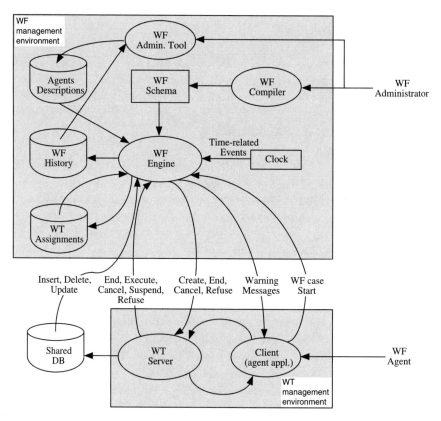

Figure 11.3 Schematic description of the architecture of a WFMS.

termination from the *inhibited* state. Task termination is represented by two exclusive states: a task can be *done*, in which case the WF continues with the task's successors selected according to the WF schema; or it can be *re-assign*, in which case the task's execution must be repeated by re-assigning it to a different agent.

When a task is activated, its execution state is decided by the agent. Initially, a created task is in the *waiting* state, and the agent changes the task's state to *executing* as soon as it starts operating on the task (for instance, by opening a window on his screen which corresponds to the task). He can suspend execution, by entering a *suspended* state, and then resume execution. Eventually, the agent indicates that the task is *ended*, *canceled*, or *refused*; in all these cases, the control returns to the WF engine. The first case corresponds to a normal termination; the second case corresponds to an abnormal termination which, however, does not suspend the WF execution. Thus, in both cases the task enters the *done* state; the two cases, however, are distinguished in the WF history. Finally, the *refused* state on the task environment corresponds to the *re-assign* state on the WF engine. When a task is *waiting, executing,* or *suspended*, it can be forced into a final state by exceptions which are generated by the WF engine.

STs have three associated states: they are *active* due to the completion of their predecessors, *suspended* due to an exception raised at the ST level, and *done* when

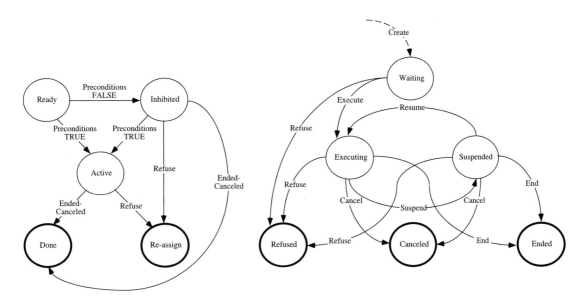

Figure 11.4 Left side: State diagram describing task execution in the WF engine. Done and Reassign are final states. Right side: State diagram describing task execution in the task server. Refused, Canceled, Ended are final states.

their execution is completed. State changes of the STs may cause state changes of the component tasks; for instance, ST suspension causes the suspension of all component tasks, and ST termination causes the completion (in the *canceled* state) of components' active tasks.

11.3.3   Flow Execution

The WFDL schema expresses the interaction and cooperation among tasks. In particular, splits and joins enable parallelism among tasks. Thus, based on the termination events from tasks (`end`, `cancel`, `refuse`), the WF engine is capable of deciding which tasks become *ready*. When a task or a ST is ready, the WF engine becomes also sensible to the (asynchronous) exceptions which are associated with the task, until the task is *done*. Exceptions normally correspond to actions that must be performed upon active tasks (thus, also the task server must be able of accepting asynchronous commands) and to messages that should be sent to agents.

Finally, the WF engine is responsible of performing several actions when a WF is completed, so that the current WF instance is eliminated from structures defining active flows and summary information is entered into the WF history.

11.3.4   Operational Semantics for Workflows and WorkTasks

The above execution models, so far expressed by means of state-transition diagrams, can be conveniently expressed by means of active rules. We briefly classify the active

Events

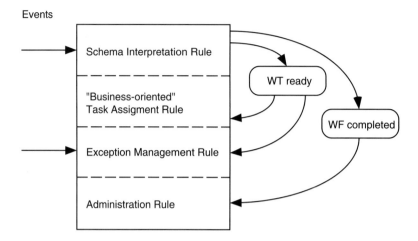

Figure 11.5   Schematic description of WF engine functionalities.

rules which should be provided for the WF engine (the specification of WT execution is much simpler). Active rules are classified as follows:

■ *Schema Interpretation Rules*: these rules implement the flow description part of a WFDL specification. When a WT enters the *ended*, *canceled* or *refused* state, these rules determine which WTs must be prepared for execution, or if the WF case must be considered finished;

■ *Task Assignment Rules*: these rules describe the privileges of agents upon WTs and express the application-specific policies for WT assignment to agents. We expect these rules to be easily customizable.

■ *Exception Management Rules*: on the basis of WT state transitions, DB modifications and time events, these rules determine if an exception was raised and perform the corresponding reactions; these rules are also responsible of recognizing that preconditions of inhibited WTs are satisfied.

■ *Administration Rules*: these rules react to the completion of WF instances and transform its associated information into historical data.

A summary of these 4 classes of rules is illustrated in Figure 11.5. Note that schema interpretation rules and exception rules react to external events, while WT assignment and administration rules react to internal events (WT ready, WF completed).

11.4   An Example of WFDL: The Car Rental Process

This section presents an example, taken from the car-rental case study (24), to illustrate how to define a WF in our conceptual model.

Workflow Booking and Picking up depicted in Figure 11.6 describes how the process of booking and picking up cars can be modeled in WFDL. The first task, Get_Customer's_Data, represents the clerk inserting customer's personal data, received either by phone or directly at the desk. For simplicity, we assume that the customer already exists in the EU-Rent database, and then all is needed to identify the customer is the driving license number (get Driv_Lic_No).

The system then gets customer data (select-one ...), that will be used in the following of the workflow. Next, the clerk records the rental period, the desired car type, and the return branch (instruction get Rental_Data in task Get_Rental_Data); the conditional fork that follows checks if the customer is blacklisted (i.e. if customer's attribute Level is negative). If the customer is blacklisted, the booking is refused (automatic task Set_Refusing_Cause_Blacklisted sets the Cause of refusal, which will then be used by the following task, Refuse_Booking, as attribute value when recording the refusal (i.e. creating a new object in the Refused object class). If the customer is not blacklisted, supertask Check_for_Car_Availability (described in detail later in this section) checks if a car is available for the selected time period. At the end the supertask sets the WF variable Available to Y if a car is found, and to N otherwise.

If no car is available, once again the booking is refused. Otherwise, the booking is recorded (task Record_Booking instantiates a new object in the Booking class, inserting rental data).

The next task, Check_Customer's_Driving_License, starts at the day scheduled for rental (note the precondition Rental_Data.Pickup_Day=Today()). The task represents the clerk checking the customer driving license; the result of the checking is recorded in the WF variable Driving_License_Status. This task has two exceptions: one is risen when 90 minutes have elapsed since the scheduled pick up time and the customer has not checked-in. The reaction causes the booking to be canceled, notifying the refusal by instantiating a new object of the Refused class. The second exceptions reacts to bookings canceled for any other reason (e.g., car accident, or delay in returns of cars from previous rentals); the reaction simply causes the end of the case (we assume that the WF manages the unplanned event also cancels the booking from the database and notifies the customer). After task Check_Customer's_Driving_License has been performed, if the driving license is correct(Driving_License_Status="OK"), the contract is printed and the car is given to the customer, otherwise the booking is canceled and cause of cancellation is recorded (task Cancel_Booking).

Figure 11.7 details the supertask Check_for_Car_Availability. The supertask first checks if a car is available in the branch (task Search_for_Car). If yes, the supertask simply finishes, otherwise different actions are performed according to the customer position with respect to the Customer Loyalty Incentive Scheme: if Level is greater than zero (i.e. the customer is a frequent renter), a car in the higher group is searched, to be offered for rental at the same price (variable upgrade checks that at maximum a car of one group higher is offered to the customer). If the customer has no privilege, or if the customer has privilege but no car in the higher

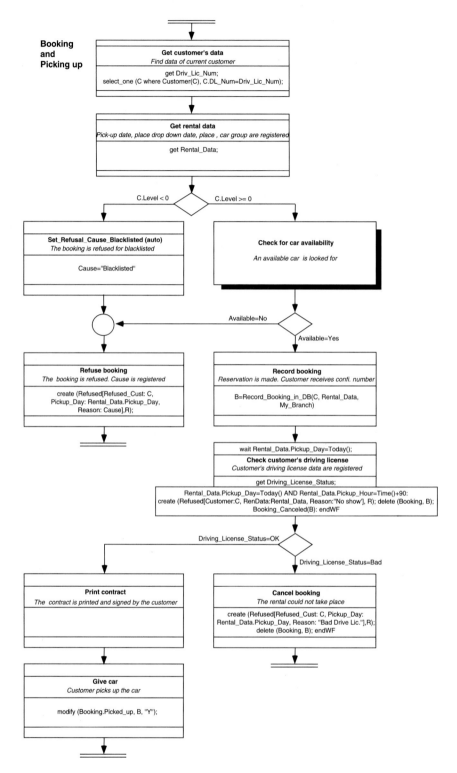

Figure 11.6   Example of booking a car for rental

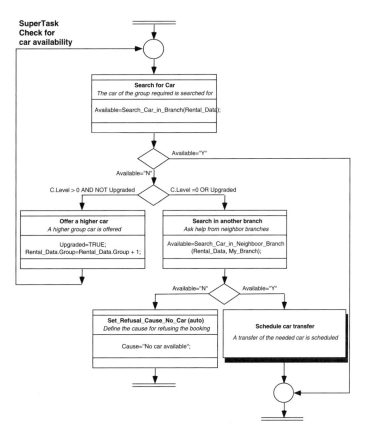

Figure 11.7   SuperTask of the example of booking a car for rental

group was found, a car is searched in neighbor branches (function `Search_Car_in_Neighbor_Branch(Rental_Data)`, not detailed further in this example). Finally, if no car is found, the cause for refusal (`No car available`) is recorded. Otherwise, if a car is found, the transfer of the car is scheduled from the neighbor branch (supertask `Schedule_Car_Transfer`, not detailed further in this example).

The WFDL textual specification for the given example is given in Appendix .

11.5   Conclusions

This chapter has presented a conceptual model and language for the specification of WF applications. Although this model reuses several concepts from existing models, it contributes to the clarification of both the behavior of WFs and their relationship to the environment and to external databases. This specification is sufficiently rich and formal to enable a syntax-directed translation of WFDL definition into active rules, thereby providing an operational semantics and an implementation scheme for many components of a WFMS. We have developed a prototype implementation running on the top of the active object-oriented database Chimera. We further anticipate the use of this conceptual model for addressing other critical problems of WF applications, namely the integration of distinct WFs and schema updates to manage application domain requirements that may change over time. In particular, the use of external databases by WFs constitutes a simple yet practical and efficient solution to WF interoperability. At the conceptual level, we plan to study the interaction between distinct WFs, developing a methodological background as well as some concrete techniques for checking that distinct WFs can correctly interact and cooperate.

The work described in this chapter is part of a large research effort on Workflow management; in particular, active database technology has been adopted within ESPRIT Project WIDE (Workflow on Intelligent and Distributed database Environments), whose goal is the development of an industrial-strength Workflow manager specifically based on active database technology.

Appendix

WFDL syntax

WFDL syntax is organized as a federated grammar (11). Top-level productions, described in the *WF Schema* section, generate the productions for each flow, ST, and WT. Each flow, in turn, includes the sections *Flow Definition* and *Flow Description*; each WT includes sections for *Task Definition*, *Task Control*, and *Task Actions*. STs, which behave partially as flows and partially as tasks, include three sections defined above: *Flow Definition*, *Task Control*, and Task Actions. Additional sections of the grammar, describing WFDL expressions and database manipulations, are not described in this chapter. Figure 11.8 shows this hierarchical grammar organization.

In the following we present a simplified syntax of WFDL, expressed in BNF notation. We use the following conventions: nonterminal symbols are enclosed within a pair of $<$ $>$ delimiters, terminal symbols are enclosed by quotes, optionality is denoted by square brackets, alternatives are separated by the | delimiter; plurals in a nonterminal symbol denote sequences of that nonterminal symbol; the suffixes *Set* and *List* added to a nonterminal symbol denotes sets or sequences of that nonterminals, e.g.:

⟨Types⟩ = ⟨Type⟩ [⟨Types⟩]
⟨TypeSet⟩ = ⟨Type⟩ ["," ⟨TypeSet⟩]
⟨TypeList⟩ = ⟨Type⟩ ";"[⟨TypeList⟩]

Top-Level Productions

The top-level productions describe the first two levels of the directed acyclic graph representing the grammar in Figure 11.8.

⟨WFSchema⟩ = ⟨Flow⟩ ⟨Supertasks⟩ ⟨Tasks⟩

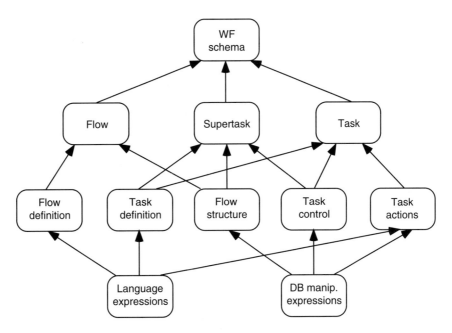

Figure 11.8   WFDL syntax tree.

⟨Flow⟩ = "WF" ⟨WFName⟩ "{" ⟨FlowDefinition⟩ ⟨FlowStructure⟩ "}"

⟨Supertask⟩ = "supertask" ⟨TaskName⟩ "{" ⟨TaskDefinition⟩ ⟨TaskControl⟩
     ⟨FlowStructure⟩ "}

⟨Task⟩ = ⟨BaseTask⟩ | ⟨Multitask⟩

⟨BaseTask⟩ = ["task"] ⟨TaskName⟩ ["(auto)"] "{"⟨TaskDefinition⟩
     ⟨TaskControl⟩ ⟨TaskAction⟩ "}

⟨Multitask⟩ = "multitask" ⟨TaskName⟩ ["(auto)"] "{"⟨NumberOfInstances⟩
     ⟨Quorum⟩ ⟨TaskDefinition⟩ ⟨TaskControl⟩ ⟨TaskActionList⟩ "}"

⟨NumberOfInstances⟩ = "NumberOfInstances =" ⟨IntegerExpression⟩ ";"

⟨Quorum⟩ = "Quorum =" ⟨IntegerExpression⟩ ";"

⟨IntegerExpression⟩ = ⟨CHIMERAselect⟩ | ⟨Var⟩ | ⟨Const⟩ | ⟨Function⟩

Flow Definitions

Flow definitions introduce constants, types, variables, functions, external schemas, and access privileges of the WF. User-defined types include simple records with atomic fields and enumeration types; WFDL supports standard atomic types. This section also includes the definition of WF agents and of their responsibilities as well as transactional and isolation properties of WFs, but we omit these features from this chapter for brevity.

⟨FlowDefinition⟩ = [⟨ConstantDefinitions⟩] [⟨TypeDefinitions⟩]
   [⟨VarDefinitions⟩] [⟨Functions⟩] [⟨TableDefinitions⟩] [⟨Grants⟩]

⟨ConstantDefinition⟩ = "#define" ⟨Const⟩ ⟨Value⟩ ";"

⟨TypeDefinition⟩ = "struct" ⟨RecordType⟩ "{"⟨FieldList⟩ "};"
   | "enum" ⟨EnumType⟩ "{" ⟨Values⟩"};"

⟨Field⟩ = ⟨TypeName⟩ ⟨FieldName⟩

⟨TypeName⟩ = ⟨EnumType⟩ | ⟨AtomicType⟩

⟨VarDefinition⟩ = ⟨TypeName⟩ ⟨Var⟩ ["[" ⟨Const⟩ "]"] ";"

⟨TableDefinition⟩ = "uses" ⟨TableName⟩ ⟨TableSchema⟩ ";"

⟨Grant⟩ = "grant " ⟨AccessSet⟩ "on" ⟨TableName⟩ ";"

⟨Access⟩ = "insert" | "select" | "delete" | "modify"

Task Definitions

Task definitions introduce constants, types, variables, functions, external schemas, and access privileges of the WT. As before, we omit the definition of transactional and isolation properties of WTs. A task is `cancellable` when it can be canceled by an agent or by an exception.

⟨TaskDefinition⟩ = [⟨Description⟩] [⟨ConstantDefinitions⟩]
   [⟨TypeDefinitions⟩] [⟨VarDefinitions⟩] [⟨Functions⟩]
   [⟨TableDefinitions⟩] [⟨Grants⟩] ["cancellable"]

⟨Description⟩ = ⟨Comment⟩

Flow Structure

This section of the grammar defines a WF as a collection of interacting tasks and supertasks. The description of task interconnections is divided into blocks. Each block is a set of instructions delimited by curly brackets. The main block is called *StartBlock* and it is activated when the WF starts.

⟨FlowStructure⟩ = ⟨StartBlock⟩ ⟨SplitBlocks⟩

⟨StartBlock⟩ = "start {" ⟨Instructions⟩ "}"

⟨ForkBlock⟩ = "after" ⟨TaskName⟩ "do {" ⟨InstructionList⟩ "}"

⟨JoinBlock⟩ = "after join" ⟨TaskName⟩ [["every"] ⟨IntegerExpression⟩
    "among ("⟨TaskNameSet⟩")"] "do {" ⟨InstructionList⟩ "}"

⟨Instruction⟩ = (⟨TaskName⟩ | ⟨Split⟩ | ⟨IfClause⟩ | ⟨Loop⟩ | "end" |
    "endWF"

⟨Split⟩ = "split" [⟨IntegerExpression⟩ "among"] "(" ⟨TaskNameSet⟩ ");"

⟨IfClause⟩ = "if (" ⟨BooleanExpression⟩ ") {" ⟨InstructionList⟩ "}"
    [⟨ExclIf⟩ | ⟨AlsoIf⟩]

⟨ExclIf⟩ = "exclif (" ⟨BooleanExpression⟩ ") {" ⟨InstructionList⟩ "}"
    [⟨Exclif⟩] | "else" ⟨InstructionList⟩

⟨AlsoIf⟩ = "alsoif (" ⟨BooleanExpression⟩ ") {" ⟨InstructionList⟩ "}"
    [⟨Alsoif⟩]

⟨Loop⟩ = "while ("⟨BooleanExpression⟩") {" ⟨Instructions⟩"}" |
    "do {"⟨Instructions⟩"}while ("⟨BooleanExpression⟩");"

Task Control

⟨TaskControl⟩ = [⟨Preconditions⟩] [⟨Exceptions⟩]

⟨Precondition⟩ = "wait" ⟨BooleanExpression⟩ ";"

⟨BooleanExpression⟩ = ⟨ExpCond⟩ ⟨AND⟩ ⟨ExpCond⟩ | ⟨ExpCond⟩
⟨OR⟩ ⟨ExpCond⟩

⟨ExpCond⟩ = ⟨Condition⟩ | ⟨NOT⟩ ⟨Condition⟩

⟨Condition⟩ = "exists ("⟨CHIMERAselect⟩")" | ⟨Function⟩ |
    ⟨Term⟩"=="⟨Term⟩

⟨Term⟩ = ⟨Const⟩ | ⟨Var⟩ | ⟨Function⟩

⟨Exception⟩ = "on" ⟨Condition⟩ "do" ⟨Reaction⟩

⟨Reaction⟩ = "END" | "CANCEL" | "NOTIFY" ⟨String⟩ | "REFUSE" |
    "ABORT" | "endWF" | "CHIMERAaction"
    ⟨AND⟩ = "AND" | "&" ⟨OR⟩ = "OR" | "||" ⟨NOT⟩ = "NOT" | "!"

Task Action

Actions of tasks manipulate temporary data (defined in WFDL) and persistent
data (by means of the CHIMERA primitives create, delete, modify, and the

select-one query primitive). These are not further discussed in the chapter (note that we don't anticipate the need of complex cursor mechanisms in WFDL).

⟨TaskAction⟩ = ⟨Var⟩ "=" ⟨Expression⟩ | ⟨Var⟩ "=" ⟨Function⟩ |
    "get" ⟨VarSet⟩ | ⟨Var⟩ = "("⟨CHIMERAselect-one⟩")" |
    ⟨CHIMERA create⟩ | ⟨CHIMERAdelete⟩ | ⟨CHIMERAmodify⟩

Example of WFDL for the Car Rental Case Study

```
WF BOOKING_AND_PICKING_UP {

/* consts declaration */
#define My_Branch 37

/* types declaration */
struct Rental_Data_Type{
        int Book_Id
        Group Booked_Group
        Branch Rental_Branch
        date Pickup_Day
        time Pickup_Time
        date Return_Day
        time Return_Time
        Branch Return_Branch
} Rental_Data;

/* vars declarations */
string Available, Driving_License_Status;

/* These refer to objects in the database: */
Customer C;
Refused R;
Bookings B;

/* declaration of accessed Chimera objects */
uses Customer (
attributes DL_Num: string,
        Name: string,
        Address: string,
        TelNo: string,
        Points: integer,
        Level: integer, derived
key     (DL_Num)
);

/* These two Chimera objects are used by functions that
determine car availability */
uses CarGroup (
```

```
attributes Group_Id: integer,
          Rental_Price: integer
key     (Group_Id)
);

uses Car (
superclass Car_Group
attributes Car_Id: integer,
          Purchased_In: date,
          Owner: Branch,
          Mileage: integer,
          Last_Service: date
key     (Car_Id)
)

uses Bookings(
attributes
          Book_Id: integer,
          Booking_Cust: Customer,
          Booked_Group Group,
          Rental_Branch Branch,
          Pickup_Day date,
          Pickup_Time time,
          Return_Day date,
          Return_Time time,
          Return_Branch Branch,
          Status: string(20)
key     (Book_Id)
);

uses Refused (
attributes RefusedCust: Customer
          Reason: string(20)
          Refused_Rental: Bookings
);

grant select on Car;
grant create on Refused;
grant create on Bookings;
grant select on Customer;

/* functions */
Bookings Record_Booking_in_DB(Customer C,
     Rental_Data_Type Rental_Data, int My_Branch) {
/*function DefineBookID returns an integer representing the booking
     number */
Rental_Data.Book_ID=DefineBookID();
```

```
Bookings B;
create (Bookings [Bookings.Book_Id: Rental_Data.Book_ID,
     Booking_Cust: C, Rental_Branch: Rental_Data.Rental_Branch,
     Pickup_Day: Rental_Data. Pickup_Day,
     Pickup_Time: Rental_Data.Pickup_Time,
     Return_Day: Rental_Data.Return_Day,
     Return_Time: Rental_Data.Return_Time,
     Return_Branch: Rental_Data.Return_Branch],B);
return B;
}

Bool Booking_Canceled(Bookings B) {
Bookings Btemp;
return EXISTS (select-one Btemp where Bookings (Btemp),
Btemp.Book_Id = B.Book_Id);
}

/* flow structure declaration */
start {
     Get_Customer_s_Data;
     Get_Rental_Data;
if (CustomerLevel<0) {
         Set_Refusal_Cause_Blacklisted;
         Refuse_Booking;
         endWF;
     }
Check_for_Car_Availability;
     if (Available="N") {
         Refuse_Booking;
         endWF;
     }
     Record_Booking;
     Get_Customer's_Driving_License;
     if (Driving_License_Status="Bad") {
         Cancel_Booking;
         endWF;
     }
     Print_Contract;
     Give_Car;
}    /* end of WF flow structure*/

/* Declaration of the supertask */
supertask Check_for_Car_Availability {
     bool Upgraded false
     string Cause;
     start{
         do{
```

```
                Search_for_Car;
                if (Available="Y") endWF;
                if (C.Level>0 and !Upgraded) Offer_A_Higher_Car;
            } while ((C.Level>0) & (!Upgraded));
            Search_in_Another_Branch;
            if (Available="Y") {
                Schedule_Car_for_Transfer;
                endWF;
            }
             Set_Refusal_Cause_No_Car;
        }
} /* end supertask flow description */

Search_for_Car {
        Available=Search_Car_in_Branch(Rental_Data, My_Branch);
}

Offer_a_Higher_Car {
        Upgraded = true;
        Rental_Data.Group = Rental_Data.Group + 1;
}

Search_in_Another_Branch{
        Available=Search_ in_Neighbor_Branch(Rental_Data, My_Branch);
}

Set_Refusal_Cause_No_Car{
        Cause = "No car available"
}
/* End of supertask declaration */

Set_Refusal_Cause_Blacklisted {
        Cause = "Blacklisted"
}

Refuse_Booking{
        create (Refused[Refused_Cust: C, Pickup_Day:
        Rental_Data.Pickup_Day, Reason: Cause],R);
}

Get_Customer's_Data{
        get Driv_Lic_Num;
        select (C where Customer(C), C.DL_Num= Driv_Lic_Num);
}

Get_Rental_Data{
        get Rental_Data;
```

```
}

Record_Booking{
    Record_Booking_in_DB(C, Rental_Data, My_Branch);
}

Get_Customer's_Driving_License{
/* precondition */ wait Rental_Data.Pickup_Day=Today();
/* action */       get Driving_License_Status;
/* exception 1: customer did not check-in*/
    on (Rental_Data.Pickup_Day=Today() AND
        Rental_Data.Pickup_Time= time()+90) do
    create (Refused [Customer: C, Pickup_Day:
        Rental_Data.Pickup_Day, Reason: "No Show"], R);
    delete (Bookings, B);
/* exception 2: booking is canceled (indep. from causes)*/
    on Booking_Canceled(B) do  endWF; }

Give_Car{
    modify (Booking.Picked_up, B, "Y"; }

Cancel_Booking {
    create (Refused [Customer: C, Pickup_Day:
        Rental_Data.Pickup_Day, Reason: "Bad Driving License"), R];
    delete (Booking, B);
    endWF; }
```

References

1. P. Attie, M. Singh, A. Sheth, and M. Rusinkiewicz. Specifying and enforcing intertask dependencies. In *Proceedings of the 19th International Conference on Very Large Data Bases (VLDB'93)*, Dublin, Ireland, February 1993.

2. S. Bandinelli, A. Fuggetta, and C. Ghezzi. Software process model evolution in the SPADE environment. *IEEE Transactions on Software Engineering*, December 1993.

3. D. Beringer, C. Tornabene, P. Jain, and G. Wiederhold. A language and system for composing autonomous, heterogeneous and distributed megamodules. In *Proceedings of the DEXA International Workshop on Large-Scale Software Composition*, Vienna, Austria, August 1998.

4. G. Bracchi and B. Pernici. The design requirements of office systems. *ACM Transactions on Office Information Systems*, April 1984.

5. F. Casati, S. Ceri, B. Pernici, and G. Pozzi. Conceptual modeling of workflows. Technical Report 95.018, Dipartimento di Elettronica e Informazione, Politecnico di Milano, 1995.

6. F. Casati, S. Ceri, B. Pernici, and G. Pozzi. Deriving active rules for workflow enactment. In *Proceedings of the 7th Coference on Database and Expert Systems Applications (DEXA'96)*, LNCS Springer Verlag, Zurich, Switzerland, September 1996.

7. F. Casati, S. Ceri, B. Pernici, and G. Pozzi. Workflow interoperability. In *Proceedings of the 5th International Conference on Extending Database Technology (EDBT'96)*, LNCS Springer Verlag, Avignon, France, March 1996.

8. F. Casati, S. Ceri, B. Pernici, and G. Pozzi. Workflow evolution. *Data and Knowledge Engineering, Elsevier Science*, January 1998.

9. S. Ceri and R. Manthey. Consolidated specification of Chimera CM and CL. Technical Report IDEA deliverable IDEA.DE.2P.006.01, ESPRIT project 6333 IDEA, 1993.

10. S. Ceri and R. Manthey. Chimera: A model and language for active DOOD systems. In *Proceedings of the East/West Database Workshop*, Klagenfurt, Austria, September 1994.

11. S. Crespi-Reghizzi and G. Psaila. Federal grammars and modular compilers. Technical Report 93.054, Dipartimento di Elettronica e Informazione, Politecnico di Milano, 1993.

12. U. Dayal, M. Hsu, and R. Ladin. Organizing long-running activities with triggers and transactions. In *Proceedings of the 1990 ACM SIGMOD International Conference on Management of Data (SIGMOD'90)*, Atlantic City, New Jersey, 1990.

13. C. Ellis and G. Nutt. Modeling and enactment of workflow systems. In M. A. Marsan, editor, *Application and Theory of Petri Nets*. Springer Verlag, New York, 1993.

14. S. Ellis, K. Keddara, and G. Rozenberg. Dynamic change within workflow systems. In *Proceedings of the ACM Conference on Organizational Computing Systems*, Milpitas, California, August 1995.

15. D. Georgakopoulos, M. Hornick, and A. Sheth. An overview of workflow management: from process modeling to workflow automation infrasctructure. *Distributed and Parallel Databases*, April 1995.

16. A. Geppert and D. Tombros. Event-based distributed workflow execution with EVE. Technical Report 96.05, University of Zurich, 1996.

17. D. Hollingsworth. The workflow reference model. Technical Report WFMC-WG01-1000, The Workflow Management Coalition, 1994.

18. M. Hsu and C. Kleissner. Objectflow: Towards a process management infrastructure. *Distributed and Parallel Databases*, April 1996.

19. M. Kamath and K. Ramamritham. Failure handling and coordinated execution of concurrent workflows. In *Proceedings of the 14th International Conference on Data Engineering (ICDE'98)*, Orlando, Florida, February 1998.

20. G. Kappel, P. Lang, S. Rausch-Schott, and W. Retschitzegger. Workflow management based on objects, rules and roles. *IEEE Data Engineering*, March 1995.

21. C. Liu, M. Orlowska, and H. Li. Automating handover in dynamic workflow environments. In *Proceedings of the 10th Conference on Advanced Information Systems Engineering (CAiSE'98)*, LNCS Springer Verlag, Pisa, Italy, June 1998.

22. M. Hsu ed. Special issue on worflow and extended transaction systems. *Data Engineering Bulletin*, June 1993.

23. R. Medina-Mora, T. Winograd, R. Flores, and F. Flores. The ActionWorkflow approach to workflow management technology. In *Proceedings of the Conference On Computer Supported Cooperative Work*, Toronto, Canada, 1992.

24. MS Brian Wilsons Ass. Eu-rent car rentals case study. Technical report, Model Systems & Brian Wilsons Ass., 1994.

25. M. Papazoglou, A. Delis, A. Bouguettaya, and M. Haghjoo. Class library support for workflow environments and applications. *IEEE Transactions on Computers*, June 1997.

26. M. Rusinkiewicz and A. Sheth. Specification and execution of transaction workflows. In W. Kim, editor, *Modern Database Systems: the Object Model, Interoperability, and beyond*. Addison-Wesley, 1994.

27. A. Sheth and M. Rusinkiewicz. On transactional workflows. *Data Engineering Bulletin*, June 1993.

28. J. Widom and S. Ceri. *Active Database Systems*. Morgan-Kaufmann, San Mateo, CA, 1995.

29. D. Wodtke, J. Weissenfels, G. Weikum, and A. K. Dittrich. The Mentor project: Steps towards enterprise-wide workflow management. In *Proceedings of the 12th International Conference on Data Engineering (ICDE'96)*, New Orleans, Lousiana, February 1996.

12 *Coordinated Collaboration of Objects*

G. Engels
Dept. of Computer Science
University of Paderborn
Warburger Str. 100, D-33098 Paderborn
Germany
engels@uni.paderborn.de

Luuk Groenewegen
Dept. of Computer Science
University of Leiden
P.O. Box 9512, NL-2300 RA Leiden
The Netherlands
luuk@wi.leidenuniv.nl

Gerti Kappel
Dept. of Computer Science
University of Linz
Altenbergerstr. 69, A-4040 Linz
Austria
gerti@ifs.uni-linz.ac.at

The computer has evolved from the purpose of pure number cranching to supporting the coordinated collaboration between human and/or artificial beings to reach a certain goal. Object-oriented modelling techniques based on the central notions of object interaction and object collaboration should provide the semantic expressivity to model such coordinated collaboration. Based on an investigation of the object-oriented modelling standard UML, however, the weaknesses of the existing modelling concepts are revealed. SOCCA is presented instead, which is an object-oriented specification language supporting the arbitrarily fine-grained synchronisation of processes, i.e., active objects. Based on several examples of the EU rental car system the expressive power of SOCCA is discussed and compared to relatd work.

12.1 Introduction

In modern software systems one can observe a tendency towards supporting ongoing work of concurrently active individuals. These individuals might be human beings, or artificial objects like software components. They are somehow interrelated and interconnected and they communicate with each other to share and exchange information.

This tendency can for instance be observed in the growing importance as well as gradual shift in meaning of the notion of user-friendliness. User-friendliness is no longer restricted to warnings in case of input errors or to extensive help facilities. Nowadays, it comprises informing a user about possible consequences of an action taken and of possible next steps after such an action. This information also reflects the state of a system as a whole. So possible effects of other users actions are taken into account, too. At this point the original notion of user-friendliness is gradually shifting towards the notion of process support. Typical examples of systems reflecting the above development are workflow systems as successors to office information systems, and software process environments as successors to CASE tools.

This shift of focus in modern software systems is mirrored by current developments in the area of modelling techniques. These modelling techniques should support a more accurate specification of relevant interrelations, interconnections, communications and mutual influences between all objects involved. The objects involved comprise human beings and other problem domain objects, as well as (artificial) software objects. The problem of choosing the "right" modelling techniques and their appropriate conceptual models is still an open research question. Object-oriented approaches with the conceptual model of object societies consisting of interacting objects are a promising candidate to fulfill the above mentioned requirements.

In more detail, object-oriented modelling techniques are based on the notion of an object. Objects are instances of a corresponding class. They have a unique identifier, and a hidden internal state. They communicate with each other by sending messages. Messages have a name, and optionally a number of argument types and a result type.

Each class provides a public interface, which comprises messages which are understood by the instances of this class. Messages are implemented by operations (also called methods). They realize the behaviour of an object. Two kinds of (sub-)behaviour of an object can be distinguished. First, operations realize the local behaviour of an object, i.e., how the internal state of an object is modified during execution. Second, operations realize the global behaviour, i.e., how different objects collaborate with each other by sending and receiving messages. In order to reach a certain goal, objects have to collaborate in a structured and coordinated way. Thus, the *coordinated collaboration* of objects in a society thereof is a major research challenge (14).

Currently available object-oriented modelling techniques deploy diagrammatic languages to model these aspects of an object society, i.e., the structure of objects, their local behaviour as well as their coordinated collaboration. All techniques agree on the use of class diagrams to model the structure of objects. The modelling of object structures has a long tradition in the field of conceptual modelling of databases. Based on the original work on Entity-Relationship models (3), standard modelling structures have been identified and are nowadays used in object-oriented class diagrams. In contrast to this, standard modelling structures for behaviour modelling do not yet exist. Different diagrammatic techniques are used to model behavioural aspects, such as state diagrams, statecharts, data flow diagrams, Petri nets, message sequence charts, and collaboration diagrams. All of them, or rather variants of them, have been brought together in the recently accepted standard notation for object-oriented modelling, the Unified Modelling Language (UML, (7, 8, 16)). However, only some means are offered by current object-oriented techniques such as UML to model the coordinated collaboration of objects. The expressivity of the behavioural modelling concepts is limited to distinguishing between synchronous and asynchronous forms of message passing. But to model realistic situations, much more detailed and fine-grained modelling expressivity is needed.

It is the goal of this contribution to elaborate on this weakness of current object-oriented modelling techniques. We will illustrate the limitations of existing object-oriented techniques by investigating UML, and explain an approach to improve the modelling of coordinated collaboration. Thus, extending the modelling expressivity with respect to coordinated collaboration provides an accordingly more refined basis for the specification of modern software systems nowadays needed. Such a specification in turn provides a more accurate basis for the eventual implementation of such systems.

In view of this goal the structure of the paper is as follows. Section 12.2 presents more details relevant for possible specification variants of coordinated collaboration. Section 12.3 summarizes the modelling means offered by UML as the most prominent object-oriented modelling technique to model coordinated collaboration. In particular, collaboration diagrams are investigated in more detail in order to understand how different forms of collaboration may be modelled. Section 12.4 presents an extension to current object-oriented techniques to model any variant of synchronous and asynchronous communication. Section 12.5 contains some conclusions, discusses related work and gives some ideas for future research.

12.2   Classification of Collaboration

Object-oriented modelling techniques use object societies as conceptual model, where a set of objects exist and where objects communicate with each other by message passing. A closer look at these conceptual models reveals differences concerning the allowed number of threads of control concurrently active within the object society and concerning the various kinds of message passing between the objects.

Concerning the number of threads of control purely sequential systems are possible, where at a certain point of time exactly one object is active. Thus, at a certain point of time there exist exactly one thread of control within the whole society. Conversely, all objects may be concurrently active, where each object has its own thread of control. The possibility of concurrently active objects might be even further extended if intra-object concurrency is supported, i.e., an object is involved in several processes, i.e., threads of control, at the same time.

Concerning the kind of message passing, different variants can be identified, too. Message passing in general means that an object, the sender, sends a message to another object, the receiver. In most approaches, two variants are distinguished. The message passing is called synchronous, if the sender is blocked after having sent the message to the receiver until the receiver has finished the activity asked by the message and has given an appropriate reaction. This kind of behaviour of two collaborating objects can be found as procedure call mechanism in sequential programming languages. Conversely, message passing is called asynchronous, if the sender is not blocked after having sent the message to the receiver. In this case, the sender continues with other activities without explicitly waiting for a reaction to the message sent. It is possible that the receiver accepts the message sometime in the future, and that it might or might not react to this message by sending an answer to the former sender.

This brief and informal explanation of the differences between synchronous and asynchronous message passing corresponds to explanations as they can be found in text books on object-oriented modelling techniques. This superficial style of explanation as well as the limited expressive power of these two kinds of synchronisation, however, are not sufficient for a software analyst to model realistic situations in an appropriate way. For example, the restriction to choose only between synchronous and asynchronous collaboration does not allow to model situations like the one, where a sender sends a message to a receiver asynchronously, continues with other activities, but would like to get an answer at some point in the future before it continues with a certain activity.

In order to improve this situation, possible interaction patterns between two objects are studied in detail in the remaining part of this section. In particular, similar to the framework of interaction rule patterns in (13) a distinction is made between the start and the end of an interaction between a sender and a receiver. The resulting classification of interaction patterns will be used in Section 12.3 to investigate whether and how UML, as typical representative of widely used object-oriented modelling techniques, supports the modelling of such a behaviour. In Section 12.4, the object-oriented modelling language SOCCA is presented, which provides explicit means to model all variants of synchronous and asynchronous behaviour.

In the following it is assumed that in the underlying object model each object has its own thread of control. This implies that two objects which are involved in an interaction may be concurrently active.

For a detailed study of the start of an interaction we distinguish the following constituents. Each object has an associated set of states. In a state, an object has three actions to choose from, namely an object may send a message, it may receive a message, and it may perform some local computations. By choosing an action, the object enters another state or reenters the same state. Any allowed state/action sequence is called behaviour of an object. The execution of some behaviour of an object is called the execution of the object in the following. In addition, each object has an associated buffer, where incoming messages are queued. The execution

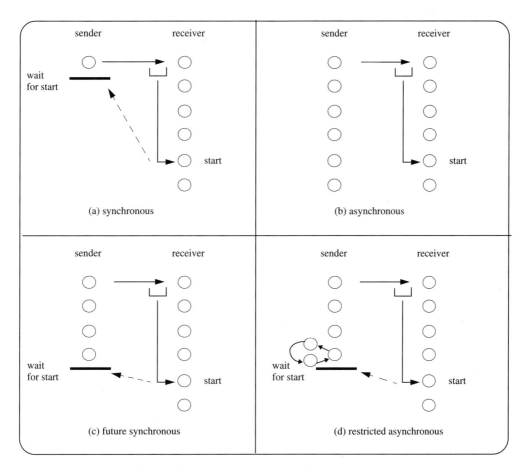

Figure 12.1   Patterns for the start of an interaction

of a sender may be blocked after sending some message to a receiver, if the continuation is depending on whether the receiver has reached a certain state. Figure 12.1 illustrates the different situations at the start of an interaction. Possible states of an object are drawn as circles, and time proceeds from top to bottom. Thus, the sequence of states from top to bottom displays the effect of the execution of one behaviour of an object solely in terms of states entered. The sending of a message is shown by an arrow, and a blocking situation is indicated by a horizontal bar.

Four different situations at the start of an interaction can be distinguished:

1. The start of an interaction is called *synchronous*, if the sending object is blocked immediately after having sent the message until the receiving object accepts that message by reading it from the input buffer (cf. Figure 12.1.a). (Note, for the purpose of this paper we do not further distinguish different blocking intervals, such as infinite, time bound, and balking (1)).

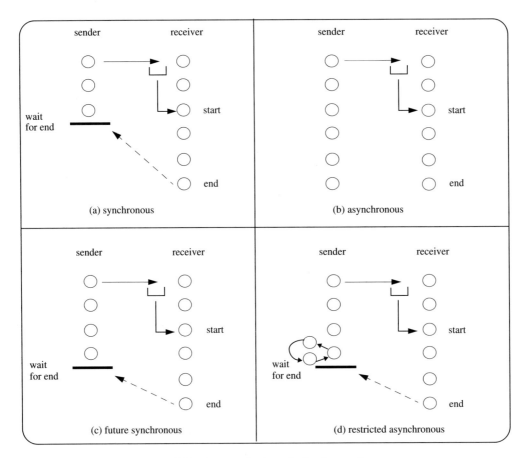

Figure 12.2   Patterns for the end of an interaction

2. The start of an interaction is called *asynchronous*, if the sending object continues with other actions independently from whether the receiver accepts the message immediately or sometime in the future or not at all (cf. Figure 12.1.b).

3. The start of an interaction is called *future synchronous*, if the sender is allowed to continue with other actions after having sent the message, but is blocked at some state until the receiver accepts that message by reading it from the input buffer (cf. Figure 12.1.c).

4. The start of an interaction is called *restricted asynchronous*, if the sender is allowed to continue with other activities after having sent the message, but is restricted to a certain (sub)behaviour until the receiver accepts the message sent (cf. Figure 12.1.d). The restricted behaviour is indicated by a loop of states in front of the horizontal blocking bar.

Analogously, the end of an interaction can be studied in detail. As before, we distinguish four different situations, but now at the end of an interaction, i.e., when the receiver has finished the execution of the operation invoked by the message sent.

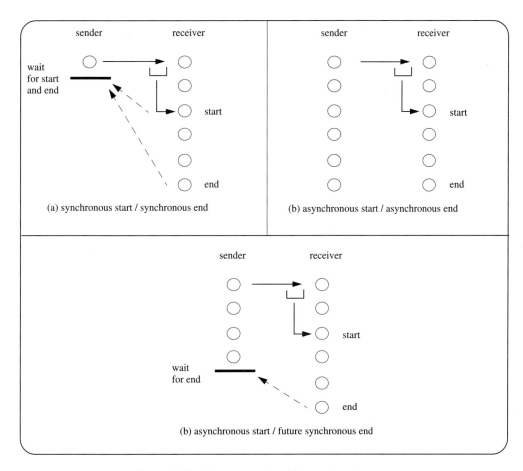

Figure 12.3   Three examples of interaction patterns

1. The end of an interaction is called *synchronous*, if the sender is blocked from the start of the invoked operation's execution on, originally initiated by the message sent, until the end of that execution (cf. Figure 12.2.a).

2. The end of an interaction is called *asynchronous*, if the end of the execution of the invoked operation has no effect on the sender (cf. Figure 12.2.b). In fact, the sender becomes not aware of the end.

3. The end of an interaction is called *future synchronous*, if the sender of a message is allowed to continue with various actions, but is blocked at some state to wait until the receiver of the message informs the sender that the execution of the invoked operation has been finished (cf. Figure 12.2.c).

4. The end of an interaction is called *restricted asynchronous*, if the sender of a message is restricted to a certain (sub)behaviour until the receiver of the message informs the sender that the execution of the invoked operation has been finished (cf. Figure 12.2.d).

The combinations of one out of the four patterns for the start of an interaction with one out of the four patterns for the end of an interaction sum up into 16 different interaction patterns for the interaction between the sender and the receiver of a message. In Figure 12.3, we depict three different combinations as examples. We will use these examples in the forthcoming sections to explain how such coordinated collaborations are modelled with UMLs collaboration diagrams and with SOCCA, respectively. The three examples are

- synchronous start and synchronous end (cf. Figure 12.3.a),

- asynchronous start and asynchronous end (cf. Figure 12.3.b), and

- asynchronous start and future synchronous end (cf. Figure 12.3.c).

The first example models what is usually called a procedure call mechanism. The second example models what is commonly referred to as asynchronous communication. In this case, the sender does not mind that it has sent a message. It does neither wait for the start nor the end of the receiver's execution of the operation invoked by the message. The third example shows that an asynchronous start does not necessarily imply for the sender to forget about having sent a message. In this case, the sender is not forced to wait until the receiver accepts the message sent. But it is forced to wait at a certain state until the receiver has finished the execution of the operation invoked by the message sent.

12.3   UML

The Unified Modeling Language UML has been approved by the OMG on November 17, 1997 as the standard notation for object-oriented analysis and design (16). Quickly, industry and research alike have adopted UML for their every day work, although parts of UML are still in their infancy (12). After providing a short intro into UML, we will concentrate on UMLs mechanisms for collaboration modeling.

The basic concepts and description techniques of UML support the modeling of the three interrelated perspectives of an information system, which are the structural perspective, the behavioural perspective, and the process perspective (15). Although the object-oriented approach clearly emphasises structural and behavioural modeling and diminishes the importance of process modeling compared to traditional approaches it is commonly accepted that the functionality of the system at hand has to be specified at first place. For this purpose, UML introduces use cases as integral part of object-oriented analysis. Based on use case diagrams the required object classes with their static and dynamic features are identified and depicted in class diagrams. The necessary interaction between objects is represented in terms of sequence diagrams and collaboration diagrams in turn. Use cases are further formalised in terms of sequence diagrams and activity diagrams alike. In contrast to the global system behaviour, which is described with the before mentioned diagrams, local object behaviour is depicted in terms of statechart diagrams. To model both application

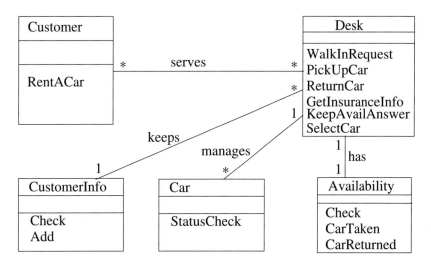

Figure 12.4   Class diagram fragment for a car rental information system

independent and application dependent constraints, UML provides the OCL, the object constraint language.

To introduce the object classes involved in our running example taken from the "EU-Rent Car Rentals Case Study" (22), Figure 12.4 depicts the corresponding class diagram fragment in UML notation. We see the most important classes involved in car renting according to the above mentioned case study. Classes are depicted in terms of rectangles showing their names, attributes (if any), and operations in three different compartments. As we are going to discuss some collaboration details based on an example built around a so-called walk-in request, we see customers as well as desks in that class diagram fragment. Furthermore, we see some other problem domain objects as far as they are being administrated by such a desk when handling a walk-in request, namely the general customer information concerning malicious customer behaviour, the list of currently available cars, and the cars themselves. Associations between these classes have been indicated by linking the respective rectangles, but only to the extent they are interesting for such a walk-in request.

12.3.1   Collaboration Modeling with UML

For interaction respectively collaboration modeling, UML provides two kinds of diagrams, namely sequence diagrams and collaboration diagrams. Following the standard document (16), both diagrams are equal concerning their semantic expressiveness, but they stress two different views. Whereas the sequence diagram emphasises the temporal perspective of interaction, the collaboration diagram emphasises the various kinds of relationships between the interacting objects. For the purpose of this paper, we concentrate on the latter. We will explain the intrinsics of collaboration diagrams by means of the collaboration examples introduced in Section 12.2.

Figure 12.5 depicts a collaboration diagram describing the case of synchronous start and synchronous end with respect to the message WalkInRequest sent from some customer to some desk (cf. the operation WalkInRequest in Figure 12.4). A collaboration diagram consists of prototypical objects depicted as rectangles with the (optional) name of the object and the name of its class prefixed with a colon shown inside the rectangle. The links between the objects are annotated with the messages sent between the objects. The direction of a message sent is given by an annotated arrow. Two kinds of arrows allow to distinguish between synchronous and asynchronous collaboration. The "normal" arrow head stands for synchronous collaboration, the half arrow head for asynchronous one. Messages are numbered concerning their execution order. Nested numbering refers to the implementation of the message with the corresponding number. Conditional execution of a message may be represented in two ways. First, by so-called guards in square brackets, and second, by preceding message numbers indicating that the execution of the corresponding messages has to be finished before the execution of the message under investigation may start.

Back to our example in Figure 12.5. Synchronous start and synchronous end of some collaboration actually comes down to the well-known procedure call mechanism, in the sense that as soon as the message asking for an activity has been sent the sender waits not only until the start but even until the end of the activity. In Figure 12.5 this is reflected by using the synchronous arrow belonging to the message WalkInRequest numbered 1 and directed from object thisCustomer to an object of type Desk.

As we can conclude from that diagram, after sending the message WalkInRequest thisCustomer has to wait until the end of the activity asked for by that message. This is synchronous start and synchronous end. In particular, the diagram specifies that the implementation of WalkInRequest consists of the messages 1.1, 1.2, and 1.3, which are sent by some object of type Desk. The result of WalkInRequest is returned as parameter answer. It is later on used as precondition for sending the messages PickUpCar (numbered 3) and ReturnCar (numbered 4). The message GetInsuranceInfo is independent of the result of WalkInRequest. But due to the synchronous behaviour modeling in this case, the message GetInsuranceInfo will only be sent after the implementation of WalkInRequest has been completely finished.

The second collaboration diagram given in Figure 12.6 visualises the asynchronous start and future synchronous end case, again with respect to the message WalkInRequest. To this end, message 1 has an asynchronous arrow directed from object thisCustomer to an object of type Desk. This indicates that thisCustomer's next message GetInsuranceInfo numbered 2 may be sent without any waiting for activity WalkInRequest to start or end. Thus, this modeling comes much closer to the real life situation, where a customer may already proceed to ask for information about insurances, while it is checked whether a car of a certain type is available for the desired period.

The message GetInsuranceInfo is sent asynchronously, too. Therefore, in principle the following message, numbered 3, could be sent without any waiting for start or

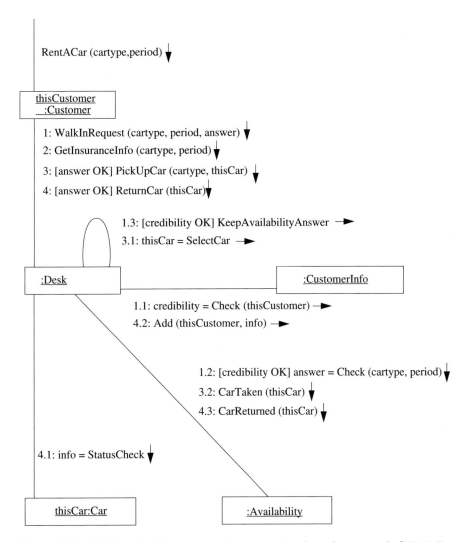

Figure 12.5   Collaboration diagram—synchronous start and synchronous end of WalkInRequest

end of the execution of GetInsuranceInfo. But in this case the sending of message PickUpCar depends on the result of the previously sent message WalkInRequest. As the message WalkInRequest has been sent asynchronously, the resulting answer is not contained as return paramter in the parameter list of WalkInRequest, but explicitly sent in a separate message (numbered 1.4) from the Desk object to the object thisCustomer. The waiting of message numbered 3 for the result of message numbered 1 is a typical example for the future synchronous end case. In the collaboration diagram, this is indicated by prefixing the message number 3 with "1.4 / ". So, here is the delayed wait for the end of activity WalkInRequest, whereas there is no wait at all for its start.

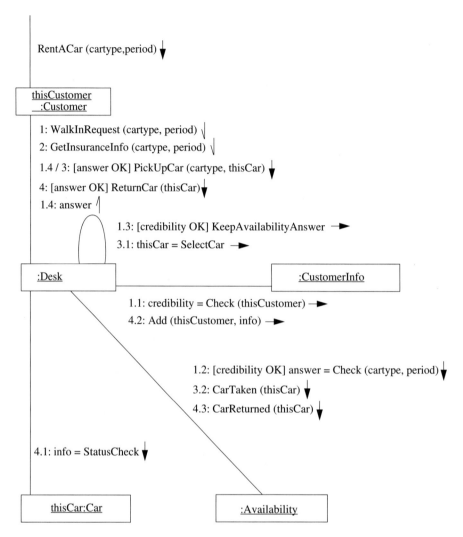

RentACar (cartype,period)

thisCustomer
 :Customer

1: WalkInRequest (cartype, period)
2: GetInsuranceInfo (cartype, period)
1.4 / 3: [answer OK] PickUpCar (cartype, thisCar)
4: [answer OK] ReturnCar (thisCar)
1.4: answer

1.3: [credibility OK] KeepAvailabilityAnswer
3.1: thisCar = SelectCar

:Desk   :CustomerInfo

1.1: credibility = Check (thisCustomer)
4.2: Add (thisCustomer, info)

1.2: [credibility OK] answer = Check (cartype, period)
3.2: CarTaken (thisCar)
4.3: CarReturned (thisCar)

4.1: info = StatusCheck

thisCar:Car   :Availability

Figure 12.6 Collaboration diagram - asynchronous start and future synchronous end of WalkInRequest

Summarising, UML allows to model other interaction patterns next to plain synchronous and asynchronous communication. However, there is no explicit support for those patterns, and they have to be specified from scratch.

12.4 SOCCA

In this section, we will discuss how SOCCA models coordinated collaboration. The next subsection gives a brief introduction to SOCCA. Subsection 12.4.2 presents the synchronous start and synchronous end case of collaboration, while subsection 12.4.3 covers the asynchronous start and future synchronous end case. From

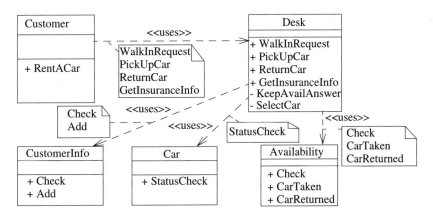

Figure 12.7   Class diagram fragment depicting the uses relationship

these fragment examples together one can get a good impression on how all other cases may be covered. Section 12.4.4 discusses pros and cons of using UML versus SOCCA.

12.4.1   Introduction to SOCCA

SOCCA is an object-oriented specification approach (2, 6). SOCCA is an eclectic formalism, whose constituent formalisms are somewhat comparable to the formalisms used in OMT (17) and UML (16). Thus, there is a substantial relationship between SOCCA and UML. In its specifications, SOCCA concentrates on four perspectives, namely data, behavior, functionality, and communication. How this is done, will be discussed successively.

As in UML, SOCCA's data perspective is covered by a class diagram. This description not only contains the classes with their operations and attributes, but also the various relationships between them, such as associations, inheritance relationships, and aggregations. Similar to UML, SOCCA supports also the uses relationship for specifying which of a class' public visible operations are actually imported in the functionality of another class (cf. the class diagram fragment in Figure 12.7). In contrast to UML, the annotated imported operations not only may be used in the implementation of the functionality of the client object class, but they really have to be used. The class diagram fragment in Figure 12.7 shows the classes of our running example an EU-Rent branch office as well as the uses relationships between these classes.

Also similar to UML, SOCCA's behavior perspective is covered by a state transition diagram (STD) for each class (called statechart diagram in UML). Such a STD specifies the allowed sequences of operations which get executed when answering messages sent to the corresponding object. As SOCCA is meant to express multithreading, handling a message in the order of such a sequence has to be understood as starting the execution of the corresponding operation, but not as completely executing that operation.

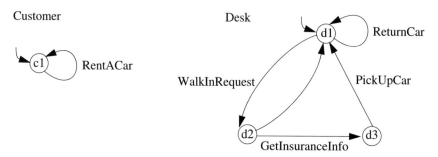

Figure 12.8 External STDs of Customer and Desk

Different to UML, the functionality perspective in SOCCA is covered by STDs, too, one separate STD for each operation of a class. These STDs are being called the internal STDs, whereas the STDs used in the behavior perspective are being called external. An external STD specifies what is usually called the visible behavior of a class. An internal STD specifies the hidden implementation of an operation. In other words, the functionality of an operation is described in terms of its hidden behavior.

To reflect the differences in perspective, the two different kinds of STDs obey two different sets of rules for labeling the transitions.

An external STD has as labels for its transitions the operation names of the corresponding class. As an example see Figure 12.8, where the external visible behavior of class Customer and of class Desk from Figure 12.7 has been visualised in terms of two external STDs. Note that unlabeled transitions may occur, too. In the case of Desk, the unlabeled transition reflects the possibility that a WalkInRequest results in a negative answer, so WalkInRequest then is not to be followed by GetInsuranceInfo and PickUpCar. State labels (or state names) are indicated within the state symbol, which is a circle. They are used for discriminating purposes, only. A starting state is indicated by means of an incoming directed edge without a source node.

The labeling rules for internal STDs are as follows. An internal STD, corresponding to an operation OperA belonging to a class A, has its first transition, the one leaving the starting state, labeled with 'act_OperA'. This actually reflects the activation of operation OperA inside whatever instance of class A. Furthermore, as transition label 'call B.Oper@' may occur, provided that Oper@ is an operation belonging to class B, and this Oper@ is actually imported in A. This means that Oper@ is to be found in the list of operations annotating the uses relationship in the class diagram pointing from class A to class B. In addition, transitions may be unlabeled, or may have a comment. Comments are indicated between < and >.

Figure 12.9 depicts the internal STDs for the operation RentACar of class Customer, and for the operation WalkInRequest of class Desk. Note that WalkInRequest, GetInsuranceInfo, PickUpCar and ReturnCar may be called from within RentACar, i.e., may occur as transition labels in RentACar's internal STD (cf. Figure 12.7 for the corresponding uses relationship). They also must be called, i.e., must occur as such labels, since RentACar is the only operation of Customer. Similarly, Check of CustomerInfo as well as of Availability and KeepAvailAnswer of Desk are called from

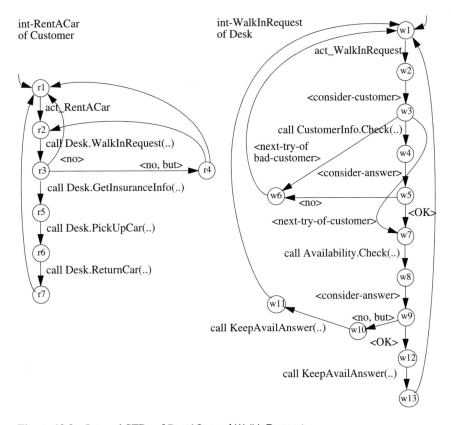

Figure 12.9   Internal STDs of RentACar and WalkInRequest

within WalkInRequest, as they occur in one of the lists of the corresponding uses relationships. The operations Add, CarTaken, StatusCheck and CarReturned are not called here, although they also occur in the related lists of used operations. This is allowed, provided that each of them is at least called from within GetInsuranceInfo, PickUpCar or ReturnCar (due to space limitations, we have omitted the internal STDs of the latter three operations). The internal STD's of RentACar and WalkInRequest give a more detailed description of the functionality compared to the above given UML collaboration diagrams, as in addition the cases of negative answers are treated, too.

The communication perspective in SOCCA is covered by a third formalism of SOCCA known as Paradigm, which specifies collaborations between STDs by using the notions of manager (process), employee (process), subprocess, trap and collaboration constraints[1] (21).

---

1. Collaboration constraints have been called state-action-interpreter in earlier publications on Paradigm.

Managers as well as employees are just STDs, but with a certain role in coordinating their collaboration. Subprocesses and traps are some special restrictions on employees.

Each external STD of a class A is considered a manager of the following employees: all internal STDs of operations belonging to A (the callees), as well as all internal STDs from which a call to one or more of A's operations occurs (the callers), i.e., containing a transition labeled with 'call A.OperA', where OperA is an operation of A. Such a group of STDs, consisting of a manager and its employees, actually constitutes a group of collaborating classes. Such a group or team is gathered around the class with the manager role, i.e., which has the external STD that is the manager. In order to act as a manager, the original external STD is extended in two directions.

The first direction is a refinement. States and transitions are added for representing possible results, even intermediate results of the actually called export operations. In (2) this refinement has been called the communicative view of the external STD. The new transitions might be labeled with some <comment>. These labels have no formal meaning at all, they only serve as some intuitive clarification.

The second direction of extending a manager is a completely new labeling of all its states and transitions, included those added in the refinement. These labels express the actual collaboration constraints. Collaboration constraints restrict both the visible behavior of the manager and the hidden behavior of its employees, i.e., they restrict (mostly hidden) behavior of collaborating objects in one collaboration team.

The restricted behavior of each employee is specified by means of subprocesses, which are subdiagrams of the internal STD being that employee. An (eventual) effect of such restricted behavior is represented by the notion of a trap of a subprocess, which is a subset of the subprocess' states such that this subset cannot be left as long as that subprocess is the current behavior restriction. The manager actually restricts the behavior of its employees, by telling them what is their current subprocess. On the other hand, the manager's behavior is restricted by its employees. As long as a certain trap has not been entered, the manager may not change the current subprocess into a next one. It is the collaboration constraint that expresses these dependencies. It does so by relating through labeling manager states to subprocesses, and by relating manager transitions to traps. A manager, by being in a state, exactly indicates the subprocesses related to that state, as the current ones for its employee - therefore a manager is said to prescribe the subprocesses. Conversely, one or more employees, by being in a trap, exactly indicate the transitions related to the combination of those traps, as currently permitted - therefore the manager is said to obey the traps. Furthermore, to start consistently, the first prescribed subprocess for an employee is such that the employee's starting state belongs to that subprocess' set of states. In addition, a trap not only is a trap of a certain subprocess. A trap is also a trap to a next subprocess, which means the following. The states of that trap also belong to the set of states of this next subprocess. So a manager, prescribing this next subprocess after obeying that trap, does not force its employee to continue its behavior in a discontinuous manner. The states to which this employee has been restricted most recently also occur in the currently prescribed next subprocess.

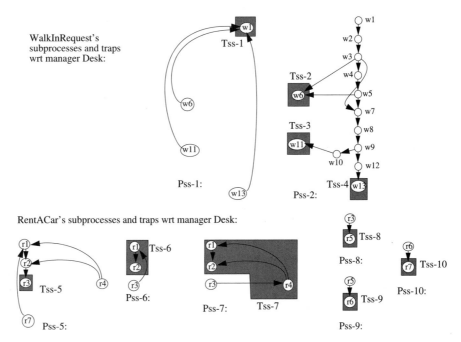

WalkInRequest's
subprocesses and traps
wrt manager Desk:

RentACar's subprocesses and traps wrt manager Desk:

Figure 12.10 Subprocesses and traps of caller RentACar and callee WalkInRequest (synchronous communication)

In the next two subsections we give two concrete examples of SOCCA specifications, i.e., for the purely synchronous case as well as for the asynchronous start and future synchronous end case.

12.4.2   Modeling of synchronous collaboration in SOCCA

The subprocesses and traps relevant for the coordinated collaboration in the synchronous start and synchronous end case are described in Figure 12.10. The figure presents the subprocesses of the internal STDs for caller RentACar and for callee WalkInRequest. Although the employees for GetInsuranceInfo, PickUpCar and for ReturnCar belong to the same team of collaborating classes, their subprocesses and traps have been omitted for the sake of brevity. For similar reasons of brevity we have omitted the transition labeling as it is present in the complete internal STDs (cf. Figure 12.9). First of all, we see the subprocesses Pss-1 and Pss-2 of WalkInRequest. Pss-1 represents the phase where the actual operation execution has been stopped and a new execution has not yet been started. Pss-2 represents the phase where the call to the operation is being executed. Trap examples are visualised by a shaded area around the trap's state(s). As we see, Pss-2 has three different traps, reflecting the three possible answers to the request: 'no' (because of malicious customer behavior), 'no, but' (perhaps a car from a different category is available), 'OK' (a car from the asked for category is available). Pss-1 has one trap only, simply indicating the end of that phase, so the operation can be restarted if needed. The trap Tss-1

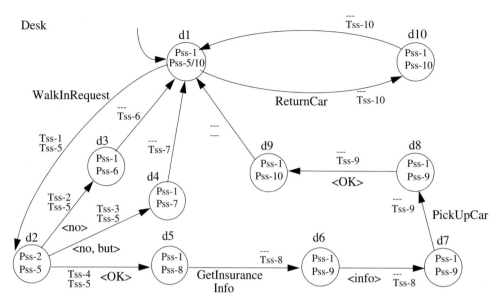

Figure 12.11   Manager Desk of employees Custromer.RentACar and Desk.WalkInRequest (synchronous communication)

of subprocess Pss-1 is a trap to subprocess Pss-2. The three traps Tss-2, Tss-3 and Tss-4 of subprocess Pss-2 are traps to Pss-1.

Second we see the subprocesses Pss-5, Pss-6, Pss-7, Pss-8, Pss-9, and Pss-10 of caller RentACar. Pss-8, Pss-9, and Pss-10 are mainly relevant with respect to the callees GetInsuranceInfo, PickUpcar and ReturnCar, which will be left out of our discussion. Pss-5 represents the phase of RentACar where a call for WalkInRequest is permitted as far as Desk is concerned. Its trap indicates the actual call. As this is a case of synchronous start, the trap consists of exactly one state, only allowing for waiting until at least the asked for operation execution has been started. Pss-6 reflects the phase of the behavior after WalkInRequest's execution, where the answer is a plain 'no'. Pss-7 reflects a similar phase, but now the answer is a 'no, but', as a car from a different category might be an option. Pss-6 as well as Pss-7 have as large traps as possible, as immediately after receiving the answer a new walk-in request is to be permitted as soon as possible, although in case of a plain 'no' this means an explicit restart of the operation RentACar. Pss-8 reflects the phase after the answer 'OK' has been received. Pss-9, and Pss-10, resp., reflect an even later phase, after call GetInsuranceInfo and call PickUpCar have been called. Here trap Tss-5 is trap to Pss-6 and also to Pss-7 and to Pss-8. The traps Tss-6, Tss-7, and Tss-10 are traps to Pss-5. Trap Tss-8 is trap to Pss-9, and trap Tss-9 is a trap to Pss-10.

Although the above explanation already suggests that this is indeed a synchronous start and synchronous end case with respect to calling WalkInRequest, the formal indication for it comes from the actual collaboration coordination by the manager. This coordination is enforced through the collaboration visualised in Figure 12.11. The state-related subprocesses are indicated as state labels, and the transition-related traps are indicated as transition labels. This labeling is a rather complicated matter because of the generally large number of employees belonging to the manager's collaboration group. Thus, some organisation has been added to the labeling. Labels are being represented according to a fixed ordering of the employees. Here we choose the upmost label as referring to employee WalkInRequest, and the undermost label as referring to employee RentACar. As the other employees have not been discussed, we also omit the labels referring to their subprocesses and traps. Moreover, where the trap does not matter, this is being indicated through "—". Formally this refers to a so-called trivial trap, consisting of all states of the (current) subprocess. Usually a trivial trap of any subprocess is trap to only the subprocess itself. In the figures we have omitted these trivial traps.

According to the above formulation of the collaboration constraints, Desk in its state d1 either indicates Pss-5 as the current subprocess to RentACar of Customer or Pss-10. In addition, Desk prescribes Pss-1 to WalkInRequest of Desk. As RentACar's starting state only occurs in Pss-5 (and not in Pss-10), this is the first subprocess indicated by Desk for RentACar. Only after both RentACar has entered its trap Tss-5 through the transition 'call Desk.WalkInRequest', and WalkInRequest has entered its trap Tss-1, Desk transits to state d2, thereby prescribing Pss-2 to WalkInRequest, and still keeping RentACar in its old subprocess in the trap. Thus, WalkInReqest actually starts a new execution and RentACar continues to wait for the result. As RentACar could do nothing else then waiting since it entered its one-state trap, the collaboration case certainly is of the type synchronous start. Subsequently, only after WalkInRequest has entered one of its traps Tss-2, Tss-3 or Tss-4, Desk prescribes Pss-1 as the next subprocess to WalkInRequest and simultaneously either Pss-6 or Pss-7 or Pss-8 to RentACar, depending on what is Desk's next state (d3, d4, or d5). This in turn depends on the exact trap entered in Pss-2. The caller RentACar is indeed kept in its single state trap Tss-5 until WalkInRequest is finished, i.e., has entered either trap Tss-2, Tss-3 or Tss-4. So we see here that the collaboration case is of type synchronous end. Moreover, the transition <no> indeed corresponds to malicious customer information found (Tss-2), the transition <no,but> indeed corresponds to the required category is not available (Tss-3), and <OK> indeed corresponds to the request can be honoured (Tss-4).

This finishes the discussion of the SOCCA modeling of purely synchronous collaboration.

12.4.3   Modeling of asynchronous collaboration in SOCCA

Mainly by choosing the size of traps differently, different types of collaboration cases can be modeled, although sometimes also subprocesses and even STDs have to be adapted accordingly. For instance, consider the collaboration case of asynchronous start and future synchronous end, again with respect to calling of WalkInRequest.

Figure 12.12 presents a slightly adapted internal STD for RentACar and for WalkInRequest, together with their subprocesses and traps with respect to manager Desk. The small difference with RentACar from Figure 12.9 is that after the call to

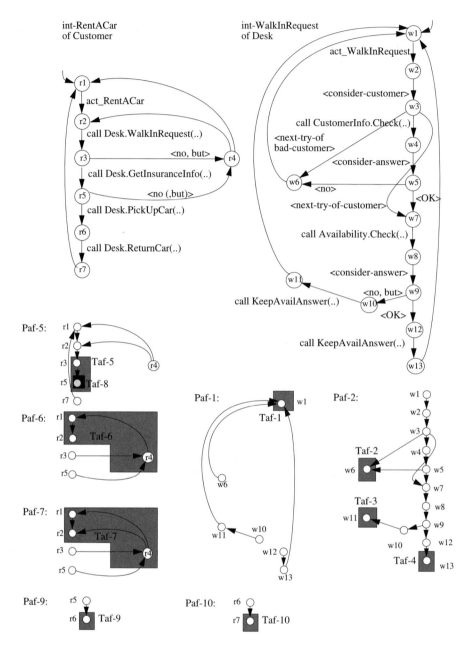

Figure 12.12   Internal STD of RentACar and WalkInRequest together with their subprocesses and traps (asynchronous communication)

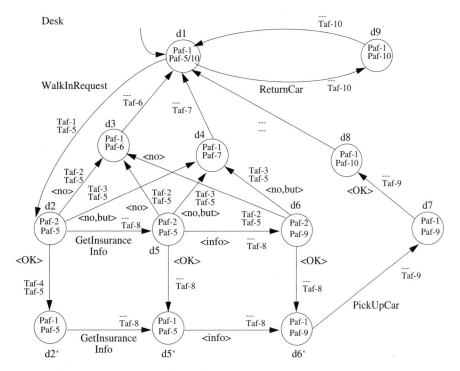

Figure 12.13 Manager Desk of employees Customer.RentACar and Desk.WalkInRequest (asynchronous communication)

GetInsuranceInfo the effect of a refusal to the preceding call of WalkInRequest must be taken into account, too. So, there is an extra transition labeled with <no>. The small difference in the subprocesses mainly consists of combining Pss-5 and Pss-8 into one new subprocess Paf-5, as after the call of WalkInRequest the possibility to continue asynchronously is to be offered. This continuation may only be the calling of GetInsuranceInfo, as for all other possible continuations the result of WalkInRequest has to be available. Moreover, in order to be able to continue after that call to GetInsuranceInfo the result of WalkInRequest has to be available anyway. The trap representing the call to WalkInRequest is Taf-5. It consists of two states, one more than the corresponding trap Tss-5 from the previous collaboration case. This very accurately expresses how the behavior of RentACar is indeed to continue asynchronously after the call to WalkInRequest. The small trap Taf-8 inside trap Taf-5 is the analogue to trap Tss-8 from Figure 12.10. It serves to indicate that Paf-9 might be prescribed as next subprocess, thus signaling that PickUpCar has been called. Moreover, trap Taf-8 still allows for Paf-6 or Paf-7 as next subprocess, as even after the call to GetInsuranceInfo the result of the preceding call to WalkInRequest might be a <no> (Paf-6), or a <no, but> (Paf-7). This is exactly captured by the requirement that Taf-8 is trap to Paf-6, to Paf-7, and to Paf-9. This is also captured by the manager /sf /small Desk (cf. Figure 12.13), where the external STD of Desk is refined by additional states (d2, d5, d6, d2', d5', d6') to model the different interleaved behaviors of finishing WalkInRequest and executing GetInsuranceInfo. Please note that the modeling does not show the internal behavior of GetInsuranceInfo. The overall specification would become even more detailed, if this would be considered, too.

While WalkInRequest and GetInsuranceInfo might be executed in parallel, PickUpCar has to wait for the end of WalkInRequest. This is the case in state d6', where the two subprocesses Paf-1 and Paf-9 have been reached.

This finishes the discussion of the asynchronous start and future synchronous end case of collaboration. Both examples have shown how any degree of asynchronous collaboration between several participants can be modelled by choosing the right subprocesses and traps of internal STDs, as well as by refining and extending external STDs appropriately by additional intermediate states and collaboration constraints.

12.4.4 Discussion

In the following, SOCCA and UML are compared concerning their supported collaboration mechanisms.

Looking back at SOCCA, how it establishes the coordination of the various collaborations, we can conclude the following. First, the collaborations are organized in groups. Each collaboration group is centered around one external state transition diagram, the visible behavior of an object class. Such a group consists of the external STD itself, of the callers of its operations and of the callees, its own operations. Second, the collaborations are explicitly described in terms of effects on the behavior of the members of such a collaboration group. That is to say, not only the immediate effect in terms of one step of the behavior, but also the longer run effect in terms of the complete future behavior gets specified, until the next coordinating action is taken. In that respect the SOCCA approach has two strong advantages. First, SOCCA is explicitly prescriptive in its collaboration specification instead of declarative. This means that every degree of (a)synchronism is accurately expressed as which part of the full behavior is permitted at which moment. Second, SOCCA structures the collaboration coordination by not only describing the immediate, short term effect of whatever communication, but also by describing the long term effect through the notions of subprocess and trap.

If one tries to express this information in some collaboration diagram, the notation becomes complicated. For example, in Figure 12.5 the message PickUpCar numbered 3 should have some precondition like [(answer OK) OR (answer 'not yet received')]. Moreover, if in the same collaboration diagram one also wants to express the iteration modelled as returning from state r4 to state r2 in Figure 12.9, it is not at all clear how to do this. Similar considerations are found in the literature concerning UML's interaction diagrams comprising sequence diagrams and collaboration diagrams (8, page 112): "They are good at showing collaborations among objects; they are not so good at precise definition of behavior." Fowler has an even stronger opinion on this point at (8, page 11): "You can easily see the messages by looking at the diagram.

However, if you try to represent something other than a single sequential process without much conditional or looping behavior, the technique begins to break down."

This is exactly what SOCCA is good at, namely specifying the precise behavioral consequences of coordinated collaborations. SOCCA does so by two different ways of sequentialising separate steps of hidden behavior, i.e., the steps the functionality consists of. First, SOCCA sequentialises the detailed steps to be taken in view of the eventual implementation of the operations by means of separate internal STDs. Each STD is modeling behavior needed for one operation. Second, SOCCA sequentialises the global steps to be taken in view of the collaborations between operations of classes by means of communicative views of external STDs together with collaboration constraints.

12.5   Conclusions and Related Work

In this paper we have presented SOCCA as an object-oriented specification language supporting an arbitrarily fine-grained synchronisation of processes, i.e., active objects. Since we are focusing on collaboration concepts between objects, a critique of UML's collaboration concepts has been given as a precursor and motivation to SOCCA's advanced synchronisation mechanisms. To complete the picture, out of the huge amount of object-oriented modeling approaches, two areas of related work are briefly discussed in the following, first some competitive approaches to UML, and second two representatives of object-oriented coordination languages.

Concerning the former, Catalysis (20), Syntropy (4), and OML (9) are nowadays the most influential object-oriented modeling approaches next to UML. All three are very strong in providing a development process and design guidelines, however, they fall short when it comes down to specific interaction mechanisms. Concerning the degree of synchronisation, they only support synchronous communication. Concerning concurrency, only Syntropy discusses this issue in detail (4). In contrast, the real-time object-oriented modeling technique ROOM (18) supports both synchronous and asynchronous communication, and the specification of concurrently active threads of control. There is an ongoing effort to integrate the real-time concepts of ROOM into UML (19). Last but not least, also Harel's extension of the statechart mechanism incorporating object-oriented concepts has to be mentioned (10). Statecharts together with O-charts support multiple-thread concurrency together with a broadcast mechanism for communication between concurrent components.

The second kind of approaches concentrate on the specification of obligatory and/or allowed interaction patterns between objects of the same or of different object classes. *Contracts* (11) are specifications of such interaction patterns with obligations on the participating objects. Each object fulfilling the corresponding obligation may participate in some contract. Contracts may be inherited and refined by adding participating objects, and by specializing besides others the inherited invariants and obligations. Since contracts are defined independently of object classes, class definitions must ultimately be mapped to participant specifications, which is done through conformance declarations. A contract is instantiated by identifying objects as participants and invoking the methods specified in the contract's instantiation statement. A similar approach is followed in *CoLa (Communication Language)* (5), which allows to model the obligatory/prohibited/permitted interaction patterns between several objects. These interaction patterns are specified in terms of contracts between two or more so-called agents. In other words, contracts specify a set of norms which give rise to a certain interaction protocol between different agents, which is implemented in turn. CoLa has been used to implement different kinds of speech acts (5).

Modern software systems require specifications of complex interactions as they are available, for example, in SOCCA, but lacking in UML. Hence, we are investigating means of incorporating SOCCA's collaboration features in UML by changing UML's meta model as little as possible. One promising approach is based on UML's extension mechanism, which is currently investigated in more detail. Our long term goal is the identification of interaction patterns encapsulating the most important recurring collaboration structures.

References

1. G. Booch, *Object-Oriented Analysis and Design with Applications (2nd edition)*, Benjamin Cummings, 1994.

2. T. de Bunje, G. Engels, L. Groenewegen, A. Matsinger and M. Rijnbeek, "Industrial Maintenance Modelled in SOCCA: an Experience Report," in *Proc. of the 4th Int. Conf. on the Sofware Process*, ed. W. Schaeffer, pp. 13-26, IEEE Press, 1996.

3. P.P. Chen, "The Entity-Relationship Model - Toward a unified view of data," in *ACM Transcations on Database Systems*, vol. 1, pp. 9-36, 1976.

4. S. Cook and J. Daniels, *Designing Object Systems - Object-Oriented Modelling with Syntropy*, Prentice Hall, 1994.

5. F. Dignum, "Modelling Communication between Cooperative Systems," in *Proceedings of the Conference on Advanced Information Systems Engineering (CAiSE'95)* , ed. J. Iivari, K. Lyytinen and M. Rossi, pp. 140-153, Springer LNCS 932, 1995.

6. G. Engels and L.P.J. Groenewegen, "SOCCA: Specifications of Coordinated and Cooperative Activities," in *Software Prices Modelling and Technology*, ed. A. Finkelstein, J. Kramer, and B. Nuseibeh, pp. 71-102, Research Studies Press, 1994.

7. H.-E. Eriksson and M. Penker, *UML Toolkit*, John Wiley and Sons, 1998.

8. M. Fowler, *UML Distilled: Applying the Standard Oject Modeling Language*, Addison-Wesley, Reading, Massachusetts, 1987.

9. I. Graham, B. Henderson-Sellers and H. Younessi, *The OPEN Process Specification*, Addison-Wesley, 1997.

10. D. Harel and E. Gery, "Executable Object Modeling with Statecharts," in *IEEE Computer*, vol. 30, pp. 31-42, July 1997.

11. R. Helm, I. Holland and D. Gangopadhyay, "Contracts: Specifying Behavioral Compositions in Object-Oriented Systems," in *Object-Oriented Programming Systems Languages and Applications (OOPSLA), Special Issue of SIGPLAN Notices*, ed. N. Meyrowitz , vol. 25, pp. 169-180, Oct. 1990.

12. M. Hitz and G. Kappel, "Developing with UML - Goodies, Pitfalls, Workarounds," in *<<UML>>'98: Beyond the Notation, 1st Int. Workshop on UML*, ed. Jean Bezivin and Pierre-Allain Muller, Springer LNCS, Mulhouse (France), 1998.

13. G. Kappel, S. Rausch-Schott, W. Retschitzegger and M. Sakkinen, "Rule Patterns - Bottom-up Design of Active Object-Oriented Databases," in *Communications of the ACM (CACM, accepted for publication)*, 1998.

14. M. Klein, "Coordination Science: Challenges and Directions," in *Coordination Technology for Collaborative Applications - Organizations, Processes, and Agents*, ed. W. Conen, G. Neumann, pp. 161-176, Springer LNCS 1364, 1998.

15. T.W. Olle, J. Hagelstein, I.G. Macdonald, C. Rolland, H.G. Sol, F.J.M. Van Assche and A.A. Verrijn-Stuart, *Information Systems Methodologies: A Framework for Understanding, 2nd edition*, Addison-Wesley, 1991.

16. Rational Software et al., *UML Documentation Version 1.1*, September 1, 1997.

17. J. Rumbaugh, M. Blaha, W. Premerlani, F. Eddy and W. Lorensen, *Object-Oriented Modelling and Design*, Prentice-Hall, 1991.

18. B. Selic, G. Gullekson and P.T. Ward, *Real-Time Object-Oriented Modeling*, Wiley, 1994.

19. B. Selic and J. Rumbaugh, *Using UML for Modeling Complex Real-Time Systems*, Technical Report, ObjecTime Lmtd., March 1998.

20. D. D'Souza and A.C. Wills, *Objects, Components, and Frameworks with UML - The Catalysis Approach*, Addison-Wesley, 1998.

21. M.R. van Steen, L.P.J. Groenewegen and G. Oosting, "Parallel control processes: modular parallelism and communication," in *Intelligent Autonomous Systems*, ed. L.O. Herzberger, pp. 562-579, North-Holland , 1987.

22. B. Wilson, *EU-Rent Car Rentals Case Study*, Model Systems & Brian Wilson Associates, May 1994.

VI   Beyond Modeling

13   *An Active, Object-Oriented, Model-Equivalent Programming Language*

Stephen W. Liddle
School of Accountancy and Information Systems
Brigham Young University
Provo, Utah 84602, U.S.A.

David W. Embley
Scott N. Woodfield
Department of Computer Science
Brigham Young University
Provo, Utah 84602, U.S.A.

The intricate and complex structure of existing advanced database applications results in part from poor integration of the models and languages used in building those applications. This complexity is a barrier to effectively understanding and developing advanced applications. We can significantly reduce the complexity of advanced-application specification and implementation by using a model-equivalent language (a language with a one-to-one correspondence to an underlying, executable model as defined herein). In this chapter we explain the difficulties encountered in making models and languages equivalent, and we resolve these difficulties for a particular language and model.

13.1   Introduction

One of the formidable barriers to effective understanding and development of advanced applications is the poor integration of model and language. We use semantic models to facilitate our understanding, but we implement our systems using languages that are neither fully integrated nor fully compatible with our models. This causes numerous problems, including:

- difficult and lossy transitions between models, languages, and tools,
- inhibited communications (e.g., due to differing definitions or assumptions),
- roadblocks to developing tools that support state-of-the-art techniques,
- variable quality in system implementation under similar quality designs, and
- lack of comprehensibility.

Herein we propose the concept of a model-equivalent language to help solve these problems. By "model" we mean a software model for systems analysis and design (e.g., ER, NIAM, OMT, UML); and by "language" we mean a programming language (e.g., Pascal, Ada, Eiffel, C++, Java). In this context, a language L *is model-equivalent with respect to a model* M if for every model instance I_M of M, there exists a program I_L of L whose semantics are one-to-one with I_M, and conversely, for every program I_L of L, there exists a model instance I_M of M whose semantics are one-to-one with I_L. By "semantics are one-to-one with" we mean that for every construct in the program, there is a corresponding construct in the model instance and vice versa. Consequently, a program written in a model-equivalent language is nothing more than an alternative view of some model instance and vice versa. Hence, every program written in a model-equivalent language is fully integrated with and fully compatible with a model instance.

A model-equivalent language allows us to resolve the problems listed above in interesting and novel ways:

- transitions are merely shifts in point of view,
- definitions and assumptions are identical for model and language,
- tools can span language and model without paradigm shifts,
- high quality designs can uniformly yield high quality implementations, and
- understandability can be improved since there is only one paradigm with which to be familiar.

The primary advantage of a model-equivalent language is that it eliminates the need for transformations when moving between different aspects of system development. For example, the shift from analysis to implementation using a model-equivalent language does not require that the system be transformed from data-flow diagrams to COBOL code, or from UML statecharts to C++ code. Using a model-equivalent language, transformations are merely shifts in point of view and thus model-equivalence can lead to faster and smoother application development with correspondingly fewer problems and higher quality results.

We are not aware of any existing language that fits our definition of model-equivalence, though there are systems that move in this direction. For example, IEF (17) provides both analysis/design tools and code generators, but only for a narrow application domain, and object-oriented database systems such as O_2 (2) provide a general language and implementation model, but support no analysis and design models. In practice, either the language does not directly support all the features of an underlying software model, or the software model is not sufficiently general or fails to satisfy the needs of the entire lifecycle of advanced-application development from analysis through implementation. In general, the current state of the art in software and data engineering combines too many distinct models that have both overt and subtle incompatibilities.

In this chapter, we illustrate the model-equivalent language concept by proposing a new language, called Harmony, that is fully integrated and compatible with an object-oriented model, the Object-oriented Systems Model (OSM) (13, 24, 23). The purpose of this chapter is to explore the issues behind the design of a model-equivalent language and to describe how we address these issues. Whether the language is Harmony and the model is OSM, or whether some other language and model are investigated, the principles, issues, and major challenges are likely to be largely the same.

The first major challenge in building model-equivalent programming languages is to ensure that the underlying model is sufficiently rich and flexible to support all application modeling and development activities, and is sufficiently powerful to allow the expression of all possible computations. OSM is a suitable candidate model because of its expressiveness, tunable formalism, varying levels of completion, and multiple-view capabilities, and because it is computationally complete. We discuss this first challenge and give an overview of OSM in Section 13.2.

The second challenge in designing a model-equivalent language is to fully integrate the language with the model. The language must not add fundamental constructs that do not arise from the model, nor may a model-equivalent language omit fundamental constructs found in the model. Maintaining bijectivity is what defines a model-equivalent language, and it is critical to achieving the expected benefits. This is the subject of Section 13.3.

The third major design challenge is to provide features in the language that support both traditional and advanced application programming. Over the years, certain features of traditional programming approaches have proven their worth. However, new techniques are continually being developed to meet the challenges of advanced applications. Traditional and advanced mechanisms are often incompatible, but a good model-equivalent language must integrate new elements with proven technology from established languages. Section 13.4 describes our approach to this problem.

We conclude in Section 13.5 and also give the status of our implementation.

13.2   The OSM Model

The Object-oriented Systems Model (OSM) is a derivative of OSA, which was originally developed for systems analysis (13). OSM is a non-traditional object-oriented model because there are no attributes—only objects and relationships (22)—and because behavior is active, driven by events and conditions, rather than being passive and driven by method invocation. Objects and relationships among objects are captured in a submodel called the Object-Relationship Model (ORM). OSM captures object behavior in two ways: individual object behavior and object interaction. The former is specified using a submodel called the Object Behavior Model (OBM), and the latter using a submodel called the Object Interaction Model (OIM).

In order for the idea of a model-equivalent language to work, we require that the model be formally defined and computationally complete. OSM is ideal in these respects, as will be discussed in Section 13.2.4. First, however, in Sections 13.2.1 through 13.2.3 we give an overview of OSM in terms of its submodels.

13.2.1 Object-Relationship Model

The ORM has several fundamental constructs, including objects, object sets, relationships, and relationship sets. There are also powerful general constraints and rich cardinality constraints (21). Objects have unique identity and are grouped (or classified) into sets called object sets. An object set may be a generalization and/or a specialization of other object sets. A specialization is a subset of each of its generalizations. A relationship set is a collection of relationships among objects of particular object sets. A relationship set has a scheme defined by two or more connected object sets, together with a relationship-set name. In addition to standard relationship sets, the ORM has aggregation and association relationship sets to model, respectively, subpart/superpart and set/member relationships. Relationship sets may be treated as object sets through a relational object set whose members are in a bijection with the relationship-set members.

Figure 13.1 shows an example of an ORM model instance for the *EU Rent* car rental agency. The examples in this paper will be drawn from this domain. In ORM's, object sets are represented as names enclosed by rectangles. The triangle that points to EU Rent Branch and also attaches to Airport Branch, Major City Branch, and Local Branch denotes that Airport Branch, Major City Branch, and Local Branch are specializations of EU Rent Branch. The other lines in the figure represent relationship sets. This figure shows four relationship sets: EU Rent Branch has Name, EU Rent Branch has Address, Supervisor manages Major City Branch, and Mechanic is assigned to Major City Branch. The text items near the relationship-set connections are participation constraints. Participation constraints indicate the number of times objects from a connected object set must participate in the relationship set. For example, the 1..* near Address indicates that each address object in the Address set must relate to one or more EU Rent Branch objects through the EU Rent Branch has Address relationship set. The dashed boxes around Name and Address indicate that these object sets contain objects that can be printed or read (such as strings, numbers, images, etc.).

13.2.2 Object Behavior Model

An instance of the OBM is called a state net, because we model object behavior in terms of transitions among states. An object may have one or more threads of control associated with it. Each thread is either in a state or firing a transition. Threads may be created or destroyed in the process of firing transitions.

States and transitions in a state net pertain to object sets in an ORM model instance. When a thread is in a state or firing a transition, then the object owning the thread is considered to be a member of the object set to which the particular state or transition pertains. Since a specialization is a subset of its generalizations, an object that is a member of a specialization object set is also a member of each of the corresponding generalization object sets. Thus, object-set membership in OSM can be a highly dynamic property, defined in conjunction with object behavior. (Because of

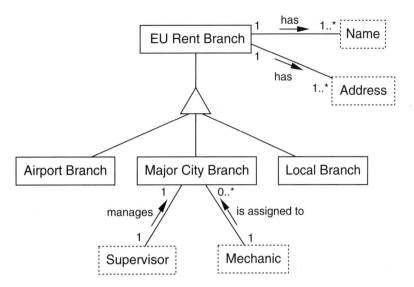

Figure 13.1   Simple Object-Relationship Model Instance.

this property and for other reasons, we have chosen to avoid the more common term *object class* and instead use *object set* to refer to object containers in OSM.)

Figure 13.2 shows a simple state net for the EU Rent Branch object set. The state net has two states (represented by ovals), named Open and Closed, and two transitions (represented by divided rectangles). Transitions consist of a trigger (written in the top half) and an action (written below the trigger). A transition can fire when its trigger is true and a thread is in the prior state(s) of the transition. When a transition fires, it may merge threads from its prior states or it may create a new thread to fire the transition. When a transition finishes firing, it may merge threads or it may destroy the firing thread. An object is destroyed with the destruction of its last thread.

13.2.3   Object Interaction Model

The OIM allows us to model object interactions in OSM. An interaction is a point of synchronization and communication between two or more threads. When an interaction occurs, the associated threads are synchronized, and information may be distributed from the sender to the receiver(s). Interactions may be broadcast to multiple receivers. A special form of interaction, called a two-way interaction, also allows information to be returned from the receiver to the sender. In a two-way interaction, the sending thread blocks until the receiving thread has finished firing its transition, signalling that the two-way interaction is complete. If we think of object interactions as service requests, we see that OSM exhibits non-uniform service availability (27), since interactions can only occur when objects are in appropriate states.

Figure 13.3 shows a simple interaction diagram. Arrows with a circled lightning bolt at the center represent interactions. Interactions may be specified at two levels of

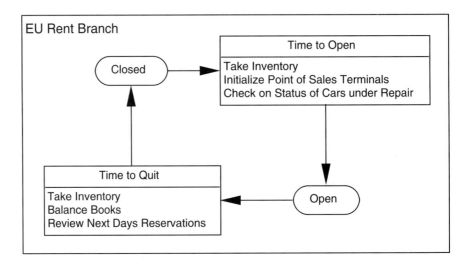

Figure 13.2   Simple Object-Behavior Model Instance.

abstraction: interactions between objects, or interactions between threads (which are associated with objects). In this example we have three object-level interactions and one thread-level interaction. The first, Make Reservation, is originated by a Customer object and sent to a EU Rent Branch object, together with a set of objects called Reservation Information. The second is a Confirm Reservation interaction initiated by the EU Rent Branch, which sends back a Confirmation Number. The third is a Pick Up Car interaction initiated by a Customer. The shading in the circles of the first three interactions indicate that they are high level, and that further details about the interactions would be revealed by examining the contents of the high-level interactions. The more detailed fourth interaction shows how two threads could interact. This is a two-way interaction; Sent Data is passed from sender to receiver, and Returned Data is passed from receiver to sender.

13.2.4   Model Foundation

OSM has several features that make it suitable as the foundation for a model-equivalent language. OSM is highly expressive, and it has the computational power of a Turing machine. Moreover, OSM is formally defined, its formalism is tunable, and OSM model instances can exhibit varying levels of completion. Furthermore, OSM provides many different kinds of views. It is because of these unique features of OSM that we have chosen to use our own model rather than adopt one of the more popular object-oriented models (such as OMT (31) or UML (30)). We will explore each of these features in turn.

Since expressiveness is often in the eye of the beholder, it is usually fruitless to present an argument about expressiveness, and full-fledged psychology experiments are time consuming and expensive. We thus do not comment here on OSM's ex-

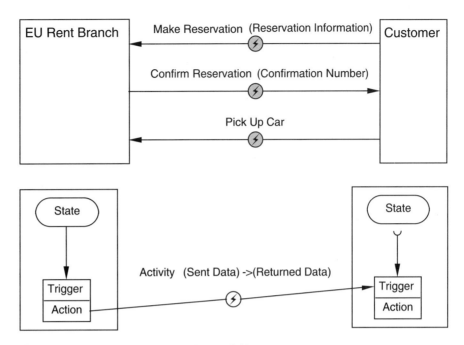

Figure 13.3   Simple Object-Interaction Model Instance.

pressiveness other than to state that we believe OSM to be highly expressive. (The interested reader may consult (12) where there is a comparative discussion, including expressiveness, among several different analysis models.)

In order to achieve bijectivity between a model and a language, we must ensure that the computational power of the model is equivalent to the computational power of the language. This implies that for any serious model-equivalent language, the underlying model must be computationally complete, meaning that it can compute any function computable by a Turing machine.

We demonstrate OSM's computational completeness by sketching how to convert any $\mathcal{S}$-language program to an OSM model instance. Since the $\mathcal{S}$ language is computationally complete (9), if OSM can represent any $\mathcal{S}$-language program, then OSM is also computationally complete. The definition of $\mathcal{S}$ is simple. Let V be a variable, and L be a statement label; then an $\mathcal{S}$-language program is a sequence of statements, each of which has one of the following forms:

$V \leftarrow V + 1$ (increment the value of V)
$V \leftarrow V - 1$ (decrement the value of V if $V > 0$)
if $V \neq 0$ goto L (transfer control to the statement labeled L if $V \neq 0$)

Variables have non-negative integer values, and there are three classes of variables: input, local, and output. Input variables have values that are specified before a program executes, but local and output variables have initial values of 0. The value of any

Figure 13.4   Variables.

variable may be modified by the program during execution. If a program terminates, its result is the values of its output variables.

The OSM representation of an S-language program is straightforward. We start with the model instance of Figure 13.4. The object set Variable represents all the variables of a program. Before executing a model instance that simulates a S-language program, we introduce a unique object in Variable for each distinct program variable. The relationship set Variable is associated with Counter allows us to associate a non-negative integer value with each variable. The value of a variable in our simulation is the number of relationships in which it participates. Statement sequencing is accomplished as Figure 13.5 illustrates. We implement the increment statement by creating a new Counter object and relating it to the appropriate Variable object. The decrement operation involves finding a relationship in which the Variable object participates (if such a relationship exists), and then deleting the relationship and its associated Counter object. The statement if $V \neq 0$ goto L is implemented with two transitions, as Figure 13.6 shows. The first has a trigger that is true if V has a zero value, and the second is true if V has a non-zero value. By connecting these constructs appropriately we can write any S-language program in OSM, which demonstrates the desired computational completeness.

This description of OSM's computational completeness is informal, but it is sufficient for our purpose here. We point out, however, that we can go a step further. Another important characteristic of OSM is that it is formally defined (6). The formal definition provides the rigorous foundation required to support a model-equivalent language. Also, using the formal definition of OSM, we can rigorously construct the simulation described above, and show that our simulation is correct. The formal definition of OSM gives the complete syntax and semantics of OSM in terms of a first-order temporal logic language called OSM-Logic. Having defined OSM formally, we can then use OSM to describe itself formally; thus, we create the OSM meta-model, which is an OSM model of OSM. Having a formal definition of OSM allows us to make rigorous statements about OSM model instances, but it also has the important consequence of making model instances directly executable. Thus, we can implement systems directly in OSM, without moving to another language.

Interestingly, our approach to formalism is tunable (7). Not all users of a system will be capable of dealing in terms of detailed formalism. The needs of theoreticians, tool builders, programmers, and customers all differ with respect to the degree of formal understanding required or expected. An OSM system can be viewed in terms of its OSM-Logic definition for those who need the full formality, or it can be viewed directly in OSM itself for those who prefer a more user-oriented, graphical view, or it can be viewed in a mixture of OSM-Logic and OSM graphical notation.

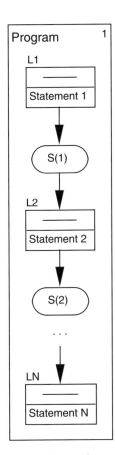

Figure 13.5   Statement Sequencing.

OSM also allows varying levels of completion. For example, constraints, triggers, and actions may be written informally, in a natural language, or they may be written formally, say, in Harmony or OSM-Logic. We call an informal constraint *incomplete* because we do not have a sufficiently precise specification to interpret it. As we evolve an incomplete model instance, more of the pieces become formally executable, until finally the entire system is complete. This concept of varying levels of completion makes OSM applicable to a wide variety of uses from pure analysis to detailed implementation.

A final aspect of OSM that helps with model-equivalent languages is the various views that can be associated with a model instance. OSM supports abstraction through high-level components, including high-level object sets, relationship sets, states, transitions, and interactions. These high-level components may contain other components, including other high-level components. High-level components are fully reified as first-class constructs, meaning that they are treated just like the corresponding low-level components (e.g., a high-level object set is an object set in every sense). Each high-level component constitutes a view of a system. A high-level

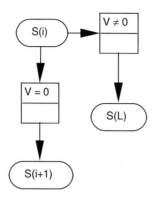

Figure 13.6   Goto Statement.

abstraction can represent a very complex or a rather simple concept. For example, we can model a weather system, an automobile engine, or a light switch with high-level object sets of varying degrees of internal complexity. But in each case, the overall concept is visible in the model as a single object set.

A further consequence of views is that OSM can seen in a completely textual form. When the view is textual and complete (and thus fully formal and executable), we call it Harmony, the model-equivalent language for OSM. Because of model-equivalence, we can also mix the two notations. Part can be Harmony text and part can be OSM graphical notation.

13.3   Integrating a Model and a Language

A model-equivalent language must maintain bijectivity between features in the model and features in the language—there must be uniformity and cohesiveness between both views. This section describes how we addressed these issues in the design of Harmony. Again, we organize our discussion in terms of structure, behavior, and interaction.

13.3.1   A Uniform Structural Model

To provide a uniform structural model, we must resolve the "impedance mismatch" (34) for types between imperative and declarative languages, and we must provide for a seamless integration of persistent and non-persistent data. We discuss the first of these two problems in Section 13.3.1.1 and the second in Section 13.3.1.2.

13.3.1.1   *Resolving Variable/Type/Class Conflict*

Structural type systems in programming languages evolved to help manage the layout of physical data structures for these languages. Data models, on the other hand, were designed to capture the logical structure of systems. Because of these distinct goals, type systems and data models have been at odds more often than not. Furthermore, as models and languages have evolved, the complexity of data models and type systems has generally increased, making the challenge to unite them much more difficult.

With the advent of object-oriented models and languages, we have seen more opportunity to consolidate elements from programming languages and database systems. However, most object-oriented systems have a physical definition of what an object is. It is typical, for example, to define an object as an instantiation of a class, and a class as a list of attributes together with a set of methods to operate on those attributes. Prototype-based (as opposed to class-based) object-oriented systems (e.g., (32)) are more dynamic in their definition of what an object is, but it is still evident that implementation and optimization issues have affected the type-system design. This creates a direct conflict with the desire to be free from physical concerns at the model level. Thus, there is an "impedance mismatch" between the semantics of a general, logical model, and a more-specific, efficiently-implemented programming-language type system.

This impedance mismatch raises a potential objection to the very idea of having a uniform structural model for all phases of application development. Is it possible to meet the needs of physical design/implementation and logical analysis/design within the bounds of a single model? We believe that the answer is affirmative.

In Harmony, we resolve this conflict by providing language elements that are logical, and yet look and behave much like their traditional counterparts. The key to our approach is the substitution of *object set* (a logical construct) for the concept of *variable* (a physical construct that represents a typed location in memory). In OSM an object set is a collection of objects; it can thus be considered a container. A variable in Harmony is an object set. Thus, a Harmony variable is a container that represents a *set* of objects. (Harmony variables containing a single element can be considered to be scalar values.) Types in Harmony are restrictions on object-set membership as constrained by the generalizations of an object set. To be a member of an object set, an object must also be a member of all generalizations of that object set. Thus, if we fix the membership of one or more generalizations, we can restrict the set of objects that are candidates for membership in a specific object set. This achieves the effect of typing a variable in a standard programming language.

We illustrate these principles with the example in Figure 13.7. Here, we have two constant object sets (indicated by the additional rectangle around the object sets named Real and Integer), and two specialization object sets, x and y. The effect of this model instance is to create two containers (x and y) whose members can change over time. However, the members are restricted by the definitions of Real and Integer, whose members are fixed. This would be similar to defining variables x and y of type Real and Integer in a programming language. Indeed, in Harmony we allow the following textual representation of the graphical model instance shown in Figure 13.7:

```
x: Real;
y: Integer;
```

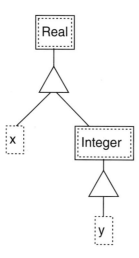

Figure 13.7 "Variables" in Harmony.

Observe, however, that this does not quite give the traditional declaration semantics because x is a *set* of Reals and y is a *set* of Integers. We can achieve scalar semantics by associating an object-set cardinality constraint of 1 with an object set. For example, x: Real[1]; constrains x to have exactly one member. The corresponding graphical notation is to place a 1 in the upper right corner of an object-set rectangle (as in Figure 13.5).

In addition to the *variable* concept, there is the related concept of *type constructor*. For example, programming languages usually provide record and array type constructors that allow the physical combination of data types to form new aggregate types. In Harmony, relationship sets play the role of type constructors. A relationship set holds relationships, each of which is an association between two or more objects. A relationship set has a scheme that tells how it connects to associated object sets. Thus, relationships are like tuples, and relationship sets are like relations or record types.

Figure 13.8 shows an example of a structure that might be used in a Harmony program. The relationship set with a star on one end is an association, indicating that EU Rent Car Rental Agency is a set of EU Rent Branch objects. The black triangle is an aggregation, or superpart/subpart, relationship set. The textual equivalent of the graphical model instance of Figure 13.8 is the following:

```
EU Rent Car Rental Company[1..*] is set of EU Rent Branch[0..*] |
      EU Rent Branch is member of EU Rent Car Rental Company;
EU Rent Branch[1] has Name[1..*];
EU Rent Branch[1] has Address[1..*];
Address has subparts [1..*] Street   [1..*],
                      [1]    City     [1..*],
                      [1]    Country [1..*];
```

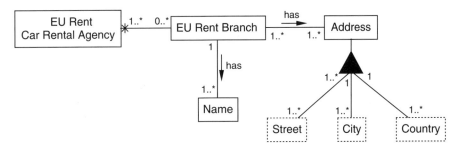

Figure 13.8   Relationship Sets for Type Constructors.

The ranges in brackets are participation constraints, indicating the number of times objects from a particular object set may participate in a given relationship set. Using this model instance, we can create data in Harmony as follows:

```
add EU Rent Branch(x) has Name("Berlin"),
        EU Rent Branch(x) is member of
                EU Rent Car Rental Agency("EU Rent"),
        EU Rent(x) has Address(y),
        Street("50 Kurfurstendamm") is subpart of Address(y),
        City("Berlin") is subpart of Address(y),
        Country("Germany") is subpart of Address(y);
```

The add statement executes as a single, atomic transaction, so either all or none of the objects and relationships are created. There are two object sets, x and y, that act as unifying variables in this statement. Since x and y are initially unbound (empty) in the add statement, the system creates new objects (internal object identifiers) and binds them to x and y. Then for each predicate in the add statement, the parameter objects are inserted in the corresponding object sets (if necessary), and then the parameter objects are related to form new relationships in the named relationship sets.

Any logical structure can be modeled in OSM using object sets and relationship sets, and so any physical structure, such as an array, can be emulated. For those bulk structures that are common, we provide optimized physical structures in the implementation of Harmony. However, the optimized form of a particular structure does not show through to the Harmony program. Only the logical structure is available to a Harmony programmer.

Note that our approach to data structures in Harmony constitutes a change in paradigm from scalar to set-oriented semantics. This implies the need for set operators in addition to or in place of traditional scalar operators. To cover this need, we provide set comparison operators, a generalized assignment statement, quantifiers, logic unification, and cardinality expressions. We give more details about these topics later, in Sections 13.3.2 and 13.4.

13.3.1.2 Type-Complete Persistence

The idea of type-complete persistence is becoming increasingly important for advanced applications. *Persistence* is defined as the ability of a program's data to outlast the execution of a program. Persistence is *type-complete* if any kind of object can persist (i.e., persistence is a property orthogonal to type; see (1) for a thorough discussion of this topic).

Harmony supports persistence by declaring that object sets and relationship sets persist for the duration of their scope. When a thread enters a nested scope, a nested model instance associated with the scope is instantiated. Objects and relationships in such a nested model instance exist as long as the thread is inside the corresponding scope. When a thread leaves a scope, associated object sets and relationship sets (together with their members) are destroyed. Nested scopes in Harmony are associated with transition actions. Because high-level transitions in OSM can be nested to an arbitrary level, scopes in Harmony likewise can be nested to an arbitrary level. Fully persistent objects are those defined in the outermost (global) scope of a model instance, which like a database can exist for an arbitrary length of time. Transient objects are those defined within a nested scope. Naturally, there are different levels of transience, depending on how rapidly threads enter and leave nested scopes. This straightforward model of persistence allows type-complete persistence and provides a clean mechanism for separating persistent data from transient data. Furthermore, it corresponds well to the structure of modern block-scoped languages, and so the framework is familiar.

Consider the example in Figure 13.9. Credit Monitor and Customer Credit History are object sets defined at the global level, so they are persistent, as is the relationship set Credit Monitor maintains Credit History of Customer. The built-in object set Integer is also pre-defined at the global scope by Harmony. However, the object set x, which is a specialization of Integer, comes into existence for a thread when the thread enters the transition, and is destroyed for the thread when the transition finishes firing. Note that for each thread firing this transition, there will be a separate copy of x, and one thread's x cannot access another thread's x. The arc on the transition arrow's tail means that a new thread is created to fire the transition and the old thread remains in the Ready state. Thus, there can be potentially many threads in Credit Montior that are simultaneously processing new credit information.

13.3.2 A Uniform Behavior Model

Programming languages are good at specifying low-level behavior, but they are poor at capturing high-level abstractions of that behavior. Thus, the usual approach to combining modeling and implementation involves creating multiple descriptions of system behavior, using distinct models and languages. In order to create a successful model-equivalent language, we must provide a rich model that can express multiple views of system behavior. Moreover, the model must do this without sacrificing the effectiveness of a programming language for the lowest-level behavior specification. Section 13.3.2.1 describes our approach to this problem.

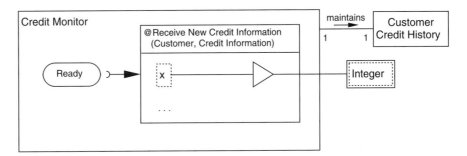

Figure 13.9   Example of Nested Scopes.

A second issue regarding the behavior model is that many disparate implementation paradigms are vying for our attention in programming languages. For example, there is the traditional von Neumann-styled imperative paradigm, logic programming, constraint programming, functional languages, object-orientation, visual programming, and so forth. The number of programming paradigms continues to increase as we seek improved vehicles for software implementation. One of the reasons for this phenomenon is that no one paradigm is most appropriate for all problems. The transitive closure problem of finding ancestors, for example, is easily solved in a two-rule logic program, but comparatively difficult to express in a standard imperative language. This gives rise to another aspect of the impedance mismatch problem—database systems are usually declarative while programming languages are usually imperative (34). How do we ensure that our behavior model will be adequate for a wide variety of problems, and in particular will span the declarative/imperative spectrum? Section 13.3.2.2 addresses this concern.

13.3.2.1   Multiple Views of Behavior

OSM and Harmony provide multiple views of behavior specification, from purely graphical to purely textual representations. Figure 13.10 shows an example of the same behavior expressed in various representations. A state net is essentially a set of rules that describe when and how an object will perform particular actions (25) and is similar in many ways to rule components in active systems such as (5), (10), and (16). An object behaves by continually evaluating its triggering rules and performing appropriate actions. The textual view in Figure 13.10(c) looks much like a propositional production system (28), emphasizing this rule orientation. More complex state nets would have many such when rules. The graphical view of this same state net in Figure 13.10(a), emphasizes the states of an object. Figure 13.10(b), a mixed view, shows the transition from ready to done in a graphical form, but gives the details of the transition action in terms of a more traditional programming style. Graphical and textual representations have differing strengths and weaknesses. For example, graphical forms tend to represent information more clearly and sparsely than textual forms and thus are especially good for high-level communication. On the other hand, many people, especially programmers, find text easier to create and read than graphics. Thus, by providing a combination of graphical and textual views, we make OSM and Harmony easy to use for people with differing needs, goals, and abilities.

We emphasize that Figures 13.10(a), (b), and (c) express identical semantics. Harmony's statements are simply alternative ways of writing state nets. Similarly, Harmony's control-flow statements (i.e., statement sequencing, if . . . then . . . else . . ., while . . . do . . ., for each . . . do . . .) are directly representable as state nets, thus maintaining direct bijectivity between model and language.

13.3.2.2   *Combining Imperative and Declarative Elements*

Besides providing multiple views of an OSM system at varying levels of abstraction, our approach also incorporates elements of both imperative and declarative programming paradigms. A state net is essentially an imperative system, though it is not restricted to a single thread of control like traditional programming languages. Also, a state net incorporates declarative elements, such as its triggers and real-time constraints. On the other hand, an ORM is essentially declarative in nature, though its instances are dynamic. Furthermore, OSM general and cardinality constraints are also declarative. Thus, OSM inherently incorporates both imperative and declarative paradigms.

Harmony builds on this multi-paradigm foundation, integrating programming features from imperative, logic, and constraint paradigms. Basically, Harmony programs can be thought of as having an imperative skeleton, with logic elements fleshing out the structure. The imperative skeleton acts by evaluating constraints and triggers and executing transition actions. Using OSM-equivalent statements as explained above, a transition action can be thought of as a sequence of statements, with flow-control constructs for repeated and conditional execution.

Within this imperative framework, Harmony provides a mechanism for deriving high-level object sets and high-level relationship sets, and this provides the means to integrate logic within the imperative-paradigm skeleton. Consider, for example, the problem of finding a person's ancestors, given the recursive relationship set Person has Parent, shown in Figure 13.11. We can define a derived high-level relationship set, Person has Ancestor, as follows:

```
Person(x) has Ancestor(y) :- Person(x) has Parent(y);
Person(x) has Ancestor(y) :- Person(x) has Parent(z),
                             Person(z) has Ancestor(y);
```

This simple logic program provides a derived (intensional) relationship set, Person has Ancestor, that is accessible in the same way as any non-derived (extensional) relationship set (but it cannot be updated like an extensional relationship set). For example, expr1 in Figure 13.10(a), (b), or (c) could be replaced with the following closed formula:

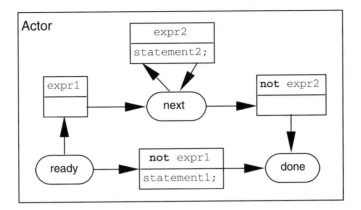

(a)

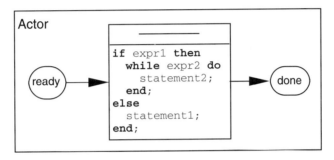

(b)

```
Actor includes
  when ready and expr1 then enter next; end;
  when ready and not expr1 then
      statement1;
    enter done; end;
  when next and expr2 then
      statement2;
    enter next; end;
  when next and not expr2 then enter done; end;
end;
```

(c)

Figure 13.10   Multiple Views of Object Behavior.

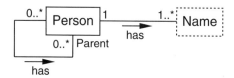

Figure 13.11   Ancestor Example.

```
exists Person(x) exists Person(y)
    (Person(x) has Ancestor(y) and
      Person(x) has Name("Steve Young") and
      Person(y) has Name("Brigham Young"))
```

which is true if Steve Young is a descendent of Brigham Young but is false otherwise. As indicated in this example, Harmony supports predicate calculus directly. OSM also directly supports predicate calculus (see (11) and Appendix A of (13)).

Within the body of a transition action, logic rules can be freely interspersed with other Harmony statements. Thus, we could place the Person has Ancestor high-level relationship set statements in Figure 13.10(c) either before or after the when statement. All rules in a given scope are gathered together, and collectively define a set of derived object sets and relationship sets that can be accessed within the scope of their definition. A logic rule derives a high-level object set if it has only one place (one variable) in the head predicate, and it derives a high-level relationship set if there are two or more places (two or more variables) in the head predicate. (For a more formal and detailed treatment of logic in Harmony, see (14).)

13.3.3 A Uniform Interaction Model

The third area of model/language integration we must consider is the interaction model. In order for a model-equivalent language to be successful, the object inter-action mechanism must be equally suited to analysis and implementation. While interaction perspectives such as data flows are common in modeling, function calls are ubiquitous in languages. We find a harmony between the two in object orientation, where message passing is the predominant concept. The key difference between OSM and traditional object orientation in this area is that in traditional OO, objects are passive in that they only execute when methods are invoked. But in OSM, objects are active and can execute independently. The OSM version of object interaction is particularly amenable to use in various development phases, because it is a richer form that can subsume the traditional, passive case.

The fundamental idea behind interactions is that threads synchronize and have an opportunity to communicate when they interact. We provide for interactions in the Harmony language by allowing interactions to be received in transition triggers, and allowing interactions to be initiated from within transition actions. Objects and relationships may be passed from a sender to its receiver(s). We also introduce a special two-way interaction, involving a single sender and a single receiver. A two-way interaction allows the receiver to communicate information back to the sender. We describe the Harmony one-way interaction in Section 13.3.3.1 and the two-way interaction mechanism in Section 13.3.3.2.

Polymorphism is also an important concept for object-oriented communication. We briefly discuss Harmony polymorphism in Section 13.3.3.3.

13.3.3.1   *One-Way Interactions in Harmony*

We described the OSM interaction mechanism in Section 13.2.3. As a basic principle, threads may send interactions within transition actions, and threads may receive interactions within transition triggers. To support this model, Harmony needs a way to specify send and receive events.

The general form of a one-way interaction send statement is the following:

[to all] [*destination-constraint*.] *interaction-name* [([*send-parameters*])]

Items in square brackets are optional. The key phrase to all indicates that the interaction is broadcast to all potential receivers; when omitted, only one of the potential receivers receives the interaction. The *destination-constraint* phrase limits the set of potential objects or threads that can receive this specific interaction send event. It is common to limit the set of potential receivers to only one. If *destination-constraint* is omitted, the sending thread has placed no restriction on who may receive the interaction. The *interaction-name* is a name that is intended to describe what the interaction is to accomplish (e.g., Reserve Vehicle). Finally, *send-parameters* is a comma-separated list of object sets and relationship sets (or expressions that yield object sets and relationship sets) that are sent from the sender to the receiver. Here are two examples of one-way interaction send statements:

```
Charge(Credit Card Number, Credit Card Type, Amount);
to all Customer.Report Status(Frequent Driver Kilometers);
```

A one-way interaction receive expression has the following form:

@ [*origin-constraint*.] *interaction-name* [([*send-parameters*])]

where *origin-constraint* is a set of objects or threads from which the interaction event may be received, *interaction-name* is as defined above, and *send-parameters* is a comma-separated formal parameter list. Thus, the following are valid one-way interaction receive expressions:

```
@Customer Arrives at Desk
@Log Message(Event: string)
@Charge(Credit Card Number:  Account Number,
        Credit Card Type:    Card Type,
        Amt:                 Dollar Amount)
```

If send parameters are listed in a one-way interaction receive expression, they are formal, meaning that each parameter is a specialization of some object set or relationship set.

One-way interactions allow object threads to synchronize and potentially communicate information. We say that an interaction *occurs* when an interaction-send event is matched with an interaction-receive event and *does not occur* if an interaction-send event does not have a corresponding receive event. Threads are in synchronization when an interaction occurs between them. Threads are not in synchronization if they are not interacting. We say that an interaction *completes* when the interaction is finished and the threads leave synchronization. In the case of a one-way interaction, the interaction completes as soon as the receiver has received all data associated with send parameters. This is different for two-way interactions, which we describe in the next section.

13.3.3.2   Two-Way Interactions in Harmony

A one-way interaction accomplishes simple message passing, thread synchronization, and one-way communication. However, threads often need to engage in bidirectional communication. While one-way interactions are probably powerful enough to accomplish any desired communication, they are not necessarily convenient for accomplishing two-way communication. For example, a thread could send a one-way interaction to another, and the sender could listen for a message from the receiver. However, it is difficult in the presence of multiple independently behaving objects to specify appropriate constraints to guarantee that the return message is causally linked with the original interaction. To overcome this difficulty, we provide a two-way interaction, which is similar in several ways to the concept of function call found in traditional languages.

The general form of a two-way interaction send statement is:

> [*destination-constraint.*] *interaction-name* ([*send-parameters*])
> -> ([*return-parameters*])

And the corresponding two-way interaction receive expression is:

> @ [*origin-constraint.*] *interaction-name* ([*send-parameters*])
> -> ([*return-parameters*])

Here, *origin-constraint*, *destination-constraint*, *interaction-name*, and *send-parameters* are as defined for one-way interactions. The new element is *return-parameters*, which is a comma-separated list of formal parameters in both the send statement and the receive expression.

In its general form, a two-way interaction corresponds to a mapping from its send parameters to its return parameters. Unlike a one-way interaction, when a thread sends a two-way interaction, it blocks until the interaction completes. A two-way interaction completes when the receiving transition finishes firing. When a two-way interaction completes, the receiver's return parameters go out of scope, so they are no longer accessible by the receiving thread.

Let us consider an example. Suppose we have the following two-way interaction send statement:

request: Reservation Request;

. . .

Reserve Car(request)->(reservation: Confirmed Reservation);

and the receiving transition's trigger is the following:

@Reserve Car (request: Reservation Request)->
(confirm: Confirmed Reservation)

When the interaction occurs, objects from request in the sending thread are added to the request object set in the receiving thread. When the interaction completes, objects from confirm in the receiving thread are added to the reservation object set in the sending thread. In this way, information can be transferred in both directions between threads communicating via a two-way interaction.

13.3.3.3   *Polymorphism*

Harmony interactions exhibit forms of ad-hoc and inclusion polymorphism (3). Harmony has ad-hoc polymorphism, or overloading, because the same interaction name can be used in arbitrarily many different receive expressions, with potentially differing parameters and origin constraints. Harmony exhibits a form of inclusion polymorphism because receive expressions can be specialized, and actual parameters may be specializations of corresponding formal parameters. This implies that Harmony dynamically dispatches some forms of interactions. For more details, see (20).

13.4   Preserving Advances of the Past

A great deal of resources are invested in current programming-language techniques. It would be unwise to propose an entirely new language that radically departs in every way from existing technology. To the extent possible, we should preserve those structures, techniques, and concepts that have proven their worth over the years. Function call and variable assignment, for example, are ubiquitous in traditional languages because they are useful abstractions and are easy to use and understand. Although we have introduced many new constructs and have redefined some existing ideas in our design of Harmony, we have also taken steps to reintroduce familiar constructs as shorthand notation, often in a somewhat more generalized form. This section describes how Harmony accommodates the following familiar constructs:

- functions, operators, and expressions, and
- assignment statements and path expressions.

13.4.1 Functions, Operators, and Expressions

As mentioned in Section 13.3.3.2, two-way interactions are very much like functions. With some "syntactic sugar," we can recover the forms for function calls and operators found in many common programming languages. For example, if we choose "+" as an interaction name, write its send parameters using infix notation, and assume an anonymously named return parameter, we have the familiar x + y expression for addition. Similarly, we achieve a traditional-looking function call by assuming a single return parameter when an interaction is sent within an expression. For example, consider the expression 10 + floor(x - 3.5). The system must have a receiver for a two-way interaction similar to the following:

@floor(arg: Real)->(res: Integer)

Then the result of x - 3.5 is passed as the arg parameter to floor, and the result res of the floor interaction becomes the second argument of the + interaction. By providing familiar operator and function-call forms for two-way interactions, we achieve a significant reuse of traditional syntax and semantics, while providing more generality (which comes from the underlying Harmony interaction model).

13.4.2 Assignment Statements and Path Expressions

Since Harmony's underlying model is based on object sets and relationship sets, containers do not necessarily represent scalar values and there are no rigid boundaries for data structures. Thus, we need to provide a way to handle these more logical, less physical structures conveniently. We do this in several ways: (1) we provide a general graph traversal operator for forming path expressions, (2) we support generalized set operations, and (3) we define a generalized assignment statement.

Path traversal is a common activity in object-oriented database programs, and so it is with Harmony, where we often need to traverse relationship sets. In its Object Query Language (OQL), the *Object Database Standard* defines a path traversal operator, ".", that allows navigation from an object into its attributes or through simple relationships (4). Harmony has a similar, but more general traversal operator. As with OQL, the Harmony dot operator traverses relationship sets, but Harmony also allows parts of a path expression to be omitted if the resulting path is unambiguous. (We define A.B to be unambiguous if there is only one minimal spanning tree between A and B in the object-relationship graph.) For example, given the model instance of Figure 13.8, we can understand the query Name("Downtown").City to be the set of cities for all branches named "Downtown". Note that Harmony's dot operator subsumes attribute selection and pointer de-referencing found in traditional programming languages.

Another interesting aspect of the Harmony dot operator is that it hides the differences between queries (selection of stored or derived information) and two-way interactions (transformational computations). Consider the expression Customer.Amount Due. This could either be a query traversing from the Customer object set to find a

related amount due from an Amount Due object set, or it could be a functional interaction with Customer as the destination, and Amount Due as the interaction activity
description.

Since Harmony is set-based, it is easy to add several useful, but non-traditional
operators that can be applied to sets. These include set cardinality, random selection,
and subset and inclusion operators. In addition, we define the inequality operators ($<$,
$<=$, $>$, $>=$) as follows. Let S and T be set expressions, and let ρ be an inequality
operator. We say that $S \rho T$ is true if $\forall x \in S \ \forall y \in T (x \rho y)$. Note that in the case
where the sets are singleton, this definition reduces to the standard definition of
inequality. We define the equality operators ($=$, $<>$) as follows. Again, let S and
T be set expressions. Then $S = T$ is true if $S \subseteq T$ and $S \supseteq T$, and $S <> T$ is defined
as the Boolean negation of $S = T$.

In traditional programming languages an assignment statement generally takes the
form *variable := expression*. The effect of an assignment statement is to replace the
contents of a memory cell of fixed size and type with a new value. The left-hand side
of an assignment statement evaluates to a storage location (called an *l-value*), and the
right-hand side is an expression that returns a value to be stored (called an *r-value*).
In Harmony, we do not have fixed-sized cells holding data values; rather, we have
object sets as containers holding zero or more objects. Furthermore, these objects
may be involved in relationships with other objects. Because we have generalized
the concept of data storage, we also need to generalize the concept of assignment
statement for Harmony. The full details are extensive (20), so we only give several
examples here.

The general form of Harmony assignment is *path.objectset := expression*. Given
the model instance of Figure 13.1, suppose we have the following Harmony code
fragment:

```
b: Major City Branch; s: Supervisor; m: Mechanic;
...
b := Supervisor("Karl Schmidt").Major City Branch;
...
m := b.Mechanic;
...
b.Address := "50 Kurfurstendamm";
```

The first assignment statement has the effect of removing any current members of b,
then selecting and assigning to b the Major City Branch object that is related to the City
object whose supervisor is "Karl Schmidt". Note that in general, we cannot guarantee
the cardinality of a variable after an assignment statement; it may be empty, or it
may contain one or more objects. However, in this case we know that the cardinality
of b after the first assignment statement is either 0 or 1, because the participation
constraints on the Major City Branch has Supervisor relationship set guarantee that
Major City Branch objects and Supervisor objects are in a one-to-one correspondence.
In the case of the second assignment statement, which assigns to m the mechanics
of branch b, we do not know what the cardinality of m will be, because there may
be many mechanics for a main city branch. The third assignment statement is more

complex. Because the left-hand side is a path expression, the assignment relates each object in b to the Address object "50 Kurfurstendamm", replacing any existing relationships between b objects and Address objects. If "50 Kurfurstendamm" is not a member of the Address object set, it is added, and any address that is no longer associated with a branch as a result of the assignment is deleted.

13.5   Conclusion

We have proposed a new pattern for model/language integration. We call this pattern a model-equivalent programming language. We have discussed some of the important principles and properties of model-equivalent programming languages, in general, and the design of the model-equivalent programming language Harmony, in particular.

The advantages of a model-equivalent language are clear. Because the application never leaves its single, unified model/language, there is no need to translate from one language or model to another. Thus, there is no loss of information or added complexity due to transformations. Furthermore, the semantics of the analysis of a system are directly observable in its implementation. This makes communication easier because an object and its behavior in the model mean the same thing as an object and its behavior in the language, and because all parties are operating from the same lexicon and with the same set of definitions.

Moreover, OSM and Harmony also have a strong concept of multiple views, varying levels of abstraction, varying degrees of formalism, and varying levels of completion. Hence, they can meet the needs of a wide variety of users, from analysts to programmers.

As we consider the ramifications of our approach, however, one question comes to the forefront. Will a model-equivalent language necessarily be rather complex, bulky, and inefficient? The answer, at least initially, appears to be affirmative. However, we need to view a model-equivalent language with proper perspective, comparing a single model and language with the multiple models, languages, and tools brought together in other approaches. We claim that a model-equivalent language approach is less complex and bulky, on balance, than an approach that uses disparate models and languages. Efficiency, however, is still in question. But as the database community in particular has shown, we can turn this challenge into an opportunity using principles of design together with the principle of data independence to achieve satisfactory efficiency, and perhaps even greater efficiency than has hitherto been achieved. As use increases, optimization will follow. Furthermore, because we have made a substantial effort to preserve traditional concepts in Harmony where possible, there are already many well-studied optimizations we can apply to our language.

Our implementation of Harmony has been under way for some time now. We have created an OSM diagramming tool, called the OSM Composer, that forms the basis for our Harmony programming environment (29). With the OSM Composer, a user can create model instances for systems analysis, specification, design, and implementation. The Composer also provides a platform for integrating other tools to assist in the development of OSM-based systems. For example, we have a rapid-prototyping component (18, 19), a graphical query language (8, 33), and a database normalization assistant (15, 26). Other related projects are also planned or under way. We have implemented a subset of Harmony's precursor language, and we are working on the implementation of Harmony.

References

1. M.P. Atkinson and O.P. Buneman. Types and persistence in database programming languages. *ACM Computing Surveys*, 19(2):105–190, 1987.

2. F. Bancilhon, C. Delobel, and P. Kanellakis, editors. *Building an Object-Oriented Database System: The Story of O2*. Morgan Kaufmann, San Mateo, California, 1992.

3. L. Cardelli and P. Wegner. On understanding types, data abstraction, and polymorphism. *ACM Computing Surveys*, 17(4):471–522, 1985.

4. R.G.G. Cattell, editor. *The Object Database Standard: ODMG-93*. Morgan Kaufmann Publishers, San Mateo, California, 1994.

5. S. Chakravarthy et al. HiPAC: A research project in active, time-constrained database management. Technical Report XAIT-89-02, Xerox Advanced Information Technology, August 1989.

6. S.W. Clyde, D.W. Embley, and S.N. Woodfield. The complete formal definition for the syntax and semantics of OSA. Technical Report BYU-CS-92-2, Computer Science Department, Brigham Young University, 1992.

7. S.W. Clyde, D.W. Embley, and S.N. Woodfield. Tunable formalism in object-oriented systems analysis: Meeting the needs of both theoreticians and practitioners. In *OOPSLA '92 Conference Proceedings*, pages 452–465, Vancouver, British Columbia, Canada, October 1992.

8. B.D. Czejdo, R.P. Tucci, D.W. Embley, and S.W. Liddle. Graphical query specification with cardinality constraints. In *Proceedings of the Fifth International Conference on Computing and Information*, pages 433–437, Sudbury, Ontario, May 1993.

9. M.D. Davis and E.J. Weyuker. *Computability, Complexity, and Languages*. Academic Press, New York, 1983.

10. U. Dayal. Active database management systems. In *Proceedings of the Third International Conference on Data and Knowledge Bases: Improving Usability and Responsiveness*, pages 150–169, Jerusalem, Israel, June 1988.

11. D.W. Embley. *Object Database Development: Concepts and Principles*. Addison-Wesley, Reading, Massachusetts, 1998.

12. D.W. Embley, R.B. Jackson, and S.N. Woodfield. Object-oriented systems analysis: Is it or isn't it? *IEEE Software*, 12(3):19–33, July 1995.

13. D.W. Embley, B.D. Kurtz, and S.N. Woodfield. *Object-oriented Systems Analysis: A Model-Driven Approach*. Prentice Hall, Englewood Cliffs, New Jersey, 1992.

14. D.W. Embley, S.W. Liddle, and Y.K. Ng. On harmonically combining active, object-orientated, and deductive databases. In *Proceedings of the Third International Workshop on Advances in Databases and Information Systems, ADBIS '96*, pages 21–30, Moscow, Russia, September 1996.

15. D.W. Embley and T.W. Ling. Synergistic database design with an extended entity-relationship model. In *Proceedings of the Eighth International Conference on Entity-Relationship Approach*, pages 118–135, Toronto, Canada, October 1989.

16. N.H. Gehani, H.V. Jagadish, and O. Shmueli. Event specification in an active object-oriented database. In *Proceedings of the 1992 ACM SIGMOD International Conference on Management of Data*, pages 81–90, San Diego, California, June 1992.

17. *A Guide to Information Engineering Using the IEF*. Texas Instruments, Dallas, Texas, second edition, 1990. Part Number 2739756-0001.

18. R.B. Jackson. *Object-Oriented Requirements Specification: A Model, A Tool and A Technique*. PhD thesis, Computer Science Department, Brigham Young University, Provo, Utah, 1994.

19. R.B. Jackson, D.W. Embley, and S.N. Woodfield. Automated support for the development of formal object-oriented requirements specifications. In *Proceedings of the 6th International Conference on Advanced Information Systems Engineering, Lecture Notes in Computer Science, 811*, Berlin, June 1994. Springer Verlag.

20. S.W. Liddle. *Object-Oriented Systems Implementation: A Model-Equivalent Approach*. PhD thesis, Computer Science Department, Brigham Young University, Provo, Utah, June 1995.

21. S.W. Liddle, D.W. Embley, and S.N. Woodfield. Cardinality constraints in semantic data models. *Data and Knowledge Engineering*, 11(3):235–270, December 1993.

22. S.W. Liddle, D.W. Embley, and S.N. Woodfield. Attributes: Should we eliminate them from semantic and object-oriented data models? In *Proceedings of the 22nd Annual ACM Computer Science Conference*, pages 340–347, Phoenix, Arizona, March 1994.

23. S.W. Liddle, D.W. Embley, and S.N. Woodfield. A seamless model for object-oriented systems development. In *Proceedings of the International Symposium on Object-Oriented Methodologies and Systems, ISOOMS 94*, pages 123–131, Palermo, Italy, September 1994.

24. S.W. Liddle, D.W. Embley, and S.N. Woodfield. Unifying Modeling and Programming Through an Active, Object-Oriented, Model-Equivalent Programming Language. In *Proceedings of the Fourteenth International Conference on Object-Oriented and Entity Relationship Modeling (OOER'95), Lecture Notes in Computer Science, 1021*, pages 55–64, Gold Coast, Queensland, Australia, December 1995. Springer Verlag.

25. S.W. Liddle, D.W. Embley, S.N. Woodfield, S.W. Clyde, and B.D. Czejdo. Analysis and design for active object bases. In *Proceedings of the Sixth International Conference on Computing and Information*, pages 1553–1568, Sudbury, Ontario, May 1994. This is available through the World Wide Web at URL http://www.cs.tufts.edu/icci/94/TOC.html.

26. J. Light. The implementation of a technique for ORM model-instance normalization. Master's thesis, Computer Science Department, Brigham Young University. In progress.

27. O. Nierstrasz. Regular types for active objects. In *OOPSLA '93 Conference Proceedings*, pages 1–15, Washington, D.C., October 1993.

28. D.R. Olsen. *User Interface Management Systems: Models and Algorithms*. Morgan Kaufmann Publishers, San Mateo, California, 1992.

29. OSM Lab Home Page. URL: http://osm7.cs.byu.edu.

30. UML Home Page. URL: http://www.rational.com/uml.

31. J. Rumbaugh, M. Blaha, W. Premerlani, F. Eddy, and W. Lorensen. *Object-Oriented Modeling and Design*. Prentice Hall, Englewood Cliffs, New Jersey, 1991.

32. D. Ungar and R.B. Smith. Self: The power of simplicity. In *OOPSLA '87 Conference Proceedings*, pages 227–242, Orlando, Florida, October 1987.

33. H.A. Wu. OSM-QL: A Calculus-Based Graphical Query Language for Object-Oriented Systems Modeling. Master's thesis, Computer Science Department, Brigham Young University, 1993.

34. S.B. Zdonik and D. Maier. Fundamentals of object-oriented databases. In S.B. Zdonik and D. Maier, editors, *Readings in Object-Oriented Database Systems*, pages 1–32. Morgan Kaufmann, San Mateo, California, 1990.

Index